The Idea
of an American Novel

Edited by

LOUIS D. RUBIN, JR.

and

JOHN REES MOORE

Hollins College

THOMAS Y. CROWELL COMPANY

New York, Established 1834

TO MARY VINCENT LONG

Library of Congress Catalog Card Number: 61–6174

Designed by Laurel Wagner

Manufactured in the United States of America
by the Vail-Ballou Press, Inc., Binghamton, N. Y.

The Idea of an American Novel:
An Introduction

In THE PREFACE TO *The Shock of Recognition,* Edmund Wilson said he was presenting literary documents that would show "the developing self-consciousness of the American genius" from the middle of the nineteenth century to the end of the nineteen twenties. In *The Idea of an American Novel,* a fascinating collection, Louis Rubin and John Rees Moore have brought together literary documents that bear on our intense and longstanding self-consciousness about the American novel.

At first young America talked about a national epic. Rome had her *Aeneid,* England her Arthurian legends, and France her *Song of Roland.* Before long, however, Americans were saying that the spirit of the new country would not be caught in the epic— it would be caught in the novel. And in looking back we can see it is in the novel, rather than in poetry, that America has sought her own image.

The Idea of an American Novel presents the arguments, the pleas, the analyses, sometimes chauvinistic but often detached and instructive, that we continue, even now, well into the second half of the twentieth century, to read in our magazines and newspapers and to talk about in classrooms and elsewhere. In these documents, early and late, we can listen to the never ceasing discussion of what it is like to be an American. In the process too we can learn a good deal about the novel as an art form.

America differs from other countries in having been founded on an idea. As some historian has said, it had no pre-history, no dim and mythy past. Seventeenth and eighteenth century man, born into the new age when rationality was supposed to have freed him from superstition, now had his chance. During the Renaissance, More, Campanella, Bacon and others imagined and described utopian societies. Here in North America was the opportunity.

Men, even the men of the enlightenment, however, are not merely social and political creatures. They study themselves in mirrors, in the memorials they erect honoring their own achievements, and in the dreams constructed inside the covers of their books. Young America was carrying a terrible burden—the need to be a perfect society, or as near perfect as possible. Crèvecoeur, who wrote *Letters from an American Farmer,* a utopian vision of the new society, also wrote *Sketches of Eighteenth Century America,* a disillusioned and bitter account of "patriots" he had known. Significantly, the former was published and widely acclaimed. The latter was put in a trunk and rediscovered, with no great fanfare, only in the twentieth century. There may be a clue here to the American imagination.

With his characteristic perceptiveness, D. H. Lawrence put his finger on two preoccupations of James Fenimore Cooper:

In his Leatherstocking books, Fenimore is off on another track. He is no longer concerned with social white Americans that buzz with pins through them, buzz loudly against every mortal thing except the pin itself. The pin of the Great Ideal. One gets irritated with Cooper because he never for once snarls at the Great Ideal Pin which transfixes him. No, indeed. Rather he tries to push it through the very heart of the Continent.

To some extent almost every American novelist is haunted by the Great Ideal and by the Continent; they are related. In essence the Great Ideal is a search for innocence, and the virgin continent was the innocent wilderness. Or was it? Man carried himself into the wilderness, and however fast he moved westward he was dogged by a sense that society, reality, and his own instincts were close behind. For the American novelist the dream of innocence is always there in one form or another. If he is a Cooper or a William Saroyan there is no irony in contemplating it. If he is a Hawthorne, a Melville, a James or a Robert Penn Warren the irony may be gentle or harsh.

We are sometimes told the novel begins with *Don Quixote*. Certainly Cervantes understood the kinds of aspiration that were to dominate the American novel. On the one side, in Don Quixote, there is the practical world, the sort of world in which a young man will be seen marrying for money, in which innocent servants are seduced, and the master of the household calmly cheats a business associate. On the other side, there is gallantry, love, self-sacrifice, and dedication to noble causes. Which side wins in the lists? Does the practical-realistic man easily unseat the dedicated idealist, or does the conduct of the latter so enliven the former's imagination that they join forces? Presumably the novel is at its best when the understanding of the "illusion" and the understanding of the "reality" are profound or at least sufficiently sophisticated to satisfy our awareness that neither "illusion" nor "reality" is wholly separable and definable—we cannot always tell the dancer from the dance. Put in another way, we want to feel sure that the dedicated idealist is tilting at something more than a windmill.

In *Don Quixote*, Cervantes began on the side of reality; he ridiculed and poked fun at the romantic. Then, in midstream, as we say, he changed horses. He began to see that fantasy can influence the human heart and idealize human conduct. The American novel appears to have reversed Cervantes' procedure. It began with a preference for the ideal, for the dream. But reality has a way of following, nipping at the heels of the romantic-minded hero.

As early as 1828, in "American Literature," Cooper was making the distinction between the novel (by which he meant a treatment of manners, the social novel) and the romance (apart from, or indifferent to, society). The former was European, the latter American. There were, according to Cooper, three reasons for this difference: America offered a "poverty of materials," "no costume for the peasant, . . . no wig for the judge, no baton for the general, no diadem for the magistrate"; there was a heaviness and lack of individuality to the American character; and, anyway, an American publisher would rather steal the rights to British novels than pay any American for his book. Cooper, of course, is not wholly consistent.

One can wonder why Boston, Philadelphia, or Charleston—which cannot have been so greatly different from provincial cities in Europe—produced no social novelists. What if Ben Franklin had been inclined toward fiction? Presumably he'd have written social novels, stories about housemaids and the young master, indentured servants, apprentices, gala dances, the slave quarters out back, the pursuit of learning in an attic room, the pull of Europe, the ways of politicians, and getting on in the world. But Franklin didn't write novels, nor did anyone of his temperament. As Cooper says, this type had more assured ways of making successful careers. And we can at least speculate that the pull of the collective American imagination was away from the social community because society has a way of dimming and tarnishing the brilliant shine on the dream.

In an interesting essay, "Manners, Morals and the Novel," Lionel Trilling says that snobbery about one's function as well as about one's status and money, having or not having it, are or should be at the very center of the novel; in other words, the novel ought to be about society. The English and the French novel are centered in society, and even D. H. Lawrence, in comparison with most American writers, is a social novelist. Mr. Trilling says that only Theodore Dreiser and Sinclair Lewis wrote social novels but he adds that neither handled social difference with sufficient cogency. John Dos Passos, he says, was preoccupied with social forces, but he employed them only as background. Following Mr. Trilling's thesis, we can assume that James has been gathered into "Balzac's bosom." And perhaps we should assign Fitzgerald, especially for *Tender Is the Night,* and Edith Wharton, for her *The Age of Innocence,* to the Balzac section in heaven. And more recently, of course, John O'Hara and James Gould Cozzens have written the social novel. As life in the United States becomes "more complex and pressing," to borrow Mr. Trilling's phrase, the American social novel will be more commonly written.

Recently an English critic has said that most American novelists tend to imitate their "own engineers," and to think of the novel in terms of "the Empire State Building or the George Washington Bridge"—he writes "on a scale other than that of everyday life." Our short novels, incidentally, tend not to sprawl; they have the neatness of a convex mirror. This English critic might have had Thomas Wolfe, William Faulkner, Robert Penn

Warren or even Saul Bellow in mind. If he had a nineteenth century novelist in the back of his head, probably it was Melville.

However important the architecture or the sprawl of the American novel in accounting for differences, there is another characteristic that may be even more significant. As backdrop, and subject too, the American novelist tends to employ something vast, the sky, the prairie, the wilderness, the ocean, war, humanity, and even eternity. Man-as-American stands in the foreground. As illustrations we may take *Wieland, The Prairie, The Scarlet Letter, The Adventures of Huckleberry Finn, Moby Dick, McTeague, The Red Badge of Courage, The Country of the Pointed Firs, A Farewell to Arms, The Professor's House, U.S.A., World Enough and Time,* and *A Fable.*

A series of arguments and manifestos that run through *The Idea of an American Novel* have to do with the terms *regionalism, nationalism,* and *universality.* By and large, the regionalists have the best of the argument. If a novelist produces a significant work, it inevitably has a wide, a universal appeal. Inevitably too, and unplanned, it has a national character.

Many of these discussions bear on the notion of the Great American Novel. Simply because we no longer use the phrase, we should not assume that the notion itself no longer engages us.

In the past few years there has been an effort to locate the American vernacular. Twain, Crane, Anderson, and Hemingway are sometimes said to represent it in its purest or at least its earliest forms. Faulkner, when not employing his high rhetoric, is said to employ it, and even Warren. And, of course, Salinger's *Catcher in the Rye* is the vernacular in its New York City guise.

There has also been a search for the American hero—Huck Finn, Nick Adams, Leatherstocking, Ishmael, Pierre, Christopher Newman, Tom Outland, Jay Gatsby, and Holden Caulfield. Obviously there is a certain family resemblance among all of these characters. Others could be added.

Recently, too, we have been told by R. P. Blackmur that the American novelist—he is referring mostly to the short novel—tends to express himself in allegories. And we seem to have come full circle, back to Cooper with Richard Chase's thesis that the American novel, unlike the English, is romance.

The Idea of an American Novel presents most of the documents, many of them not hitherto reprinted, that any student of these matters will want to know. There is no other volume quite like it. We owe Mr. Wilson a considerable debt for his volume on the "American genius." We now owe an equal debt to Messrs. Rubin and Moore.

WILLIAM VAN O'CONNOR

Preface

WHEN our thirteen original states declared their independence of the mother country, they made a declaration that was not to become fact in the cultural realm for over a century. American readers depended upon the British for most of their novels, poetry, and literary criticism; they even subscribed widely to British newspapers. Yet from the beginning Americans made bold pronouncements of faith in the future of the arts in this country. A young Harvard student predicted that America would soon become "the seat of the Muses, the Athens of our age, the admiration of the world," and Noah Webster, a Connecticut schoolmaster soon to win fame as a lexicographer, admonished: "This country must, at some future time, be as distinguished by the superiority of her literary improvements as she is already by the liberality of her civil and ecclesiastical institutions."

But to call for a distinct American literature was one thing, to produce it another. Not that distinguished writing was lacking in the days of Jefferson and John Adams—far from it. But the best literary talent was applied to what seemed more urgent tasks than the creation of fiction and poetry. There was truth, if not the whole truth, in Sydney Smith's famous pronouncement made in 1820 in the Edinburgh Review that "during the thirty or forty years of their independence, [the United States] have done absolutely nothing for the Sciences, for the Arts, for Literature, or even for the statesmen—like studies of Politics or Political Economy." No wonder that he asked, "In the four quarters of the globe, who reads an American book?"

That very year, however, an author who was to be widely read on both sides of the Atlantic published anonymously his first novel, *Precaution*. Encouraged by favorable reviews in British periodicals, James Fenimore Cooper began his second novel, *The Spy*, dealing with events of the Revolutionary War. Published in 1821, its success was so great that it was not only pirated in England but translated into French, German, Spanish, Italian, Russian, Swedish, Danish, Low Dutch, and several other languages. In Cooper, America had the answer to the question put by Sydney Smith.

The novel was still a relatively new literary genre. In England, Defoe, Richardson, Fielding, Sterne, and Smollett had developed the form in the eighteenth century and brought into being a large new reading public. By the middle of the nineteenth century the novel had displaced poetry as the dominant medium of the literary imagination, and instead of demanding a national epic, American critics began to call for the Great American Novel. Their desire was largely motivated by a concern for the national unity that had been so disastrously interrupted by the Civil War, for it was not till the 1860's that the demand specifically for a *novel* began to appear. Meanwhile Hawthorne and Melville, if not Cooper, had written great novels without waiting to be bidden.

With its structural fluidity, its commitment to a language derived from speech, its (at least intended) fidelity to everyday experience, the novel was the literary form best fitted to express the combination of realism and idealism that seemed needed by our emerging capitalistic society after the Civil War. The increasing population was moving into the cities, the older aristocracy was being displaced by the rising plutocracy, new sections of the country were being opened up, and social relations were uncertain and insecure. Although the war did not create this pattern, it accelerated the perhaps inevitable changes taking place. The novel reflected these changes with gradually increasing verisimilitude. As we shall see, there has been a constantly recurring argument in the literary life of our country over the proper decorum for the writer who wishes to confront the reality of experience honestly. Americans, at least until recently, have always been especially sensitive to the moral impact of literature, though not always either subtle or intelligent in judging the moral qualities of their artists. In this, of course, Americans are not unique. What *is* peculiarly American is the unwillingness of our best novelists and critics to settle for either the "real" or the "ideal" at the sacrifice of the other. We want an American myth, but it must be one we can believe in.

This book starts with a group of famous (and not so famous) statements reflecting an awakening national consciousness of the desirability, and even the necessity, of developing a self-reliant, indigenous culture. Next we move on to our subject proper, the idea of the American novel. The discussion turns out to include far more than purely esthetic considerations. Perhaps the basic question is whether *any* novel can adequately sum up the complex realities and aspirations of a nation. At any rate, from Harriet Beecher Stowe to Thomas Wolfe the attempt has frequently been made. With the increasing concern in the eighties and nineties about the national image reflected in the novel, "realism" became the focus of critical debate. How far could the truth be allowed to appear ugly? In fact, can the ugly really be true? As the novelist gradually gained the right to include more and more of the raw experience of life in his work, critical attention shifted to another problem, one that had already preoccupied Henry James for some time. Granted the right to any subject matter, what approach would allow the novelist to extract the maximum significance from the reality he chose to portray? This is the problem of form.

The demand for *the* Great American Novel has come to seem naive, but the questions about form and content that arose during the debate can never be finally answered. If the American novelist is allowed considerably more detachment in his attitude toward his country and its institutions than he once was, his responsibilities as an artist and citizen are nevertheless still lively issues. In this book you will find some of the questions and answers proposed by thoughtful men vitally concerned with the novel in America.

For assistance in the preparation of this work, the editors wish to acknowledge the help of the following persons: Miss Dorothy A. Doerr, Miss Charlotte Tiplady, and the staff of the Fishburn Library of Hollins College; Mr. John Cook Wyllie and the staff

of the Alderman Library, University of Virginia; former President
John R. Everett of Hollins College; and Dr. Stuart H. L. Degginger,
chairman of the faculty committee on research and travel, Hollins
College.

LOUIS D. RUBIN, JR.

JOHN REES MOORE

Contents

VII. *Novels and Novelists*

JAMES FENIMORE COOPER

Here

Contents

NATHANIEL HAWTHORNE

"But

NATHANIEL HAWTHORNE

"But, one idle and rainy day"   205
NATHANIEL HAWTHORNE

"Out of the very heart of New England"   210
HENRY JAMES

"That blue-eyed darling Nathaniel knew disagreeable things in his inner soul"   213
D. H. LAWRENCE

HERMAN MELVILLE

"He can neither believe, nor be comfortable in his unbelief"   216
NATHANIEL HAWTHORNE

"I have written a wicked book, and feel spotless as the lamb"   217
HERMAN MELVILLE

"A new work by Herman Melville"   220
GEORGE RIPLEY

"The alternative of Narcissus"   222
RICHARD CHASE

WILLIAM DEAN HOWELLS

"Mr. James is cosmopolitan and Mr. Howells is American"   230
THE SATURDAY REVIEW

"A vivifying faith Mr. Howells may distinctly be said to possess"   235
HENRY JAMES

"He was the dean of the national letters"   238
H. L. MENCKEN

HENRY JAMES

MARK TWAIN

ERNEST HEMINGWAY

F. SCOTT FITZGERALD

JOHN DOS PASSOS

JAMES T. FARRELL

I

The Call for a National Literature

"It would baffle the strength of a giant"

JAMES FENIMORE COOPER

The first American novelist to attain literary fame beyond the
boundaries of his own country was James Fenimore Cooper
(1789–1851). This upstate New Yorker of aristocratic
lineage and cantankerously democratic leanings was greatly
concerned with the problem of creating imaginative literature
in a new world, and in the passage that follows he cites
several of the obstacles. His second objection in particular was
one that other writers, notably Hawthorne and Henry James,
would continue to find quite pertinent.

A CAPITAL American publisher has assured me that
there are not a dozen writers in this country whose works he
should feel confidence in publishing at all, while he reprints hundreds of English books without the least hesitation. This preference is by no means so much owing to any difference in merit,
as to the fact that, when the price of the original author is to be
added to the uniform hazard which accompanies all literary speculations, the risk becomes too great. The general taste of the reading world in this country is better than that of England. The fact
is both proved and explained by the circumstances that thousands
of works that are printed and read in the mother country are
not printed and read here. The publisher on this side of the Atlantic has the advantage of seeing the reviews of every book he
wishes to reprint, and, what is of far more importance, he knows,

From James Fenimore Cooper, Letter XXIII in *Notions of the Americans*
(Philadelphia, 1828).

3

with the exception of books that he is sure of selling, by means
of a name, the decision of the English critics before he makes
his choice. Nine times in ten, popularity, which is all he looks
for, is a sufficient test of general merit. Thus, while you find
every English work of character, or notoriety, on the shelves of
an American bookstore, you may ask in vain for most of the trash
that is so greedily devoured in the circulating libraries of the
mother country, and which would be just as eagerly devoured over
here, had not a much better taste been created by a compelling
abstinence. That taste must now be overcome before such works
could be sold at all.

When I say that books are not rejected here, from any want of
talent in the writers, perhaps I ought to explain. I wish to express
something a little different. Talent is sure of too many avenues to
wealth and honor in America, to seek, unnecessarily, an unknown
and hazardous path. It is better paid in the ordinary pursuits of
life than it would be likely to be paid by an adventure in which
an extraordinary and skillful, because practiced, foreign competition is certain. Perhaps high talent does not often make the trial
with the American bookseller; but it is precisely for the reason I
have named.

The second obstacle against which American literature has to
contend is in the poverty of materials. There is scarcely an ore
which contributes to the wealth of the author that is found here
in veins as rich as in Europe. There are no annals for the historian;
no follies (beyond the most vulgar and commonplace) for the
satirist; no manners for the dramatist; no obscure fictions for the
writer of romance; no gross and hardy offenses against decorum
for the moralist; nor any of the rich artificial auxiliaries of poetry.
The weakest hand can extract a spark from the flint, but it would
baffle the strength of a giant to attempt kindling a flame with a
pudding-stone. I very well know there are theorists who assume
that the society and institutions of this country are, or ought to
be, particularly favorable to novelties and variety. But the experience of one month, in these States, is sufficient to show any
observant man the falsity of their position. The effect of a promis-
cuous assemblage anywhere is to create a standard of deportment; and great liberty permits every one to aim at its attainment. I have never seen a nation so much alike in my life, as the
people of the United States, and what is more, they are not only

like each other, but they are remarkably like that which common sense tells them they ought to resemble. No doubt, traits of character that are a little peculiar, without, however, being either very poetical, or very rich, are to be found in remote districts; but they are rare, and not always happy exceptions. In short, it is not possible to conceive a state of society in which more of the attributes of plain good sense, or fewer of the artificial absurdities of life, are to be found, than here. There is no costume for the peasant (there is scarcely a peasant at all), no wig for the judge, no baton for the general, no diadem for the chief magistrate. The darkest ages of their history are illuminated by the light of truth; the utmost effects of their chivalry are limited by the laws of God; and even the deeds of their sages and heroes are to be sung in a language that would differ but little from a version of the ten commandments. However useful and respectable all this may be in actual life, it indicates but one direction to the man of genius.

"We will walk on our own feet"

RALPH WALDO EMERSON

Ralph Waldo Emerson (1803–1882) was the first American essayist to attract a wide audience as a philosopher. In his transcendentalist idealism he envisioned for the new American nation a spiritual emancipation from the bonds of Old World thought and custom. American scholars—and by "scholar" Emerson included all who write and think—would proclaim and lead the way.

W̲E HAVE LISTENED too long to the courtly muses of Europe. The spirit of the American freeman is already suspected

From Ralph Waldo Emerson, "The American Scholar," in *Nature: Addresses and Lectures,* Vol. I of the Centenary Ed., *Complete Works,* ed. Edward Waldo Emerson (Boston, 1903), pp. 114–115. Originally an address delivered in 1837.

to be timid, imitative, tame. Public and private avarice make the air we breathe thick and fat. The scholar is decent, indolent, complaisant. See already the tragic consequence. The mind of this country, taught to aim at low objects, eats upon itself. There is no work for any but the decorous and the complaisant. Young men of the fairest promise, who begin life upon our shores, inflated by the mountain winds, shined upon by all the stars of God, find the earth below not in unison with these, but are hindered from action by the disgust which the principles on which business is managed inspire, and turn drudges, or die of disgust, some of them suicides. What is the remedy? They did not yet see, and thousands of young men as hopeful now crowding to the barriers for the career do not yet see, that if the single man plant himself indomitably on his instincts, and there abide, the huge world will come round to him. Patience,—patience; with the shades of all the good and great for company; and for solace the perspective of your own infinite life; and for work the study and the communication of principles, the making those instincts prevalent, the conversion of the world. Is it not the chief disgrace in the world, not to be an unit;—not to be reckoned one character;—not to yield that peculiar fruit which each man was created to bear, but to be reckoned in the gross, in the hundred, or the thousand, of the party, the section, to which we belong; and our opinion predicted geographically, as the north, or the south? Not so, brothers and friends—please God, ours shall not be so. We will walk on our own feet; we will work with our own hands; we will speak our own minds. The study of letters shall be no longer a name for pity, for doubt, and for sensual indulgence. The dread of man and the love of man shall be a wall of defence and a wreath of joy around all. A nation of men will for the first time exist, because each believes himself inspired by the Divine Soul which also inspires all men.

"No shadow, no antiquity, no mystery"

NATHANIEL HAWTHORNE

For the would-be American writer, the newness of his country, its lack of a long history and tradition of its own, presented difficulties. Nathaniel Hawthorne (1804–1864), who in his own work drew effectively upon the two hundred years of fact and legend concerning his Puritan New England ancestors, expressed the American writer's problem succinctly in the Preface to his last completed novel, *The Marble Faun* (1860).

ITALY, AS THE SITE of his Romance, was chiefly valuable to him as affording a sort of poetic or fairy precinct, where actualities would not be so terribly insisted upon as they are, and must needs be, in America. No author, without a trial, can conceive of the difficulty of writing a romance about a country where there is no shadow, no antiquity, no mystery, no picturesque and gloomy wrong, nor anything but a commonplace prosperity, in broad and simple daylight, as is happily the case with my dear native land. It will be very long, I trust, before romance-writers may find congenial and easily handled themes, either in the annals of our stalwart republic, or in any characteristic and probable events of our individual lives. Romance and poetry, ivy, lichens, and wall-flowers need ruin to make them grow.

From Nathaniel Hawthorne, "Preface to *The Marble Faun*," in *Works of Nathaniel Hawthorne* (Boston, 1871), pp. viii–ix.

"Let him write like a man"

HERMAN MELVILLE

In 1850 Herman Melville (1819–1891), already preparing
to write his great *Moby Dick* (1851), contributed to the
New York *Literary World* a two-part review of Hawthorne's
Mosses From An Old Manse (1851), in which he boldly
proclaimed Hawthorne's genius, as well as the right of the
American author to be judged on his own terms rather than
by his success in conforming to European models.

SOME MAY START to read of Shakespeare and Hawthorne
on the same page. They may say that if an illustration were
needed, a lesser light might have sufficed to elucidate this Hawthorne, this small man of yesterday. But I am not willingly one of
those who, as touching Shakespeare at least, exemplify the maxim
of Rochefoucauld, that "we exalt the reputation of some, in order
to depress that of others"—who, to teach all noble-souled as-
pirants that there is no hope for them, pronounce Shakespeare
absolutely unapproachable. But Shakespeare has been approached.
There are minds that have gone as far as Shakespeare into the
universe. And hardly a mortal man, who, at some time or other,
has not felt as great thoughts in him as any you will find in Hamlet. We must not inferentially malign mankind for the sake of
any one man, whoever he may be. This is too cheap a purchase
of contentment for conscious mediocrity to make. Besides, this
absolute and unconditional adoration of Shakespeare has grown

[Herman Melville], "Hawthorne and His *Mosses:* By a Virginian Spending
July in Vermont," *The Literary World* VII (August 17, 1850), 126 and (August
24, 1850), 145–146. Reprinted in *The Shock of Recognition,* ed. Edmund Wil-
son (New York: Farrar, Straus & Cudahy, Inc., 1955), pp. 194–198. (*The
Shock of Recognition,* in two volumes, is available in a paperback edition (New
York: Grosset & Dunlap).)

to be a part of our Anglo-Saxon superstitions. The Thirty-Nine Articles are now forty. Intolerance has come to exist in this matter. You must believe in Shakespeare's unapproachability, or quit the country. But what sort of a belief is this for an American, a man who is bound to carry republican progressiveness into Literature as well as into Life? Believe me, my friends, that men not very much inferior to Shakespeare are this day being born on the banks of the Ohio. And the day will come when you shall say, Who reads a book by an Englishman that is a modern? The great mistake seems to be, that even with those Americans who look forward to the coming of a great literary genius among us, they somehow fancy he will come in the costume of Queen Elizabeth's day; be a writer of dramas founded upon old English history or the tales of Boccaccio. Whereas, great geniuses are parts of the times, they themselves are the times, and possess a corresponding coloring. It is of a piece with the Jews, who, while their Shiloh was meekly walking in their streets, were still praying for his magnificent coming; looking for him in a chariot, who was already among them on an ass. Nor must we forget that, in his own lifetime, Shakespeare was not Shakespeare, but only Master William Shakespeare of the shrewd, thriving business firm of Condell, Shakespeare and Co., proprietors of the Globe Theater in London; and by a courtly author, of the name of Chettle, was looked at as an "upstart crow," beautified "with other birds' feathers." For, mark it well, imitation is often the first charge brought against originality. Why this is so, there is not space to set forth here. You must have plenty of sea-room to tell the Truth in; especially when it seems to have an aspect of newness, as America did in 1492, though it was then just as old, and perhaps older than Asia, only those sagacious philosophers, the common sailors, had never seen it before, swearing it was all water and moonshine there.

Now I do not say that Nathaniel of Salem is a greater man than William of Avon, or as great. But the difference between the two men is by no means immeasurable. Not a very great deal more, and Nathaniel were verily William.

This, too, I mean: that if Shakespeare has not been equaled, give the world time, and he is sure to be surpassed in one hemisphere or the other. Nor will it at all do to say that the world

is getting gray and grizzled now, and has lost that fresh charm
which she wore of old, and by virtue of which the great poets of
past times made themselves what we esteem them to be. Not so.
The world is as young today as when it was created; and this
Vermont morning dew is as wet to my feet as Eden's dew to
Adam's. Nor has nature been all over ransacked by our progeni-
tors, so that no new charms and mysteries remain for this latter
generation to find. Far from it. The trillionth part has not yet
been said; and all that has been said but multiplies the avenues
to what remains to be said. It is not so much paucity as super-
abundance of material that seems to incapacitate modern authors.

Let America, then, prize and cherish her writers; yea, let her
glorify them. They are not so many in number as to exhaust her
good-will. And while she has good kith and kin of her own to
take to her bosom, let her not lavish her embraces upon the
household of an alien. For believe it or not, England, after all,
is in many things an alien to us. China has more bonds of real
love for us than she. But even were there no strong literary indi-
vidualities among us, as there are some dozen at least, nevertheless, let America first praise mediocrity even, in her children,
before she praises (for everywhere, merit demands acknowledgment from everyone) the best excellence in the children of any
other land. Let her own authors, I say, have the priority of appreciation. I was much pleased with a hot-headed Carolina cousin
of mine, who once said, "If there were no other American to stand
by, in literature, why, then, I would stand by Pop Emmonds and
his *Fredoniad,* and till a better epic came along, swear it was not
very far behind the *Iliad.*" Take away the words, and in spirit
he was sound.

Not that American genius needs patronage in order to expand.
For that explosive sort of stuff will expand though screwed up in
a vise, and burst it, though it were triple steel. It is for the nation's sake, not for her authors' sake, that I would have America
be heedful of the increasing greatness among her writers. For
how great the shame, if other nations should be before her, in
crowning her heroes of the pen! But this is almost the case now.
American authors have received more just and discriminating
praise (however loftily and ridiculously given, in certain cases)
even from some Englishmen, than from their own countrymen.

There are hardly five critics in America; and several of them are asleep. As for patronage, it is the American author who now patronizes his country, and not his country him. As if at times some among them appeal to the people for more recognition, it is not always with selfish motives, but patriotic ones.

It is true that but few of them as yet have evinced that decided originality which merits great praise. But that graceful writer who perhaps of all Americans has received the most plaudits from his own country for his productions—that very popular and amiable writer, however good and self-reliant in many things, perhaps owes his chief reputation to the self-acknowledged imitation of a foreign model, and to the studied avoidance of all topics but smooth ones. But it is better to fail in originality than to succeed in imitation. He who has never failed somewhere, that man cannot be great. Failure is the true test of greatness. And if it be said that continual success is a proof that a man wisely knows his powers, it is only to be added that, in that case, he knows there is no hope for us in these smooth, pleasing writers that know their powers. Without malice, but to speak the plain fact, they but furnish an appendix to Goldsmith and other English authors. And we want no American Goldsmiths, nay, we want no American Miltons. It were the vilest thing you could say of a true American author that he were an American Tompkins. Call him an American and have done, for you cannot say a nobler thing of him. But it is not meant that all American writers should studiously cleave to nationality in their writings; only this, no American writer should write like an Englishman or a Frenchman; let him write like a man, for then he will be sure to write like an American. Let us away with this leaven of literary flunkeyism toward England. If either must play the flunkey in this thing, let England do it, not us. While we are rapidly preparing for that political supremacy among the nations which prophetically awaits us at the close of the present century, in a literary point of view, we are deplorably unprepared for it; and we seem studious to remain so. Hitherto, reasons might have existed why this should be, but no good reason exists now. And all that is requisite to amendment in this matter is simply this: that while fully acknowledging all excellence everywhere, we should refrain from unduly lauding foreign writers, and, at the same time, duly recognize the meritorious writers that are our own; those writers who breathe that unshackled, democratic spirit of Christianity in all things, which now takes the practical lead in this world, though at the same time led by ourselves—us Americans. Let us boldly condemn all imitation, though it comes to us graceful and fragrant as the morning; and foster all originality, though at first it be crabbed and ugly as our own pine knots. And if any of our authors fail, or seem to fail, then, in the words of my Carolina cousin, let us clap him on the shoulder and back him against all Europe for his second round. The truth is, that in one point of view this matter of a national literature has come to such a pass with us, that in some sense we must turn bullies, else the day is lost, or superiority so far beyond us, that we can hardly say it will ever be ours.

"Democratic vistas"

WALT WHITMAN

Walt Whitman (1819–1892), poet and American, expressed in his prose work "Democratic Vistas" (1882–1883) the same thoughts he had set forth in his poems, concerning the great possibilities and needs of an American imaginative literature.

BUT IT IS NECESSARY to return to our original premises. In view of them, we have again pointedly to confess that all the objective grandeurs of the world, for highest purposes, yield themselves up, and depend on mentality alone. Here, and here only, all balances, all rests. For the mind, which alone builds the permanent edifice, haughtily builds it to itself. By it, with what follows it, are convey'd to mortal sense the culminations of the

From Walt Whitman, "Democratic Vistas," in *Specimen Days and Collect. Prose Works of Walt Whitman* (Philadelphia, n.d.), pp. 238–239.

materialistic, the known, and a prophecy of the unknown. To take expression, to incarnate, to endow a literature with grand and archetypal models—to fill with pride and love the utmost capacity, and to achieve spiritual meanings, and suggest the future—these, and these only, satisfy the soul. We must not say one word against real materials; but the wise know that they do not become real till touched by emotions, the mind. Did we call the latter imponderable? Ah, let us rather proclaim that the slightest song-tune, the countless ephemera of passions arous'd by orators and tale-tellers, are more dense, more weighty than the engines there in the great factories, or the granite blocks in their foundations.

Approaching thus the momentous spaces, and considering with reference to a new and greater personalism, the needs and possibilities of American imaginative literature, through the medium-light of what we have already broach'd, it will at once be appreciated that a vast gulf of difference separates the present accepted condition of these spaces, inclusive of what is floating in them, from any condition adjusted to, or fit for, the world, the America, there sought to be indicated, and the copious races of complete men and women, along these Vistas crudely outlined. It is, in some sort, no less a difference than lies between that long-continued nebular state and vagueness of the astronomical worlds, compared with the subsequent state, the definitely-form'd worlds themselves, duly compacted, clustering in systems, hung up there, chandeliers of the universe, beholding and mutually lit by each other's lights, serving for ground of all substantial foothold, all vulgar uses—yet serving still more as an undying chain and echelon of spiritual proofs and shows. A boundless field to fill! A new creation, with needed orbic works launch'd forth, to revolve in free and lawful circuits—to move, self-poised, through the ether, and shine like heaven's own suns! With such, and nothing less, we suggest that New World literature, fit to rise upon, cohere, and signalize in time, these States.

"*We are in a condition to be criticized*"

EDGAR ALLAN POE

Edgar Allan Poe (1809–1849) not only all but created the
modern short story and wrote some widely popular poems,
but was one of America's first and most influential literary
critics. His impatience with mediocre American work, and with
the tendency of many readers to excuse literary shortcomings
on the grounds that the work was American, is illustrated in
his strictures on the poems of J. G. C. Brainard, originally
published in *Graham's Magazine* in 1842. American literature,
he declares, was of sufficient stature now to be subjected to
the same kind of criticism on its merits that English literature
faced.

A MONG ALL THE PIONEERS of American literature,
whether prose or poetical, there is *not one* whose productions
have not been much overrated by his countrymen. But this fact
is more especially obvious in respect to such of these pioneers as
are no longer living; nor is it a fact of so deeply transcendental a
nature as only to be accounted for by the Emersons and Alcotts.
In the first place we have but to consider that gratitude, surprise,
and a species of hyper-patriotic triumph have been blended, and
finally confounded with mere admiration, or appreciation, in respect to the labors of our earlier writers; and, in the second
place, that Death has thrown his customary veil of the sacred over
these commingled feelings, forbidding them, in a measure, to be
now separated or subjected to analysis. "In speaking of the de-

From Edgar Allan Poe, "A Few Words about Brainard," in Vol. XI, *Com-
plete Works*, ed. James A. Harrison (New York, 1902), pp. 15–17. Reprinted in
The Shock of Recognition, ed. Edmund Wilson (New York: Farrar, Straus &
Cudahy, Inc., 1955), pp. 85–86.

ceased," says that excellent old English Moralist, James Puckle, in his *Gray Cap for a Green Head,* "so fold up your discourse that their virtues may be outwardly shown, while their vices are wrapped up in silence." And with somewhat too inconsiderate a promptitude have we followed the spirit of this quaint advice. The mass of American readers have been, hitherto, in no frame of mind to view with calmness, and to discuss with discrimination, the true claims of the few who were *first* in convincing the mother country that her sons were not all brainless, as, in the plenitude of her arrogance, she, at one period, half affected and half wished to believe; and where any of these few have departed from among us, the difficulty of bringing their pretensions to the test of a proper criticism has been enhanced in a very remarkable degree. But even as concerns the living: is there anyone so blind as not to see that Mr. Cooper, for example, owes much, and that Mr. Paulding owes *all* of his reputation as a novelist to his early occupation of the field? Is there anyone so dull as not to know that fictions which neither Mr. Paulding nor Mr. Cooper *could* have written are daily published by native authors without attracting more of commendation than can be crammed into a hack newspaper paragraph? And, again, is there anyone so prejudiced as not to acknowledge that all this is because there is no longer either reason or wit in the query,—"Who reads an American book?" It is not because we lack the talent in which the days of Mr. Paulding exulted, but because such talent has shown itself to be common. It is not because we have *no* Mr. Coopers; but because it has been demonstrated that we might, at any moment, have as many Mr. Coopers as we please. In fact, we are now strong in our own resources. We have, at length, arrived at that epoch when our literature may and must stand on its own merits, or fall through its own defects. We have snapped asunder the leading-strings of our British grandmamma, and, better still, we have survived the first hours of our novel freedom,—the first licentious hours of a hobbledehoy braggadocio and swagger. At last, then we are in a condition to be criticized—even more, to be neglected; and the journalist is no longer in danger of being impeached for *lèse majesté* of the Democratic Spirit, who shall assert, with sufficient humility, that we have committed an error in mistaking Kettell's *Specimens* for the Pentateuch, or Joseph Rodman Drake for Apollo.

"A false and narrow criterion"

HENRY TIMROD

It is not the subject matter that an American writer chooses,
but his underlying attitudes as expressed in the way he
manages his material, that will demonstrate the American
character of his work, declared the poet Henry Timrod
(1828–1867). In his discussion of Southern literature, the
South Carolina poet notably anticipated twentieth-century
discussions of regionalism in literature.

Iɴ ᴛʜᴇ ᴄᴏᴜʀsᴇ of these remarks, we have alluded to
three classes of critics, the bigot, the slave, and we cannot better
characterize the third, than as the autocratic. There is yet a
fourth, which feels, or professes to feel, a warm interest in Southern literature, and which so far is entitled to our respect. But,
unfortunately, the critical principles of this class are quite as
shallow as those of any of the others; and we notice it chiefly
to expose the absurdity of one of its favourite opinions, adopted
from a theory which some years ago arose at the North, and
which bore the name of Americanism in literature. After the lapse
of a period commensurate with the distance it had to travel, it
reached the remote South, where it became, with an intensity of
absurdity which is admirable indeed, Southernism in literature.
Now, if the theory had gone to the depth of that which constitutes
true nationality, we should have no objections to urge against it.
But to the understandings of these superficial critics, it meant
nothing more than that an author should confine himself in the
choice of his subjects to the scenery, the history, and the traditions of his own country. To be an American novelist, it was

From Henry Timrod, "Literature in the South," *Russell's Magazine*, V
(August, 1859). Reprinted in *The Essays of Henry Timrod*, ed. Edd Winfield
Parks (Athens, Ga.: University of Georgia Press, 1942), pp. 87–90.

sufficient that a writer should select a story, in which one half the characters should be backwoodsmen, who talked bad Saxon, and the other half should be savages, who talked Choctaw translated into very bombastic English. To be an American poet, it was sufficient either in a style and measure imitated from Pope and Goldsmith, or in the more modern style and measure of Scott and Wordsworth, to describe the vast prairies of the West, the swamps and pine forests of the South, or the great lakes and broad rivers of the North. It signified nothing to these critics whether the tone, the spirit, or the style were caught from European writers or not. If a poet, in genuine Scott, or genuine Byron, compared his hero to a cougar or grisly bear—patriotically ignoring the Asiatic tiger or the African lion—the exclamation of the critic was, "How intensely American!"

We submit that this is a false and narrow criterion, by which to judge of the true nationality of the author. Not in the subject, except to a partial extent, but in the management of the subject, in the tone and bearings of the thought, in the drapery, the colouring, and those thousand nameless touches, which are to be felt rather than expressed, are the characteristics of a writer to be sought. It is in these particulars that an author of original genius—no matter what his subject—will manifest his nationality. In fact, true originality will be always found identical with true nationality. A painter who should paint an American landscape exactly in the style of Salvator or of Claude ought scarcely to be entitled an American painter. A poet who should write a hymn to Niagara in the blank verse of the Ulysses or the Princess, ought not to be entitled an American poet. In a word, he alone, who, in a style evolved from his own individual nature, speaks the thoughts and feelings of his own deep heart, can be a truly national genius. In the works of such a man, the character which speaks behind and through him—as character does not always speak in the case of men of mere talent, who in some respects are usually more or less under the sway of more commanding minds—will furnish the best and highest types of the intellectual character of his countrymen, and will illustrate most correctly, as well as most subtly—perhaps most correctly because most subtly—the nature of the influences around him. In the poetry of such a man, if he be a poet, whether its scenes be laid in his native country or the land of faery, the pines of his own forests shall be heard to murmur, the music of his own rivers shall swell the diapason, the flowers of his own soil shall bud and burst, though touched perhaps with a more ethereal and lasting grace; and with a brighter and more spiritual lustre, or with a darker and holier beauty, it will be his own skies that look down upon the loveliest landscapes of his creation.

We regard the theory of Southernism in literature as a circumscription, both unnecessary and unreasonable, of the privileges of genius. Shakespeare was not less an Englishman when he wrote Antony and Cleopatra, than when he dramatized the history of the kings of England. Sir Walter was not less a Scotchman when he drew the characters of Louis XI and Charles the Bold, than when he conceived the characters of Edie Ochiltree and Balfour of Burley. We do not suppose that until this theory germinated in the brain of its foolish originator, it ever occurred to an author that in his selection of subjects, he was to be bounded by certain geographical limits. And if in addition to the many difficulties which he has to overcome, the Southern author be expected, under the penalty of being pronounced un-Southern in tone, and unpatriotic in spirit, never to pass the Potomac on one side, or the Gulf on the other, we shall despair of ever seeing within our borders a literature of such depth and comprehensiveness as will ensure it the respect of other countries, or permanence in the remembrance of posterity. No! the domain of genius is as wide as the world, and as ancient as creation. Wherever the angel of its inspiration may lead, it has the right to follow—and whether exhibited by the light of tropic suns, or of the Arctic morning, whether embodied in the persons of ancient heroes, or of modern thinkers, the eternal verities which it aims to inculcate shall find in every situation, and under every guise, their suitable place, and their proper incarnation.

"Universality is better"

HENRY WADSWORTH LONGFELLOW

Henry Wadsworth Longfellow (1807–1882) achieved
tremendous popularity in Europe and America with his
poems. A Greek and Latin scholar, Longfellow wrote epic
poems in classical measure, and had little sympathy with
those who advocated a conscious rejection of the European
literary tradition, as witness this passage from his novel
Kavanagh (1849), in which he discusses the subject of
American literature.

H E ANNOUNCED himself as Mr. Hathaway. Passing
through the village, he could not deny himself the pleasure of
calling on Mr. Churchill, whom he knew by his writings in the
periodicals, though not personally. He wished, moreover, to secure the cooperation of one, already so favorably known to the
literary world, in a new Magazine he was about to establish, in
order to raise the character of American literature, which, in his
opinion, the existing reviews and magazines had entirely failed
to accomplish. A daily increasing want of something better was
felt by the public, and the time had come for the establishment
of such a periodical as he proposed. After explaining, in rather
a florid and exuberant manner, his plan and prospects, he entered
more at large into the subject of American literature, which it was
his design to foster and patronize.

"I think, Mr. Churchill," said he, "that we want a national
literature commensurate with our mountains and rivers,—commensurate with Niagara, and the Alleghenies, and the Great
Lakes!"

"Oh!"

From Henry Wadsworth Longfellow, "Kavanagh," in *Hyperion and Kavanagh*, Vol. II of the *Prose Works of Henry Wadsworth Longfellow* (Boston,
1886), pp. 365–369.

"We want a national epic that shall correspond to the size of the country; that shall be to all other epics what Banvard's Panorama of the Mississippi is to all other paintings,—the largest in the world!"

"Ah!"

"We want a national drama in which scope enough shall be given to our gigantic ideas, and to the unparalleled activity and progress of our people!"

"Of course."

"In a word, we want a national literature altogether shaggy and unshorn, that shall shake the earth, like a herd of buffaloes thundering over the prairies!"

"Precisely," interrupted Mr. Churchill; "but excuse me!—are you not confounding things that have no analogy? Great has a very different meaning when applied to a river, and when applied to a literature. Large and shallow may perhaps be applied to both. Literature is rather an image of the spiritual world, than of the physical, is it not?—of the internal, rather than the external. Mountains, lakes, and rivers are, after all, only its scenery and decorations, not its substance and essence. A man will not necessarily be a great poet because he lives near a great mountain. Nor, being a poet, will he necessarily write better poems than another, because he lives near Niagara."

"But, Mr. Churchill, you do not certainly mean to deny the influence of scenery on the mind?"

"No, only to deny that it can create genius. At best, it can only develop it. Switzerland has produced no extraordinary poet; nor, as far as I know, have the Andes, or the Himalaya mountains, or the Mountains of the Moon in Africa."

"But, at all events," urged Mr. Hathaway, "let us have our literature national. If it is not national, it is nothing."

"On the contrary, it may be a great deal. Nationality is a good thing to a certain extent, but universality is better. All that is best in the great poets of all countries is not what is national in them, but what is universal. Their roots are in their native soil; but their branches wave in the unpatriotic air, that speaks the same language unto all men, and their leaves shine with the illimitable light that pervades all lands. Let us throw all the windows open; let us admit the light and air on all sides; that we may look towards the four corners of the heavens, and not always in the same direction."

"But you admit nationality to be a good thing?"

"Yes, if not carried too far; still, I confess, it rather limits one's views of truth. I prefer what is natural. Mere nationality is often ridiculous. Every one smiles when he hears the Icelandic proverb, 'Iceland is the best land the sun shines upon.' Let us be natural, and we shall be national enough. Besides, our literature can be strictly national only so far as our character and modes of thought differ from those of other nations. Now, as we are very like the English,—are, in fact, English under a different sky,—I do not see how our literature can be very different from theirs. Westward from hand to hand we pass the lighted torch, but it was lighted at the old domestic fireside of England."

"Then you think our literature is never to be anything but an imitation of the English?"

"Not at all. It is not an imitation, but, as some one has said, a continuation."

"It seems to me that you take a very narrow view of the subject."

"On the contrary, a very broad one. No literature is complete until the language in which it is written is dead. We may well be proud of our task and of our position. Let us see if we can build in any way worthy of our forefathers."

"But I insist upon originality."

"Yes; but without spasms and convulsions. Authors must not, like Chinese soldiers, expect to win victories by turning somersets in the air."

"Well, really, the prospect from your point of view is not very brilliant. Pray, what do you think of our national literature?"

"Simply, that a national literature is not the growth of a day. Centuries must contribute their dew and sunshine to it. Our own is growing slowly but surely, striking its roots downward, and its branches upward, as is natural; and I do not wish, for the sake of what some people call originality, to invert it, and try to make it grow with its roots in the air. And as for having it so savage and wild as you want it, I have only to say, that all literature, as well as all art, is the result of culture and intellectual refinement."

"Ah! we do not want art and refinement; we want genius,—untutored, wild, original, free."

"But, if this genius is to find any expression, it must employ art, for art is the external expression of our thoughts. Many have genius, but, wanting art, are forever dumb. The two must go together to form the great poet, painter, or sculptor."

"In that sense, very well."

"I was about to say also that I thought our literature would finally not be wanting in a kind of universality. As the blood of all nations is mingling with our own, so will their thoughts and feelings finally mingle in our literature. We shall draw from the Germans, tenderness; from the Spaniards, passion; from the French, vivacity,—to mingle more and more with our English solid sense. And this will give us universality, so much to be desired."

"In a thousand fresh and original forms"

MARGARET FULLER

Margaret Fuller (1810–1850), literary critic and social commentator, did not doubt that a distinctive American literature would come, but predicted that it would have to wait until the new nation was much more united politically, culturally, and socially than was possible in her own time.

W E HAVE NO SYMPATHY with national vanity. We are not anxious to prove that there is as yet much American literature. Of those who think and write among us in the methods and of the thoughts of Europe, we are not impatient; if their minds are

From Margaret Fuller, "American Literature," in *Papers on Literature and Art* (2 vols.: New York, 1846). Reprinted in *The Writings of Margaret Fuller*, ed. Mason Wade (New York: The Viking Press, Inc., 1941), pp. 358–360.

still best adapted to such food and such action. If their books express life of mind and character in graceful forms, they are good and we like them. We consider them as colonists and useful schoolmasters to our people in a transition state; which lasts rather longer than is occupied in passing bodily the ocean which separates the New from the Old World.

We have been accused of an undue attachment to foreign continental literature, and it is true that in childhood we had well nigh "forgotten our English" while constantly reading in other languages. Still what we loved in the literature of continental Europe was the range and force of ideal manifestation in forms of national and individual greatness. A model was before us in the great Latins of simple masculine minds seizing upon life with unbroken power. The stamp both of nationality and individuality was very strong upon them; their lives and thoughts stood out in clear and bold relief. The English character has the iron force of the Latins, but not the frankness and expansion. Like their fruits, they need a summer sky to give them more sweetness and a richer flavor. This does not apply to Shakespeare, who has all the fine side of English genius, with the rich coloring and more fluent life of the Catholic countries. Other poets of England also are expansive more or less, and soar freely to seek the blue sky, but take it as a whole, there is in English literature, as in English character, a reminiscence of walls and ceilings, a tendency to the arbitrary and conventional that repels a mind trained in admiration of the antique spirit. It is only in later days that we are learning to prize the peculiar greatness which a thousand times outweighs this fault, and which has enabled English genius to go forth from its insular position and conquer such vast dominion in the realms both of matter and of mind.

Yet there is often between child and parent a reaction from excessive influence having been exerted, and such a one we have experienced in behalf of our country against England. We use her language and receive in torrents the influence of her thought, yet it is in many respects uncongenial and injurious to our constitution. What suits Great Britain, with her insular position and consequent need to concentrate and intensify her life, her limited monarchy and spirit of trade, does not suit a mixed race continually enriched with new blood from other stocks the most unlike that of our first descent, with ample field and verge enough to range in and leave every impulse free, and abundant opportunity to develop a genius wide and full as our rivers, flowery, luxuriant, and impassioned as our vast prairies, rooted in strength as the rocks on which the Puritan fathers landed.

That such a genius is to rise and work in this hemisphere we are confident; equally so that scarce the first faint streaks of that day's dawn are yet visible. It is sad for those that foresee, to know they may not live to share its glories, yet it is sweet, too, to know that every act and word uttered in the light of that foresight may tend to hasten or ennoble its fulfillment.

That day will not arise till the fusion of races among us is more complete. It will not rise till this nation shall attain sufficient moral and intellectual dignity to prize moral and intellectual no less highly than political freedom, not till the physical resources of the country being explored, all its regions studded with towns, broken by the plow, netted together by railways and telegraph lines, talent shall be left at leisure to turn its energies upon the higher department of man's existence. Nor then shall it be seen till from the leisurely and yearning soul of that riper time national ideas shall take birth, ideas craving to be clothed in a thousand fresh and original forms.

Without such ideas all attempts to construct a national literature must end in abortions like the monster of Frankenstein, things with forms and the instincts of forms, but soulless and therefore revolting. We cannot have expression till there is something to be expressed.

II

The Scope of the "Great American Novel"

"A single tale which paints American life"

THE NATION

The demand that went up for the "Great American Novel" after the Civil War, when spiritual unification of the divided land seemed so necessary, caught the fancy of many literary critics and authors. An editorial in *The Nation* for January 9, 1868, presented a reasoned appraisal of the literary situation in America, and calmly surveyed the claims of various novels (neglecting, of course, to mention Melville's *Moby Dick*, by now an almost forgotten sea story). Some of the difficulties of authorship in America were also noted, notably the raging controversy over international copyright, the lack of laws for which permitted American publishers to pirate editions of British novels without payment to the British owners. Not until 1891 was the copyright law extended to foreign publications.

A FRIEND OF OURS, a fairly clever person, and by no means lacking in common sense on common subjects, has the craze in his head that he will some day write a great American novel.

"If I can do it," he says, "I shall perform a national service, and be hailed as a national benefactor. It will be acknowledged that I have broken another of the bonds which make us spiritually colonists and provincials. Who does not like to have his portrait taken? If I ever can give expression to the idea which is in my brain, the American people will say, 'That is my picture,' and

From an editorial, "The Great American Novel," *The Nation*, VI (January 9, 1868), 27–29.

will lavish heart and pocket in remuneration. It is a feat worthy of vast labor and suffering."

During eight or ten years he has struggled for his prize. He has published two or three experiments which have been more or less well spoken of by the critics, and rather more than less neglected by the purchasing public. Now and then, collared by the material necessities of life, or by some national enthusiasm even stronger than his own, he has turned aside into other pursuits, has fought at the front, has aided in the work of reconstruction, has written articles and other things which he calls trivialities. But at every leisure moment he returns to his idea of producing "the Great American Novel."

Will he produce it? Will any one of this generation produce it? It is very doubtful, for the obstacles are immense. To write a great American poem is at present impossible, for the reason that the nation has not yet lived a great poem. It cost unknown centuries of Greek faiths and fightings to produce the "Iliad." It cost all the Roman kings and all the Roman republic to produce the "Aeneid." The "Divina Commedia" is the result of a thousand years of the Papal Church. Europe had to live politically through the crusades and the feudal system before it could earn the "Gierusalemme Liberata" and the "Orlando Furioso." "Paradise Lost" is the summary of all gnosticism and Protestantism. We may be confident that the Great American Poem will not be written, no matter what genius attempts it, until democracy, the idea of our day and nation and race, has agonized and conquered through centuries, and made its work secure.

But the "Great American Novel"—the picture of the ordinary emotions and manners of American existence—the American "Newcomes" or "Misérables" will, we suppose, be possible earlier. "Is it time?" the benighted people in the earthen jars of commonplace life are asking. And with no intention of being disagreeable, but rather with sympathetic sorrow, we answer, "Wait." At least we fear that such ought to be our answer. This task of painting the American soul within the framework of a novel has seldom been attempted, and has never been accomplished further than very partially—in the production of a few outlines. Washington Irving was too cautious to make the trial; he went back to fictions of Knickerbockers and Rip Van Winkles and Ichabod Cranes; these he did well, and we may thank him for not attempting more and failing in the attempt. With the same consciousness of incapacity Cooper shirked the experiment; he devoted himself to Indians, of whom he knew next to nothing, and to backwoodsmen and sailors, whom he idealized; or where he attempted civilized groups, he produced something less natural than the wax figures of Barnum's old museum. If all Americans were like the heroes and heroines of Cooper, Carlyle might well enough call us "eighteen millions of bores." As for a tableau of American society, as for anything resembling the tableaux of English society by Thackeray and Trollope, or the tableaux of French society by Balzac and George Sand, we had better not trouble ourselves with looking for it in Cooper.

There come to us from the deserts of the past certain voices which "syllable men's names"—names that seem to sound like "Paulding," "Brown," "Kennedy"—and we catch nothing further. These are ghosts, and they wrote about ghosts, and the ghosts have vanished utterly. Another of these shadowy mediums, still living, if we are not misinformed, is W. Gilmore Simms, of whom the best and worst thing to be said is this—that he is nearly as good as Cooper, and deserves fame nearly as much.

Thus do we arrive, without frequent stoppage, at our own times. Hawthorne, the greatest of American imaginations, staggered under the load of the American novel. In "The Scarlet Letter," "The House of the Seven Gables," and "The Blithedale Romance" we have three delightful romances, full of acute spiritual analysis, of the light of other worlds, but also characterized by only a vague consciousness of this life, and by graspings that catch little but the subjective of humanity. Such personages as Hawthorne creates belong to the wide realm of art rather than to our nationality. They are as probably natives of the furthest mountains of Cathay or of the moon as of the United States of America. They are what Yankees might come to be who should shut themselves up for life to meditate in old manses. They have no sympathy with this eager and laborious people, which takes so many newspapers, builds so many railroads, does the most business on a given capital, wages the biggest war in proportion to its population, believes in the physically impossible and does some of it. Hawthorne's characters cannot talk. Certainly not in the style of this western world; rather in the language of men who never expressed themselves but on paper, and on paper in dreams. There is a curious lack of natural dialogue in Hawthorne's books, and with this, of course, a lack of almost all other signs of the dramatic faculty. Besides, his company is so limited. New Englanders they profess to be: to be sure, they are of the queerest; men and women of the oddest, shyest, most recluse nature, and often creatures purely ideal; but they never profess to be other than New Englanders. The profoundest reverence for this great man need prevent no one from saying that he has not written "the Great American Novel."

The nearest approach to the desired phenomenon is "Uncle Tom's Cabin." There were very noticeable faults in that story; there was a very faulty plot; there was (if idealism be a fault) a black man painted whiter than the angels, and a girl such as girls are to be, perhaps, but are not yet; there was a little village twaddle. But there was also a national breadth to the picture, truthful outlining of character, natural speaking, and plenty of strong feeling. Though comeliness of form was lacking, the material of the work was in many respects admirable. Such Northerners as Mrs. Stowe painted we have seen; and we have seen such Southerners, no matter what the people south of Mason and Dixon's line may protest; we have seen such negroes, barring, of course, the impeccable Uncle Tom—uncle of no extant nephews, so far as we know. It was a picture of American life, drawn with a few strong and passionate strokes, not filled in thoroughly, but still a portrait. It seemed, then, when that book was published, easy to have more American novels. But in "Dred" it became clear that the soul which a throb of emotion had enabled to grasp this whole people was losing its hold on the vast subject which had so stirred us. Then, stricken with timidity, the author shrank into her native shell of New England. . . .

We shall always be grateful to Oliver Wendell Holmes for "The Autocrat of the Breakfast Table," and hardly less grateful for "The Professor." Lighter, brighter, keener, defter prose has rarely been written in America. It would not be unworthy of a Parisian; it would not be scorned by Taine or Veuillot or Henri de Rochefort. . . . We acknowledge that "Elsie Venner" and "The Guardian Angel" are interesting books. They show us faithfully the exterior of commonplace New England life, and they travesty the solemnities of New England's spiritual life with an amusing manual dexterity. But the artist is hampered by his scientific theories and by his lack of fervent emotional sympathy. His characters do not go; they do not drag him along; they do not drag us. . . .

Moreover, these two tales are not American novels; they are only New England novels; they are localisms. We shall not be suspected of desiring to belittle New England, of denying its moral strength, keen intellect, and wide influence. But Dr. Holmes has not sketched that Yankeehood which goes abroad and leavens the character of the Republic. The Yankeehood which he exhibits is that which stays in corners, speechless and impotent—a community of old maids, toothless doctors, small-souled lawyers, village poets, and shelved professors; the coterie of an antique borough, amusing, queer, and of no account. We do not say that he should have put a Wendell Phillips or an Emerson on the canvas; we only say that he has given no prominence to those moral characteristics of New England which produce such movers of the national heart and teachers of the national intellect. . . .

There are other experiments. There are novels by Mr. Mitchell, and Mr. Bayard Taylor, and Mr. Beecher, and many more, but none is better than those already mentioned and few are nearly as good. Is there in the whole catalogue a "Newcomes," a "Vanity Fair," a "Misérables," or even a "Little Dorrit" or a "Small House at Allington"? Is there, in other words, a single tale which paints American life so broadly, truly, and sympathetically that every American of feeling and culture is forced to acknowledge the picture as a likeness of something which he knows? Throwing out "Uncle Tom's Cabin," we must answer, Not one!

And why not? There are several reasons, some material, some spiritual, some pertaining to the artists, some to the subject. It is not necessary to dwell upon the fact that, as we produce few books of any kind, we must consequently produce a duly small proportion of good ones. Another cause of barrenness is not less obvious; but it has been upheld by selfishness, shortsightedness, and national prejudice; it has been so strenuously defended that argument is pardonable. For lack of an international copyright the American author is undersold in his own market by the stolen brain-labor of other countries. The ordinary reader, wanting a book and not caring what, providing it will amuse him, steps into a bookstore and finds "Little Dorrit" alongside of "Elsie Venner." He is pretty sure that both are good, but he sees that the former costs a dollar and three-quarters, and the latter two dollars. He buys the cheaper because it is the cheaper. "Little Dorrit" is stolen and sold without any profit to Dickens; and "Elsie Venner" remains unsold, to the loss of Holmes. Nine readers out of ten do this; each one is glad of the twenty-five cents saved; then he wonders "why we don't have an American literature." Depend upon it that, if "Little Dorrit" were the dearest, more "Elsie Venners" would be sold, and Dr. Holmes would give more time to planning and perfecting novels. The American reader must have his book cheap. He will pay high for his coat, his sofa, his piano, his portrait; but the furniture and clothing and adornment of his mind must be cheap, even if nasty. To charge the English price for a good novel might provoke an indignation meeting, if not a riot. When the "young man called John" buys a book for two dollars, he wants very nearly the worth of his "stamps" in paper and binding. The intellectual or moral value of his purchase is a trifle in his estimation, and he does not mean to pay much for it. In short, the American author has first a small sale, and second a small profit on his sale. His business does not keep him, and so he works carelessly at it, or he quits it. His first book is marked by inexperience; his second is produced in haste to meet a board-bill; and he stops disgusted before he has learned his trade. If he could make a living, and if in addition he saw a chance, the merest chance, of doing as well as a grocery merchant, he would go on and perhaps be our glory; who knows?

We do not say that he would do miraculously well, even under favoring pecuniary circumstances. The child of a community which is given to estimating the claims of books by their cheapness, his culture is not of the highest. Clever, but not trained, he knows better what to write than what not to write. Just consider the educational advantages of an English writer of by no means the highest rank, Miss Thackeray, the author of "The Village on the Cliff." Surrounded from infancy by such men as the creator of "Vanity Fair," the creator of "David Copperfield," and their compeers, she may be said to have inherited the precious knowledge of what not to write. You can see it in her books; there is no great power, but there is nothing threadbare, nothing sophomorical; there is a careful, intelligent workmanship, like that of an old hand. The power of an author is frequently, if not generally, no more than the expression of the community which produced him. Have we as yet the literary culture to educate Thackerays and Balzacs? Ah! we only buy them—cheap.

So much for the artist; now for the sitter. Ask a portrait-painter if he can make a good likeness of a baby, and he will tell you that the features are not sufficiently marked nor the expression sufficiently personal. Is there not the same difficulty in limning this continental infant of American society, who is changing every year not only in physical attributes, but in the characteristics of his soul? Fifteen years ago it was morality to return fugitive slaves to their owners—and now? Five years ago everybody swore to pay the national debt in specie—and now? Our aristocracy flies through the phases of Knickerbocker, codfish, shoddy, and petroleum. Where are the "high-toned gentlemen" whom North and South gloried in a quarter of a century since? Where are the Congressmen who could write "The Federalist"? Where is everything that was? Can a society which is changing so rapidly be painted except in the daily newspaper? Has any one photographed fireworks or the shooting-stars? And then there is such variety and even such antagonism in the component parts of this cataract. When you have made your picture of petrified New England village life, left aground like a boulder near the banks of the Merrimac, does the Mississippian or the Minnesotian or the Pennsylvanian recognize it as American society? We are a nation of provinces, and each province claims to be the court.

When Mr. Anthony Trollope commences a novel, he is perplexed by no such kaleidoscopic transformations and no such conflicting claims of sections. Hundreds of years ago English aristocracy assumed the spiritual nature which it holds with little change to the present day. It had made its code of honor; it had established its relations with the mass of the nation; it had become the model for all proper Englishmen. At this time it is a unit of social expression throughout the kingdom. A large class of people go up to London at the same season, go into the country at the same season, lead very nearly the same lives, have the same ideas and tastes. There you have something fixed to paint; there you have the novelist's sitter; there you have his purchaser. All successful English romances are written with reference to this class; they may attack it, they may defend it, they always paint it. Wealthy, it pays high prices for books; anxious to be amused, it buys them freely. For such a sitter who would not, if possible, learn to paint well? Thus, also, in France, only that the subject is always in your studio, for the studio is Paris. If George Sand writes a provincial novel, she does it not for the people of the province described but for the Parisians, who occasionally like a novelty. But the French author need not know more than that one city to have his subject and his public. In divided Germany there have been few good novels. In distracted Italy there has been, perhaps, but one—"I Promessi Sposi"—and that historical, the result of half a lifetime, the task of a great poet. Even Manzoni found it a mighty labor to depict the life of a nation of provinces.

Well, what are our immediate chances for a "great American novel?" We fear that the wonder will not soon be wrought unless more talent can be enlisted in the work, and we are sure that this sufficient talent can hardly be obtained without the encouragement of an international copyright. And, even then, is it time?

"The country sorely needs great unifying forces"

HAMILTON W. MABIE

The demand for unity, for national self-consciousness, was voiced on many sides during the decades after the Civil War, and continued well into the present century. The essay that follows, by Hamilton W. Mabie (1845?–1916), though published as late as 1899, is representative of the continuing hue and cry for a literature that would cement sections and classes into a single indivisible nation.

ONE OF THE CHIEF USES of literature is to give the inner life clear and commanding expression; for it is only in and through some form of expression that the quality and significance of the inner life are comprehended. Inarticulate life may have reality and depth: it cannot have expansiveness and contagious power. It is essential, therefore, that a nation should understand itself

From Hamilton W. Mabie, "American Literature and American Nationality," *The Forum*, XXVI (January, 1899), 636–638.

through the disclosure of its instincts and ideals, in order that its spiritual life may dominate and form its material life. It may, for a time, make its way by instinct and feeling; but it cannot develop its full power, nor do its work with adequate force, until it has supplemented instinct and feeling with intelligence.

The American people stand in great need of this adequate expression of their life. They are spread over an immense territory. The industrial and social centres are separated from one another by great distances. The body of the nation is so vast that its safety depends upon a highly organized spiritual life. More than once it has faced the peril of sectional misunderstandings and antagonisms which have been made possible by the extent of ground which it covers. In no compact country would the dense ignorance of one another's character and resources, which prevailed in the North and South before the Civil War have been possible. In no compact country would the failure to understand one another, shown of late years in the East and West, have been possible. . . . Boston and New Orleans are almost as far apart as London and St. Petersburg: New York and San Francisco are separated from one another more widely than Paris and Damascus. The distance from Portland, Maine, to Portland, Oregon, is considerably greater than that from Greece to Norway. The magnitude of the continent is continually put to the front as one of the great advantages which the Republic enjoys in its competition with the world, or, to use the language of the future, in its coöperation with the world. Other things being equal, terms of territorial superiority are also terms of moral superiority; but the vastness of the national estate, like every great opportunity, involves grave perils.

That these perils are not imaginary the history of the last half of this century has tragically shown. That they still exist those who know the country are firmly persuaded. As a rule, cultivated Americans know Europe more thoroughly and more sympathetically than they know their own country. They cannot know Europe too well for their own education; but they owe it to themselves to know their own country first. The knowledge of Europe by an American is, in a sense, a privilege and a luxury: knowledge of his own country is a necessity. . . .

. . . . .

The higher interests of the nation are imperilled by the lack of a coördination of intellectual standards and aims, and by the tendency to let the development of the soul of the country wait on the development of its land, its mineral resources, and its trade. The magnitude of its material resources makes an intense and a highly organized spiritual life a sovereign necessity in America. It is an open question whether we shall be makers of things or creators of ideas and ideals. If we are to be materialists in the final character of our civilization, we shall fill a great place in the activities of the modern world; but we shall do nothing for its spiritual fortunes: we shall fill pages of statistics in the encyclopaedias; but we shall have small space in the history of art, culture, religion. The ingrained idealism of the American nature will probably preserve us from the dismal fate of being rich without being significant or interesting; but that idealism needs constant classification and reinforcement. It needs clear and commanding expression.

And that expression it must find mainly in its literature; for literature, in its greater forms, is both a revelation of national character and a force to form national character. Its influence, though not computable by any external records, is diffused through the atmosphere which a people breathes. It has recently been said, and not without a degree of truth, that the modern movement for expansion, which has made England active and potential at the ends of the earth, did not originate in the mind of a statesman, and was not the result of the scheming of a shrewd politician like Beaconsfield, but received its most powerful impulse from three writers: Carlyle, Tennyson, and Kipling. These men of letters, like many of their predecessors, have not urged definite policies upon their countrymen; but they have given the English spirit and temper the impulse of sharp definition, and of deep and passionate faith. Indeed, the service of English literature as a practical force in English life cannot be overstated. It has done more than any other single force to give the English race clear consciousness of its strength, its aims, and its work: it has bound the race together in the consciousness of a rich and enduring community of history and fortune. Shakespeare has done more for England in forming this consciousness than Pitt or Peel or Gladstone.

If this service was needed in a country of such narrow territory, with a population so compact, as England, it is sorely needed in this country, with its immense distances and its widely separated communities. And when one adds to these natural conditions the complexity of races now learning to live together in the Republic, the necessity of a literature that shall develop first a national consciousness, and then clarify national spiritual ideals and make them authoritative, becomes even painfully apparent. A literature adequate in its power and vision to the range of life on this continent is a prime necessity for our safety. We need a literature which shall speak to and for the consciousness of the nation as the New England literature spoke to and for the consciousness of New England. The note of nationality was struck with resonant clearness by Emerson, Lowell, and Whittier; but the force and depth of conscious national life were not behind these earlier poets as they will be behind their successors. The time was not ripe; but it is fast ripening.

This more inclusive literature will not be written by intention: it must come spontaneously and by the pressure of a wider and richer experience. The way has been prepared by every true man of letters from Irving to Howells. It is being prepared today by the widespread activity in the field of history; for the later historians, by making us aware of the stirring and romantic history behind us, are developing a consciousness of our racial resources and of the experience which has made us a nation. It is being prepared by the writers of fiction, whose work in many instances has depth and reality, and is a true revelation of American character. Such a story as Mr. Thomas Nelson Page's "Red Rock" is a contribution of lasting value to our knowledge of our own past, a veritable human document, because it deals in a serious spirit with a significant and tragic experience; a genuine interpretation of the spirit, the vicissitudes, and the historical attitude of a great section in one of the shaping crises of its history. A book of this seriousness of temper and artistic insight is to be welcomed, not only for what it brings us of enlightenment and pleasure, but still more for what it predicts in the way of large, conscientious, patient endeavor to make Americans conscious of the shaping forces of their history, and of the deeper ties and fortunes which unite them. In this spiritual history of the New World the novelists have already discovered material of such depth and richness that a generation of great writers could not exhaust it. One of the highest uses of that material in the forms of art will be the clear development of national self-consciousness.

"The point of view is the point"

JULIAN HAWTHORNE

Many authors and readers tended, just as Henry Timrod had noted much earlier, to confuse American literature with American subject matter. Julian Hawthorne (1846–1934), son of Nathaniel Hawthorne and a novelist and essayist in his own right, scouted the kind of nationalism that would insist that American authors write about American people and places alone. In the years to come this would be a frequent point of controversy in discussions of the American novel.

THAT MUST BE a very shallow literature which depends for its national flavor and character upon its topography and its dialect; and the criticism which can conceive of no deeper Americanism than this is shallower still. What is an American book? It is a book written by an American, and by one who writes as an American; that is, unaffectedly. So an English book is a book written by an unaffected Englishman. What difference can it make what the subject of the writing is? Mr. Henry James lately brought out a volume of essays on "French Poets and Novelists." Mr. E. C. Stedman recently published a series of monographs on "The Victorian Poets." Are these books French and English, or are they nondescript, or are they American? Not only are they American, but they are more essentially American than if they had been disquisitions upon American literature. And the reason is, of course, that they subject the things of the old world to the tests of the new, and thereby vindicate and illustrate the characteristic mission of America to mankind. We are here to hold up European

Julian Hawthorne, "Americanism in Fiction," in *Confessions and Criticisms* (Boston, 1879), pp. 77–79.

conventionalisms and prejudices in the light of the new day, and thus afford everybody the opportunity, never heretofore enjoyed, of judging them by other standards, and in other surroundings than those amidst which they came into existence. In the same way, Emerson's "English Traits" is an American thing, and it gives categorical reasons why American things should be. And what is an American novel except a novel treating of persons, places, and ideas from an American point of view? The point of view is *the* point, not the thing seen from it.

But it is said that "the great American novel," in order fully to deserve its name, ought to have American scenery. Some thousands of years ago, the Greeks had a novelist—Homer—who evolved the great novel of that epoch; but the scenery of that novel was Trojan, not Greek. The story is a criticism, from a Greek standpoint, of foreign affairs, illustrated with practical examples; and, as regards treatment, quite as much care is bestowed upon the delineation of Hector, Priam, and Paris, as upon Agamemnon, Menelaus, and Achilles. The same story, told by a Trojan Homer, would doubtless have been very different; but it is by no means certain that it would have been any better told. It embodies, whether symbolically or literally matters not, the triumph of Greek ideas and civilization. But, even so, the sympathies of the reader are not always, or perhaps uniformly, on the conquering side. Homer was doubtless a patriot, but he shows no signs of having been a bigot. He described that great international episode with singular impartiality; what chiefly interested him was the play of human nature. Nevertheless, there is no evidence that the Greeks were backward in admitting his claims as their national poet; and we may legitimately conclude that were an American Homer—whether in prose or poetry—to appear among us, he might pitch his scene where he liked—in Patagonia, or on the banks of the Zambezi—and we should accept the situation with perfect equanimity. Only let him be a native of New York, or Boston, or San Francisco, or Mullenville, and be inspired with the American idea, and we ask no more. Whatever he writes will belong to our literature, and add lustre to it.

*"The more smiling
aspects of life"*

WILLIAM DEAN HOWELLS

No American writer played a more useful and vigorous role
in championing the cause of American fiction than
William Dean Howells (1837–1920). As editor of *The
Atlantic* and later columnist for *Harper's,* Howells urged the
claims of contemporary Russian and French realists for
attention by American readers, and both as critic and
novelist he strove for a literature that would image the
realities of everyday life in the United States. Yet Howells was
curiously limited in his definition of realism. He thought
American life should be portrayed only in its "more smiling
aspects," since, he insisted, such aspects are really more
typical. The excerpts from Howells' essays that follow,
published originally in *Harper's* in 1879 and 1890 in a
somewhat different form, show both Howells' range of interest
and his limitations.

It used to be one of the disadvantages of the practice of
romance in America, which Hawthorne more or less whimsically
lamented, that there were so few shadows and inequalities in our
broad level of prosperity; and it is one of the reflections suggested
by Dostoievsky's novel, *The Crime and the Punishment,* that
whoever struck a note so profoundly tragic in American fiction
would do a false and mistaken thing—as false and as mistaken
in its way as dealing in American fiction with certain nudities
which the Latin peoples seem to find edifying. Whatever their
deserts, very few American novelists have been led out to be

From William Dean Howells, *My Literary Passions—Criticism and Fiction*
(New York: Harper & Brothers, 1910), pp. 252–253, 257–259.

shot, or finally exiled to the rigors of a winter at Duluth; and in a land where journeymen carpenters and plumbers strike for four dollars a day the sum of hunger and cold is comparatively small, and the wrong from class to class has been almost inappreciable, though all this is changing for the worse. Our novelists, therefore, concern themselves with the more smiling aspects of life, which are the more American, and seek the universal in the individual rather than the social interests. It is worth while, even at the risk of being called commonplace, to be true to our well-to-do actualities; the very passions themselves seem to be softened and modified by conditions which formerly at least could not be said to wrong any one, to cramp endeavor, or to cross lawful desire. Sin and suffering and shame there must always be in the world, I suppose, but I believe that in this new world of ours it is still mainly from one to another one, and oftener still from one to one's self. We have death, too, in America, and a great deal of disagreeable and painful disease, which the multiplicity of our patent medicines does not seem to cure; but this is tragedy that comes in the very nature of things, and is not peculiarly American, as the large, cheerful average of health and success and happy life is. It will not do to boast, but it is well to be true to the facts, and to see that, apart from these purely mortal troubles, the race here has enjoyed conditions in which most of the ills that have darkened its annals might be averted by honest work and unselfish behavior.

Fine artists we have among us, and right-minded as far as they go; and we must not forget this at evil moments when it seems as if all the women had taken to writing hysterical improprieties, and some of the men were trying to be at least as hysterical in despair of being as improper. Other traits are much more characteristic of our life and our fiction. In most American novels, vivid and graphic as the best of them are, the people are segregated if not sequestered, and the scene is sparsely populated. The effect may be in instinctive response to the vacancy of our social life, and I shall not make haste to blame it. There are few places, few occasions among us, in which a novelist can get a large number of polite people together, or at least keep them together. Unless he carries a snap-camera his picture of them has no probability; they affect one like the figures perfunctorily associated in such deadly old engravings as that of "Washington Irving and his Friends." Perhaps it is for this reason that we excel in small pieces with three or four figures, or in studies of rustic communities, where there is propinquity if not society. Our grasp of more urbane life is feeble; most attempts to assemble it in our pictures are failures, possibly because it is too transitory, too intangible in its nature with us, to be truthfully represented as really existent. . . .

. . . . .

In fine, I would have our American novelists be as American as they unconsciously can. Matthew Arnold complained that he found no "distinction" in our life, and I would gladly persuade all artists intending greatness in any kind among us that the recognition of the fact pointed out by Mr. Arnold ought to be a source of inspiration to them, and not discouragement. We have been now some hundred years building up a state on the affirmation of the essential equality of men in their rights and duties, and whether we have been right or been wrong the gods have taken us at our word, and have responded to us with a civilization in which there is no "distinction" perceptible to the eye that loves and values it. Such beauty and such grandeur as we have is common beauty, common grandeur, or the beauty and grandeur in which the quality of solidarity so prevails that neither distinguishes itself to the disadvantage of anything else. It seems to me that these conditions invite the artist to the study and the appreciation of the common, and to the portrayal in every art of those finer and higher aspects which unite rather than sever humanity, if he would thrive in our new order of things. The talent that is robust enough to front the every-day world and catch the charm of its work-worn, care-worn, brave, kindly face, need not fear the encounter, though it seems terrible to the sort nurtured in the superstition of the romantic, the bizarre, the heroic, the distinguished, as the things alone worthy of painting or carving or writing. The arts must become democratic, and then we shall have the expression of America in art; and the reproach which Arnold was half right in making us shall have no justice in it any longer; we shall be "distinguished."

In the meantime it has been said with a superficial justice that our fiction is narrow, though in the same sense I suppose the present English fiction is as narrow as our own; and most modern fiction is narrow in a certain sense. In Italy the best men are writing novels as brief and restricted in range as ours; in Spain the novels are intense and deep, and not spacious; the French school, with the exception of Zola, is narrow; the Norwegians are narrow; the Russians, except Tolstoy, are narrow, and the next greatest after him, Tourguenief, is the narrowest great novelist, as to mere dimensions, that ever lived, dealing nearly always with small groups, isolated and analyzed in the most American fashion. In fact, the charge of narrowness accuses the whole tendency of modern fiction as much as the American school. But I do not by any means allow that this narrowness is a defect, while denying that it is a universal characteristic of our fiction; it is rather, for the present, a virtue. Indeed, I should call the present American work, North and South, thorough rather than narrow. In one sense it is as broad as life, for each man is a microcosm, and the writer who is able to acquaint us intimately with half a dozen people, or the conditions of a neighborhood or a class, has done something which cannot in any bad sense be called narrow; his breadth is vertical instead of lateral, that is all; and this depth is more desirable than horizontal expansion in a civilization like ours, where the differences are not of classes, but of types, and not of types either so much as of characters. A new method was necessary in dealing with the new conditions, and the new method is worldwide, because the whole world is more or less Americanized. Tolstoy is exceptionally voluminous among modern writers, even Russian writers; and it might be said that the forte of Tolstoy himself is not in his breadth sidewise, but in his breadth upward and downward. *The Death of Ivan Ilyitch* leaves as vast an impression on the reader's soul as any episode of *War and Peace*, which, indeed, can be recalled only in episodes, and not as a whole. I think that our writers may be safely counselled to continue their work in the modern way, because it is the best way yet known. If they make it true, it will be large, no matter what its superficies are; and it would be the greatest mistake to try to make it big. . . .

"O for a few more
—many more—
broad characters"

"A SOUTHERNER"

Howells had contended that if the realistic novel in America tended to focus upon a rather small, narrow scene, then so did the modern novel everywhere; narrowness, he said, is strength. In *The Critic* for November 7, 1885, a writer who signed himself "A Southerner" disputed this claim. The slightness of the contemporary American novel when compared with the great works of English, French, and Russian fiction constituted a refusal to be deep and broad, he said, and in so doing failed to portray American character properly. He cited the protagonist of Howells' own novel, *The Rise of Silas Lapham* (1885), as an example of what the American character in fiction could be.

WHAT, THEN, IS MEANT by the statement that the tendency of all modern fiction is narrowness? First, is not fiction that prose form of modern literature in which the imagination undertakes to embody unfolding human personality? And how in all modern, or indeed any progressive, civilization has human personality tended to unfold itself but in the directions of breadth and depth? Posnett is an authority whom Mr. Howells has quoted with approval: but the basic principle of Posnett's entire work on Comparative Literature is stated thus: "We accept, then, as the principle of literary growth the progressive deepening and widening of personality." He elsewhere describes this as the twofold

"Mr. Howells on the Tendency of Fiction," by "A Southerner," in *The Critic* n.s., IV (November 7, 1885), 147–148.

process of individuality, deepening in the separate units while expanding in the number of separate units it includes, and further maintains that only when depth and extent of individuality are concurrently developed can we feel confidence in the permanence of literary growth.

What have we, therefore? We have the principle of historic evolution—the development of personality; we have the principle of literary growth matching it—the deepening and widening of personality; and we have the literary form—the novel—matching the principle of literary growth. What, then, is the inevitable conclusion respecting that literary form? Is it that the form grows narrow as the material grows wide and deep? Or is it—is it not—that the form must broaden and deepen as well? As opposed to the principle, stated by Mr. Howells, that the whole tendency of modern fiction is toward narrowness, we submit it as true, therefore, that the whole tendency of modern fiction is toward greater breadth and depth. But as the movement of history is not unbrokenly progressive, as the principle of literary growth is not traceable throughout, so the development of fiction is not everywhere continuous; and to assert that its general tendency is toward more breadth and depth, does not necessarily mean that the novelists of every school of generation represent a higher stage of that development, by being broader and deeper than any who have gone before. On the contrary, should the novels of any school be confessedly narrower than the novels of preceding ones, the conclusion to be drawn from this fact would seem to be, not that the general tendency of fiction was toward narrowness, but that the novels of the school in question had not reached the high-water-mark of prior development in respect to breadth. At the same time, it should be borne in mind that these same novels might not only equal but far surpass all prior development in respect to other qualities, such as delicacy, finish, symmetry, purity, absolute veracity; so that while marking no advanced stage of general tendency in all things, they might properly be cited as marking it in some.

Now, unquestionably, a tendency of the time is toward shorter novels. This naturally; for if the novelist must give a broader and deeper account of personality, he must provide against unmanageable bulkiness in the result by taking fewer personalities. But given this shorter American novel, the question remains, Is it narrow compared with the greatest English, French, Russian fiction? To fall back upon our suggested definitions, does it equal the latter in social breadth (the representative quality of its social type), or in generic breadth (the rich essential variety of its human type), or in metaphysical breadth (the fulness of its psychological insight and verification)? It might be objected that our general level of social conditions and decentralization measurably forbid the first, and that it is too soon to call for the second; but what explains the third? For here, right here lies the principle of tendency. Is it not the peculiar claim of our civilization that by it human nature stands liberated as never before in the breadth and depth of its vital elements? But is it not in respect of these that American fiction suffers most by comparison with the greatest fiction of other countries and times? Does it portray men and women at the close of the Nineteenth Century for the most and the best that is in them? Is it deep? Does it stir the deepest feelings, bring the deepest thoughts, help the deepest convictions, feed the desire to be fed on the utmost truth and beauty and goodness that human life provides? Or does it *refuse* to be deep and broad, and *aim* to be light and narrow—and thorough?

We hold to our conviction that the main essential tendency of the novel is to become broader and deeper in the study of personality, though in doing so it may become narrower in the variety of human types, and may of necessity have to deal with social types less broadly representative and powerful; and that American fiction has not yet attained the high-water-mark of previous development in any one of these respects, however far it may have gone ahead in others.

O for a few more—many more—broad characters like that man of pure American granite, Silas Lapham! And O for a little more heart, a little more soul, in Silas!

"A broader outlook for American literature"

HAMLIN GARLAND

With the publication of Mark Twain's "The Celebrated
Jumping Frog of Calaveras County" in 1867 and Bret Harte's
"Luck of Roaring Camp" the year afterward, a new
dimension was added to American fiction—the West. Not in
the Eastern states, with "your nipping accent, your nice
phrases, your balanced sentences and your neat proprieties
inherited from the eighteenth century," would the only true
literary culture of the nation be found, declared Hamlin
Garland (1860–1940) in the passage that follows. Instead,
Americans should look westward, to the prairies and
mountains, for their true inspiration. Garland expressed an
attitude that even today has its vociferous champions.

SHALL OUR LITERATURE be a literature of the East, in
mode if not in subject, or shall it be national? Is it to be only so
large as the conception of New York and Boston critics, or shall
it be as big and broad and democratic as the best thought of the
whole nation? Is every work of art of every Western or Southern
man or woman to be submitted with timid air to a jury that represents only a section of American society, a section which is really
nearer the Old World than the New? Or shall the writing be addressed to the whole nation? Editors and critics are human. They
are likely at best to be biassed by their section and their ad-
herents. As a matter of fact, there are groups of people all over
the interior America, in towns and cities, who have not only all
the substantial acquirements of the Eastern readers, but a broader
and more intimate knowledge of American life. The culture repre-

Hamlin Garland, "Literary Emancipation of the West," *The Forum,* XVI
(October, 1893), 161–166.

sented by these people is not alone based upon knowledge of dead forms of art, but it includes living issues of art. The number of these people increases year by year. They stand for ideas and conditions of the future, and from them artists are rising filled with courage and moved by convictions of their allegiance to truth. These people demand something more than smooth conventional work. They realize the tendency of young authors not to write as they really feel, but as they think the editors of the great magazines of the East would have them write. They realize the danger which lies in putting into the hands of a few men, no matter how fine they may be, the directing power of American literature.

These cultivated and fearless Western readers are beginning to understand the situation and to say, By what right do you of the East assume the position of final judges of what American literature shall be? What special qualifications does a residence on the extreme eastern shore of our nation give you, by which to settle all questions of a national literature? "The West is crude," Eastern critics are fond of saying. What do you mean by that? Do you mean that there are not men and women of the highest type in the West? Do you mean that we do not conform to your specific ideal of culture? Or do you mean that we have not been self-respecting enough in our own thinking? In what lies your assumed superiority over the West?

To this the East replies: We are the occupying claimants of the glory of the great men of this century's literature. We have also the great libraries, the museums, the great universities which make us the centre of critical intelligence. Granting your great railways, your stupendous enterprises, your great cities, the East still remains and must remain the centre of the highest literary culture in America.

The West rejoins: That is the point at issue. We deny that the East is the exclusive home of the broadest culture. We feel that much of this culture is barren and insincere. It has a hopeless outlook. It leads nowhere. It treads a circle, like the logic of the Koran. Culture is not creative power. Scholarship does not imply wisdom. We do not believe a city at our farthest East can remain the city most progressive in its art, most unbiassed in its judgments. The American city of broadest culture is henceforth to be that where the broad, free currents of American life daily ebb and flow. Such a city can know (and will know) all that the East knows of fundamental principles of art and literature and will have a wider knowledge of the scope and action of American life.

The East then says: It will take a hundred years to make a Western city like New York or Boston. The mellow charm of our literary atmosphere is the growth of two centuries. Our very streets are lined with suggestive walls and historical tablets. Our drawing-rooms and our clubs represent the flowering culture of ten generations.

The West quickly responds: Keep your past. Hug your tablets to your shirtfront; you are welcome to all that; we are concerned with the present, and with the splendor of the future. Your culture is too largely of the moribund. You fail to conceive that our idea of culture is a different and, we assert, a higher form because it refers to a culture of living forms. Besides, culture even of the broadest is only part of it; creative power is the crowning splendor of a nation's life. Scholarship does not necessarily imply wisdom. The study of the past does little for original genius. Libraries and universities produce few of the great leaders of American thought; all that books can give is our inheritance as well as yours. We deny that the Eastern "art atmosphere" is necessary to the production of original works of art. We doubt the ability of New York or Boston criticism to pass final judgment upon a Western work of art, because the conditions of our life are outside the circle of its intimate knowledge. A criticism which stands for old things, we repeat, is not the criticism which is to aid the production of characteristic American art. America is not to submit itself to the past, it is to be free.

Do you mean to say that you propose to cut loose from the past? asks the East.

By no means. We expect to assert our right to our day, as Russia, Norway, Germany and others of our neighbor nations have done. The youth of all nations are in the fight. We are in the midst of one of those returning cycles of progress in art when the young man attains his majority. America has begun to attain her majority, to claim the right to a free choice in art as well as in government, to speak her own mind in her own way.

Permit us—are you to use as a medium, Choctaw or English? the East inquires, in strenuously polite phrase.

That illustrates the inadequateness and the illiberality of your attitude toward us. We propose to use the speech of living men and women. We expect to use actual speech as we hear it and to record its changes. We expect to treat of the town and city as well as of the farm, each in its place and through the medium of characteristic speech. We propose to discard your nipping accent, your nice phrases, your balanced sentences and your neat proprieties inherited from the eighteenth century. Our speech is to be as individual as our view of life.

Says the East: Your view of life is of no interest to us. We do not see the necessity of Americans troubling to write or paint at all in future. We have books and paintings enough in the market. When we want a book, we buy a classic and know what we are getting. When we want a painting, there are Corots and Rousseaus and Bouguereaus in the markets. Produce wheat and corn and railway-stocks yet awhile, and don't trouble yourself about literary problems. Read the classics for the improvement of your style. In the meantime, we will see that American literature is not vulgarized.

Again the West retorts hotly: Who constituted you the guardian of American literature? What do you know of the needs or tastes of the people—

Testily the old gentleman breaks in: My dear sir, I care nothing for any tastes but my own. I don't like the common American in life and I don't like him in books. Therefore—

There! rejoins the West triumphantly. There is a second point admitted. You have no sympathy with the American people of middle condition. You are essentially aristocratic and un-American in your position. From your library, or from the car-window, you look upon our life; that is the extent of your knowledge of our conditions at best. For the most part you have never been west of Niagara Falls. How can you be just to this literature which springs from a life you do not know or sympathize with? We are forming a literature from direct contact with life, and such a literature can be estimated only by unbiassed minds and by comparison with nature and the life we live. Are you fitted to be the court of last resort upon our writing by reason of your study of English novels and your study of last-century painting? The test of a work of art is not, Does it conform to the best models? but, Does it touch and lift and exalt men? And we profess ability to perceive these qualities even west of the Mississippi River. We care little for the free-masonry of literary phrases which relates one spectacled enthusiast over dead men's books to another and a similar devotee of dead men's pictures. The West should aim to be wise rather than cultured. Wisdom is democratic, culture is an aristocrat. Wisdom is knowledge of principles, culture is a knowledge of forms and accepted conceptions.

In this way has the battle begun to take shape, as I know, having lived for ten years in the East and still retaining close connection with the West. Lines are, of course, only broadly thus drawn. For there are fine critics of the comparative philosophy in the East and in London, men who perceive these conditions and understand them. On the other hand, the West is full of timid souls who tremble in constant fear of being incorrect. But broadly, the West by virtue of its needs is coming to perceive its relation to the Old World and to the literature of the past. With the coming to power and importance in material ways, Chicago is soon to be the centre of unfettered and unconventional criticism. It is probably the most representative Western city. It is central. It cannot be one-sided, because of the equal pressure brought to bear upon it. It must be democratic and progressive, for it will stand for a mighty people who will not abide slavish genuflections before any idol. Finally, therefore, America should be free—free from any domination. It should not cringe or bow to the past nor to the East, nor to any coterie, for that matter. The American idea has hardly yet entered into literature; and one reason why it has not, is because of the inherited idea of a central academy, whereas true American literature must differ as radically from the literature of England, as the life we live differs from theirs.

Original creation moves in cycles. Each age of strong creative capability reveals life in its own fashion. That is, each creative age in the past uttered its own truth as over against the conventionalized dogmas of its teachers. I believe such a period of literary breaking-away has come in America. Whitman announced it, but could not exemplify it in popular form. He voiced its force, its love of liberty and love of comrades, but he was the prophet, not the exemplar. He said well that the real literature of America could not be a polite literature. The nation is too great, too sincere. There is coming in this land the mightiest assertion in art of the rights of man and the glory of the physical universe ever made in the world. It will be done not by one man, but by many men and women. It will be born not of drawing-room culture, nor of imitation, nor of fear of masters, nor will it come from homes of great wealth. It will come from the average American home in the city, as well as in the country. It will deal with all kinds and conditions. It will be born of the mingling seas of men in the vast interior of America, because there the problem of the perpetuity of our democracy, the question of the liberty as well as the nationality of our art, will be fought out. This literature will be too great to submit to the domination of any literary centre or literary master. With cities of half-a-million inhabitants scattered from Pittsburgh to Seattle, New York and Chicago will alike be made humble. Stand up, O young man and woman of the West! Stand erect! Face the future with a song on your lips and the light of a broader day in your eyes. Turn your back on the past, not in scorn, but in justice to the future. Reject the scholasticism of the East. Cease trying to be correct, and become creative. This is our day. The past is not vital. It is a highway of dust, and Homer, Æschylus, Sophocles, Dante, Shakespeare are milestones. Libraries do not create great poets and artists; they seldom aid, and they often warp and destroy them. To know Shakespeare is good. To know your fellow-men is better. All that Shakespeare knew of his fellows you may know of your fellows, but not at second-hand, not through Shakespeare, not through the eyes of the dead, but at first hand.

In closing let me say: I hope I have made it clear that our position is not one of attacking the East, or Eastern literary men. We are simply attacking the false and fatal idea of culture, based upon past models rather than upon truth. We are speaking for a broader outlook for American literature. We are standing for a literature which shall rise above culture, above library centres and literary masters, to sincerity of accent and to native democracy of sentiment, and, above all, to creative candor.

"Not extinct like the Dodo, but mythical like the Hippogriff"

FRANK NORRIS

Frank Norris (1870–1902), like Hamlin Garland, was a strong advocate of regionalism. In the essay that follows, published posthumously in his *The Responsibilities of the Novelist* (1903), he cites the distinct character of the various American regions as a condition making impossible the writing of any single "Great American Novel." Norris' chief importance in American literature, however, lies not in his regionalism but in his strongly naturalistic fiction, with its picture of man's bitter struggle against a hostile environment.

O F ALL THE OVERWORKED phrases of overworked book reviewers, the phrase, the "Great American Novelist," is beyond doubt worn the thinnest from much handling—or mishandling. Continually the little literary middlemen who come between the producers and the consumers of fiction are mouthing the words with a great flourish of adjectives, scare-heading them in Sunday supplements or placarding them on posters, crying out, "Lo, he is here!" or "Lo, there!" But the heathen rage and the people imagine a vain thing. The G.A.N. is either as extinct as the Dodo or as far in the future as the practical aëroplane. He certainly is not discoverable at the present.

The moment a new writer of fiction begins to make himself felt he is gibbeted upon this elevation—upon this *false,* insecure elevation, for the underpinning is of the flimsiest, and at any moment is liable to collapse under the victim's feet and leave him

From Frank Norris, "The Great American Novelist" in *The Responsibilities of the Novelist and the Joyous Miracle,* Vol. III of the *Collected Works* (New York: Doubleday, Doran & Company, Inc., 1928), pp. 65–67.

hanging in midair by head and hands, a fixture and a mockery.

And who is to settle the title upon the aspirant in the last issue? Who is to determine what constitutes the G.A.N. Your candidate may suit you, but your neighbour may have a very different standard to which he must conform. It all depends upon what you mean by *Great*, what you mean by *American*. Shakespeare has been called great, and so has Mr. Stephen Phillips. Oliver Wendell Holmes was *American*, and so is Bret Harte. Who is to say?

And many good people who deplore the decay of American letters are accustomed to refer to the absence of a G.A.N. as though there were a Great English Novelist or a Great French Novelist. But do these two people exist? Ask any dozen of your friends to mention the Great English Novelist, and out of the dozen you will get at least a half-dozen different names. It will be Dickens or Scott or Thackeray or Brontë or Eliot or Stevenson, and the same with the Frenchman. And it seems to me that if a novelist were great enough to be universally acknowledged to be the great one of his country, he would cease to belong to any particular geographical area and would become a heritage of the whole world; as for instance Tolstoi; when one thinks of him it is—is it not?—as a novelist first and as a Russian afterward.

But if one wishes to split hairs, one might admit that while the Great American Novelist is yet to be born, the possibility of *A*— note the indefinite article—*A*—Great American Novel is not too remote for discussion. But such a novel will be sectional. The United States is a Union, but not a unit, and the life in one part is very, very different from the life in another. It is as yet impossible to construct a novel which will represent all the various characteristics of the different sections. It is only possible to make a picture of a single locality. What is true of the South is not true of the North. The West is different, and the Pacific Coast is a community by itself.

Many of our very best writers are working on this theory. Bret Harte made a study of the West as he saw it, and Mr. Howells has done the same for the East. Cable has worked the field of the Far South, and Eggleston has gone deep into the life of the Middle West.

But consider a suggestion. It is an argument on the other side, and to be fair one must present it. It is a good argument, and if based on fact is encouraging in the hope that the Great man may yet appear. It has been said that "what is true—vitally and inherently true—for any one man is true for all men." Accordingly, then, what is vitally true of the Westerner is true of the Bostonian —yes, and of the creole. So that if Mr. Cable, say, should only go *deep enough* into the hearts and lives of his creoles, he would at last strike the universal sub-stratum and find the elemental thing that is common to the creole and to the Puritan alike—yes, and to the Cowboy and Hoosier and Greaser and Buckeye and Jay Hawker, and that, once getting hold of *that,* he could produce the Great American Novel that should be a picture of the entire nation.

Now, that is a very ingenious argument and sounds very plausible. But it won't do, and for this reason: If an American novelist should go so deep into the lives of the people of any one community that he would find the thing that is common to another class of people a thousand miles away, he would have gone *too* deep to be exclusively American. He would not only be American, but English as well. He would have sounded the world note; he would be a writer not national but international, and his countrymen would be all humanity, not the citizens of any one nation. He himself would be a heritage of the whole world, a second Tolstoi, which brings us back to the very place from which we started.

And the conclusion of the whole matter? That fiction is very good or very bad—there is no middle ground; that writers of fiction in their points of view are either limited to a circumscribed area or see humanity as a tremendous conglomerate whole; that it must be either Mary Wilkins or George Eliot, Edward Eggleston or William Shakespeare; that the others do not weigh very much in the balance of the world's judgment; and that the Great American Novel is not extinct like the Dodo, but mythical like the Hippogriff, and that the thing to be looked for is not the Great American Novelist, but the Great Novelist who shall also be an American.

"We already talk too much about the novel"

HENRY JAMES

Meanwhile, in London, Henry James (1843–1916), brother
of the philosopher William James, was steadily producing
the novels, many of them centered about Americans in
Europe, that in our own day would make him a crucial
influence in American literature. A close follower of the
American literary scene, James shared little of the
enthusiasm that many of his fellow American authors held
for regionalism or for the idea of the "Great American
Novel." It was "life," and more than that, the techniques
for creating "life" in fiction, that interested James most.
When he was invited to attend the Summer School at
Deerfield, Massachusetts, in 1889, for a discussion of the
art of the novel, James declined, sending instead the
following letter which was read during the proceedings.

I AM AFRAID I can do little more than thank you for
your courteous invitation to be present at the sittings of your
delightfully sounding school of romance, which ought to inherit
happiness and honour from such a name. I am so very far away
from you that I am afraid I can't participate very intelligently
in your discussions, but I can only give them the furtherance of
a dimly discriminating sympathy. I am not sure that I apprehend
very well your apparent premise, 'the materialism of our present
tendencies,' and I suspect that this would require some clearing
up before I should be able (if even then) to contribute any sug-

Henry James, "Letter to the Deerfield Summer School," first published in
the New York *Tribune*, August 4, 1889. Reprinted in *Selected Letters of
Henry James*, ed. Leon Edel (New York: Farrar, Straus and Cudahy, Inc.,
1955), pp. 92–94.

gestive or helpful word. To tell the truth, I can't help thinking that we already talk too much about the novel, about and around it, in proportion to the quantity of it having any importance that we produce. What I should say to the nymphs and swains who propose to converse about it under the great trees at Deerfield is: "Oh, do something from your point of view; an ounce of example is worth a ton of generalities; do something with the great art and the great form; do something with life. Any point of view is interesting that is a direct impression of life. You each have an impression coloured by your individual conditions; make that into a picture, a picture framed by your own personal wisdom, your glimpse of the American world. The field is vast for freedom, for study, for observation, for satire, for truth." I don't think I really do know what you mean by 'materializing tendencies' any more than I should by 'spiritualizing' or 'etherealizing.' There are no tendencies worth anything but to see the actual or the imaginative, which is just as visible, and to paint it. I have only two little words for the matter remotely approaching to rule or doctrine; one is life and the other freedom. Tell the ladies and gentlemen, the ingenious inquirers, to consider life directly and closely, and not to be put off with mean and puerile falsities, and be conscientious about it. It is infinitely large, various and comprehensive. Every sort of mind will find what it looks for in it, whereby the novel becomes truly multifarious and illustrative. That is what I mean by liberty; give it its head and let it range. If it is in a bad way, and the English novel is, I think, nothing but absolute freedom can refresh it and restore its self-respect. Excuse these raw brevities and please convey to your companions, my dear sir, the cordial good wishes of yours and theirs,

III

The American Novel and "Reality"

"See how free those French fellows are"

WILLIAM DEAN HOWELLS

How far should American fiction go in its effort to give
a realistic portrait of American life? With the 1880's and
1890's there began to come a literature that examined the
hitherto unrespectable question of sex, as well as some of
the darker aspects of the human psyche. The dispute which
ensued has not ended yet. William Dean Howells, for all
his championing of the cause of realism, came out
emphatically on the side of decency and convention. In
an essay published originally in *Harper's* for June, 1889,
he declared that the notion that American novelists
should write nothing unsuitable for reading by innocent
young ladies was not an excessive restriction of realism.

ONE OF THE GREAT newspapers the other day invited
the prominent American authors to speak their minds upon a
point in the theory and practice of fiction which had already
vexed some of them. It was the question of how much or how
little the American novel ought to deal with certain facts of life
which are not usually talked of before young people, and especially young ladies. Of course the question was not decided, and
I forget just how far the balance inclined in favor of a larger
freedom in the matter. But it certainly inclined that way; one
or two writers of the sex which is somehow supposed to have

From William Dean Howells, *My Literary Passions—Criticism and Fiction*
(New York: Harper & Brothers, 1910), pp. 261–267.

purity in its keeping (as if purity were a thing that did not practically concern the other sex, preoccupied with serious affairs)
gave it a rather vigorous tilt to that side. In view of this fact it
would not be the part of prudence to make an effort to dress the
balance; and indeed I do not know that I was going to make
any such effort. But there are some things to say, around and
about the subject, which I should like to have some one else say,
and which I may myself possibly be safe in suggesting.

One of the first of these is the fact, generally lost sight of by
those who censure the Anglo-Saxon novel for its prudishness,
that it is really not such a prude after all; and that if it is sometimes apparently anxious to avoid those experiences of life not
spoken of before young people, this may be an appearance only.
Sometimes a novel which has this shuffling air, this effect of
truckling to propriety, might defend itself, if it could speak for
itself, by saying that such experiences happened not to come
within its scheme, and that, so far from maiming or mutilating
itself in ignoring them, it was all the more faithfully representative of the tone of modern life in dealing with love that was
chaste, and with passion so honest that it could be openly spoken
of before the tenderest society bud at dinner. It might say that
the guilty intrigue, the betrayal, the extreme flirtation even, was
the exceptional thing in life, and unless the scheme of the story
necessarily involved it, that it would be bad art to lug it in, and
as bad taste as to introduce such topics in a mixed company. It
could say very justly that the novel in our civilization now always
addresses a mixed company, and that the vast majority of the
company are ladies, and that very many, if not most, of these
ladies are young girls. If the novel were written for men and for
married women alone, as in continental Europe, it might be altogether different. But the simple fact is that it is not written for
them alone among us, and it is a question of writing, under
cover of our universal acceptance, things for young girls to read
which you would be put out-of-doors for saying to them, or of
frankly giving notice of your intention, and so cutting yourself
off from the pleasure—and it is a very high and sweet one—of
appealing to these vivid, responsive intelligences, which are none
the less brilliant and admirable because they are innocent.

One day a novelist who liked, after the manner of other men, to repine at his hard fate, complained to his friend, a critic, that he was tired of the restriction he had put upon himself in this regard; for it is a mistake, as can be readily shown, to suppose that others impose it. "See how free those French fellows are!" he rebelled. "Shall we always be shut up to our tradition of decency?"

"Do you think it's much worse than being shut up to their tradition of indecency?" said his friend.

Then that novelist began to reflect, and he remembered how sick the invariable motive of the French novel made him. He perceived finally that, convention for convention, ours was not only more tolerable, but on the whole was truer to life, not only to its complexion, but also to its texture. No one will pretend that there is not vicious love beneath the surface of our society; if he did, the fetid explosions of the divorce trials would refute him; but if he pretended that it was in any just sense characteristic of our society, he could be still more easily refuted. Yet it exists, and it is unquestionably the material of tragedy, the stuff from which intense effects are wrought. The question, after owning this fact, is whether these intense effects are not rather cheap effects. I incline to think they are, and I will try to say why I think so, if I may do so without offence. The material itself, the mere mention of it, has an instant fascination; it arrests, it detains, till the last word is said, and while there is anything to be hinted. This is what makes a love intrigue of some sort all but essential to the popularity of any fiction. Without such an intrigue the intellectual equipment of the author must be of the highest, and then he will succeed only with the highest class of readers. But any author who will deal with a guilty love intrigue holds all readers in his hand, the highest with the lowest, as long as he hints the slightest hope of the smallest potential naughtiness. He need not at all be a great author; he may be a very shabby wretch, if he has but the courage or the trick of that sort of thing. The critics will call him "virile" and "passionate"; decent people will be ashamed to have been limed by him; but the low average will only ask another chance of flocking into his net. If he happens to be an able writer, his really fine and costly work will be unheeded, and the lure to the appetite will be chiefly remembered. There may be other qualities which make reputations for other men, but in his case they will count for nothing. He pays this penalty for his success in that kind; and everyone pays some such penalty who deals with some such material.

But I do not mean to imply that his case covers the whole ground. So far as it goes, though, it ought to stop the mouths of those who complain that fiction is enslaved to propriety among us. It appears that of a certain kind of impropriety it is free to give us all it will, and more. But this is not what serious men and women writing fiction mean when they rebel against the limitations of their art in our civilization. They have no desire to deal with nakedness, as painters and sculptors freely do in the worship of beauty; or with certain facts of life, as the stage does, in the service of sensation. But they ask why, when the conventions of the plastic and histrionic arts liberate their followers to the portrayal of almost any phase of the physical or of the emotional nature, an American novelist may not write a story on the lines of *Anna Karénina* or *Madame Bovary*. They wish to touch one of the most serious and sorrowful problems of life in the spirit of Tolstoy and Flaubert, and they ask why they may not. At one time, they remind us, the Anglo-Saxon novelist did deal with such problems—De Foe in his spirit, Richardson in his, Goldsmith in his. At what moment did our fiction lose this privilege? In what fatal hour did the Young Girl arise and seal the lips of Fiction, with a touch of her finger, to some of the most vital interests of life?

Whether I wished to oppose them in their aspiration for greater freedom, or whether I wished to encourage them, I should begin to answer them by saying that the Young Girl has never done anything of the kind. The manners of the novel have been improving with those of its readers; that is all. Gentlemen no longer swear or fall drunk under the table, or abduct young ladies and shut them up in lonely country-houses, or so habitually set about the ruin of their neighbors' wives, as they once did. Generally, people now call a spade an agricultural implement, they have not grown decent without having also grown a little squeamish, but they have grown comparatively decent; there is no doubt about that. They require of a novelist whom they respect unquestionable proof of his seriousness, if he proposes to deal with certain phases of life; they require a sort of scientific decorum. He can no longer expect to be received on the ground of entertainment only; he assumes a higher function, something like that of a physician or a priest, and they expect him to be bound by laws as sacred as those of such professions; they hold him solemnly pledged not to betray them or abuse their confidence. If he will accept the conditions, they give him their confidence, and he may then treat to his greater honor, and not at all to his disadvantage, of such experiences, such relations of men and women as George Eliot treats in *Adam Bede*, in *Daniel Deronda*, in *Romola*, in almost all her books; such as Hawthorne treats in *The Scarlet Letter;* such as Dickens treats in *David Copperfield;* such as Thackeray treats in *Pendennis*, and glances at in every one of his fictions; such as most of the masters of English fiction have at some time treated more or less openly. It is quite false or quite mistaken to suppose that our novels have left untouched these most important realities of life. They have only not made them their stock in trade; they have kept a true perspective in regard to them; they have relegated them in their pictures of life to the space and place they occupy in life itself, as we know it in England and America. They have kept a correct proportion, knowing perfectly well that unless the novel is to be a map, with everything scrupulously laid down in it, a faithful record of life in far the greater extent could be made to the exclusion of guilty love and all its circumstances and consequences.

I justify them in this view not only because I hate what is cheap and meretricious, and hold in peculiar loathing the cant of the critics who require "passion" as something in itself admirable and desirable in a novel, but because I prize fidelity in the historian of feeling and character. Most of these critics who demand "passion" would seem to have no conception of any passion but one. Yet there are several other passions: the passion of grief, the passion of avarice, the passion of pity, the passion of ambition, the passion of hate, the passion of envy, the passion of devotion, the passion of friendship; and all these have a greater part in the drama of life than the passion of love, and infinitely greater than the passion of guilty love. Wittingly or unwittingly, English fiction and American fiction have recognized this truth, not fully, not in the measure it merits, but in greater degree than most other fiction.

*"A new order of things has
been coming into vogue"*

JULIAN HAWTHORNE

With realism, and more particularly with naturalism, a
school of writing which conceived of man as a creature of
biology trapped in a mechanistic universe, a new note
appeared in American fiction—agnosticism, even atheism.
Very naturally such an attitude did not appeal to many
readers whose view of the role of fiction was idealistic.
Julian Hawthorne, who felt that great fiction must entertain
a lofty view of man's nature, and who opposed the realistic novel
of everyday life because of its lack of idealism, described
the growth of the skeptical attitude towards divinity
in the American fiction of his day.

IN PROCEEDING FROM the general to the particular,
—to the novel as it actually exists in England and America,—
attention will be confined strictly to the contemporary outlook.
The new generation of novelists (by which is intended not those
merely living in this age, but those who actively belong to it)
differ in at least one fundamental respect from the later representatives of the generation preceding them. Thackeray and
Dickens did not deliberately concern themselves about a philosophy of life. With more or less complacency, more or less
cynicism, they accepted the religious and social canons which
had grown to be the commonplace of the first half of this century.
They pictured men and women, not as affected by questions, but
as affected by one another. The morality and immorality of their
personages were of the old familiar Church-of-England sort;
there was no speculation as to whether what had been supposed

From Julian Hawthorne, "Novels and Agnosticism," in *Confessions and
Criticisms* (Boston, 1887), pp. 39–43.

to be wrong was really right, and *vice versa*. Such speculations, in various forms and degrees of energy, appear in the world periodically; but the public conscience during the last thirty or forty years had been gradually making itself comfortable after the disturbances consequent upon the French Revolution; the theoretical rights of man had been settled for the moment; and interest was directed no longer to the assertion and support of these rights, but to the social condition and character which were their outcome. Good people were those who climbed through reverses and sorrows towards the conventional heaven; bad people were those who, in spite of worldly and temporary successes and triumphs, gravitated towards the conventional hell. . . .

. . . As to Nathaniel Hawthorne, he cannot properly be instanced in this connection; for he analyzed chiefly those parts of human nature which remain substantially unaltered in the face of whatever changes of opinion, civilization, and religion. The truth that he brings to light is not the sensational fact of a fashion or a period, but a verity of the human heart, which may foretell, but can never be affected by, anything which that heart may conceive. In other words, Hawthorne belonged neither to this nor to any other generation of writers further than that his productions may be used as a test of the inner veracity of all the rest.

But of late years a new order of things has been coming into vogue, and the new novelists have been among the first to reflect it; and of these the Americans have shown themselves among the most susceptible. Science, or the investigation of the phenomena of existence (in opposition to philosophy, the investigation of the phenomena of being), has proved nature to be so orderly and self-sufficient, and inquiry as to the origin of the primordial atom so unproductive and quixotic, as to make it convenient and indeed reasonable to accept nature as a self-existing fact, and to let all the rest—if rest there be—go. From this point of view, God and a future life retire into the background; not as finally disproved,—because denial, like affirmation, must, in order to be final, be logically supported; and spirit is, if not illogical, at any rate outside the domain of logic,—but as being a hopelessly vague and untrustworthy hypothesis. The Bible is a human book; Christ was a gentleman, related to the Buddha and Plato families; Joseph was an ill-used man; death, so far as we have any reason to believe, is annihilation of personal existence;

life is the predicament of the body previous to death; morality
is the enlightened selfishness of the greatest number; civilization
is the compromises men make with one another in order to get the
most they can out of the world; wisdom is acknowledgment of
these propositions; folly is to hanker after what may lie beyond
the sphere of sense. The supporter of these doctrines by no means
permits himself to be regarded as a rampant and dogmatic atheist;
he is simply the modest and humble doubter of what he cannot
prove. He even recognizes the persistence of the religious instinct
in man, and caters to it by a new religion suited to the times—
the Religion of Humanity. Thus he is secure at all points: for if
the religion of the Bible turn out to be true, his disappointment
will be an agreeable one; and if it turns out false, he will not be
disappointed at all. He is an agnostic—a person bound to be
complacent whatever happens. He may indulge a gentle regret,
a musing sadness, a smiling pensiveness; but he will never refuse
a comfortable dinner, and always wear something soft next his
skin, nor can he altogether avoid the consciousness of his intellectual superiority.

"It must not fear the reproach of realism"

WILLIAM B. CHISHOLM

Directly contrary to the advice of Julian Hawthorne and
other advocates of an idealistic function for literature,
an essayist in *The Critic*, influential New York literary
periodical, called for novels that were thoroughly immersed
in present day political, social, and business life. William
B. Chisholm declared that it would be folly to construct
contemporary novels upon legendary or romantic lines.
There is also more than a hint, in Chisholm's analysis, of
the necessity for social consciousness in the novel, a demand
that would increase as the twentieth century came in.

William B. Chisholm, "American Themes in Fiction," *The Critic*, XXVII
(April 10, 1897), 245–246.

Iᴛ ɪs ɴoᴛ ᴅɪғғɪᴄᴜʟᴛ to find the causes which have militated against a literature of local coloring, and it is no reproach against our patriotism that we have so little distinctly American fiction. There is a law at work which has impelled so many of our best writers either to choose foreign subjects or to shift the scene of action as expeditiously as possible from American to transatlantic surroundings. The inspiration of the average American novel may be stated tersely thus: A new-rich family, seeking broader fields of culture or social display in foreign capitals or at foreign pleasure resorts. The young women of the family are attractive. They have everything to make them so. They are robust in spite of being "lithe" or "svelte." There would be some incongruity in making the daughter of a modern millionaire a plant of hot-house growth. The family began with nothing and worked their way up. To this extent they represent new blood and considerable brawn. In other words, it would be inconsistent to picture them as effete. The father of the family is sturdy and sensible, despising the tawdriness of social distinctions, every successive one of which has to be bought with cold cash. He reads the daily papers and winces under the lash which is so plainly designed for the ambitions of his own household. Not so, however, with the partner of his joys and sorrows. Her interest in the world of fashion has kept steady pace with the advance of her husband's bank account. Money was made to act as an Aladdin's lamp in procuring the grand *entrée*. The girls have been made ready for the social mart by every appliance in the shape of fashionable boarding-schools, ability to call for bread-and-cheese and a good many other things in Parisian French, and, above all, an exhaustive knowledge of gowns, jewelry and the code of observances in society. To this great end everything has been subordinated. The subsequent history of such a family is almost necessarily transferred to foreign capitals, and the still hunt after coronets is made the theme of the favorite American satire.

But such a presentment of American life and aims can hardly be accepted as the final type, any more than can the dialect stories which have pictured a state of life and manners which is rapidly disappearing. Even sectional *differentiae* have been so much modified, that a novel of twenty or thirty years ago would hardly picture the average American of today. The novel of the future

must therefore adapt itself to the conditions of a more homogeneous population and more distinctly national aims and inspirations.
It must throw vividly upon the camera the types of social and
political leadership which are best studied in cities, and which
the newspapers of the day can only give us in segmentary and
entirely concrete fashion. It must be able to deal with these without gloves, and not as they are presented to us too often in interviews. In fact, the American politician, the promoter, the reformer,
has never been "written up" as nature intended that he should be.
The caricature has been too broad, or the eulogy too fulsome. If
the picture of national life and manners in the closing years of
the century is to be handed down with faithful coloring, it must
be through romance, for biography is of necessity partial. It may
be that in such a delineation more than one of our present men
of the hour might see themselves held up to the mirror of nature,
even if not by name—but fidelity in such portraits would be the
first thing demanded. It will be as essential to do full justice to
the commercialism of the age and the general leveling influences
which make one man so like another, and most of them to a certain extent business machines. Whether such a story would have
the charm of feudal romance, is a question. But there is no question that the American novel of the day must eschew imitation
of old models, for the subjects are of necessity new.

If there is no romance in the restless progress of this age, then
the novel of the future must not call itself a romance. It must not
fear the reproach of realism. It would, indeed, be absolute folly
to construct the novel of the latter part of the nineteenth century in the United States upon legendary or romantic lines. Any
departure from the probabilities of the case would be instantly
detected by a whole host of readers, all of whom know that in
this age of steam and telegraph and myriad daily papers, nothing
is easier to do than to verify the leading facts of national history
as they transpire, and nothing is more easily dissipated than fond
delusions about this or that national hero. It is not the accidental
or the sudden that most interests American people. In a sense,
almost every event of real interest is foreshadowed. We are a
nation of previous engagements and announcements, and even
the most sensational of daily papers cannot often take its readers
entirely by surprise. All these peculiarities of our modern environment must be taken into consideration by the coming

novelist, and so, with these strong curbs upon his imagination, it seems almost certain that the successful picture of the future must call for far finer strokes than any which have preceded. A mere portraiture of national life hung on a peg of romance as between some one man and woman, will not be enough. Such a novelist must grasp the significance of great popular movements—what it means to the men and women of today, and whither it seems to point in the study of our national destiny. Is this equivalent to saying that the novel of the future must be a purely philosophical novel? Hardly.

There need be no restraint as to the number of bright pictures of domestic and social life, travel, incident and even private love-making. But it must be a picture of men as they are, of the language as it is, with a due intermixture of dialect and slang, but no more than the probabilities of the case will bear. It must especially emphasize the life of the people as affected by rapidly changing conditions and an imperious business system. But it must seize rather upon the salient points of a nation's laborious life than upon the drier details of this or that special work.

In its nicety of delineation it must not contract the horizon of its outlook. It may be, indeed, with reference either to our foreign relations of the future, or to revolutionary forces within our own jurisdiction, that the novel of the future will be called upon to deal with intensely stirring events. If the law of periodicity means anything, the sword has rusted full long. It is in the drama of martial events that the most fascinating and easily delineable of a nation's characteristics are most readily flashed forth. From the present eyrie of observation we gaze upon a field of fiercely combating opinions and hear vague but disquieting threats. Let us hope that these will prove unmeaning. Still, with reference to the possibilities of national literature, it is of interest to keep abreast with every phase of national discontent, so that, if storms arise, the causes may be intelligently grasped. It was the unsettled conditions of Scottish society which formed the framework of most of the Waverley novels. It is the almost unbroken latter quietude of England's internal affairs which has driven historians as well as romancers to go back to unquiet times for their most elaborate themes. It is the epoch and the crisis which develop the most effective genius in these lines of national delineation. Yet if peace and orderly progress are to be the conditions of a long golden age, if the present conflicts are merely those of opposing opinions, not affecting the course of social harmony and average popular content, then the novel of the future must deal in finer strokes and may satirize the more amiable delusions, or picture the rise and progress of this and that educational or moral crusade. Thus there is no immediate means of forecasting the special character of the coming American romance. We must know something of the future in order to hazard a guess. But with reference to the complexity of our modern life, its high intellectual development, the ceaseless play of competition in every line of social, business and mental progress, it is evident that a truly national novel must prove one of the most serious of undertakings. He must indeed be broadminded and prophetic by instinct who shall take up the four corners of our national advance and present a homogeneous and graphic likeness of the whole.

"So ridiculous as to be made only by a madman"

RICHARD BURTON

Against the new naturalism, the novel of social protest,
the novel of power and sex, the advocates of idealism in
American literature continued to voice their strident
objections—(and, indeed, still do; compare the selection
that follows, by Richard Burton (1861–1940) in *The Forum*
for April, 1895, with the editorial from *Life* on page 172.)
Written the year after the Pullman strike in Chicago and
the march of Coxey's army of unemployed on Washington,
this selection called for "a literature which is bracing
and splendid" for America.

From Richard Burton, "The Healthful Tone for American Literature," *The Forum*, XIX (April, 1895), 251–252, 255–256.

L̲ET US NOT DODGE the fact: the morbid, the cynical, the naturalistic, and the decadent in our present-day literature,—all of this is, more than aught else, a sure emanation from the lack of faith and courage following on the loss (or at least change) of definite and canonical religious conviction. That it cannot always be traced to this efficient cause proves nothing; it is said that a mushroom will appear above the earth an eighth of a mile from the fungus wood whence it springs; yet dependent thereupon by a filament many times too small for seeing by the unaided human eye.

But it would be a false representation of our age and country to bear down on its intellectual struggle in this most important of thought-domains and omit to speak of its affirmative and altruistic side—the side of practical humanitarianism broader, more enlightened, more in the spirit of Christ, in short, than the world has before witnessed. The overthrow of letter-perfect Bible-infallibility will do good in the end and has already liberated people as well as dismayed them; while the great lesson that a life of good is far more to be desired than a hard and fast adherence to a conservative creed, begins to put forth lovely fruit in church and society. This spirit, too, is finding its strong expression in literature, and may be relied upon as a foil to the protuberant ugliness of the theory we are diagnosing. But this should not put us at ease with "art for art's sake." It is to literature what materialism is to thought; and no robing in the splendors of Solomon can conceal the awful truth that death, not life, is in its person. Religion without spiritual activity is pithless formalism; art without spirituality (or ethical beauty, which I hold to be the same thing) is again a whited sepulchre, full of stinking bones.

It is not difficult to expose the fallacy of the creed which cries up manner as the be-all and end-all of art. A mere glance at world-literature proves beyond peradventure that the moving and permanent forces are those which are healthful, vital, positive, optimistic. Homer, Dante, Shakespeare, Cervantes, Milton, and Browning are not decadents; men, all of them, cognizant of life's depths as well as heights, but never forgetting that accomplishment, aspiration, and peace are articulated into our living quite as truly as doubt, denial, and death. Hence these masters are open-air-influences and a tonic to distraught humanity. The history of any puissant nation teaches the same thing; its athletic evolution and crest of power mean a literature which is bracing and splendid, its devolution a product into which the minor note has crept and through which runs the self-questioning of decay. All records yield an irresistible Yea to the query, Does not the decadent in literature (when sincere and not an affectation) always square with a similar state of social and intellectual life in the nation? To accept the poems, stories, and essays of the school in mind as legitimate and natural is to self-doom the country's career and pronounce its noble work done and its maturity past— a claim so ridiculous as to be made only by a madman. . . .

. . . . .

The younger literary folk of the United States, then, are brought face to face with certain hard facts and are bidden choose. They may follow older lands, letting the popular theory of the day generate and guide their work, thereby laying themselves open to the charge of imitation, un-Americanism, false aesthetics and false psychology. Contrariwise, keeping a firm grip on the essential truth that a sound and efficient technique must bottom American literature as it must that of any and all lands, they may nevertheless have clear in sight the still broader and deeper verity that "beauty is truth, truth beauty," that in the ethic atmosphere only can the creative find its homeland and natural breathing-place, beauty being, in the words of Matthew Arnold, "truth seen from another side." We are aware that some critics, good men and true, having the best interests of our native literary- and art-production at heart, are fond of laying chief stress on the need of an unprovincial comparison of our work with other centres of civilization, in order to avoid a fatal self-sufficiency and the exclusive use of local standards—a kind of literary Chauvinism. And coincident with this they talk continually of technique and deem it our crying duty just now to ensure that, lest talent and enthusiasm run to waste. Their word has its share of truth, but in view of this infinitely graver menace implied in the acceptance of an illogical and soulless principle and method, sure if generally received to result in malformation in place of wholesome growth, it may well be ranked as of secondary importance. I believe heartily that our *litératures* are by comparison scot-free from the worst phases of the delusion; the work being done on all sides is vital and vigorous, and Mr. Howells was never more illuminative than in his critical *aperçus* recognizing the independent worth of our native product.

Indeed, the negative spirit, the cynic mood, and the manner of the realist or the pessimist belong, with us, rather to the critics than to the creators, the latter being as a class (though exceptions will occur to all) sound at heart and only eager to do work which shall be sane, broad, truthful, and wholesome. The criticism which continually depresses a fine young extravagance, which reiterates the sacerdotal function of art-minus-morals, and which sneers down admiration for local impulses and data, is not wanting in the United States. Though perhaps not representative, it exists, and so does a corresponding coterie among the literary folk themselves.

Returning to the original questions then, it may be said that what our writers are doing is endangered by what there is a temptation for them to believe; a temptation valiantly resisted in the main, but still present. An American literature such as is in mind, and which if true to our literary forebears we must make, shall be at once practical and ideal; practical, since it is the honest expression of national life and thought; ideal, for that it presents not facts alone but symbols, is not merely photographic but artistic by reason of its sensing the relative proportion of things and the all-important rôle of imaginative representation. Such a school of writers will beget poets and novelists who are also patriots, clasping clean and loyal hands and taking an inextinguishable joy in their work, which they hope shall be for the healing of the nation. And all the people will say, *Amen.*

"Thin and impermanent—
and not a little shoddy"

ROBERT HERRICK

Robert Herrick (1868–1938), like Richard Burton in
the selection previously reproduced, found the American
novel inadequate—but for greatly different reasons.
Herrick, a transplanted New Englander who wrote from
Chicago a series of discerning novels portraying the
defects of the American social and economic scene, felt
that our fiction ignored the most pressing social
and cultural questions of the day, was pale, insipid, and
sentimental. His lengthy analysis of the current literary scene
in the *Yale Review* for April, 1914, provides a good look
at the American novel as the twentieth century got under
way.

IN THE FIRST PLACE, our novels are weakly sentimental.
As a people we have always been excessively sentimental beneath our practical surface. Among the great mass, sentimentality
is one of our blind spots, and "the mass" here does not imply
poverty or ignorance. "The Rosary," which might justly be described as the most syrupy concoction of current years, found its
immense market among American women. But we are no longer
as sentimental as the novelists think us to be: at least, our more
intelligent readers are fast losing the vice. The tone of public
discussion, the note of the newspaper world, no longer has the
sickly sentimentality that has characterized it largely since the
Civil War. Our charities no longer dare to put forward the sentimental plea. The vice conditions of our cities are not only being
exposed with sensational candor, but are being met with unsenti-

From Robert Herrick, "The American Novel," *The Yale Review*, III (April,
1914), 425–431. Copyright Yale University Press.

mental efforts at reform. When we consider the verdict of the press and of the people upon the McNamara case, we cannot be accused of the maudlin, sentimental squint that has often made our criminal procedure a farce. But with all the evidence of a growing appetite for healthy fact, sentimentalism persists in our novels. We sentimentalize in them success and business warfare; above all we sentimentalize our women—both the amorous relation of the sexes and the home. One of the benefits we may expect from the present woman movement is that American women will rise in resentment and kick over the false pedestal of chivalrous sentimentality on which (in our novels) American men have posed them inanely for so long.

. . . . .

Again, our novels are weak religiously. For the most part, they avoid altogether the religious side of life, perhaps as unfit for the tired reader in his hour of relaxation; and at the best they represent a conventionally or negatively religious social world. In a few cases, survivals of the New England tradition, they iterate the old Puritan themes of sin, self-sacrifice, and regeneration. The Puritan tradition is dead, however: for good or for bad it no longer expresses the spiritual life of the people. Yet there is abundant religious feeling in America. We have always had a strain of transcendental mysticism, cropping out in the least expected spots, developing latterly into Christian Science and other healing cults. The ancient creed of Catholicism still has a vital hold, especially in the cities, and the older Protestant creeds have some influence in the smaller towns. It is perhaps not surprising that these formal religions have not shown their influence in our literature. For as a people, our attitude towards the whole subject of religion has fundamentally changed. We demand increasingly an effective religion—a religion that shall have its *point d'appui* on this terrestrial abode. Moreover, American life is becoming peculiarly paganized, yet without renouncing a vital religious interest. It is not a sensual or self-indulgent paganism, but a vital, active, effective paganism, with a popular creed that might read like this:—"Life is good! I desire to make it better. For me life is here and now, and what I can do to make it better must be done here and now, and done not by prayer and fasting but by strong deeds." All our interest in social betterment, which is literally immense, is permeated with this spirit, at once scientific, pagan, and mystic. But very little of this spirit gets into our novels. . . .

In the third place, there is our prudery in the sex realm. This attitude was perfectly expressed recently in a little essay by one of "The Outlook" pundits, in which he said with a good deal of moral unction that Americans would not tolerate in their literature the treatment of "certain subjects." Ours had been always a "pure literature," he boasted, and seemed to imply that our social life was peculiarly free from certain forms of vice due to a lax attitude on the sex question. Our literature has certainly been an emasculated literature, if that is what he means by "pure." As a matter of statistical fact, of which we are becoming painfully aware, American civilization is by no means as free from sexual vice as the editor of "The Outlook" would have us assume, even among the superior classes that make the typical American home. The vice reports of New York and Chicago have wakened us to the meaning of our increased public expenditure for asylums for the blind and feeble-minded, which even the newer western States are forced to maintain. All this would seem to indicate that as a people we must squarely face sex questions, and there is much evidence of our will to do so. Of course, the recognition of sex problems in novels is another matter, and it is not my intention to debate at length that threadbare topic of the proper treatment of sex in literature. The only arguments that are of importance on either side are specific instances of sex relations described by novelists, and this is not the place for such an extended discussion. It is obvious to me that a literature which persistently ignores any subject of considerable human interest is an imperfect and superficial literature. That is exactly what we have tried to do in America, what the editor of "The Outlook" prides himself on our novelists having done successfully in regard to sex—with the result that our more intelligent people read with apparent interest and profit English and German books that deal with the subject from the modern point of view. That amiable generation of Americans who preferred to look the other way when any perplexing or "dangerous" topic was broached and preserved an unspotted optimism by strenuously refusing to use their intelligence on "certain subjects," is fast disappearing, fortunately. Our magazines are still hypocritical, for magazine editors are a timid race. But our press is frank enough and hopelessly vulgar about all sorts of sex matters. What we need is the same honest, unwavering, unsqueamish treatment of this eternal human subject as of any other.

. . . . .

Lastly, for a democratic people, as we call ourselves, we have a singularly unreal and aristocratic literature. The preoccupation of our popular novelists with the lives and the possessions of the rich, who perforce are our aristocrats, is something amazing. Even that much read novel "The House of Mirth," which came near being the woman's epic of our day, betrays this unbalanced absorption in the lives of the privileged, with little or no shading of the commoner experience. American women must be held responsible for this aristocratic taste. They are still by far the chief reading public, and they prefer books about rich and luxurious people. Their favorite epic still remains the old barbaric one of the triumphant male who conquers the riches and the powers of this earth, only to lay them at the feet of his loved one, chivalrously surrounding her with all the glories of his conquest, and rewarded by her with faithfulness and love. . . .

To return for a moment to the aristocratic aspect of our novels, wealth has been the great American fact for the past generation —the making, the conquest, the control, the disposal of money. The figures that have fascinated the imagination of our people have been the forceful men who have taken, often ruthlessly, what they wanted out of life, who have directed the economic energies of the race. The capitalist has been both our buccaneer and our epic hero. So we had for a time a great many business novels that described commercial struggles and money conquests. But this rich material of the pioneer days of capitalism was largely wasted: it never gave us one great epic figure, enduring, illustrative for all time of our predatory period. The future American will have to go to the magazine biographies of Gould, Rockefeller, Harriman, or Morgan to get the epic, not to our novels. The pity of it! For it was the one big theme of the past twenty years—the story of the money-maker, his inner meaning and his self-explanation. We are already passing out of that period of towering industrial creators: we have come to the era of luxury and trusteeship—the family life of wealth in the second and third generations. And what we get of them in our novels is a profusion of motors, country houses,—Palm Beach and Fifth Avenue. We do not get the stories of the little people, and they make up the living of most of our ninety millions. . . .

On these four grounds, then, among others, I find the American novel to-day lacking in importance, not really representative of our richest and most significant life. I find it thin and impermanent —and not a little shoddy.

"A vast home-grown provision for entertainment"

HENRY JAMES

In 1904 Henry James came back to America from England, and surveyed the scene afresh. The result was the series of essays and commentaries later collected in *The American Scene* (1907). The novelist Wright Morris says of this work that "no other book contains so much of the American scene, since no other book has so much to give out." James toured the country from coast to coast, then returned to England to compose his memoirs. What he found—as one might expect—was innocence; American literature, like the rest of America, needed most to grow up.

B<small>UT OH, AS I WAS</small> to observe, the school of "black and white" trained up by the magazines has much, in the American air, to answer for: it points so vividly the homely moral that when you haven't what you like you must perforce like, and above all misrepresent, what you have. Its translation of these perfunctory passions into pictorial terms saddles it with a weight of responsibility that would be greater, one can only say, if there ever were a critic, some guardian of real values, to bring it to book. The

From Henry James, "Florida," in *The American Scene*, pp. 439–441. Copyright 1907 by Harper & Brothers, renewed 1935 by Henry James. Reprinted by permission of Harper & Brothers.

guardians of real values struck me as, up and down, far to seek. The whole matter indeed would seem to come back, interestingly enough, to the general truth of the aesthetic need, in the country, for much greater values, of certain sorts, than the country and its manners, its aspects and arrangements, its past and present, and perhaps even future, really supply; whereby, as the aesthetic need is also intermixed with a patriotic yearning, a supply has some-how to be extemporized, by any pardonable form of pictorial "hankey-pankey"—has to be, as the expression goes, cleverly "faked." But it takes an inordinate amount of faking to meet the supposed intensity of appetite of a body of readers at once more numerous and less critical than any other in the world; so that, frankly, the desperate expedient is written large in much of the "artistic activity" of the country.

The results are of the oddest; they hang all traceably together; wonderful in short the general spectacle and lesson of the scale and variety of the faking. They renew again the frequent admoni-tion that the pabulum provided for a great thriving democracy may derive most of its interest from the nature of its testimony to the thriving democratic demand. No long time is required, in the States, to make vivid for the visitor the truth that the nation is almost feverishly engaged in producing, with the greatest pos-sible activity and expedition, an "intellectual" pabulum after its own heart, and that not only the arts and ingenuities of the drafts-man (called upon to furnish the picturesque background and peo-ple it with the "aristocratic" figure where neither of these revela-tions ever meets his eye) pay their extravagant tribute, but that those of the journalist, the novelist, the dramatist, the genealogist, the historian, are pressed as well, for dear life, into the service. The illustrators of the magazines improvise, largely—that is when not labouring in the cause of the rural dialects—improvise the field of action, full of features at any price, and the characters who figure upon it, young gods and goddesses mostly, of super-human stature and towering pride; the novelists improvise, with the aid of the historians, a romantic local past of costume and compliment and sword-play and gallantry and passion; the drama-tists build up, of a thousand pieces, the airy fiction that the life of the people in the world among whom the elements of clash and contrast are simplest and most superficial abounds in the sub-jects and situations and effects of the theatre; while the genealogists touch up the picture with their pleasant hint of the number, over the land, of families of royal blood. All this constitutes a vast home-grown provision for entertainment, rapidly superseding any that may be borrowed or imported, and that indeed already begins, not invisibly, to press for exportation. As to quantity, it looms immense, and resounds in proportion, yet with the property, all its own, of ceasing to be, of fading like the mist of dawn —that is of giving no account of itself whatever—as soon as one turns on it any intending eye of appreciation or of inquiry. It is the public these appearances collectively refer us to that becomes thus again the more attaching subject; the public so placidly uncritical that the whitest thread of the deceptive stitch never makes it blink, and sentimental at once with such inveteracy and such simplicity that, finding everything everywhere perfectly splendid, it fairly goes upon its knees to be humbuggingly humbugged. It proves ever, by the ironic measure, quite incalculably young.

"The talent is there, high and dry"

VAN WYCK BROOKS

Van Wyck Brooks entered the American literary scene
with a smashing attack on gentility and propriety in
the novel. In *America's-Coming-of-Age* (1915) he excoriated
the tendency toward conformity in the American scene,
and called for a literature and a culture that was vigorous
and democratic. At this period in his career Brooks was
distinctly a rebel against national complacency, as the
excerpt that follows shows.

ALMOST ALL THE greater American writers, placed beside their English contemporaries, have a certain all too unworldly

From the book *Three Essays on America* by Van Wyck Brooks, p. 78. Copyright 1934 by E. P. Dutton & Co., Inc. Reprinted by permission of the publishers.

refinement. Purity of style and delicacy of touch at once distinguish Emerson from Carlyle and Hawthorne from any Victorian novelist; but the abyss between their writings and the world in which they lived is immeasurably greater. The American character speaks through them, of course, but it is the American character only in its most sublimated form, carefully cleansed as it were and highly rarefied. Nothing is more marked than their disinclination to take a plunge, reckless and complete, as Carlyle and Dickens did, into the rudest and grossest actualities. The poet Camoens on his deathbed observed that his whole life had been spent in trying to keep himself afloat in a stormy sea, and his only care had been to exercise his left hand with double energy so that his right hand might be free to hold his *Luciad* aloft, uncontaminated by the waves. This is the whole story of American literature: in a more than usually difficult and sordid world it has applied its principal energies to being uncontaminated itself. It has held aloof, as a consciously better part, like all American idealism. The talent is there, high and dry; and if it is not always too high, it is very often a great deal too dry.

"To a pin-point in limitless space"

VERNON LOUIS PARRINGTON

The intellectual forces at work in American life during the years before and after the turn of the century, which played so important a role in the development of an uncompromising naturalism in the American novel, are summed up by Vernon Louis Parrington (1871–1929) in his influential *Main Currents in American Thought* (1927–1930), an ideological interpretation of the literature of the United States. The rise of scientific determinism,

From *Main Currents in American Thought*, Vol. III, by Vernon L. Parrington, pp. 316–319. Copyright 1930 by Harcourt, Brace and Company, Inc.; renewed, 1958, by Vernon L. Parrington, Jr., Louise P. Tucker, and Elizabeth P. Thomas. Reprinted by permission of the publishers.

with its mechanistic interpretation of man's nature, rendered
increasingly obsolete the idealistic, optimistic fiction of
an earlier day, replacing it with the novel as practiced by
Stephen Crane, Frank Norris, and Theodore Dreiser—
somber, pessimistic, obsessed with the pitiful helplessness
of man in nature, and the animalistic brutality of man
toward man.

So LATE AS 1893, in spite of the stark ugliness of Hamlin
Garland's pictures of the Middle Border, American realism was
still unlike in temper those somber etchings, burnt into dark patterns by the caustic acids of European experience, that came from
the hands of Russian and German and French naturalists—
sketches that in their bitter gloom seemed tragically untrue to the
homelier experience of America. In appraising such difference in
temper Howells ascribed it to the gulf that separated American
well-being from the poverty and injustice of European societies.
American realism was hopeful because American life was hopeful.
The novelist in this singularly favored land must reflect the temper
of a people made kindly by an abundant prosperity and democratic justice, and in the sincerity of his realism he will necessarily
concern himself with the "more smiling aspects of life, which are
the more American." Whoever should strike a "note so profoundly
tragic in American fiction" as was struck in Dostoevski's *Crime
and Punishment,* he asserted in 1891, "would do a false and mistaken thing." And in a later work he spoke casually of our "gay
American horizons"—surely the most romantic phrase ever applied to a sad and joyless people by a professed realist.

But while Howells was thus summing up the achievements of
American realism and somewhat overconfidently forecasting its
future temper, he was in fact writing the history of a past phase.
Already the clouds were gathering upon our "gay" horizons, and
the current optimisms were finding less food to feed on. The economics of this happy America were coming to be regarded by vast
numbers as a class economics, forecasting a less democratic future.
Young men born in the early seventies, when Mr. Howells was
entering upon his new realistic studies, were coming to intellectual
maturity in a very different age; a new science and a consolidating
economics were creating a somber temper that was eventually to

produce in *An American Tragedy,* a story not greatly unlike that
Russian tale which Mr. Howells, a short generation before, had
pronounced impossible to American experience. Stephen Crane
and Frank Norris and Theodore Dreiser were the intellectual
children of the nineties, and their art was a reflection of that
sober period of American disillusion.

The artist, of course, in his creative work is only mediately influenced by the current science and philosophy; yet even in his
aloofness from the specific problems of the laboratory and the
study he can scarcely escape the pervasive influence of the *Zeit-
geist.* And so, after Hamlin Garland, the realistic novel again took
a new course from the shifting winds of scientific doctrine. The
generation that succeeded the rebellious son of the Middle Border
came too late to maturity to share his faith in the benevolent
universe of Herbert Spencer, and got little comfort from a prom-
ised Utopia that only awaited the enactment of certain statutory
laws—laws that would assure economic justice to all—to lay open
its hospitable realm. Far-reaching changes were coming over the
temper of scientific thought. The conclusions of the physical
sciences were ravaging the orderly preserves of biological evolution, with its cardinal doctrine of organic growth and historical
continuity; the hurrying march of scientific investigation was
leaving far behind the benevolent universe conceived of by Victorian thinkers and was coming out upon higher and bleaker
tablelands of speculation. The universe that unfolded itself to
chemistry and physics was vaster and colder than biological evolution, with its doctrine of the conservation of energy, had imagined
—a vibrating mechanism shot through with energy, that revealed
itself in action and reaction, impersonal, amoral, dwarfing all the
gods dreamed of hitherto; a universe in which the generations of
men have shrunk to a pin-point in limitless space and all teleological hopes and fears become the emptiest of futilities. It was the
conception of determinism that after long denial was at last coming to wide acceptance—a conception that underlay the thinking
of such diverse men as Comte and Spencer and Marx, a conception
implicit in the doctrine of continuity, in the law of causality, in
the Marxian law of concentration; and now disencumbered of its
teleological wrappings, disillusioned with the doctrine of progress,
it was to shape the new intellectual attitude towards life.

In presence of such an extraordinary intellectual revolution the old anthropomorphisms of metaphysics and ethics were doomed, and from the revelations of physics and chemistry and psychology must come an endeavor after a fresh evaluation of man's duty and destiny in a universe of immeasurable energy. An ethics that should square with the new data of science must take its departure from the bleak fact of a depersonalized universe, wherein man is but a single form of imprisoned energy, localized for a brief instant and rising to momentary consciousness in the eternal flux, about and through whom flows the energy of an unprobed universe. As this mechanistic conception found lodgment in minds prepared by a mechanical economics, the last remaining vestiges of the old French romanticism were swept away; a benevolent, egocentric universe was become unthinkable; progress was no longer the inherent law of matter and of life; but instead, everywhere change, disintegration and reintegration, a ceaseless and purposeless flux to what final end the human mind could not forecast. Thus at a stroke the benevolent cosmos of the fathers, wherein for generations men had been providing themselves with sure refuges, was swept away; and with its passing passed the old faiths—faith in freedom of the will, in a purposive providence, in a universe that had been long in travail to bring forth man, its last and dearest offspring for whom all things work together for good. And with the decay of the traditional faiths the younger generation was left to wander as best it might upon the bleak tablelands of impersonal energy. Spencer's "ultimate of ultimates," the Permanence of Force, that follows the law of evolution and dissolution, had given way to Faraday's electro-energy that is indifferent to purpose.

The intellectual backgrounds were thus preparing for a gloomier realism than Howells's or Garland's, a realism that took its departure from two postulates: that men are physical beings who can do no other than obey the laws of a physical universe; and that in the vast indifferentism of nature they are inconsequential pawns in a game that to human reason has no meaning or rules. To assume that fate which rules human destiny is malignant, is to assume a cosmic interest in man which finds no justification in science; Man at best is only an inconsequential atom in a mechanical flux, or at worst, as Jurgen puts it picturesquely, only a bubble in fermenting swill. Such a conception, of course, made slow headway against the traditional order of thought; and if it had not been aided by a changing economics it would have found few to follow a line of reasoning that led to such unpleasant conclusions. The mind of the artist is more susceptible to concrete social fact than to abstract physical principle, and the swift centralizing of economics in the eighties and the nineties provided the stimulus for the extraordinary reversal of thought marked by the contrast between Emerson and Theodore Dreiser. Emerson was the apotheosis of two centuries of decentralization that destroyed the pessimism brought to the new world by refugees from the old, and found its inevitable expression in the exaltation of the individual, free and excellent, the child of a beneficent order; whereas Dreiser was the first spokesman of a later America once more falling within the shadow of the pessimism that springs from every centralized society shut up within the portals of a static economics; that dwarfs the individual and nullifies his will, reducing him from a child of God to a serf.

IV

The American Character

"This magnificent image
of themselves"

ALEXIS DE TOCQUEVILLE

Can any novel properly image the American character?
And can a democracy produce not only the proper image
for the writer, but the literary sensibility necessary for the
creation of literature? In all the debates over the role of
the American novel, the claims of idealism and realism, the
later controversy over the proper use of art and experience,
there would always be that underlying question of whether
America presented the necessary subject, and object,
for its writers. In an early (1840) analysis of the American
character, the Frenchman Alexis de Tocqueville discussed
the relationship of political democracy and imaginative
literature. His comments are a useful preface to the
discussion of the American character in fiction that
will follow.

I AM PERSUADED that in the end democracy diverts the
imagination from all that is external to man, and fixes it on man
alone. Democratic nations may amuse themselves for a while
with considering the productions of Nature; but they are only excited in reality by a survey of themselves. Here, and here alone,
the true sources of poetry among such nations are to be found;
and it may be believed that the poets who shall neglect to draw
their inspirations hence, will lose all sway over the minds which

From Alexis de Tocqueville, *Democracy in America*, translated by Henry
Reeve as revised and annotated from the author's last edition by Francis
Bowen (New York: The Century Company, 1890), pp. 89–90.

they would enchant, and will be left in the end with none but un-impassioned spectators of their transports. I have shown how the ideas of progression and of the indefinite perfectibility of the human race belong to democratic ages. Democratic nations care but little for what has been, but they are haunted by visions of what will be; in this direction their unbounded imagination grows and dilates beyond all measure. Here, then, is the wildest range open to the genius of poets, which allows them to remove their performances to a sufficient distance from the eye. Democracy shuts the past against the poet, but opens the future before him. As all the citizens who compose a democratic community are nearly equal and alike, the poet cannot dwell upon any one of them; but the nation itself invites the exercise of his powers. The general similitude of individuals, which renders any one of them taken separately an improper subject of poetry, allows poets to include them all in the same imagery, and to take a general survey of the people itself. Democratic nations have a clearer perception than any others of their own aspect; and an aspect so imposing is admirably fitted to the delineation of the ideal.

I readily admit that the Americans have no poets; I cannot allow that they have no poetic ideas. In Europe people talk a great deal of the wilds of America, but the Americans themselves never think about them: they are insensible to the wonders of inanimate Nature, and they may be said not to perceive the mighty forests which surround them till they fall beneath the hatchet. Their eyes are fixed upon another sight: the American people views its own march across these wilds—drying swamps, turning the course of rivers, peopling solitudes, and subduing Nature. This magnificent image of themselves does not meet the gaze of the Americans at intervals only; it may be said to haunt every one of them in his least as well as in his most important actions, and to be always flitting before his mind. Nothing conceivable is so petty, so insipid, so crowded with paltry interests, in one word so anti-poetic, as the life of a man in the United States. But among the thoughts which it suggests there is always one which is full of poetry, and that is the hidden nerve which gives vigor to the frame.

"He trun up bote hands"

WILLIAM ALLEN WHITE

William Allen White (1868–1944), essayist, novelist,
and newspaper editor, looked back at the literary fashions
of the 1880's and 1890's and saw the scene dominated
by the magazine editors, whose view of the American
character was serene and complacent. The editors of *The
Century, Harper's* and *Scribner's,* he said, thought it proper
that fiction should carefully guard young Americans from
contact with the more sordid aspects of reality. The
American was a good creature; the American home was
immaculate and beautiful. The American writer's task,
therefore, was to preserve and cherish that ideal.

Forty years ago and more Hamlin Garland was a new
writer. He wrote of the Middle West. He was a Populist, a restless soul. He wrote of the dirt and the dust, the shimmering heat
and the stinks of the farm. His people talked in the farm vernacular.
His was a protesting voice against the smugness of the pastoral
writers who told of the delights of the rural scene. Garland knew
of the sweat and the despair, of the futile hopes and mocking
ironies of American farm life. He knew how the farmer talked
and he set down what he knew. And one day he sent a story to
Mr. Richard Watson Gilder, editor of *The Century.* Mr. Gilder
wrote Garland a letter about it. Mr. Gilder doubted whether *The
Century* could print it because Garland's fictional farmers did not
use good English, and the colloquialisms which Garland used
Mr. Gilder feared would corrupt the youth of his subscribers. He
said so, simply and directly; not that Mr. Garland had introduced

From William Allen White, "Fiction of the Eighties and Nineties," in
American Writers on American Literature, ed. John Macy (New York: Liveright Publishing Corporation, 1934), pp. 390–393.

anything so profane as "damn." It was not profanity, it was loose English, anachronisms, vulgarisms, to which Mr. Gilder objected.

Mr. Gilder was the literary arbiter of the times. His magazine, *The Century*, represented in the mid-eighties and nineties the heights to which American literary culture had risen. The stories he printed carefully guarded youth from contact with reality. Mr. Henry L. Alden was editor of *Harper's Magazine* in that period. He also was a sentinel of the hearthstone. From *Harper's Magazine* no raucous voice could come, no low, earthbound spirits could escape to disturb the serenity of the house beautiful, the home immaculate. Mr. Burlingame of *Scribner's Magazine* held to the same high ideals of the functions of literature that inspired and ennobled Mr. Gilder and Mr. Alden. They were three in one and one in three, a blessed trinity that beamed over the America of that day, kindly lights of literature and learning, beacons that shone benignly unto the perfect day.

Yet there were other voices. Hooting, ribald, outlaw mobs of jeering, brick-throwing, window-breaking literary gangsters infested the lower walks of what must by courtesy be called the literature of the period. The comic papers—and a score of them were scattered across the length and breadth of the land—led by *Life, Truth, Puck* and *Judge* in New York City, hurled their poisoned darts and javelins at the high gods enthroned in the golden editorial chairs. Peck's *Sun* at Milwaukee, the Detroit *Free Press*, Bill Nye's Laramie *Boomerang*, Sam Clover's Estelline (Dakota) *Bell*, the Arkansas *Traveler*, the Danbury *News*, the Toledo *Blade*, *Texas Siftings* and half a score of others, evanescent, protesting weekly newspapers, carried the serious doubts of a young and impudent nation about the infallibility of the holy trinity of Burlingame, Alden and Gilder. A decade earlier Mark Twain had begun to poke fun at the plaster of Paris perfection in contemporary literature.

Now viewing the situation casually, these local spokesmen of the restless dissenters who passed with the eighties seemed to have lived and died in vain. But the nineties came, and with the nineties came new magazines with new editors; the *Cosmopolitan* and *McClure's* and *Munsey's*, whose ideals differed from the loftier ideals of the editors of *The Century, Harper's* and *Scribner's*. Yet the difference was a difference in degree of sweetness and light which they shed; it was not a new kind of light. Even when certain of these newer popular low-priced magazines went into muck-raking, their fiction for the most part was cut from the old piece of goods which the masters had been weaving.

James L. Ford, who was a pre-Menckenite literary protestant, wrote in the early nineties. He was a scorner of the ideals of the times. It was Ford who wrote a skit famous in the early nineties about Richard Watson Gilder. In this skit Ford represented Gilder "within the tabooed district" crawling "cautiously through the barbed-wire fence which was long ago stretched from his sanctum across the city at Cooper Union." According to Ford, Gilder was "pursuing his studies of what was known in the magazine offices as 'low life'."

" 'He's just been down to Ludlow Street and troo one o' dem houses where the Jew sweaters is.'

" 'And what did he say to it all?' I inquired.

" 'He trun up bote hands,' said the East Sider earnestly."

It was Ford's contention in the middle of the nineties that be-low Fourteenth Street in New York was a fertile, fallow field, wait-ing for the artist's plow. It is difficult to realize now in what light and low esteem an opinion like that was held by the arbiters of American literary taste. Not that writing in those days did not have its realism of a kind, but the reality was based upon a philosophical precept, perhaps one might call it a religious tenet, which prevailed generally through the latter half of the nineteenth century and had its roots in an elder day. Those who held this hypothesis believed in a moral government of the universe so well policed that material rewards were always returned for spiritual excellence. When realism dealt with the lower orders as it did sometimes in American writing, realism described more or less meticulously their clothes, their houses, their works and ways, but the deep injustice which often frustrated their inner and spiritual lives was ignored. They were regarded as amusing creatures and the toad on the harrow was not supposed to feel seriously its devastating pain.

To understand the popular fiction of the last quarter of the old century in America, one must go back to the spiritual pabulum upon which the writers of that fiction were fed in childhood and in youth. Even the best of them and most cultured, went as chil-dren to Sunday-school. There they learned something more than the Bible and something different from many of the Bible's stark realities. They "took out" Sunday-school books. The Sunday-school books were generally published and distributed under the auspices of the American Tract Society, a Boston concern which thrived in Tremont Street with a branch in New York in Nassau Street. These Sunday-school books essayed fiction and the fiction had one pattern. For it was based upon just one philosophical tenet—that virtue is rewarded by material counters and vice punished by material castigations. When one said that the wages of sin is death there was no nonsense about interpreting death to mean spiritual decay. Death meant death, at least a broken leg or a bashed head or a taut rope or a railroad accident provided by a careful Providence which kept books scrupulously and well with all poor sinners. These pious tales mostly concerned children, good little boys and girls and bad little boys and girls, and the bad little boys and girls were always punished by calamity or lingered in a life of sin and shame, encountering disaster along their painful way to the portals of hell, and the good little boys and girls either were rewarded with great treasure and good fortune or died and went straight to heaven. It was upon this meat that the little literary Caesars of our seventies and eighties were fed as children. Of course they grew up, read books, perhaps not Sunday-school books, written out in the big world, went to college, came to question, to challenge and to deny the moral precepts that had been pounded into them as youths. But the challenge and denial were superficial. When they set up their universes in their stories or poems, there skulking in the background were the police-court gods with whiskers who someway managed to reward virtue and to punish vice. Rarely was a writer of that gay golden day able to shake off entirely the Sunday-school philosophy with which the American Tract Society had tainted his youth.

One must not mistake the philosophy of that day for a gloomy philosophy, for it was not. Hell was cooling off. The hell of the eighteenth century was pretty well crusted over. The skating was good there. Scholarship had justified the mockers and the ribald had their following. Frank Stockton and H. C. Bunner told their merry tales and sold them to the best magazines. But in the merry tales often lurked a poisonous villain or a pestiferous saint, the one to be punished with whips and scorpions, the other to be rewarded by the hand of the king's daughter and half of the kingdom. In the popular fiction of that day were precious few unhappy endings. For unhappy endings would indicate that virtue was unrewarded by material counters or earthly blessings of some sort. Writers were probably intelligent enough to wish that they could end their stories without playing providence to their heroes and villains, but writers knew, and publishers reminded those who forgot, that the public was imbued with the philosophy of a moral government of the universe which punished sin and rewarded virtue with substantial, understandable demerits or earthly tokens of divine affection and esteem.

"There is only one expert"

MARK TWAIN

In 1893 the French author Paul Bourget visited the United States, and a year later appeared his *Outre-Mer*, in which he discussed, sympathetically but not without criticism, the American character as he saw it. Bourget's generalizations on Americans fired the wrath of Mark Twain (1835–1910), who responded with an essay entitled "What Paul Bourget Thinks Of Us." The American novelist delivered himself of some malevolently humorous observations on the moral superiority of the American character to the French, and declared that no foreigner could ever understand and portray the American character. Only the native writer could do this, and then for only a small area of America, because the United States was too large for any single novelist to capture the image of its character in a single book.

A FOREIGNER CAN photograph the exteriors of a nation, but I think that that is as far as he can get. I think that no foreigner can report its interior—its soul, its life, its speech, its

From Mark Twain, "What Paul Bourget Thinks of Us," *North American Review*, CLX (January, 1895), 50–52.

thought. I think that a knowledge of these things is acquirable in only one way; not two or four or six—*absorption;* years and years of unconscious absorption; years and years of intercourse with the life concerned; of living it, indeed; sharing personally in its shames and prides, its joys and griefs, its loves and hates, its prosperities and reverses, its shows and shabbinesses, its deep patriotisms, its whirlwinds of political passion, its adorations—of flag, and heroic dead, and the glory of the national name. Observation? Of what real value is it? One learns peoples through the heart, not the eyes or the intellect.

There is only one expert who is qualified to examine the souls and the life of a people and make a valuable report—the native novelist. This expert is so rare that the most populous country can never have fifteen conspicuously and confessedly competent ones in stock at one time. This native specialist is not qualified to begin work until he has been absorbing during twenty-five years. How much of his competency is derived from conscious "observation"? The amount is so slight that it counts for next to nothing in the equipment. Almost the whole capital of the novelist is the slow accumulation of *un*conscious observation—absorption. The native expert's intentional observation of manners, speech, character, and ways of life can have value, for the native knows what they mean without having to cipher out the meaning. But I should be astonished to see a foreigner get at the right meanings, catch the elusive shades of these subtle things. Even the native novelist becomes a foreigner, with a foreigner's limitations, when he steps from the State whose life is familiar to him into a State whose life he has not lived. Bret Harte got his California and his Californians by unconscious absorption and put both of them into his tales alive. But when he came from the Pacific to the Atlantic and tried to do Newport life from study—conscious observation—his failure was absolutely monumental. Newport is a disastrous place for the unacclimated observer, evidently.

To return to novel-building. Does the native novelist try to generalize the nation? No, he lays plainly before you the ways and speech and life of a few people grouped in a certain place—his own place—and that is one book. In time, he and his brethren will report to you the life and the people of the whole nation—the life of a group in a New England village; in a New York village; in a Texan village; in an Oregon village; in villages in fifty States and Territories; then the farm-life in fifty States and Territories; a hundred patches of life and groups of people in a dozen widely separated cities. And the Indians will be attended to; and the cowboys; and the gold and silver miners; and the negroes; and the idiots and Congressmen; and the Irish, the Germans, the Italians, the Swedes, the French, the Chinamen, the Greasers; and the Catholics, the Methodists, the Presbyterians, the Congregationalists, the Baptists, the Spiritualists, the Mormons, the Shakers, the Quakers, the Jews, the Campbellites, the infidels, the Christian Scientists, the Mind-Curists, the Faith-Curists, the train-robbers, the White Caps, the Moonshiners. And when a thousand able novels have been written, *there* you have the soul of the people, the life of the people, the speech of the people; and not anywhere else can these be had. And the shadings of character, manners, feelings, ambitions, will be infinite.

"All that has given us distinct nationality"

PAUL LEICESTER FORD

Paul Leicester Ford (1865–1902) believed that there *was* a distinct American character. It was to be found in the ideals for which the American people stood, as revealed in the great accomplishments of American democracy throughout its history. Ford, himself an historical novelist, excoriated American writers for devoting their attention to the petty, the un-typical in American life and character, and criticized those who would seek to portray the national character in terms of a single place or region.

W HAT A BLENDING of history and romance may do as to the future it is idle to attempt to prophesy. At the present moment

From Paul Leicester Ford, "The American Historical Novel," *The Atlantic Monthly*, LXXX (December, 1897), 728.

there seems a revival of interest in American history, and the novelist has been quickly responsive to it. In the resulting literature, however, we find as yet the same defects that appear in much, one is tempted to say all, of our contemporary fiction. That is, an entire disregard of the big elements of American life and an over-accentuation of the untypical. In a general survey of our fiction, one is struck with its almost universal silence on all that has given us distinct nationality. Who in reading American fiction has ever brought away a sense of real glory in his own country? We are told that our people are hopelessly occupied in money-making, and that our politics are shamefully corrupt. Yet the joint product of these forces has won, or is winning, equality of man, religious liberty, the right of asylum, freedom of the ocean, arbitration of international disputes, and universal education; and this, too, while these people were fighting a threefold struggle with man, beast, and nature across a vast continent.

Disregarding all this, the novelist has turned to the petty in American life. With the most homogeneous people in both thought and language in the world, American literature is overburdened with dialect stories; with no true class distinctions, and with an essential resemblance in American life from the Atlantic to the Pacific, the novel of locality has been accepted as typical and not exceptional; with a people less absorbed in and less influenced by so-called society than any other great nation, we are almost submerged with what may be styled the Afternoon Tea Novel. It may be good fictional material, for human nature should be after all the first consideration of the novelist, but whales are not caught in pails, nor are the great purposes and passions of mankind usually to be found in the neighborhood of "the cups that cheer but not inebriate." And so our novelists may be likened to the early miners of gold, who, overlooking the vast mountain lodes of precious metal, industriously sifted the river-bed for the little shining particles that had been washed down from the former. American history and American life have their rich lodes of gold-bearing quartz; and when our people produce as good literary workers as mechanical engineers, when the best of our imagination turns from the practical to the ideal, there will be no lack of an American fiction.

"Cultural chauvinism is the most harmless of patriotisms"

RANDOLPH BOURNE

Randolph Bourne (1886–1918) was leading spokesman
and inspiration for the group of young radicals who
challenged the complacency of the American scene during
the second decade of the twentieth century. He saw our
culture as weak and imitative, and demanded an American
fiction that would look not to Europe and the past, but to
present-day American life, for its vitality. The American
character, he said, was bound by cultural fetters to Europe,
and such groveling humility prevented the proper
development of our own writers.

T HIS VIRUS of the "best" rages throughout all our Anglo-
Saxon campaign for culture. Is it not a notorious fact that our
professors of English literature make no attempt to judge the
work produced since the death of the last consecrated saint of
the literary canon,—Robert Louis Stevenson? In strict accordance
with Arnold's doctrine, they are waiting for the judgment upon
our contemporaries which they call the test of time, that is, an
authoritative objective judgment, upon which they can unques-
tioningly rely. Surely it seems as if the principle of authority,
having been ousted from religion and politics, had found a strong
refuge in the sphere of culture. This tyranny of the "best" ob-
jectifies all our taste. It is a "best" that is always outside of our
native reactions to the freshnesses and sincerities of life, a "best"
to which our spontaneities must be disciplined. By fixing our eyes

From Randolph Bourne, *The History of a Literary Radical and Other Essays,*
ed. Van Wyck Brooks. Copyright 1920 by B. W. Huebsch, Inc., 1948 by
The Viking Press, Inc. Reprinted in *Literary Opinion in America,* rev. ed.,
ed. Morton Dauwen Zabel (New York: Harper & Brothers, 1951), pp. 71–72.

humbly on the ages that are past, and on foreign countries, we effectually protect ourselves from that inner taste which is the only sincere "culture."

Our cultural humility before the civilizations of Europe, then, is the chief obstacle which prevents us from producing any true indigenous culture of our own. I am far from saying, of course, that it is not necessary for our arts to be fertilized by the civilizations of other nations past and present. The culture of Europe has arisen only from such an extensive cross-fertilization in the past. But we have passed through that period of learning, and it is time for us now to set up our individual standards. We are already "heir of all the ages" through our English ancestry and our last half-century of European idolatry has done for us all that can be expected. But, with our eyes fixed on Europe, we continue to strangle whatever native genius springs up. Is it not a tragedy that the American artist feels the imperative need of foreign approval before he can be assured of his attainment? Through our inability or unwillingness to judge him, through our cultural humility, through our insistence on the objective standard, we drive him to depend on a foreign clientele, to live even in foreign countries, where taste is more confident of itself and does not require the label, to be assured of the worth of what it appreciates.

The only remedy for this deplorable situation is the cultivation of a new American nationalism. We need that keen introspection into the beauties and vitalities and sincerities of our own life and ideals that characterizes the French. The French culture is animated by principles and tastes which are as old as art itself. There are "classics," not in the English and Arnoldian sense of a consecrated canon, dissent from which is heresy, but in the sense that each successive generation, putting them to the test, finds them redolent of those qualities which are characteristically French, and so preserves them as a precious heritage. This cultural chauvinism is the most harmless of patriotisms; indeed it is absolutely necessary for a true life of civilization. And it can hardly be too intense, or too exaggerated. Such an international art exhibition as was held recently in New York, with the frankly avowed purpose of showing American artists how bad they were in comparison with the modern French, represents an appalling degradation of attitude which would be quite impossible in any

other country. Such groveling humility can only have the effect
of making us feeble imitators, instead of making us assert, with
all the power at our command, the genius and individuality
which we already possess in quantity, if we would only see it.

"Charity covers a multitude of mediocrities"

JAMES GIBBONS HUNEKER

James Gibbons Huneker (1860–1921), like Randolph
Bourne and Van Wyck Brooks, saw American literature as
overly saccharine and unoriginal, but unlike them he did
not see cultural patriotism as the answer. As art, music,
drama, and literature critic for the New York *Sun* and other
newspapers, he was instrumental in introducing the work
of European artists to American audiences. Huneker found
the American novel sentimental, and felt that the new
"fearlessness" in matters of sex and society was no less
stereotyped than the kind of writing it had replaced. To
write the American novel, he declared, the native novelist
needed *taste*, and a willingness to pursue the naked truth,
free of adherence to conventions of any kind.

W HEN THE SUPREME MASTER of the historical novel mod-
estly confessed that he could do the "big bow-wow strain," but to
Jane Austen must be accorded the palm of exquisite craftsman-

From James Gibbons Huneker, "The Great American Novel," pp. 82–88. Re-
printed with the permission of Charles Scribner's Sons from *Unicorns* by James
Gibbons Huneker, copyright 1917 Charles Scribner's Sons; renewal copyright
Josephine Huneker. Reprinted in *Literary Opinion in America*, rev. ed., ed.
Morton Dauwen Zabel (New York: Harper & Brothers, 1951), pp. 73, 74,
75–76.

ship, there was then no question upon the critical map of the so-called "great American novel." Sir Walter Scott—to whom such authors of historical novels as Châteaubriand and his *Martyrs,* the *Salammbô* of Flaubert, and that well-nigh perfect fiction, *The History of Henry Esmond,* by Thackeray, yield precedence— might have achieved the impossible: the writing of a library, epitomising the social history of "These States"—as Walt Whitman would say. After Scott no name but Balzac's occurs to the memory; Balzac, who laid all France under his microscope (and France is all of a piece, not the checkerboard of nationalities we call America). Even the mighty Tolstoy would have balked the job. And if these giants would have failed, what may be said of their successors? The idea of a great American novel is an "absolute," and nature abhors an absolute, despite the belief of some metaphysicians to the contrary. Yet the notion still obtains and inquests are held from time to time, and the opinions of contemporary novelists are taken toll of; as if each man and woman could give aught else but their own side of the matter, that side which is rightfully enough personal and provincial. The question is, after all, an affair for critics, and the great American novel will be in the plural; thousands perhaps. America is a chord of many nations, and to find the key-note we must play much and varied music. . . .

Mr. James is a splendid case for us; he began in America and landed in England, there to stay. Our other felicitous example of cosmopolitanism is Henry Blake Fuller, the author of *The Chevalier of Pensieri-Vani* and *The Châtelaine of la Trinité,* who was so widely read in the nineties. After those charming excursions into a rapidly vanishing Europe Mr. Fuller reversed the proceeding of James; he returned to America and composed two novels of high artistic significance, *The Cliff Dwellers* and *With the Procession,* which, while they continued the realistic tradition of William Dean Howells, were also the forerunners of a new movement in America. It is not necessary to dwell now on *The Last Refuge,* or on that masterly book of spiritual parodies, *The Puppet-Booth.* But Mr. Fuller did not write the great American novel. Neither did Mr. Howells, nor Mr. James. Who has? No one. Is there such a thing? Without existing it might be described in Celtic fashion, this mythical work, as pure fiction. Let us admit for the sake of argument that if it were written by some unknown monster of genius, it would, like Lewis Carroll's Snark, turn into a Boojum.

Henry James has said that no one is compelled to admire any particular sort of writing; that the province of fiction is all life, and he has also wisely remarked that "when you have no taste you have no discretion, which is the conscience of taste," and may we add, when you have no discretion you perpetrate the shocking fiction with which America is deluged at this hour. We are told that the new writers have altered the old canons of bad taste, but *"plus ça change, plus c'est la même chose."* A liquorish sentimentality is the ever-threatening rock upon which the bark of young American novelists goes to pieces. (Pardon the mixed metaphor.) Be sentimental and you will succeed! We agree with Dostoevski that in fiction, as well as in life, there are no general principles, only special cases. But these cases, could they not be typical? even if there are not types, only individuals. And are men and women so enthralled by the molasses of sentimentalism in life? Have the motion-pictures hopelessly deranged our critical values? I know that in America charity covers a multitude of mediocrities, nevertheless, I am loath to believe that all one reads in praise of wretched contemporary fiction is meant in earnest. . . .

As to the Puritanism of our present novels one may dare to say in the teeth of youthful protestants that it is non-existent. The pendulum has swung too far the other way. And as literary artists are rare, the result has not been reassuring. Zola seems prudish after some experiments of the younger crowd. How badly they pull off the trick. How coarse and hard and heavy their touch. Most of these productions read like stupid translations from a dull French original. They are not immoral, only vulgar. As old Flaubert used to say: such books are false, nature is not like that. How keenly he saw through the humbug of "free love"—a romantic tradition of George Sand's epoch—may be noted in his comment that Emma Bovary found in adultery all the platitudes of marriage. Ah! that much-despised, stupid, venerable institution, marriage! How it has been flouted since the days of Rousseau —the father of false romanticism and that stupefying legend, the "equality" of mankind. (O! the beautiful word, "equality," invented for the delectation of rudimentary minds.) A century and more fiction has played with the theme of concubinage. If the Nacquet divorce bill had been introduced a decade or so before it was in France, what would have become of the theatre of Dumas *fils*, or later, of the misunderstood woman in Ibsen's plays? All such tribal taboos make or unmake literature.

So, merely as a suggestion to ambitious youngsters, let the novelist of the future in search of a novelty describe a happy marriage, children, a husband who doesn't drink or gamble, a wife who votes, yet loves her home, her family, and knows how to cook. What a realistic bombshell he would hurl into the camp of sentimental socialists and them that believe a wedding certificate is like Balzac's *La Peau de Chagrin*—a document daily shrinking in happiness. Absurdities make martyrs, but of all the absurd and ineffectual martyrdoms that of running off with another's wife is usually the crowning one. "I don't call this very popular pie," said the little boy in Richard Grant White's story; and the man in the case is usually the first to complain of his bargain in pastry.

However, categories are virtually an avowal of mental impuissance, and all marriages are not made in heaven. In the kingdom of morality there are many mansions. When too late you may sport with the shade—not in the shade—of Amaryllis, and perhaps elbow epigrams as a lean consolation. That is your own affair. Paul Verlaine has told us that *"j'ai vécu énormement,"* though his living enormously did not prove that he was happy. Far from it. But he had at least the courage to relate his terrors. American novelists may agree with Dostoevski that "everything in the world always ends in meanness"; or with Doctor Pangloss that all is for the best in the best of possible worlds. An affair of temperament. But don't mix the values. Don't confuse intellectual substances. Don't smear a fact with treacle and call it truth. Above all, don't preach. Impiety is an indiscretion, yet, don't be afraid to tell the truth. From Jane Austen and Walter Scott, the parents of the modern English novel, to many modern instances, fiction has thrived best on naked truth. All the rest is sawdust, tripe-selling, and sentimentalism. Didn't Mr. Roundabout declare in one of his famous papers that "Figs are sweet, but fictions are sweeter"? In our land we can't get the latter sweet enough. Altruism, Brotherhood of Man Uplifting. These are the shibboleths of the *"nouvelles couches sociales."* Prodigious!

"*The moral hypocrisy of the American mind*"

THEODORE DREISER

In 1900 Theodore Dreiser (1871–1945) published *Sister Carrie*, the story of a woman who used her body to advance herself in the world. It was almost immediately suppressed by the publisher for its alleged immorality; not for eleven years would Dreiser bring out another novel. The excerpt that follows from Dreiser's autobiography, telling of his first encounter with realism in American literature through an unpublished novel by a fellow newspaperman, Robert Hazard, provides a suitable coda to the dispute over gentility and the portrayal of American character in fiction. For it was Dreiser more than any other single figure who would write the novels that ended the genteel tradition.

THE CENTRAL CHARACTER of Hazard's book was an actress, young and very beautiful. Her lover was a newspaper man, deeply in love with her and yet not faithful, in one instance anyhow. This brought about a Zolaesque scene in which she spanked another actress with a hairbrush. There was treacherous plotting on the part of somebody in regard to a local murder, which brought about the arrest and conviction of the newspaper man for something he knew nothing about. This entailed a great struggle on the part of Theo to save him, which resulted in her failure and his death on the guillotine. A priest figured in it in some way, grim, jesuitical.

To this day some of the scenes of this book come back to me as having been forcefully done—the fight between the two actresses,

From Theodore Dreiser, *A Book About Myself* (New York: Boni & Liveright, 1922), pp. 131–133. Reprinted by permission of The World Publishing Company, Cleveland and New York.

for one thing, a midnight feast with several managers, the gallows scene, a confession. I am not sure of the name of the newspaper man who collaborated with Hazard on this work, but the picture of his death in an opium joint later, painted for me by Hazard, and the eccentricities of his daily life, stand out even now as Poe-like. He must have been blessed or cursed with some such temperament as that of Poe, dark, gloomy, reckless, poetic, for he was a dope-fiend and died of dope.

Be that as it may, this posthumous work, never published, so far as I know, was the opening wedge for me into the realm of realism. Being distinctly imitative of Balzac and Zola, the method was new and to me impressive. It has always struck me as curious that the first novel written by an American that I read in manuscript should have been one which by reason of its subject matter and the puritanic character of the American mind could never be published. These two youths knew this. Hazard handed it to me with the statement: "Of course a thing like this could never be published over here. We'd have to get it done abroad." That struck me as odd at the time—the fact that if one wrote a fine thing nevertheless because of an American standard I had not even thought of before, one might not get it published. How queer, I thought. Yet these two incipient artists had already encountered it. They had been overawed to the extent of thinking it necessary to write of French, not American life in terms of fact. Such things as they felt called upon to relate occurred only in France, never here—or at least such things, if done here, were never spoken of. I think it nothing less than tragic that these men, or boys, fresh, forceful, imbued with a burning desire to present life as they saw it, were thus completely overawed by the moral hypocrisy of the American mind and did not even dare to think of sending their novel to an American publisher. Hazard was deeply impressed with the futility of attempting to do anything with a book of that kind. The publishers wouldn't stand for it. You couldn't write about life as it was; you had to write about it as somebody else thought it was, the ministers and farmers and dullards of the home. Yet here he was, as was I, busy in a profession that was hourly revealing the fact that this sweetness and light code, this idea of a perfect world which contained neither sin nor shame for any save vile outcasts, criminals and vagrants, was the trashiest lie that was ever foisted upon an all too human world. Not a day, not an hour, but the pages of the very news-paper we were helping to fill with our scribbled observations were full of the most incisive pictures of the lack of virtue, honesty, kindness, even average human intelligence, not on the part of a few but of nearly everybody. Not a business, apparently, not a home, not a political or social organization or an individual but in the course of time was guilty of an infraction of some kind of this seemingly perfect and unbroken social and moral code. But in spite of all this, judging by the editorial page, the pulpit and the noble mouthings of the average citizen speaking for the benefit of his friends and neighbors, all men were honest—only they weren't; all women were virtuous and without evil intent or de-sign—but they weren't; all mothers were gentle, self-sacrificing slaves, sweet pictures for songs and Sunday Schools—only they weren't; all fathers were kind, affectionate, saving, industrious—only they weren't. But when describing actual facts for the news columns, you were not allowed to indicate these things. Side by side with the most amazing columns of crimes of every kind and description would be other amazing columns of sweet mush about love, undying and sacrificial, editorials about the perfection of the American man, woman, child, his or her sweet deeds, inten-tions and the like—a wonderful dose. And all this last in the face of the other, which was supposed to represent the false state of things, merely passing indecencies, accidental errors that did not count. If a man like Hazard or myself had ventured to transpose a true picture of facts from the news columns of the papers, from our own reportorial experiences, into a story or novel, what a howl! Ostracism would have followed much more swiftly in that day than in this, for today turgid slush approximating at least some of the facts is tolerated. Fifteen years later Hazard told me he still had his book buried in a trunk somewhere, but by then he had turned to adventurous fiction, and a year later, as I have said, he blew his brains out.

V

Ideals for the American Novel

"They divide American life between them"

VAN WYCK BROOKS

With the 1920's, the battle seemed won. The genteel
tradition was of increasingly minor importance. By and
large, it seemed possible for the American novelist to treat
almost any aspect of life that he wanted, and get his work
published. Still, there was the matter of the reading public.
The novelist began to come up more and more against the
problem of maintaining his artistic integrity while appealing
to a large enough section of the reading public to enable
him to survive economically. In 1915 Van Wyck Brooks
had noted a division of American culture into what he called
"highbrow" and "lowbrow" segments, and the result, he
felt, was that our literature suffered accordingly. This
dichotomy, which has also been expressed as "class" vs.
"mass," "modern" vs. "traditional," and, nowadays, "art"
vs. "experience," would seem increasingly important as the
century grew older—for it soon developed that critics who
inveighed against "highbrow" literature tended to favor
what was "healthy" and "American," and to suspect what
they considered "ultra-intellectuality" in fiction and poetry.

Now I suppose that most of the American novelists in
our day are university men; they have learned to regard literature
as an august compound of Browning, Ben Jonson, and Hesiod;

From the book *Three Essays on America* by Van Wyck Brooks, pp. 16–18.
Copyright 1934 by E. P. Dutton & Co., Inc. Reprinted by permission of the
publishers.

and consequently when they themselves begin to write it is in a spirit of real humility that they set themselves to the composition of richly rewarded trash. I am sure of this: it is modesty that lies behind the "best-seller"; and there is an aspect in which the spectacle of writers regarding themselves as humble tradesfolk has a certain charm. But the conception of literature as something, so to speak, high and dry, gives to the craft of authorship in America a latitude like that of morality in Catholic countries: so long as the heavenly virtues are upheld mundane virtues may shift as they will. In a word, writers are relieved of responsibility, and while their ethical conscience remains quite sound they absolve themselves from any artistic conscience whatsoever. And the worst of it is that precisely these writers of immitigable trash are often the bright, vigorous, intuitive souls who *could* make literature out of American life. Has it ever been considered how great a knowledge of men, what psychological gifts of the first order, their incomparable achievement of popularity implies?

These two attitudes of mind have been phrased once for all in our vernacular as "Highbrow" and "Lowbrow." I have proposed these terms to a Russian, an Englishman, and a German, asking each in turn whether in his country there was anything to correspond with the conceptions implied in them. In each case they have been returned to me as quite American, authentically our very own, and, I should add, highly suggestive.

What side of American life is not touched by this antithesis? What explanation of American life is more central or more illuminating? In everything one finds this frank acceptance of twin values which are not expected to have anything in common: on the one hand a quite unclouded, quite unhypocritical assumption of transcendent theory ("high ideals"); on the other a simultaneous acceptance of catchpenny realities. Between university ethics and business ethics, between American culture and American humor, between Good Government and Tammany, between academic pedantry and pavement slang, there is no community, no genial middle ground.

The very accent of the words "Highbrow" and "Lowbrow" implies an instinctive perception that this is a very unsatisfactory state of affairs. For both are used in a derogatory sense. The "Highbrow" is the superior person whose virtue is admitted but felt to be an inept unpalatable virtue; while the "Lowbrow" is a good fellow one readily takes to, but with a certain scorn for him and all his works. And what is true of them as personal types is true of what they stand for. They are equally undesirable, and they are incompatible; but they divide American life between them.

"A group which says little and saws wood"

H. L. MENCKEN

H. L. Mencken (1880–1956) was a popular and influential critic of American literature and culture during the 1910's, but it was the 1920's that saw him in his heyday. Witty, irreverent, an avowed enemy to pomposity and cant in any form, Mencken seemed prophet and guide to a generation that had thrown off the genteel tradition and recoiled from the idealism of the first world war. In the essay on the American novel from which the selection below is taken, Mencken looks with satisfaction at the victory over prudery and decorum in the novel, notes the key role of Theodore Dreiser in the struggle, then looks around him at our liberated letters, to find that so far only limited use has been made of the new freedom.

THE YOUNG AMERICAN literatus of today, with publishers ready and eager to give him a hearing, can scarcely imagine the difficulties which beset his predecessor of twenty years ago; he is, indeed, far too little appreciative of the freedom he has, and far

Reprinted from H. L. Mencken, "The American Novel," pp. 285–293, in *Prejudices: Fourth Series*, by permission of Alfred A. Knopf, Inc. Copyright 1924 by Alfred A. Knopf, Inc. Reprinted in *Literary Opinion in America*, rev. ed., ed. Morton Dauwen Zabel (New York: Harper & Brothers, 1951), pp. 160–164.

too prone to flee from hard work to the solace of the martyr's shroud. When I first began practice as a critic, in 1908, there was yet plenty of excuse for putting it on. It was a time of almost inconceivable complacency and conformity. Hamilton Wright Mabie was still alive and still taken seriously, and all the young pedagogues who aspired to the critical gown imitated him in his watchful stupidity. This camorra had delivered a violent wallop to Theodore Dreiser eight years before, and he was yet suffering from his bruises; it was not until 1911 that he printed *Jennie Gerhardt.* Miss Harriet Monroe and her gang of new poets were still dispersed and inarticulate; Miss Amy Lowell, as yet unaware of Imagism, was writing polite doggerel in the manner of a New England schoolmarm; the reigning dramatists of the nation were Augustus Thomas, David Belasco, and Clyde Fitch; Miss Cather was imitating Mrs. Wharton; Hergesheimer had six years to go before he'd come to *The Lay Anthony;* Cabell was known only as one who provided the text for illustrated gift-books; the American novelists most admired by most publishers, by most readers and by all practicing critics were Richard Harding Davis, Robert W. Chambers, and James Lane Allen. It is hard indeed, in restrospect, to picture those remote days just as they were. They seem almost fabulous. The chief critical organ of the Republic was actually the Literary Supplement of the *New York Times. The Dial* was down with diabetes in Chicago; *The Nation* was made dreadful by the gloomy humors of Paul Elmer More; *The Bookman* was even more saccharine and sophomoric than it is today. When the mild and pianissimo revolt of the middle 90's—a feeble echo of the English revolt—had spent itself, the Presbyterians marched in and took possession of the works. Most of the erstwhile revoltés boldly took the veil—notably Hamlin Garland. No novel that told the truth about life as Americans were living it, no poem that departed from the old patterns, no play that had the merest ghost of an idea in it had a chance. When, in 1908, Mrs. Mary Roberts Rinehart printed a conventional mystery story which yet managed to have a trace of sense in it, it caused a sensation. And when, two years later, Dr. William Lyon Phelps printed a book of criticism in which he actually ranked Mark Twain alongside Emerson and Hawthorne, there was as great a stirring beneath the college elms as if a naked fancy

woman had run across the campus. If Hergesheimer had come
into New York in 1908 with *Cytherea* under his arm, he would
have worn out his pantaloons on publishers' benches without
getting so much as a polite kick. If Eugene O'Neill had come to
Broadway with *The Hairy Ape,* he would have been sent to
Edward E. Rose to learn the elements of his trade. The devilish
and advanced thing, in those days, was for the fat lady star to
give a couple of matinées of Ibsen's *A Doll's House.*

A great many men and a few women addressed themselves to
the dispersal of this fog. Some of them were imaginative writers
who found it simply impossible to bring themselves within the
prevailing rules; some were critics; others were young publishers.
As I look back, I can't find any sign of concerted effort; it was, in
the main, a case of each on his own. The more contumacious of
the younger critics, true enough, tended to rally 'round Huneker,
who, as a matter of fact, was very little interested in American
letters, and the young novelists had a leader in Dreiser, who, I
suspect, was quite unaware of most of them. However, it was
probably Dreiser who chiefly gave form to the movement, despite
the fact that for eleven long years he was silent. Not only was
there a useful rallying-point in the idiotic suppression of *Sister
Carrie;* there was also the encouraging fact of the man's massive
immovability. Physically and mentally he loomed up like a sort
of headland—a great crag of basalt that no conceivable assault
seemed able to touch. His predecessor, Frank Norris, was of much
softer stuff. Norris, had he lived longer, would have been wooed
and ruined, I fear, by the Mabies, Boyntons, and other such
Christian critics, as Garland had been wooed and ruined before
him. Dreiser, fortunately for American letters, never had to face
any such seduction. The critical schoolmarms, young and old,
fell upon him with violence the moment he appeared above the
horizon of his native steppe, and soon he was the storm center
of a battle-royal that lasted nearly twenty years. The man himself
was solid, granitic, without nerves. Very little cunning was in him
and not much bellicose enterprise, but he showed a truly appalling
tenacity. The pedagogues tried to scare him to death, they tried
to stampede his partisans and they tried to put him into Coventry
and get him forgotten, but they failed every time. The more he
was reviled, sneered at, neglected, the more resolutely he stuck

to his formula. That formula is now every serious American novelist's formula. They all try to write better than Dreiser, and not a few of them succeed, but they all follow him in his fundamental purpose—to make the novel true. Dreiser added something, and here following him is harder: he tried to make the novel poignant—to add sympathy, feeling, imagination to understanding. It will be a long while before that enterprise is better managed than he managed it in *Jennie Gerhardt.*

Today, it seems to me, the American imaginative writer, whether he be novelist, poet or dramatist, is quite as free as he deserves to be. He is free to depict the life about him precisely as he sees it, and to interpret it in any manner he pleases. The publishers of the land, once so fearful of novelty, are now so hospitable to it that they constantly fail to distinguish the novelty that has hard thought behind it from that which has only some Village mountebank's desire to stagger the wives of Rotarians. Our stage is perhaps the freest in the world—not only to sensations, but also to ideas. Our poets get into print regularly with stuff so bizarre and unearthly that only Christian Scientists can understand it. The extent of this new freedom, indeed, is so great that large numbers of persons appear to be unable to believe in it; they are constantly getting into sweats about the taboos and inhibitions that remain, for example, those nourished by comstockery. But the importance and puissance of comstockery, I believe, is quite as much overestimated as the importance and puissance of the objurgations still hurled at sense and honesty by the provincial professors of American Idealism, the Genius of America, and other such phantasms. The Comstocks, true enough, still raid an occasional book, particularly when their funds are running low and there is need to inflame Christian men, but that their monkeyshines ever actually suppress a book of any consequence I very much doubt. The flood is too vast for them. Chasing a minnow with desperate passion, they let a whole school of whales go by. In any case, they confine their operations to the single field of sex, and it must be plain that it is not in the field of sex that the hottest battles against the old American manner have been fought and won. *Three Soldiers* was far more subversive of that manner than all the stories of sex ever written in America—and yet *Three Soldiers* came out with the imprint of one of the most respectable American publishers, and was scarcely challenged. *Babbitt* scored a victory that was still easier, and yet more significant, for its target was the double one of American business and American Christianity; it set the whole world to laughing at two things that are far more venerated in the United States than the bodily chastity of women. Nevertheless, *Babbitt* went down so easily that even the alfalfa *Gelehrten* joined in whooping for it, apparently on the theory that praising Lewis would make the young of the national species forget Dreiser. Victimized by their own craft, the *Gelehrten* thus made a foul attack upon their own principles, for if their principles did not stand against just such anarchistic and sacrilegious books, then they were without any sense whatever, as was and is, indeed, the case.

I shall not rehearse the steps in the advance from *Sister Carrie*, suppressed and proscribed, to *Babbitt*, swallowed and hailed. The important thing is that, despite the caterwauling of the Comstocks and the pedagogues, a reasonable freedom for the serious artist now prevails—that publishers stand ready to print him, that critics exist who are competent to recognize him and willing to do battle for him, and that there is a large public eager to read him. What use is he making of his opportunity? Certainly not the worst use possible, but also certainly not the best. He is free, but he is not yet, perhaps, worthy of freedom. He lets the popular magazine, the movie and the cheap-John publisher pull him too hard in one direction; he lets the vagaries of his politics pull him too hard in another. Back in 1908 I predicted the destruction of Upton Sinclair the artist by Upton Sinclair the visionary and reformer. Sinclair's bones now bleach upon the beach. Beside them repose those of many another man and woman of great promise —for example, Winston Churchill. Floyd Dell is on his way—one novel and two doses of Greenwich Village psychology. Hergesheimer writes novelettes for the *Saturday Evening Post*. Willa Cather has won the Pulitzer Prize—a transaction comparable to the election of Charles W. Eliot to the Elks. Masters turns to prose that somehow fails to come off. Dreiser, forgetting his trilogy, experiments rather futilely with the drama, the essay, free verse. Fuller renounces the novel for book reviewing. Tarkington is another Pulitzer prizeman, always on the verge of first-rate work but always falling short by an inch. Many of the White

Hopes of ten or fifteen years ago perished in the war, as surely victims of its slaughter as Rupert Brooke or Otto Braun; it is, indeed, curious to note that practically every American author who moaned and sobbed for democracy between the years 1914 and 1919 is now extinct. The rest have gone down the chute of the movies.

But all this, after all, may signify little. The shock troops have been piled up in great masses, but the ground is cleared for those that follow. Well, then, what of the youngsters? Do they show any sign of seizing their chance? The answer is yes and no. On the one hand there is a group which, revolving 'round *The Book-man*, talks a great deal and accomplishes nothing. On the other hand there is a group which, revolving 'round *The Dial* and *The Little Review*, talks even more and does even less. But on the third hand, as it were, there is a group which says little and saws wood. There seems to be little in common between its members, no sign of a formal movement, with its blague and its bombast, but all of them have this in common: that they owe both their opportunity and their method to the revolution that followed *Sister Carrie*. Most of them are from the Middle West, but they are distinct from the Chicago crowd, now degenerated to posturing and worse. They are sophisticated, disillusioned, free from cant, and yet they have imagination. The raucous protests of the evangelists of American Idealism seem to have no more effect upon them than the advances of the Expressionists, Dadaists, and other such café-table prophets. Out of this dispersed and ill-defined group, I believe, something will come. Its members are those who are free from the two great delusions which, from the beginning, have always cursed American letters: the delusion that a work of art is primarily a moral document, that its purpose is to make men better Christians and more docile cannon-fodder, and the delusion that it is an exercise in logic, that its purpose is to prove something. These delusions, lingering beyond their time, are responsible for most of the disasters visible in the national literature today—the disasters of the radicals as well as those of the 100 per cent dunderheads. The writers of the future, I hope and believe, will carefully avoid both of them.

"The truths of the inner life"

IRVING BABBITT

The new literature was immoral, lacking in spiritual humility, materialistic, deterministic. So declared Irving Babbitt (1865–1933), leader of the so-called New Humanists, who sought to combat what he considered the godless revolt-for-revolt's-sake of the writers of the 1920's. Babbitt felt the realism of the contemporary novel was in fact less than real, because it ignored "the principle of control on which the inner life finally depends."

YET IT REMAINS TRUE that awe and reverence and humility are Christian virtues and that there was some survival of these virtues in the Puritan. For a representative Puritan like Jonathan Edwards they were inseparable from the illumination of grace, from what he terms a "divine and supernatural light." In the passage from the love and fear of God of an Edwards to the love and service of man professed by the humanitarian, something has plainly dropped out, something that is very near the center. What has tended to disappear is the inner life with the special type of control it imposes. With the decline of this inner control there has been an increasing resort to outer control. Instead of the genuine Puritan we then have the humanitarian legalist who passes innumerable laws for the control of people who refuse to control themselves. The activity of the uplifters is scarcely suggestive of any "divine and supernatural light." Here is a discrimination of the first importance that has been obscured by the muddy thinking of our half-baked intelligentsia. One is thus kept from perceiving the real problem, which is to retain

From Irving Babbitt, "The Critic and American Life," in *On Being Creative* (Boston: Houghton Mifflin Company, 1932), pp. 209–216. Reprinted in *Literary Opinion in America*, rev. ed., ed. Morton Dauwen Zabel (New York: Harper & Brothers, 1951), pp. 136–139.

the inner life, even though one refuse to accept the theological
nightmare with which the Puritan associated it. More is involved
in the failure to solve this problem than the Puritan tradition. It
is the failure of our contemporary life in general. Yet, unless some
relation is reached by a full and free exercise of the critical spirit,
one remains a mere modernist and not a thoroughgoing and complete modern; for the modern spirit and the critical spirit are in
their essence one.

What happens, when one sets out to deal with questions of this
order without sufficient depth of reflection and critical maturity,
may be seen in Mr. Sinclair Lewis's *Elmer Gantry*. He has been
lured from art into the writing of a wild diatribe which, considered even as such, is largely beside the mark. If the Protestant
Church is at present threatened with bankruptcy, it is not because
it has produced an occasional Elmer Gantry. The true reproach
it has incurred is that, in its drift toward modernism, it has lost
its grip not merely on certain dogmas, but simultaneously on the
facts of human nature. It has failed above all to carry over in
some modern and critical form the truth of a dogma that unfortunately receives much support from these facts—the dogma of
original sin. At first sight Mr. Mencken would appear to have a
conviction of evil—when, for example, he reduces democracy in
its essential aspect to a "combat between jackals and jackasses"—
that establishes at least one bond between him and the austere
Christian.

The appearance, however, is deceptive. The Christian is conscious above all of the "old Adam" in himself; hence his humility.
The effect of Mr. Mencken's writing, on the other hand, is to
produce pride rather than humility, a pride ultimately based on
flattery. The reader, especially the young and callow reader,
identifies himself imaginatively with Mr. Mencken, and conceives
of himself as a sort of morose and sardonic divinity surveying
from some superior altitude an immeasurable expanse of "boobs."
This attitude will not seem especially novel to anyone who has
traced the modern movement. One is reminded in particular of
Flaubert, who showed a diligence in collecting bourgeois im-
becilities comparable to that displayed by Mr. Mencken in his
Americana. Flaubert's discovery that one does not add to one's
happiness in this way would no doubt be dismissed by Mr.

Mencken as irrelevant, for he has told us that he does not believe
in happiness. Another discovery of Flaubert's may seem to him
more worthy of consideration. "By dint of railing at idiots," Flaubert reports, "one runs the risk of becoming idiotic oneself."

It may be that the only way to escape from the unduly complacent cynicism of Mr. Mencken and his school, is to reaffirm
once more the truths of the inner life. In that case it would seem
desirable to disengage, so far as possible, the principle of control on which the inner life finally depends from mere creeds
and traditions and assert it as a psychological fact; a fact, moreover, that is neither "cold" nor "clammy." The coldness and
clamminess of much so-called realism arises from its failure to
give this fact due recognition. A chief task, indeed, of the Socratic
critic would be to rescue the noble term "realist" from its present
degradation. A view of reality that overlooks the element in man
that moves in an opposite direction from mere temperament, the
specifically human factor, in short, may prove to be singularly
one-sided. Is the Puritan, John Milton, when he declares that "he
who reigns within himself and rules passions, desires, and fears
is more than a king," less real than Mr. Theodore Dreiser when he
discourses in his peculiar dialect of "those rearranging chemisms
upon which all the morality and immorality of the world is
based"?

As a matter of fact, according to the degree and nature of the
exercise of the principle of control, one may distinguish two main
types of realism which may be denominated respectively religious
and humanistic: as the principle of control falls into abeyance, a
third type tends to emerge, which may be termed naturalistic
realism. That the decline of the traditional controls has been
followed by a lapse to the naturalistic level is indubitable. The
characteristic evils of the present age arise from unrestraint and
violation of the law of measure and not, as our modernists would
have us believe, from the tyranny of taboos and traditional inhibitions. The facts cry to heaven. The delicate adjustment that
is required between the craving for emancipation and the need
of control has been pointed out once for all by Goethe, speaking
not as a Puritan, but as a clear-eyed man of the world. Everything, he says, that liberates the spirit without a corresponding
growth in self-mastery is pernicious. This one sentence would

seem to cover the case of our "flaming youth" rather completely.

The movement in the midst of which we are still living was from its inception unsound in its dealing with the principle of control. It is vain to expect from the dregs of this movement what its "first sprightly running failed to give." Mr. Carl Sandburg speaks of the "marvelous rebellion of man at all signs reading *Keep off*." An objection to this purely insurrectional attitude is that, as a result of its endless iteration during the past century and more, it has come to savor too strongly of what has been called the "humdrum of revolt." A more serious objection to the attitude is that it encourages an unrestricted and merely temperamental liberty which, paradoxically enough, at first sight affords the modern man no avenue of escape from the web that is being woven about him by the scientific determinist.

Realists of the current type are in point of fact intimately allied with the psychologists—glandular, behavioristic, and psychoanalytical—who, whatever their divergences among themselves, unite in their deterministic trend and therefore clash fundamentally with both religious and humanistic realists. The proper method of procedure in defending the freedom of the will would seem to insist upon it as a fact of experience, a fact so primary that the position of the determinist involves an evasion of one of the immediate data of consciousness in favor of a metaphysical dream. What is genuinely experimental in naturalistic psychology should of course be received with respect; but the facts of which it takes account in its experiments are unimportant compared with the facts it either neglects or denies. Practically it is running into grotesque extremes of pseudo-science that make it a shining mark for the Socratic critic.

Here at all events is the issue on which all other issues finally hinge; for until the question of moral freedom—the question of whether man is a responsible agent or only the plaything of his impulses and impressions—is decided, nothing is decided; and to decide the question under existing circumstances calls for the keenest critical discrimination. Creation that is not sufficiently supported by such discrimination is likely to prove premature.

"I put my faith in the modern literary adventurers"

SHERWOOD ANDERSON

Sherwood Anderson (1876–1941) was inspiration and example to many of the young writers of the 1920's. He had rejected a prosperous business career to become a writer, and his stories of small town Midwestern life displayed a keen insight into the impoverishing aspects of American village existence, together with a notable awareness of psychological motivation. Himself an accomplished stylist, he defended the necessity for crudity and ugliness in American literature, declaring that modern industrial society was itself crude and ugly, and required such treatment at the hands of its novelists.

AND WHAT ARE WE to do about it? To me it seems that as writers we shall have to throw ourselves with greater daring into the life here. We shall have to begin to write out of the people and not for the people. We shall have to find within ourselves a little of that courage. To continue along the road we are travelling is unthinkable. To draw ourselves apart, to live in little groups and console ourselves with the thought that we are achieving intellectuality, is to get nowhere. By such a road we can hope only to go on producing a literature that has nothing to do with life as it is lived in these United States.

To be sure, the doing of the thing I am talking about will not be easy. America is a land of objective writing and thinking. New

From Sherwood Anderson, "An Apology for Crudity," *The Dial*, LXIII (November 8, 1917), 438. Copyright 1917 (renewed) by Eleanor Anderson. Reprinted by permission of Harold Ober Associates Incorporated. Reprinted in *The Stature of Theodore Dreiser*, ed. Alfred Kazin and Charles Shapiro (Bloomington: Indiana University Press, 1955), pp. 82–83.

paths will have to be made. The subjective impulse is almost unknown to us. Because it is close to life, it works out into crude
and broken forms. It leads along a road that such American
masters of prose as James and Howells did not want to take, but
if we are to get anywhere, we shall have to travel that road.

The road is rough and the times are pitiless. Who, knowing our
America and understanding the life in our towns and cities, can
close his eyes to the fact that life here is for the most part an
ugly affair? As a people we have given ourselves to industrialism,
and industrialism is not lovely. If anyone can find beauty in an
American factory town, I wish he would show me the way. For
myself, I cannot find it. To me, and I am living in industrial life,
the whole thing is as ugly as modern war. I have to accept that
fact and I believe a great step forward will have been taken when
it is more generally accepted.

But why, I am asked, is crudity and ugliness necessary? Why
cannot a man like Mr. Dreiser write in the spirit of the early
Americans, why cannot he see fun in life? What we want is the
note of health. In the work of Mark Twain there was something
wholesome and sweet. Why cannot the modern man be also
wholesome and sweet?

To this I make answer that to me a man, say like Mr. Dreiser,
is wholesome. He is true to something in the life about him, and
truth is always wholesome. Twain and Whitman wrote out of
another age, out of an age and a land of forests and rivers. The
dominant note of American life in their time was the noisy,
swaggering raftsman and the hairy-breasted woodsman. To-day
it is not so. The dominant note in American life to-day is the factory hand. When we have digested that fact, we can begin to
approach the task of the present-day novelist with a new point
of view.

It is, I believe, self-evident that the work of the novelist must
always lie somewhat outside the field of philosophic thought. Your
true novelist is a man gone a little mad with the life of his times.
As he goes through life he lives, not in himself, but in many people. Through his brain march figures and groups of figures. Out of
the many figures, one emerges. If he be at all sensitive to the
life about him and that life be crude, the figure that emerges
will be crude and will crudely express itself.

I do not know how far a man may go on the road of subjective writing. The matter, I admit, puzzles me. There is something approaching insanity in the very idea of sinking yourself too deeply into modern American industrial life.

But it is my contention that there is no other road. If one would avoid neat, slick writing, he must at least attempt to be brother to his brothers and live as the men of his time live. He must share with them the crude expression of their lives. To our grandchildren the privilege of attempting to produce a school of American writing that has delicacy and color may come as a matter of course. One hopes that will be true, but it is not true now. And that is why, with so many of the younger Americans, I put my faith in the modern literary adventurers. We shall, I am sure, have much crude, blundering American writing before the gift of beauty and subtlety in prose shall honestly belong to us.

"The sad surprises which are in store"

JAMES BRANCH CABELL

Unlike most of his contemporaries, James Branch Cabell (1879–1958) did not deal with the present-day scene in his novels. The Virginia writer enjoyed a brief but tremendous vogue during the 1920's and then faded out of the literary picture, but before and after that he continued to write novels ostensibly set in a hazy, faraway medieval land called Poictesme. Written in flawless prose, these fables contained some incisive criticism of contemporary life, as well as acute speculation on the nature of man. In the passage that follows, Cabell defends his lack of concern, as a novelist, with the present-day picture.

From James Branch Cabell, "Near a Flag in Summer," in *These Restless Heads: a Trilogy of Romantics* (New York: Robert M. McBride & Company, 1932), pp. 114–121. Reprinted by permission of Margaret F. Cabell.

No PATRIOT CAN remain deaf, it is well known, to the call of his country's flag. So under these persistent urgings I have now and then wondered for what real reason I have not ever considered, in any one of my writings, some part of those matters which the flag speaks of. I wonder why, save for the unimportant and highly ambiguous instance of the first version of *The Eagle's Shadow* (that tiny comedy which presents people cloistered for a while in the unreal world of a house-party), I have at no time written any novel which pretended to touch the known life about me. Even the few stories about Lichfield which venture some little way into the present century are painstakingly antedated a decade or so of years prior to their publication. The Biography of the life of Manuel could so easily, so plausibly, and so very profitably, have been extended into the 1920's: and I, in common with the most of my contemporaries in prose, I too could have viewed, with remunerative scornfulness, the American doings of my own muddled and tumultuous era.

Yet I do not wonder about this commercial delinquency with any profound interest. I recognize the many logical reasons which will induce the ambitious writer to avoid handling contemporary life: and I remember I have listed these in another place. But I recognize too that to adopt and to cling to authorship as a profession is in itself an avoidance of every sort of logic. I know that my book has always been to me a diversion, and that the sole aim of my endless typewriting, in all the diverting while I have been about it, has been to divert, before any other person, me. I explain to the flag how I discovered, as far back as in 1916, that when I set about the adding of yet another volume affairs proceeded much more divertingly if I did not attempt to control them.

I would not be thought, I explain also, to be weighing any nonsense about "inspiration." So far as I know, inspiration is a matter, like the phoenix or the salamander, which many have talked about but none has encountered. I mean only that the practised author develops a highly specialized sub-consciousness which decides for him, far more happily than he can do, the theme and the general outline of his writing some while before he sits down at his desk. It tacitly picks out for him, I think, if only he possess the intelligence not to meddle here, such tasks as will be truly and profoundly to his liking. Like a well-trained butler, it brings up from the cellarage of the sub-conscious, without any ostentation, a vintage in all ways suited to the known tastes of the master of the house.

It has never fetched me a contemporaneous American theme in the long while that my familiar has catered to my daily needs with the half-kindly, half-contemptuous tyranny of any other old servant: and if I defer to this arrangement without rejoicing, I defer also without any profitless questions. The knowledge suffices me (as I patiently explain over and yet over again to that ever-impatient flag) that I have never written about contemporary life because—for a reason, or for a concatenation of reasons, as to which I remain contentedly ignorant—that daemon who in some sort both serves and controls my endless typing does not wish me to write about contemporary life.

This explanation does not content the flag. It still says, "Look at me! look at me!"

But I, to the contrary, I delude myself during these summer days with the improbable notion that there may be a certain inexpensive distinction in not criticizing "the American scene" at a time when no other native prose-writer appears able to avoid this pursuit. It seems to me in my vainglory, as I sit exceedingly high in the brisk air, that a number of my contemporaries have addressed themselves to the theme which is too trivial to be worth writing about when they set to commemorating these United States of America. I can see so very much of earth's surface and such appalling profundities of sky that a mere nation sandwiched somewhere in between the two appears inconsequential. I imagine that the United States of America is but a transient intruder between the incurious planet beneath me and yonder incurious heavens. I think that by-and-by all our America must pass away, perhaps as Assyria faded into nothingness, or that perhaps it will be changed as Athens was changed into a polity which kept only the name of its earlier self.

I appear to foresee a time when a book based upon any of our twentieth century *mores* will be at one with a book dealing with the mercantile code of Sidon, or with the narrow-mindedness of village life in Kish during the reign of Semiramis, or with the regrettable callousness of that younger generation which took part in the Second Punic War: and I begin to think quite affably about the sad surprises which are in store for my contemporaries.

"The feeling that what he creates does not matter"

SINCLAIR LEWIS

In 1930 the American novelist Sinclair Lewis (1885–1951), whose *Main Street* (1920), *Babbitt* (1922), *Arrowsmith* (1925) and other novels had provoked so much furor for their scathing pictures of "typical" American life, was awarded the Nobel Prize for literature. Recognizing that the award, the first made to an American writer, constituted something of a recognition of the achievement of American writing as a whole as well as of his own work, Lewis used the occasion, on December 12, 1930, to attack the attitude of America's business society toward its artists.

I AM SURE THAT you know, by now, that the award to me of the Nobel Prize has by no means been altogether popular in America. Doubtless the experience is not new to you. I fancy that when you gave the award even to Thomas Mann, whose *Zauberberg* seems to me to contain the whole of intellectual Europe, even when you gave it to Kipling, whose social significance is so profound that it has been rather authoritatively said that he created the British Empire, even when you gave it to Bernard Shaw, there were countrymen of those authors who complained because you did not choose another.

From Sinclair Lewis, "Nobel Prize Address," in *The Man from Main Street: A Sinclair Lewis Reader,* ed. Harry E. Maule and Melville H. Cane, pp. 7–10. Copyright 1953 by Harry E. Maule. Copyright 1953 by the Estate of Sinclair Lewis, Melville H. Cane and Pincus Berner Executors. Reprinted by courtesy of Random House, Inc.

And I imagined what would have been said had you chosen some American other than myself. Suppose you had taken Theodore Dreiser.

Now to me, as to many other American writers, Dreiser more than any other man, marching alone, usually unappreciated, often hated, has cleared the trail from Victorian and Howellsian timidity and gentility in American fiction to honesty and boldness and passion of life. Without his pioneering, I doubt if any of us could, unless we liked to be sent to jail, seek to express life and beauty and terror.

My great colleague Sherwood Anderson has proclaimed this leadership of Dreiser. I am delighted to join him. Dreiser's great first novel, *Sister Carrie,* which he dared to publish thirty long years ago and which I read twenty-five years ago, came to housebound and airless America like a great free Western wind, and to our stuffy domesticity gave us the first fresh air since Mark Twain and Whitman.

Yet had you given the Prize to Mr. Dreiser, you would have heard groans from America; you would have heard that his style —I am not exactly sure what this mystic quality "style" may be, but I find the word so often in the writings of minor critics that I suppose it must exist—you would have heard that his style is cumbersome, that his choice of words is insensitive, that his books are interminable. And certainly respectable scholars would complain that in Mr. Dreiser's world, men and women are often sinful and tragic and despairing, instead of being forever sunny and full of song and virtue, as befits authentic Americans.

And had you chosen Mr. Eugene O'Neill, who has done nothing much in American drama save to transform it utterly, in ten or twelve years, from a false world of neat and competent trickery to a world of splendor and fear and greatness, you would have been reminded that he has done something far worse than scoffing —he has seen life as not to be neatly arranged in the study of a scholar but as a terrifying, magnificent and often quite horrible thing akin to the tornado, the earthquake, the devastating fire.

And had you given Mr. James Branch Cabell the Prize, you would have been told that he is too fantastically malicious. So would you have been told that Miss Willa Cather, for all the homely virtue of her novels concerning the peasants of Nebraska, has in her novel, *The Lost Lady,* been so untrue to America's patent and perpetual and possibly tedious virtuousness as to picture an abandoned woman who remains, nevertheless, uncannily charming even to the virtuous, in a story without any moral; that Mr. Henry Mencken is the worst of all scoffers; that Mr. Sherwood Anderson viciously errs in considering sex as important a force in life as fishing; that Mr. Upton Sinclair, being a Socialist, sins against the perfectness of American capitalistic mass-production; that Mr. Joseph Hergesheimer is un-American in regarding graciousness of manner and beauty of surface as of some importance in the endurance of daily life; and that Mr. Ernest Hemingway is not only too young but, far worse, uses language which should be unknown to gentlemen; that he acknowledges drunkenness as one of man's eternal ways to happiness, and asserts that a soldier may find love more significant than the hearty slaughter of men in battle.

Yes, they are wicked, these colleagues of mine; you would have done almost as evilly to have chosen them as to have chosen me; and as a chauvinistic American—only, mind you, as an American of 1930 and not of 1880—I rejoice that they are my countrymen and countrywomen, and that I may speak of them with pride even in the Europe of Thomas Mann, H. G. Wells, Galsworthy, Knut Hamsun, Arnold Bennett, Feuchtwanger, Selma Lagerlöf, Sigrid Undset, Werner von Heidenstam, D'Annunzio, Romain Rolland.

It is my fate in this paper to swing constantly from optimism to pessimism and back, but so is it the fate of any one who writes or speaks of anything in America—the most contradictory, the most depressing, the most stirring, of any land in the world today.

Thus, having with no muted pride called the roll of what seem to me to be great men and women in American literary life today, and having indeed omitted a dozen other names of which I should like to boast were there time, I must turn again and assert that in our contemporary American literature, indeed in all American arts save architecture and the film, we—yes, we who have such pregnant and vigorous standards in commerce and science—have no standards, no healing communication, no heroes to be followed nor villains to be condemned, no certain ways to be pursued and no dangerous paths to be avoided.

The American novelist or poet or dramatist or sculptor or painter must work alone, in confusion, unassisted save by his own integrity.

That, of course, has always been the lot of the artist. The vaga-bond and criminal François Villon had certainly no smug and comfortable refuge in which elegant ladies would hold his hand and comfort his starveling soul and more starved body. He, veritably a great man, destined to outlive in history all the dukes and puissant cardinals whose robes he was esteemed unworthy to touch, had for his lot the gutter and the hardened crust.

Such poverty is not for the artist in America. They pay us, in-deed, only too well; that writer is a failure who cannot have his butler and motor and his villa at Palm Beach, where he is permitted to mingle almost in equality with the barons of bank-ing. But he is oppressed ever by something worse than poverty —by the feeling that what he creates does not matter, that he is expected by his readers to be only a decorator or a clown, or that he is good-naturedly accepted as a scoffer whose bark probably is worse than his bite and who probably is a good fellow at heart, who in any case certainly does not count in a land that produces eighty-story buildings, motors by the million, and wheat by the billions of bushels. And he has no institution, no group, to which he can turn for inspiration, whose criticism he can accept and whose praise will be precious to him.

"Almost like a rending of the earth"

EDMUND WILSON

In October, 1929, came the New York stock market crash, and the United States, together with most of the rest of the world, was plunged into a devastating economic depression that left millions unemployed and utterly changed the optimistic, expansive tone of American social and business life during the 1920's. The impact upon American writers was tremendous. In an essay in *The New Republic* for March 23, 1932, Edmund Wilson summed up the change in attitude.

From Edmund Wilson, "Literary Consequences of the Crash," in *The Shores of Light: A Literary Chronicle of the Twenties and Thirties* (New York: Farrar, Straus and Young, Inc., 1952), pp. 492–494, 496–499. Reprinted by permission of the author.

A CHANGE OF TONE and of point of view will be noted in my articles of the early thirties.

Even before the stock market crash of October, 1929, a kind of nervous dissatisfaction and apprehension had begun to manifest itself in American intellectual life. The liberating movement of the twenties had by that time accomplished its work of discrediting the gentility and Puritanism of the later nineteenth century; the orgy of spending of the Boom was becoming more and more grotesque, and the Jazz Age was ending in hysteria. The principal points of view of this period I tried, after the crash, to sum up in an article of March 23, 1932:

The attitudes of the decade that followed the war, before the depression set in, already seem a long way off:

The attitude of the Menckenian gentleman, ironic, beer-loving and "civilized," living principally on the satisfaction of feeling superior to the broker and enjoying the debauchment of American life as a burlesque show or three-ring circus; the attitude of old-American-stock smugness, with its drawing aloof from the rabble in the name of old Uncle Gilead Pilcher who was Governor of Connecticut or Grandfather Timothy Merrymount who was killed in the Civil War—though the parvenus kept crashing the gate so fast, while the prosperity boom was on, that it was becoming harder and harder to get one's aloofness properly recognized; the liberal attitude that American capitalism was going to show a new wonder to the world by gradually and comfortably socializing itself and that we should just have to respect it in the meantime, taking a great interest in Dwight W. Morrow and Owen D. Young; the attitude of trying to get a kick out of the sheer size and energy of American enterprises, irrespective of what they were aiming at; the attitude of proudly withdrawing and cultivating a refined sensibility or of losing oneself completely in abstruse intellectual pursuits—scholastic philosophy, symbolic logic or metaphysical physics; the attitude of letting oneself be carried along by the mad hilarity and heartbreak of jazz, living only for the excitement of the evening; the attitude of keeping one's mind and morals impregnably disinfected with the feeble fascism-classicism of humanism.

I have in one mood or another myself felt some sympathy with all of these different attitudes—with the single exception of humanism; and they have all, no doubt, had their validity for certain people, for special situations. Yet today they all look rather queer: they are no use in our present predicament, and we can see how superficial they were. We can see now that they all represented attempts on the part of the more thoughtful Americans to reconcile themselves to a world dominated by salesmen and brokers—and that they all involved compromises with the salesman and the broker. Mencken and Nathan laughed at the broker, but they justified the system which produced him and they got along with him very well, provided he enjoyed George Moore and had pretensions to a taste in liquor; the jazz-age romantics spent the broker's money as speedily and wildly as possible and tried to laugh off the office and the factory with boyish and girlish jokes; the old-American-stockers sniffed at him, but though they salved their consciences thus, they were usually glad to get in on any of his good things that were going; the liberals, who had been vaguely unhappy, later became vaguely resigned and could never bring themselves to the point of serious quarrelling with him; the poets and philosophers hid from him—and the physicists grew more and more mystical in the laboratories subsidized mainly by the profits from industrial investments; the humanists, in volume after volume, endeavored by sheer hollow thunder to induce people to find in the stock exchange the harmony and dignity of the Parthenon.

. . . . .

The stock market crash was to count for us almost like a rending of the earth in preparation for the Day of Judgment. In my articles of the months just before it, I had often urged writers to acquaint themselves with "the realities of our contemporary life," to apply themselves to "the study of contemporary reality," etc. I myself had not exercised enough insight to realize that American "prosperity" was an inflation that was due to burst. I had, however, become aware that we liberals of the *New Republic* were not taking certain recent happenings so seriously as we should. The execution of Sacco and Vanzetti in August, 1927, had made liberals lose their bearings. During the months while the case was working up to its climax, Herbert Croly had been away in Honolulu attending a conference called by the Institute of Pacific Relations.

When he returned, I was surprised to learn that he did not entirely approve of the way in which we had handled the case. Croly's method of commenting on current events was impersonal and very abstract; and, in his absence, we had given way to the impulse to print certain articles which were certainly, for the *New Republic,* unusually concrete and militant. I first became aware of a serious divergence between my own point of view and Croly's when I was talking with him one day about a leader called *A Nation of Foreigners* that I wrote for the paper in October. He did approve of this editorial, but for reasons that put me in a false position. My article had dealt with the futility of attempting to identify "Americanism" with the interests and ideas of the Anglo-Saxon element in the United States, pointing out that, in this case, the Irish, who had been snubbed by the Anglo-Saxon Bostonians, had combined with them in the most wolfish way to persecute the immigrant Italians; and I discovered that Croly was pleased at my treating a subject from this angle rather than from that of class animosities. This class aspect he wanted to deny; it was one of the assumptions of his political thinking—I had not then read *The Promise of American Life*—that the class struggle should not, and in its true form did not, occur in the United States.

I had been running the literary department, and this was my first excursion on the political side of the paper, which Croly had kept strictly in line with his own very definite ideas. Sometime in the later months of 1928, he had the first of several strokes, and was never able again to perform his full functions as editor-in-chief. When he died in May, 1930, the paper was carried on by the editors as a group, with no one in Croly's position, and we had—rather difficult with men of conflicting opinions and temperaments, with nobody to make final decisions—to work out a policy of our own. I had been troubled by another incident that took place in the autumn of 1929. The bitter and violent Gastonia strike of the textile workers in North Carolina had been going on ever since spring. It was the first major labor battle conducted by a Communist union. Sixteen union members, including three women, were being tried for the murder of a chief of police, who had invaded without a warrant the tent-colony in which the strikers had been living; and the death penalty was being asked for all of them except the women. Feeling on both sides had been roused to the point of ferocity—we were not then familiar with the Communists' habit of manufacturing martyrs—and, after the execution of Sacco and Vanzetti, one was apprehensive of another judicial lynching. John Dos Passos and Mary Heaton Vorse both asked the *New Republic* to send them to report on Gastonia, but both were thought to be too far to the Left to be reliable from our point of view. "The liberals," Dos Passos said to me, "are all so neurotic about Communists!" This was perfectly true; and the pressure on us to do something about Gastonia had at the time almost no effect. The young man who had been hooked by Orage —who had had no experience of labor disputes—was going down to a fashionable wedding at Asheville, not far from Gastonia, and he was asked to drop in at the seat of trouble. When he came back, this young man reported that there was nothing of interest going on. I do not know whom he could have talked to. He had been in Gastonia on the very day, September 14, when the hostilities were coming to a climax. In an attempt to prevent a union meeting, an armed mob had fired on unarmed strikers and had killed a woman named Ella May Wiggins, a widow with five children, who had written songs for the strikers and was extremely popular among them. Her death gave the Communists a battle-cry and the strikers an unforgettable grievance. It was obvious that the *New Republic*, which was supposed to cover labor sympathetically, was falling down on this part of its program.

The next month the slump began, and, as conditions grew worse and worse and President Hoover, unable to grasp what had happened, made no effort to deal with the breakdown, a darkness seemed to descend. Yet, to the writers and artists of my generation who had grown up in the Big Business era and had always resented its barbarism, its crowding-out of everything they cared about, these years were not depressing but stimulating. One couldn't help being exhilarated at the sudden unexpected collapse of that stupid gigantic fraud. It gave us a new sense of freedom; and it gave us a new sense of power to find ourselves still carrying on while the bankers, for a change, were taking a beating. With a businessman's president in the White House, who kept telling us, when he told us anything, that the system was perfectly sound, who sent General Douglas MacArthur to burn the camp of the unemployed war veterans who had come to appeal to Washington, we wondered about the survival of republican

American institutions; and we became more and more impressed by the achievements of the Soviet Union, which could boast that its industrial and financial problems were carefully studied by the government, and that it was able to avert such crises. We overdid both these tendencies; but the slump was like a flood or an earthquake, and it was long before many things righted themselves.

"Revolutionary literature will draw its strength from the proletariat"

GRANVILLE HICKS

An example of the Marxist critique of the novel in its most articulate form is given in this excerpt from Granville Hicks' *The Great Tradition* (1933; revised edition, 1935). Hicks viewed American writing from its beginnings to the present day in terms of its relationship to the class struggle; in the selection below, he applies the Communist dialectic to the novelists of his own day. Hicks later broke sharply with Marxism, as can be seen in a selection from his more recent work in the next section of this book (pp. 175–177).

THE PROBLEMS THAT EVENTS force upon the writer's attention as he reads the papers or talks with his friends also rise to trouble him in his work. Whether an author starts with the life of some little village or the life of fashionable New York, whether he is interested in the sexual adjustments of men and women or in the quest for a philosophy of life, in the struggles

From Granville Hicks, *The Great Tradition*, pp. 295–300. Copyright 1933, 1935 by The Macmillan Company. Used by permission of The Macmillan Company.

of youth or the tragedies of age, sooner or later, if he is astute
and persistent, he comes to certain elementary bread-and-butter
questions. These questions many writers try to evade, maintaining
that economic issues are of no importance, that human nature is
always the same, regardless of the systems under which men live,
that the basic themes of life and death have nothing to do with
the ways in which life is supported. But evasion is not easy and it
is very dangerous. Some authors, while loudly proclaiming the
right of evasion, have, like Archibald MacLeish, practiced what
they preached against, and written propaganda against propaganda. Others have half-heartedly attacked the problems they
insist are unworthy of concern: Wilder in *Heaven's My Destina-
tion,* Elizabeth Madox Roberts in *He Sent For a Raven,* and Ernest
Hemingway in such stories as "The Gambler, the Nun, and the
Radio." Their half-heartedness condemns them to worse confusion than their former indifference, but at least there is evidence that they, too, feel the pressure that forces so many of their
contemporaries to decision.

If evasion becomes more difficult, decision becomes easier and
its implications more apparent. The revolutionary writers have
proceeded from a belief that capitalism is unsound to a belief
that it must be destroyed. Most of them have gone further and
recognized that only the working class can destroy capitalism.
And many have seen that choosing the side of the proletariat in
the class struggle means working with it, becoming identified with
it, and they have joined or given their aid to militant working-
class organizations. A majority of these support the Communist
Party.

The large measure of agreement on fundamental political questions distinguishes the revolutionary movement in literature today
from any radical movement that preceded it. The muckrakers
were for the most part middle-class reformers, agreeing only partly
in their analyses of the evils of capitalism and not at all in their
remedies. The literary radicalism of the pre-war period, centering
in the *Masses,* was a phase of the revolt against nineteenth century bourgeois standards, particularly standards of sexual conduct. Made possible by the contrast between village surveillance
and urban anonymity, it constantly lapsed into Bohemian freak-
ishness. It was an emancipating force, valuably destructive, but
it had no deep roots. It was an escape from the middle class,

and yet not an identification with the working class. It left the important decision to the future.

Post-war disillusionment and Coolidge prosperity ended the careers of most of the *Masses* radicals. There were a few who, after wandering in strange places, were to return at the end of the decade. And there were a very few who continued to march under the revolutionary banner. Of these the most influential was Michael Gold, author of the first revolutionary novel to receive widespread attention, one of the founders of the New Playwrights Theatre, editor of the *New Masses,* which resumed in 1926 the *Masses-Liberator* tradition, and when the depression dispelled the dreams of the prosperous twenties, leader, by virtue both of his steadfast record and his eloquent challenges, of the new revolutionary movement. *Jews Without Money,* portions of which had appeared in the *Liberator* and the *New Masses* long before it was published as a book, was a reminder, surprisingly necessary in the twenties, that poverty had not been miraculously abolished and that the dreams and sufferings of the poor were a worthy theme for any author. Endowed with Gold's passionate romanticism, the book achieved its effect by a robust power of evocation rather than by what today we think of as revolutionary insight. Novelist, poet, dramatist, critic, columnist, Gold has been the movement's great amateur, but he has been an amateur with something close to genius. He has been the important link between the radicalism of the war period and the revolutionary movement of the present. That he remained steadfast in an era of apostasy and that he triumphed over the emotional, anarchic Bohemianism of the *Masses* group can be attributed to the depth of his roots in the working class. If he is still rather undisciplined, spending his talents at times in ways that are unproductive, it is quite clear to anyone who reads the first impassioned protests of his individualism that he has acquired a measure of discipline, and acquired it because loyalty to the working class demanded it. Otherwise his fine imaginative powers would have been wasted as so many rich talents were in the rank morasses of the twenties.

Once Gold stood almost alone, so that now, young as he is, he seems almost the dean of revolutionary literature. The writers of today have come, by easier paths than his, to his position. Though not many revolutionary writers are members of the Communist Party, most of them give it their allegiance, and all are deeply influenced by its existence. Acceptance of the logic of revolution demands participation in the struggle of the working class, and the Communist Party is the principal means for joining in the fight. When Josephine Herbst takes part in the farmer's struggles, it is in an organization that communists help to guide. When Erskine Caldwell studies conditions in Detroit, it is for the communist *Daily Worker* that he writes his reports. When Jack Conroy, Nelson Algren, and Emmet Gowan make a trip into the South, they seek to test a law that principally affects communists, and they are treated as communists by the authorities. Most of the strikes that have been portrayed in revolutionary novels have been strikes that communists led. It is in this way, and certainly not through any attempt to impose its discipline upon writers, that the Communist Party has become the unifying force in the revolutionary literary movement. Insofar as the Communist Party makes good its claim to be the only party of the militant working class, and insofar as it adheres to the theories of Marxism, it commands the allegiance of the revolutionary writers.

It should be understood that, apart from this fundamental unity, with all it entails, there is no lack of diversity. First of all, no one imagines that mere adherence to a set of political principles, or even the complete mastery of a world philosophy, is any guarantee of literary talent. . . . We have taken for granted a certain minimum qualification, so to speak, and have been principally concerned with what each writer did with the capabilities he had. This is not to say, however, that a discerning eye and a quick ear, the power of penetrating below the surface and the willingness to work for perfect expression, are unimportant. The quality that we call imagination, the ability to rearrange the elements of experience into patterns that are new and different and yet true to experience, is significant, wherever it may be found. We have tried to discover under what conditions imagination ripens into literature, and even now our chief aim is to determine whether the revolutionary movement provides such conditions, but, as we examine a group of writers who share a certain attitude towards life, we cannot ignore kinds and degrees of talent.

There are other and more subtle differences. There are writers who do not adhere to the Communist Party and yet write from the point of view of a class-conscious worker, and there are writers who are very close to the Communist Party and yet differ only slightly from their bourgeois contemporaries. B. Traven, for example, though he has respect for some communists, is contemptuous of party discipline, but he belongs to the working class, and there are no novels that speak more effectively for that class than *The Death Ship* and *The Treasure of the Sierra Madre*. Erskine Caldwell, on the other hand, or Nathan Asch, or Waldo Frank, for all their loyalty to communism, are closer to such writers as Faulkner, Joyce, and Lawrence than they are to Traven. The problem is, indeed, even more complicated, for one often finds the same writer varying from what is revolutionary to what obviously is not. Such inconsistencies, arguing, of course, imperfect integration, are not unnatural in the infancy of revolutionary literature. In some degree in fact, though often less conspicuously than in the novelists mentioned, they are to be found in every revolutionary writer.

Finally, there are the most important differences of all, the differences that are inherent in the nature of revolutionary literature. If all bourgeois survivals could be miraculously obliterated, and if the same high talent everywhere prevailed, monotony would by no means be the result. Potentially revolutionary literature, far from being committed to the narrowness about which some of its critics pretend to worry, has a broader field than any literature the world has known. To the themes the writers of the past have adopted the revolutionary artist adds a multitude of themes that they could not or would not use. It is bourgeois literature today that is narrow, with its few patterns of success and failure in love, business, and the quest for a philosophy. It is revolutionary literature that is finding new themes and new ways of treating old ones.

If, then, we insist on the unity of the revolutionary literary movement, it is not to be supposed that there is any lack of variety in the novels, poems, and plays that compose it. But it is, nevertheless, a movement, held together by certain conceptions of the relation of literature to life and of the direction that life is taking. It is not a movement in any organizational sense; there is no one who can say, except as an individual opinion, what is revolutionary in literature and what is not; there is no one who can impose themes or dictate treatment. It derives its unity from an historical process, the transition from private exploitation to social organization. It deserves the name proletarian as well as the name revolutionary, for it speaks for the class that is making the revolution. At the moment it is only imperfectly and embryonically the expression of that class, for the proletariat is only imperfectly conscious of its destiny; but as the workers are forced by the further collapse of capitalism to a full realization of their power and opportunity, revolutionary literature will draw its strength from the proletariat and be, as it cannot be today, truly and fully proletarian.

"He will deny its parenthood to his own hurt"

DONALD DAVIDSON

A very different response to the depression of the 1930's is found in the writings of the Nashville Agrarians, a group of highly articulate novelists, poets, and essayists mostly from Vanderbilt University. The Agrarians, like the regionalists of the late nineteenth century, expressed their strong distrust of the role of the Northeast, particularly New York City, as the center of American writing. They saw nationalism and industrialism as a perpetual force for standardization, and called for a vigorous regionalism to maintain the integrity of American life and letters. In the selection below, first published in *The Attack on Leviathan* (1938), the poet Donald Davidson pointed out both the dangers and the opportunities of regionalism in literature. At least part of Davidson's analysis has proved accurate: the novels of William Faulkner, Robert Penn Warren, Thomas Wolfe, and others, all drawing heavily on Southern life for their form and attitude, soon assumed a commanding position in American fiction.

From Donald Davidson, "Regionalism and Nationalism in American Literature," in *Still Rebels, Still Yankees and Other Essays* (Baton Rouge, La.: Louisiana State University Press, 1957), pp. 275–278. Copyright 1957 by Louisiana State University Press. Reprinted by permission of the author.

IN OUR OWN TIME, the metropolitan critics are making national prescriptions that are equally partial, though somewhat more confused. In one sentence they assure us that the industrial unification of America is desirable and inevitable; but in the next sentence they declare that the civilization thus produced puts upon us an intolerable spiritual bondage from which the artist cannot escape save through the shibboleths of Marxism and Freudianism. Wearily, they proclaim that America is standardized; but angrily they scorn the rural backwardness of regions that prove to be, after all, less urban than New York. Confidently they announce that America must be industrialized; but they sneer at Mr. Babbitt of the Middle West, the creature of industrialism. They urge the provinces to adopt the intellectual sophistication of the Eastern metropolis; but among themselves they bewail the poverty of the modern temper, which in its sophistication has left them nothing to enjoy.

Their error is precisely like Emerson's and has far less nobility in it. As a basis for national unity they offer the apologetic mechanisms that the metropolis sets up to explain away and palliate its own diseases. The impact of their arguments on American thought has been on the whole confusing and corrupting; but it is now clear that they cannot win out completely over the regions, except at the cost of a dangerous struggle.

For already the reaction has set in. Regionalism, so far as it is an actual literary movement, is in large measure a protest, sometimes angry and intense, but more often calm and assured, against the false nationalism that the metropolitans have been disseminating. No one who has studied American history intelligently could doubt that such a protest had to come. It is the American means of restoring our lost balance.

But the regionalists, in the extremity of their natural reaction, have also not been guiltless of oversimplification. The dangers of regionalism, if in its turn it becomes a shibboleth, begin at the point where aesthetic rationalization magnifies means into ends. Consider, for example, the new "regional" consciousness of folk art. The immense research into folk-ways that has characterized the regional movement is of enormous instrumental value. For critical and historical purposes we need to know a great deal about American ballads, songs, stories, myths. But there is some doubt whether in recovering these critically we can also recover them creatively, except by simulating a naïveté which, the critics assure us, the modern principle of sincerity will never permit. The regionalist may well retort that naïveté in literature does have a value, but only when it is assumed or simulated. The danger is, however, that the regionalist, in attempting through folklore to express the genius of place, will be content merely to dwell among the artifacts he has dug up, and will thus narrow his expression almost to documentary limits. We shall have to wait on performance to see what the function of a folk-pattern is in American literature; but meanwhile the regionalist should be warned against retiring into folklore as into an ivory tower. Folklore is good, but alone it is not good enough, it is only one feature of a regional literature. And the modernist critics are right in their claim that modern issues cannot be evaded. The writer of a given region cannot shut himself away under the name "regionalist"; but he must, from his region, confront the total and moving world.

Such calamitous retirements, however, are not implied in the organic relation of regional and national elements that I have tried to describe. When the two become warring "isms," they have the common defect of anaesthetizing the artist against reality. Of the two, considered as "isms," nationalism is the more vicious, in its present aspect at least, for it is harsh, oppressive, and swaggering. Regionalism proposes to live and let live, and its narrow or belligerent features will fall away quickly enough when the repressive force is softened or removed.

I return to my central point. Regionalism is not an end in itself, not a literary affectation, not an aesthetic credo, but a condition of literary realization. The function of a region is to endow the American artist with character and purpose. He is born of a region. He will deny its parenthood to his own hurt. Without its background he is a homeless exile in the wilderness of modern life. That self which he is, if not ignobly impugned, will readily be a modern self; and what he creates, if he can resist the perversions of our time, will be the expression of both the region and himself, no matter what the subject or what the style. It is the office of the nation to conserve and cherish this free effort, and surely never by precept or example to delude us into thinking that a novel about a plowboy is only a regional curiosity, but a novel about a bellboy, a national masterpiece.

"To the meal in the firkin, the milk in the pan"

BERNARD DE VOTO

With the onset of the second world war, and America's participation in it, cultural nationalism became popular again. Marxism as a literary force in American letters dwindled away. American novelists were urged to ground their fiction solidly in the American tradition; "highbrow" literature was criticized for its withdrawal from the "common man." In the passage that follows, Bernard DeVoto (1897–1955) criticizes the writing of his contemporaries, and calls for a literature that will faithfully mirror what he considers "the common experience of Americans."

If LITERATURE IS to be a dependable description of America, if it is to make a useful comment on America, then first of all it must know America. The word "ignorance" has had to run through these lectures like a leitmotif. For the guesses, phantasies, and deductions which contented so many of the writers we have talked about, it must substitute patient years—years of study, years of experience. Knowledge is a slow growth, a long path beset with possibilities of error. Men are not given to know the nature of things by intuition. Authority is not born full-grown in any mind, nor can anyone come to it by staring into his own soul, or at his navel, or into the high priest's emerald breastplate.

From Bernard DeVoto, *The Literary Fallacy* (Boston: Little, Brown & Company, 1944), pp. 172–175. Reprinted by permission of the Trustees of Indiana University, Bloomington, Indiana.

No one can know a country or a people, no one can know even the small portions with which most of us must be content, except by a long effort to know them, a refusal to be satisfied with the nobly vague, a distrust of the logically beautiful. Knowledge does not come from the matching up of myths, abstractions, and hypotheses that made the writers of the 1920's sure they were red to the shoulders with the blood of life when they were only watching the play of shadows across the screen of their own souls. Knowledge means sweat and doggedness, a realization that one can never know enough, and it comes from experience inappeasably sought after and tested with the most powerful reagents the mind can use. Writers must be content to hold their peace until they know what they are talking about. Readers must be willing to hold them to the job if they refuse to hold themselves. An uninstructed gentleness toward writers has been the mistake of readers in our time. Words like "fool" and "liar" might profitably come back to use. If literature is a trivial pursuit, folly and lying are of no particular moment, but if literature is to be serious then it cannot be permitted folly and lying and when they appear in it they must be labeled and denounced.

Yet knowledge can be come by. But first there is a fixed barrier which writers cannot cross except by virtue of a profound humility. The moral of our literature between the wars is that literature must come upon futility and despair unless it begins in fellowship from within. Rejection, the attitude of superiority, disdain of the experience of ordinary people, repudiation of the values to which the generality of a writer's countrymen devote their lives—the literature of my generation tried that path and found that the path ended in impotence and the courtship of death. The evils and abuses of society may be intolerable but my generation has proved that literature can do nothing whatever about them from outside. It must enter in, it must speak its "Thou shalt!" as one who shares the dust and thirst. Cut the umbilical cord and what dies is not society but literature. Form coteries of the initiate, turn in abhorrence from the village square to the High Place, consecrate yourself to anything which the louts at the foot of the High Place cannot know, however fine or noble or beautiful it may be—and in the end you have only a group of the merely literary, speaking fretfully to one another in soft voices while the tides of the world sweep by.

Either literature deals honestly with the basic experiences in which all men may see themselves, or else it is only a mannered diversion practised by the impaired and of interest only to the leisure moments of those who are whole. Either it is a man and a brother speaking to men and brothers, speaking of the things which all share and are subject to, or else it is only a private titillation. Well over a century ago Ralph Waldo Emerson ordered the American writer to his job—to the meal in the firkin, the milk in the pan. To know what it was that had appeared upon the earth, the new man, this American. To search his heart, his mind, his vision, his memory. Only in obeying that command has American literature ever found reality. Our literature can be true only as it is true of us, it can be great only as it comes to find greatness. All roots will be winter-killed and all the sweet green shoots will die except as they are warmed and fertilized by the common experience of Americans. That common experience is sufficiently wide and deep—literature has never yet drawn even with it and can never exhaust it. In it lies the future of American literature, possibly a great future, but only as the writers of the future, by their own wit or by the grace of God, may, as the writers between wars in the main did not, accept it as their own.

"There is no longer any turning back"

CONRAD AIKEN

The renewed demand for cultural nationalism, for "wholesomeness" in American literature, was strongly attacked by many of the best American writers and critics. Conrad Aiken, poet and novelist, pointed out in the essay below that

From Conrad Aiken, "American Writers Come of Age," in *A Reviewer's ABC*, pp. 107–111. Copyright © 1935, 1939, 1940, 1951, 1958 by Conrad Aiken. A Greenwich Edition, published by Meridian Books, Inc. This essay originally appeared in *The Atlantic*, CLXIC (April, 1942), 478–481.

if America was to lead the free world in its fight against
totalitarianism, our literature must not be forced into a
nationalistic strait jacket, but must be allowed and encouraged
to reflect strength and freedom of inquiry. Just as political
isolation from the rest of the world was no longer possible, so
our novelists and poets must not attempt to turn their backs on
the major intellectual currents of their time.

Two RECENT BOOKS by American critics make one wonder, with some uneasiness, whether we too are not to be treated
to some such anachronistic purge: *The Opinions of Oliver Allston,*
by Van Wyck Brooks, and *Intellectual America,* by Mr. Oscar
Cargill. Mr. Brooks, as we know, and much as we admire him
(and indeed we have long been greatly in his debt), is an im-
placable enemy of the American expatriate and all his works. Was
it his own brief taste of the Lotus—at least, the English Lotus—
that has embittered him? For one can have little doubt that his
judgment of Henry James, and especially of those wonderful "late"
novels, is more than Tolstoyan in its *parti pris* recklessness; nor
that the opinions of Oliver Allston, his ventriloquist, on Ezra
Pound, T. S. Eliot, and James Joyce, to mention only a few, will
one day seem just as surprisingly wrong-headed. As Tolstoy sought
his universal, misguidedly, in a kind of lowest common denomi-
nator of the arts which any peasant could grasp—sacrificing at
one stroke both the great and the subtle—so Mr. Brooks and Mr.
Cargill, with pretty much the same intention, might be described
as Two Critics in Search of the Wholesome. Mr. Brooks makes
the really startling admission that he prefers *Snow-Bound* to *The
Waste Land;* and at this rate it cannot be long before some even
bolder champion of the autochthonous will publicly prefer *Little
Women* to James Joyce's *Ulysses.* Mr. Cargill, for his part, displays an almost Comstockian zeal in hunting out decadents—he
finds decadents everywhere, and tears them to pieces with a
relish which looks decidedly suspicious. Evidently, as Gypsy Rose
Lee said of men, he "prefers them monstrous": he likes his decadence "high."

But what is interesting, and indeed disturbing, is that both
critics, like Tolstoy, single out with a practically unerring eye
the best, the most deeply creative writers of our time, not for

praise, but for ridicule and dismissal. Mr. Brooks dismisses them as "escapists" and "coteries"; Mr. Cargill, with a handful of loose labels, bundles them together more or less indiscriminately and inaccurately as Freudians, Intelligentsia, or Decadents: he is a kind of grocer-critic, and weighs "content" as one might weigh sugar. Both critics betray a marked, though occasionally am- biguous, animus toward modern psychology—toward Freud and the notion of the unconscious in particular; and for both the idea of the "death-drive," Freud's *Beyond the Pleasure Principle* (which Santayana wittily called "a long way round to Nirvana"), is, at any rate as embodied in contemporary poetry and fiction, the very last word in defeatism, unwholesomeness, and decay.

Now what is really being proposed here, let us be in no doubt about it, is a moral, or social, intrusion into the world of letters: the world of letters, that is to say, has become a moral peril, and must be regenerated. And the step that is suggested, at any rate by implication, is that, if we are to recover that most priceless element in a work of art, the *will* (by which is no doubt meant the will to goodness, or the will to wholesomeness), we must be- gin, as Tolstoy began, by simply shutting the door to pretty much everything else. Above all, now that the world is at war, and when cultural interchange between the nations is so difficult (thus runs a common argument), now is the very time for a complete re- treat, a return to our own inexhaustible inner resources, our own beautiful and inviolate regionalism and national purity. Let us therefore close the doors once again on these "foreign" ideas, these naughty, and alien, and for us so insoluble poisons. In short, let us now be good wholesome Americans and have a good whole- some American art. The time for decadence is past—and it was never really natural to us, anyway.

Leaving aside the somewhat frightening vision of what this "wholesomeness" would lead us to in literature—with its proto- typical Horatio Algers and Pollyannas, its rural innocence and regional Arcadias—it is perhaps more useful to take a good look at the notion of "decadence." First of all, let us note that de- cadence is always a relative thing: it is not an absolute, or de- finable as such, but merely and always a something which follows a something else—a something else to which it is assumed to be inferior. Nor is it quite as simple as that, either—for we must re- member that if this decadence follows something, it also precedes something. It is no more an end than it is a beginning: in fact, it is an organic and living part of a constantly changing and evolving continuum. And this continuum is nothing less, in turn, than the whole evolution of man's awareness. Literature, the plastic arts, the sciences—everything comprised in our cultural and intellectual evolution—are these not, insofar as they represent the steady advance in human awareness, completely identifiable with the evolution of man's "mind"—his capacity to feel, perceive, and understand?

And has this not been so from the very beginning? The inventors of the first words, the inventors of language—these were our first poets—were, like the inventors of the other arts and the sciences, biological "sports"; they were variants on the norm; it would not be amiss, perhaps, to say that they were our first decadents. As in every evolutionary process, the sieve of selective survival chose from among them those whose inventions were acceptable to the majority: these became leaders and priests, their teachings or discoveries being incorporated in the main stream of man's social growth; while those others, whose contributions were less generally suitable, were forgotten. In this trial-and-error evolution of consciousness, a new word meant, to all intents, a new feeling; a new cluster of words meant a new complex of feelings; and in each item it could perhaps properly be said that this new perception or feeling represented a splitting and refinement of the coarser and simpler perceptions which had preceded it. Practically, in short, refinement and decadence are the same thing. Parts were substituted for wholes, shades and discriminations for the more vigorous but less exact holophrases which they replaced. The evolution of form proceeded from the large to the small, from the single and simple to the comprehensive and complex; and analogously from the energetic to the subtle.

And in this evolution of language, which is also the evolution of literature and consciousness, it must be borne in mind that the process has always been a strictly individualist and minority affair, a game of follow-my-leader. There has never been, so far as we know, a "whole-society" art—the arrangement of society in the past has been just exactly as pyramidal, in its distribution of consciousness, as it is today. The very conscious have always been the very few: the comparatively unconscious the comparative majority. In any evolutionary process this condition must be inevitable. The artists, the poets, the scientists, these are the advance guard who explore or invent new mental hinterlands, which the rest of mankind adopts and validates as it can and will.

Thus man gets his "universal" in art, willy-nilly; but he gets it from the top, invariably, never from the bottom. And if we realize that this vital competitive hierarchy in levels of consciousness is indispensable to the continuation of a healthy and normal renewal and growth in man's awareness, then we can begin to see how mistaken was Tolstoy, for example, when he proposed to reduce all art to the level of understanding of the simplest peasant. At the drop of a hat, this would achieve that wholesale degradation of cultural energy (which Henry Adams foresaw) to a sterile uniformity. The creative principle of discrimination abandoned, all that marvelous process of exfoliation by which meaning has constantly given way to the more comprehensive on the one hand and the subtler on the other—the endless refinement of man's mind as externalized in his arts and sciences—all this would be at an end. For a faint notion of what it would lead to, one has only to consider the average total radio program of any given day. This is the field in which the Tolstoyan doctrine is most nearly applied.

And this, whether they know it or not, is exactly what the advocates of "nationalism," "wholesomeness," and "the closed door" are up to. They want to turn back the clock; and clearly they mean to do it if they can. At the very moment when America has reached her cultural majority, and when she is able to give the world artists and writers of the first rank, these critics propose once more to close America in, to make her once again provincial; and they begin with a threat of moral censorship on precisely those gifted writers who, in our time, have established themselves as "world" citizens, and are of international importance. We must have no decadence, they say, whether domestic or imported—no escapists, no coteries. Yet it was Baudelaire, a decadent on their own admission, who did most in the last century to restore to French poetry its greatness, giving it a power, a richness, and a beauty which it had never known before. And how few poets and artists in the history of mankind cannot be said to have been escapists, or members of a coterie! Is not art itself an escape, a sublimation —an escape *upward?*

Such mere name-calling will not stay the living forces of literature, nor re-establish outmoded customs barriers; nor can the complex, by a mere effort of the will, turn itself back into the simple, for those who fear it. At best, it will become the *faux bon,* the *faux naif;* at worst, the sentimental. The process of refinement —of "decadence"—has already gone too far. For every Henry James we get, every Proust or Eliot or Joyce (those dreadful fellows, who by some miracle of logic are "empty formalists" on the one hand and purveyors of ugliness and the "death-drive" on the other), the less likely are we ever again to have anything as genuinely naive as *Snowbound* or *Little Women;* and certainly the less likely are we to mistake an *Uncle Tom's Cabin* for a *Moby Dick.* Even in our much discussed "regionalism," what we are witnessing, one suspects, is the last stand of the naive, the final rear guard action of a "Little America" isolationism: for they too, the regional centers, are now fully and inescapably in the midstream of the one great human "thing," from which there is no longer any turning back.

It is no use fearing the complex or chaotic merely because we see all values so visibly and violently in the melting-pot—surely that is no reason for squeamishness, or timidity, or for not facing even the most disagreeable facts in human nature. Man has built himself churches in the past, and of humbler materials; he can build them again, and build them better. No, we must be open to all influences, all knowledge, all speculation, all the winds of doctrine. The arts must be free. For better or worse, American literature is henceforth a part of world literature; and to aim now at a self-conscious and limited "Americanism" would be nothing less than cowardice. The time for that sort of protective tariff, as for a limited-objective moral censorship, is past.

And we have a high responsibility. For if, at the moment, America is the arsenal of democracy, she is also the laboratory of the arts and sciences. Heir to all that is best in the history of mankind, let us hope that we can use our inheritance wisely, and that it can be said of us, as Sainte-Beuve of Goethe, that he "assimilated not merely tradition, but all traditions, and that without ceasing to be a modern of moderns; he keeps watch for every new sail on the horizon, but from the height of a Sunium. He would use the larger background and perspective to round out and support his individual insight, and so make of the present what it should be—not a servile imitation, nor yet a blank denial,

of the past, but its creative continuation. To the errors and aberrations of the hour"—he says—"we must oppose the masses of
universal history." And as a salutary reminder, let us add to this
Tolstoy's footnote to patriotism: "This disposition of preference
for one nation over all others, like egoism, can in no wise be
good."

VI

American Art and American Experience

"The profound poetry
of disorder"

RICHARD CHASE

Looking back at the development of the American novel from
its beginnings up to our own time, the critic Richard Chase
sees it as reflecting "alienation, contradiction, and disorder."
By contrast with the English novel, "notable for its great
practical sanity," the American novel has explored divisiveness
and conflict.

T HE IMAGINATION THAT has produced much of the best
and most characteristic American fiction has been shaped by the
contradictions and not by the unities and harmonies of our culture.
In a sense this may be true of all literatures of whatever time and
place. Nevertheless there are some literatures which take their
form and tone from polarities, opposites, and irreconcilables, but
are content to rest in and sustain them, or to resolve them into
unities, if at all, only by special and limited means. The American
novel tends to rest in contradictions and among extreme ranges
of experience. When it attempts to resolve contradictions, it does
so in oblique, morally equivocal ways. As a general rule it does
so either in melodramatic actions or in pastoral idyls, although
intermixed with both one may find the stirring instabilities of
"American humor." These qualities constitute the uniqueness of
that branch of the novelistic tradition which has flourished in this

country. They help to account for the strong element of "romance" in the American "novel."

By contrast, the English novel has followed a middle way. It is notable for its great practical sanity, its powerful, engrossing composition of wide ranges of experience into a moral centrality and equability of judgment. Oddity, distortion of personality, dislocations of normal life, recklessness of behavior, malignancy of motive—these the English novel has included. Yet the profound poetry of disorder we find in the American novel is missing, with rare exceptions, from the English. Radical maladjustments and contradictions are reported but are seldom of the essence of form in the English novel, and although it is no stranger to suffering and defeat or to triumphant joy either, it gives the impression of absorbing all extremes, all maladjustments and contradictions into a normative view of life. In doing so, it shows itself to derive from the two great influences that stand behind it—classic tragedy and Christianity. The English novel has not, of course, always been strictly speaking tragic or Christian. Often it has been comic, but often, too, in that superior form of comedy which approaches tragedy. Usually it has been realistic or, in the philosophical sense of the word, "naturalistic." Yet even its peculiar kind of gross poetic naturalism has preserved something of the two great traditions that formed English literature. The English novel, that is, follows the tendency of tragic art and Christian art, which characteristically move through contradictions to forms of harmony, reconciliation, catharsis, and transfiguration.

Judging by our greatest novels, the American imagination, even when it wishes to assuage and reconcile the contradictions of life, has not been stirred by the possibility of catharsis or incarnation, by the tragic or Christian possibility. It has been stirred, rather, by the aesthetic possibilities of radical forms of alienation, contradiction, and disorder.

"By that rope we know where we are"

HENRY JAMES

Art and experience. In our own day the two terms have come
to represent two basic approaches of the novelist toward the
book he is writing. Does the American novelist set out to
"create life," to refine the raw material of experience into the
artistic dimensions of the story he would tell, or is his object
that of "capturing life," of reproducing in words and sentences
the fresh impact of real experience? The difference between
the two approaches is reflected in the attitude of the writer
to his material, in the form his novels take. But of course the
major writer does both—as Henry James (1843–1916) had
pointed out long ago. The renewed importance of James'
fiction and his criticism for writers of our time has been perhaps
the most startling development in American writing since the
close of the second world war. In the passage below, from the
Preface to his novel *The American* (1877; Preface written
for the New York Edition, 1907), James discussed the
relationship of romance and realism in fiction, in terms of their
effect upon the reader.

BY WHAT ART OR MYSTERY, what craft of selection, omission or commission, does a given picture of life appear to us to
surround its theme, its figures and images, with the air of romance
while another picture close beside it may affect us as steeping
the whole matter in the element of reality? It is a question, no

doubt, on the painter's part, very much more of perceived effect, effect *after* the fact, than of conscious design—though indeed I have ever failed to see how a coherent picture of anything is producible save by a complex of fine measurements. The cause of the deflexion, in one pronounced sense or the other, must lie deep, however; so that for the most part we recognise the character of our interest only after the particular magic, as I say, has thoroughly operated—and then in truth but if we be a bit critically minded, if we find our pleasure, that is, in these intimate appreciations (for which, as I am well aware, ninety-nine readers in a hundred have no use whatever). The determining condition would at any rate seem so latent that one may well doubt if the full artistic consciousness ever reaches it; leaving the matter thus a case, ever, not of an author's plotting and planning and calculating, but just of his feeling and seeing, of his conceiving, in a word, and of his thereby inevitably expressing himself, under the influence of one value or the other. These values represent different sorts and degrees of the communicable thrill, and I doubt if any novelist, for instance, ever proposed to commit himself to one kind or the other with as little mitigation as we are sometimes able to find for him. The interest is greatest—the interest of his genius, I mean, and of his general wealth—when he commits himself in both directions; not quite at the same time or to the same effect, of course, but by some need of performing his whole possible revolution, by the law of some rich passion in him for extremes.

Of the men of largest responding imagination before the human scene, of Scott, or Balzac, even of the coarse, comprehensive, prodigious Zola, we feel, I think, that the deflexion toward either quarter has never taken place; that neither the nature of the man's faculty nor the nature of his experience has ever quite determined it. His current remains therefore extraordinarily rich and mixed, washing us successively with the warm wave of the near and familiar and the tonic shock, as may be, of the far and strange. (In making which opposition I suggest not that the strange and the far are at all necessarily romantic: they happen to be simply the unknown, which is quite a different matter. The real represents to my perception the things we cannot possibly *not* know, sooner or later, in one way or another; it being but one of the accidents of our hampered state, and one of the incidents of their quantity and number, that particular instances have not yet come our way. The romantic stands, on the other hand, for the things that, with all the facilities in the world, all the wealth and all the courage and all the wit and all the adventure, we never *can* directly know; the things that can reach us only through the beautiful circuit and subterfuge of our thought and our desire.) There have been, I gather, many definitions of romance, as a matter indispensably of boats, or of caravans, or of tigers, or of "historical characters," or of ghosts, or of forgers, or of detectives, or of beautiful wicked women, or of pistols and knives, but they appear for the most part reducible to the idea of the facing of danger, the acceptance of great risks for the fascination, the very love, of their uncertainty, the joy of success if possible and of battle in any case. This would be a fine formula if it bore examination; but it strikes me as weak and inadequate, as by no means covering the true ground and yet as landing us in strange confusions.

. . . . .

The only *general* attribute of projected romance that I can see, the only one that fits all its cases, is the fact of the kind of experience with which it deals—experience liberated, so to speak; experience disengaged, disembroiled, disencumbered, exempt from the conditions that we usually know to attach to it and, if we wish so to put the matter, drag upon it, and operating in a medium which relieves it, in a particular interest, of the inconvenience of a *related*, a measurable state, a state subject to all our vulgar communities. The greatest intensity may so be arrived at evidently —when the sacrifice of community, of the "related" sides of situations, has not been too rash. It must to this end not flagrantly betray itself; we must even be kept if possible, for our illusion, from suspecting any sacrifice at all. The balloon of experience is in fact of course tied to the earth, and under that necessity we swing, thanks to a rope of remarkable length, in the more or less commodious car of the imagination; but it is by the rope we know where we are, and from the moment that cable is cut we are at large and unrelated: we only swing apart from the globe—though remaining as exhilarated, naturally, as we like, especially when all goes well. The art of the romancer is, "for the fun of it," insidiously to cut the cable, to cut it without our detecting him.

"Bare experience"

PHILIP RAHV

American experience, the critic Philip Rahv has declared, has
been of such a nature as to cut us off from intellectual concerns,
and to direct our attention toward our own private interests.
Thus the American novelist, taking his lead from Henry James,
has sought to dramatize private life. Only now do international
forces seem more decisive than national forces in the
development of the American literary life, and the future of
our writing will lie in the response of our writers to this
new influence.

IT IS NOT THE MERE recoil from the inhibitions of puritan
and neo-puritan times that instigated the American search for experience. Behind it is the extreme individualism of a country without a long past to brood on, whose bourgeois spirit had not worn
itself out and been debased in a severe struggle against an old
culture so tenacious as to retain the power on occasion to fascinate
and render impotent even its predestined enemies. Moreover, in
contrast to the derangements that have continually shaken Europe,
life in the United States has been relatively fortunate and prosperous. It is possible to speak of American history as "successful"
history. Within the limits of the capitalist order—and until the
present period the objective basis for a different social order simply did not exist here—the American people have been able to
find definitive solutions for the great historical problems that
faced them. Thus both the Revolutionary and the Civil War were
complete actions that once and for all abolished the antagonisms
which had initially caused the breakdown of national equilibrium.
In Europe similar actions have usually led to festering compro-

From Philip Rahv, "The Cult of Experience in American Writing," in
Image and Idea (Norfolk, Conn.: New Directions, 1949), pp. 19–21. Copyright 1949 by Philip Rahv. Reprinted by permission of New Directions.

mises that in the end reproduced the same conflicts in other forms.

It is plain that until very recently there has really been no urgent need in America for high intellectual productivity. Indeed, the American intelligentsia developed very slowly as a semi-independent grouping; and what is equally important, for more than a century now and especially since 1865, it has been kept at a distance from the machinery of social and political power. What this means is that insofar as it has been deprived of certain opportunities, it has also been sheltered and pampered. There was no occasion or necessity for the intervention of the intellectuals—it was not mentality that society needed most in order to keep its affairs in order. On the whole the intellectuals were left free to cultivate private interests, and, once the moral and aesthetic ban on certain types of exertion had been removed, uninterruptedly to solicit individual experience. It is this lack of a sense of extremity and many-sided involvement which explains the peculiar shallowness of a good deal of American literary expression. If some conditions of insecurity have been known to retard and disarm the mind, so have some conditions of security. The question is not whether Americans have suffered less than Europeans, but of the quality of whatever suffering and happiness have fallen to their lot.

The consequence of all this has been that American literature has tended to make too much of private life, to impose on it, to scour it for meanings that it cannot always legitimately yield. Henry James was the first to make a cause, if not a fetish, of personal relations; and the justice of his case, despite his vaunted divergence from the pioneer type, is that of a pioneer too, for while Americans generally were still engaged in "gathering in the preparations and necessities" he resolved to seek out "the amenities and consummations." Furthermore, by exploiting in a fashion altogether his own the contingencies of private life that fell within his scope, he was able to dramatize the relation of the new world to the old, thus driving the wedge of historical consciousness into the very heart of the theme of experience. Later not a few attempts were made to combine experience with consciousness, to achieve the balance of thought and being characteristic of the great traditions of European art. But except for certain narratives of James and Melville, I know of very little American fiction which can unqualifiedly be said to have attained this end.

Since the decline of the regime of gentility many admirable works have been produced, but in the main it is the quantity of felt life comprised in them that satisfies, not their quality of belief or interpretative range. In poetry there is evidence of more distinct gains, perhaps because the medium has reached that late stage in its evolution when its chance of survival depends on its capacity to absorb ideas. The modern poetic styles—metaphysical and symbolist—depend on a conjunction of feeling and idea. But, generally speaking, bare experience is still the *Leitmotif* of the American writer, though the literary depression of recent years tends to show that this theme is virtually exhausted. At bottom it was the theme of the individual transplanted from an old culture taking inventory of himself and of his new surroundings. This inventory, this initial recognition and experiencing of oneself and one's surroundings, is all but complete now, and those who persist in going on with it are doing so out of mere routine and inertia.

The creative power of the cult of experience is almost spent, but what lies beyond it is still unclear. One thing, however, is certain: whereas in the past, throughout the nineteenth and well into the twentieth century, the nature of American literary life was largely determined by national forces, now it is international forces that have begun to exert a dominant influence. And in the long run it is in the terms of this historic change that the future course of American writing will define itself.

"In the novel manners make men"

LIONEL TRILLING

The American novelist, Lionel Trilling declares, has
refused to confront society. Because of the nature of American
experience our novelists have largely failed to concern

From "Manners, Morals, and the Novel" in *The Liberal Imagination* by Lionel Trilling, pp. 212–216. Copyright 1948, 1950 by Lionel Trilling. Reprinted by permission of The Viking Press, Inc. This essay originally appeared in *The Kenyon Review*, X (Winter, 1948), 17–22.

themselves with "the investigation of the problem of reality beginning in the social field." The call has been for "reality," but reality has meant the harsh externals of life, the surfaces, rather than the shrewd exploration of the relationships of men in a society. "In proportion as we have committed ourselves to our particular idea of reality we have lost our interest in manners. For the novel that is a definitive condition because it is inescapably true that in the novel manners make men."

T<small>HE</small> NOVEL . . . is a perpetual quest for reality, the field of its research being always the social world, the material of its analysis being always manners as the indication of the direction of man's soul. When we understand this we can understand the pride of profession that moved D. H. Lawrence to say, "Being a novelist, I consider myself superior to the saint, the scientist, the philosopher and the poet. The novel is the one bright book of life."

Now the novel as I have described it has never really established itself in America. Not that we have not had very great novels but that the novel in America diverges from its classic intention, which, as I have said, is the investigation of the problem of reality beginning in the social field. The fact is that American writers of genius have not turned their minds to society. Poe and Melville were quite apart from it; the reality they sought was only tangential to society. Hawthorne was acute when he insisted that he did not write novels but romances—he thus expressed his awareness of the lack of social texture in his work. Howells never fulfilled himself because, although he saw the social subject clearly, he would never take it with full seriousness. In America in the nineteenth century, Henry James was alone in knowing that to scale the moral and aesthetic heights in the novel one had to use the ladder of social observation.

There is a famous passage in James's life of Hawthorne in which James enumerates the things which are lacking to give the American novel the thick social texture of the English novel—no state; barely a specific national name; no sovereign; no court; no aristocracy; no church; no clergy; no army; no diplomatic service; no country gentlemen; no palaces; no castles; no manors; no old country houses; no parsonages; no thatched cottages; no ivied ruins; no cathedrals; no great universities; no public schools; no political society; no sporting class—no Epsom, no Ascot! That is, no sufficiency of means for the display of a variety of manners, no opportunity for the novelist to do his job of searching out reality, not enough complication of appearance to make the job interesting. Another great American novelist of very different temperament had said much the same thing some decades before: James Fenimore Cooper found that American manners were too simple and dull to nourish the novelist.

This is cogent but it does not explain the condition of the American novel at the present moment. For life in America has increasingly thickened since the nineteenth century. It has not, to be sure, thickened so much as to permit our undergraduates to understand the characters of Balzac, to understand, that is, life in a crowded country where the competitive pressures are great, forcing intense passions to express themselves fiercely and yet within the limitations set by a strong and complicated tradition of manners. Still, life here has become more complex and more pressing. And even so we do not have the novel that touches significantly on society, on manners. Whatever the virtues of Dreiser may be, he could not report the social fact with the kind of accuracy it needs. Sinclair Lewis is shrewd, but no one, however charmed with him as a social satirist, can believe that he does more than a limited job of social understanding. John Dos Passos sees much, sees it often in the great way of Flaubert, but can never use social fact as more than either backdrop or "condition." Of our novelists today perhaps only William Faulkner deals with society as the field of tragic reality and he has the disadvantage of being limited to a provincial scene.

It would seem that Americans have a kind of resistance to looking closely at society. They appear to believe that to touch accurately on the matter of class, to take full note of snobbery, is somehow to demean themselves. It is as if we felt that one cannot touch pitch without being defiled—which, of course, may possibly be the case. Americans will not deny that we have classes and snobbery, but they seem to hold it to be indelicate to take precise cognizance of these phenomena. Consider that Henry James is, among a large part of our reading public, still held to be at fault for noticing society as much as he did. Consider the conversation that has, for some interesting reason, become a part of our literary folklore. Scott Fitzgerald said to Ernest Hemingway, "The very rich are different from us." Hemingway replied, "Yes, they have more money." I have seen the exchange quoted many times and always with the intention of suggesting that Fitzgerald was infatuated by wealth and had received a salutary rebuke from his democratic friend. But the truth is that after a certain point quantity of money does indeed change into quality of personality: in an important sense the very rich *are* different from us. So are the very powerful, the very gifted, the very poor. Fitzgerald was right, and almost for that remark alone he must surely have been received in Balzac's bosom in the heaven of novelists.

It is of course by no means true that the American reading class has no interest in society. Its interest fails only before society as it used to be represented by the novel. And if we look at the commercially successful serious novels of the last decade, we see that almost all of them have been written from an intense social awareness—it might be said that our present definition of a serious book is one which holds before us some image of society to consider and condemn. What is the situation of the dispossessed Oklahoma farmer and whose fault it is, what situation the Jew finds himself in, what it means to be a Negro, how one gets a bell for Adano, what is the advertising business really like, what it means to be insane and how society takes care of you or fails to do so—these are the matters which are believed to be most fertile for the novelist, and certainly they are the subjects most favored by our reading class.

The public is probably not deceived about the quality of most of these books. If the question of quality is brought up, the answer is likely to be: no, they are not great, they are not imaginative, they are not "literature." But there is an unexpressed addendum: and perhaps they are all the better for not being imaginative, for not being literature—they are not literature, they are reality, and *in a time like this* what we need is reality in large doses.

When, generations from now, the historian of our times undertakes to describe the assumptions of our culture, he will surely discover that the word *reality* is of central importance in his understanding of us. He will observe that for some of our philosophers the meaning of the word was a good deal in doubt, but that for our political writers, for many of our literary critics, and for most of our reading public, the word did not open discussion but, rather, closed it. Reality, as conceived by us, is whatever is external and hard, gross, unpleasant. Involved in its meaning is the idea of power conceived in a particular way. Some time ago I had occasion to remark how, in the critical estimates of Theodore Dreiser, it is always being said that Dreiser has many faults but that it cannot be denied that he has great power. No one ever says "a kind of power." Power is assumed to be always "brute" power, crude, ugly, and undiscriminating, the way an elephant appears to be. It is seldom understood to be the way an elephant actually is, precise and discriminating; or the way electricity is, swift and absolute and scarcely embodied.

The word *reality* is an honorific word and the future historian will naturally try to discover our notion of its pejorative opposite, appearance, mere appearance. He will find it in our feeling about the internal; whenever we detect evidences of style and thought we suspect that reality is being a little betrayed, that "mere subjectivity" is creeping in. There follows from this our feeling about complication, modulation, personal idiosyncrasy, and about social forms, both the great and the small.

Having gone so far, our historian is then likely to discover a puzzling contradiction. For we claim that the great advantage of reality is its hard, bedrock, concrete quality, yet everything we say about it tends toward the abstract and it almost seems that what we want to find in reality is abstraction itself. Thus we believe that one of the unpleasant bedrock facts is social class, but we become extremely impatient if ever we are told that social class is indeed so real that it produces actual differences of personality. The very people who talk most about class and its evils think that Fitzgerald was bedazzled and Hemingway right. Or again, it might be observed that in the degree that we speak in praise of the "individual" we have contrived that our literature should have no individuals in it—no people, that is, who are shaped by our liking for the interesting and memorable and special and precious.

Here, then, is our generalization: that in proportion as we have committed ourselves to our particular idea of reality we have lost our interest in manners. For the novel this is a definitive condition because it is inescapably true that in the novel manners make men. It does not matter in what sense the word manners is taken—it is equally true of the sense which so much interested Proust or of the sense which interested Dickens or, indeed, of the sense which interested Homer. The Duchesse de Guermantes unable to delay departure for the dinner party to receive properly from her friend Swann the news that he is dying but able to delay to change the black slippers her husband objects to; Mr. Pickwick and Sam Weller; Priam and Achilles—they exist by reason of their observed manners.

"The evil now stares out of the bright sunlight"

RALPH ELLISON

The novel, says Ralph Ellison, cannot be reduced to any one form; the nature of American life today is such that the novelist must deal with new and rapidly changing materials, and the closed society that Lionel Trilling's definition of the novel would require is an impossibility. The American novelist's task is to seek ways of affirming "that which *is* stable in human life beyond and despite all processes of social change."

IN THE LEVELING PROCESS to which all things are subjected in a democracy one must depend always upon the *individual's* ability to rise out of the mass and achieve the possibility implicit in the society. One must depend upon his ability, whoever he is and from whatever class and racial group, to attain the finest perception of human value, to become as consciously aware of life, say, as any of Henry James's "super-subtle fry."

Certainly the novelist must make some such assumption if he is to allow himself range in which to work toward the finest possibilities of his talent and his form without a frustrating sense of alienation.

Which tells us something of why the novelists keep writing despite the current attempts to legislate the novel a quiet death. It also gives us a hint as to why a number of the younger novelists are not at all hindered by the attempt to reduce the novel to only one of its possible forms; yes, and why the picaresque, many-leveled novel, swarming with characters and with varied types and levels of experience, has appeared among us. Though we love the classics, some of us have little interest in what Mr. Trilling calls the "novel of manners," and I don't believe that a society hot in the process of defining itself can for long find its image in so limited a form. Surely the novel is more than he would have it be, and if it isn't then we must make it so.

One of the comic aspects to the current controversy over what a novel should be is the implicit assumption, held by Cooper, James, and Hawthorne, as well as several contemporary critics, that society was created mainly so that novelists could write about it. It is felt that society should be of such shape that the novelist can settle it neatly into prefabricated molds with the least spilling of rude life over the sides. The notion started when the forest was still being cleared, and it is understandable that a certain type of writer would have liked to deal with fine cabinetry instead of crude logs. Still, minds that were philosophically and politically most advanced and sophisticated conceived this society, but even they had nonetheless to deal with raw and rapidly moving materials. And so in the beginning did the American novel, and so today. We are not so crude now as during James's time but we have even less stability and there is no longer a stable England to which to withdraw for perspective. World War I, the Depression, World War II and Korea, the Cold War, the threat of the atom, our discovery of the reality of treason, and now Egypt and Hungary make us aware that reality, which during Dickens's time seemed fairly stable, has broken loose from its old historical base, and the Age of Anxiety is truly more than a poetic conceit. Closed societies are now the flimsy illusions, for all the outsiders are demanding in.

In fact there is no stability anywhere and there will not be for many years to come, and progress now insistently asserts its tragic side; the evil now stares out of the bright sunlight. New groups will ceaselessly emerge, class lines will continue to waver and break and re-form; great wealth there will be and a broader distribution of that wealth, and a broader distribution of ideas along with it. But the problem of what to do with the increased leisure which wealth makes possible will continue to plague us—as will the problem of deciding just what constitutes a truly human way of life. The fundamental problems of the American situation will repeat themselves again and again and will be faced more or less by peoples throughout the world: Where shall we draw the line upon our own freedom in a world in which culture, tradition, and even history have been shaken up? At how fast a pace should we move toward social ideals? What is worth having and what worth holding? Where and in what pattern of conduct does true value, at a given moment, lie? These questions will continue to press upon us even if the dream of world peace is achieved, for they are questions built into the core of modern experience.

For the novelist the existence of these questions creates a basic problem of rhetoric. How does one in the novel (the novel which is a work of art and not a disguised piece of sociology) persuade the American reader to identify that which is basic in man beyond all differences of class, race, wealth, or formal education? How does one not only make the illiterate and inarticulate eloquent enough so that the educated and more favorably situated will recognize wisdom and honor and charity, heroism and capacity for love when found in humble speech and dress? And conversely, how does one persuade readers with least knowledge of literature to recognize the broader values implicit in their lives? How, in a word, do we affirm that which *is* stable in human life beyond and despite all processes of social change? How give the reader that which we do have in abundance, all the countless untold and wonderful variations on the themes of identity and freedom and necessity, love and death, and with all the mystery of personality undergoing its endless metamorphosis?

Here are questions which cannot be answered by criticism; they call for the novel, many novels; and as long as there are writers willing to accept the challenge of reducing the reality in which they exist to living form there will be readers interested in their answers, and we need have no fear that the novel is moribund.

"*Who speaks for America today?*"

LIFE MAGAZINE

American literature should be optimistic, joyful, prosperous, should reflect the optimistic, joyful prosperity of contemporary American life. So declared *Life* magazine in an editorial that criticized the modern American novelist for writing as if the depression of the 1930's were still on. Europeans and Asians, reading the American novel, receive a false and dangerous impression of American life. *Life* singled out novels such as Herman Wouk's *Marjorie Morningstar* (1955) as constituting a healthy rebellion against "degeneracy and negation."

Sloan Wilson, a young writer whose first novel (*The Man in the Gray Flannel Suit*) is moving up best-seller lists, recently made a statement in defense of his book's happy ending which is worth repeating: "The world's treated me awfully well," he said, "and I guess it's crept into my work. . . . These are, we forget, pretty good times. Yet too many novelists are still writing as if we were back in the Depression years."

Wilson put his finger on a strange contradiction. Ours is the most powerful nation in the world. It has had a decade of unparalleled prosperity. It has gone further than any other society in the history of man toward creating a truly classless society. Yet it is still producing a literature which sounds sometimes as if it were written by an unemployed homosexual living in a packing-box shanty on the city dump while awaiting admission to the county poorhouse.

This is doubly strange because past American eras have produced art which faithfully mirrored their times; *The Great Gatsby* still speaks eloquently of Prohibition's frauds and deceits, *Main*

"Wanted: An American Novel," an editorial from LIFE Magazine, XXXIX (September 12, 1955), 48. Copyright 1955 by Time, Inc.

Street of the high tide of provincial self-satisfaction, *The Grapes of Wrath* with a just anger for the unnecessary humiliations of Depression, while *Look Homeward, Angel* may well speak for a timeless America. But who speaks for America today? One might argue, with some plausibility, that the fearful indecisions of an atomic age keep a representative literature from being born, but when has life ever been secure? Atomic fear or not, the incredible accomplishments of our day are surely the raw stuff of saga.

Wilson's uneven book may be flimsy art but it is at least affirmative. Happily there are a few other signs of a trend away from degeneracy and negation. For example, Lionel Shapiro's *Sixth of June*, though it revolves about a triangle, is not resolved by adultery. Herman Wouk's *Marjorie Morningstar* is a mutiny, says *Time*, against "three decades of U. S. fiction dominated by skeptical criticism, sexual emancipation, social protest and psychoanalytical sermonizing." Wouk's book even endorses premarital chastity. And there is visible in other work what Critic Maxwell Geismar calls "a return to the security of a religious universe."

A change is needed. Nobody wants Pollyanna literature. Poets have always had what Robert Frost admits is "a vested interest in human misery"; agony begets art. Maybe art mistrusts prosperity. But at least the breeches-busting Paul Bunyan of the U. S. today seems to deserve better literature than the papaya-smelly, overripe school of the Truman Capotes, or the obscenity-obsessed school of "new realism" exemplified by a parade of war novels which mostly read like the diary of a professional grievance collector with a dirty mind and total recall. James Gould Cozzens' *Guard of Honor* was one of the few military novels that rang true with dignity. In most of the others the enemy is not the one shooting at us but our own officers and Army.

Europeans are already prejudiced against America by savage animadversions in their own classics against our "vulgar" democracy ("If I had remained another day in that horrible . . . United States, where there is neither hope nor faith, nor charity," wrote Balzac, "I should have died without being sick"). Small wonder that our own self-depreciation helps them enlarge the evil image to that which France's Michel Mohrt describes in his new study of American novels: "a hypocritical society based on the power of money, racial prejudice, sexual taboos. Exile, alcohol, suicide seem the only escape." Such a onetime exile, Henry (*Tropic of Cancer*) Miller, puts it more savagely in the current *Chicago Review*. The American seen through the eyes of our leading writers, he asserts, is "a digit in machine-made formulas . . . he has neither face nor name but is shuffled about like the victim of a soulless society on an electronic chessboard operated by a dummy hidden in the cells of a publisher's diseased brain. . . ." The writing, he adds, "reeks of embalming fluid."

It is understandable that American groups which feel the most isolated should produce the most anguished writing, and that so much of it should come from the South. Its ante bellum slave society was in some ways similar to the feudal Russian system whose injustices and tensions produced a Dostoevski and a Tolstoi. William Faulkner has a patent kinship with Dostoevski and his preoccupation with guilt. But Faulkner, for all his enormous gifts, can be searched in vain for that quality of redemption, through love and brotherhood, which always shines amid Dostoevski's horrors. It shines also amid the worst havoc of Tolstoi's overturned world (Moscow, too, was burned, even if not by Sherman).

To find this redeeming quality of spiritual purpose today's reader must turn not to novels but to nonfiction like Russell Davenport's *The Dignity of Man* or to the British book, *The Conquest of Everest*. That conquest held a deeper meaning than the achievement. The European Hillary and the Asian Tenzing are a hopeful symbol for a wider brotherhood yet to be achieved. Their final triumph expresses the unquenchable reaching of man's soul for a truth higher than reality, for a good better than himself, the qualities which modern literature so often deny. In every healthy man there is a wisdom deeper than his conscious mind, reaching beyond memory to the primeval rivers, a yea-saying to the goodness and joy of life. This is what is most missing from our hothouse literature—the joy of life itself.

"*I view the future of the novel without alarm*"

GRANVILLE HICKS

In a day when Americans are ceaselessly exposed to the demands of mass opinion, are relentlessly pressured to conform to what the group thinks is right, the novel, says Granville Hicks, stands out as spokesman for the individual integrity. The American novelist is a misfit in the Age of Conformity, and properly so: he communicates what he sees, pitting the integrity of his imagination against "the confusion of our society, the multitudinous distractions, the almost universal apprehensiveness." Thus the novel provides us with the practice in self-scrutiny that we need to understand our own experience.

WE SHALL PREACH, of course, to the people who can read serious fiction but don't. There are arguments, I think, to which they may listen. There is, for instance, the question of conformity in our society, a question that troubles most thoughtful persons. We can point out that the act of choosing to be a serious novelist is in itself today an act of dissent, and that the cultivation of the craft is a constant discipline in nonconformity. The novelist is always learning to communicate what he sees, and this means that he is always learning to see, to see, that is, for himself. All our days we are being fed, often forcibly fed, the mush of group opinion, until many of us long to get our teeth into the honest-to-God thoughts and feelings of a single, specific person. That is what we do when we read a serious novel. We may think that a particular novelist is cockeyed, but at least we get to know what an individual pair of eyes, defective or not, is seeing.

The novelist is not only a misfit in an Age of Conformity; he is an anomaly in an Age of Inattention. For the novelist, the paying of attention is a tool, a technique, a *raison d'être*. He is as much exposed to distractions as anyone else, but an unceasing struggle against them is the condition of success in his chosen vocation. A serious novel is by definition the work of a man who has learned to pay attention to what goes on in him and about him. And it not only brings to you and involves you in some small segment of the world that has been really looked at; it also, in a mysterious fashion, increases your own capacity for experience. The more completely you yield yourself to a novel—or any other work of art—as an experience, the less likely it is that your own experiences will be wasted on you.

The serious novel is also an act of evaluation, one performed according to a set of difficult but indispensable rules. The novelist can never allow himself to present only one side of a case; the other side must always be given. He does not make judgments, but he forces the reader to make them. As Lionel Trilling puts it, he involves the reader in the moral life. In the confusions of our society, with the onrush of new experiences and new problems, we need more than ever a talent for self-scrutiny, and the serious novel gives us practice.

The serious novel is needed, and, happily for us, it is being written. If the times are in so many ways unfavorable for the serious novelist, he is still a beneficiary of the national prosperity. He may make next to nothing from his novels, but jobs can be found, and fellowships, if not exactly abundant, are more numerous than ever before. I believe that most of our serious novelists would go hungry if they had to rather than stop writing, but few of them are compelled to make that choice. And every year, it seems, more and more young people deliberately elect this financially unrewarding way of life. We can be sure that many of them have talent, and perhaps one of them is the genius who will rout the enemies of the novel once for all.

Whether a genius appears or not, I view the future of the novel without alarm: . . . The conditions that are largely responsible for the present neglect of the serious novel—the confusion of our society, the multitudinous distractions, the almost universal apprehensiveness—are conditions that make the operation of the imagination almost, if not quite, a matter of life and death. And the imagination is functioning in the novel, though of course not only there. Not fewer people but more are likely to become convinced that, whatever else may be expendable in contemporary American life, the serious novel isn't.

"Without any of the frayed edges"

MALCOLM COWLEY

Malcolm Cowley, whose *Exile's Return* (1934) had so effectively summarized the literary mood of the young writers of the 1920's, presented in *The Literary Situation* (1954) an overall survey of the prevailing tendencies of the 1950's. The typical contemporary novel is thin, limited in time, centered in a peripheral location, with the point of view carefully chosen. The characters are seldom caught up in the main activities of American life. The novel is concerned with certain themes, rather than political or social subjects; social mobility is at a minimum; the ideas dealt with are predominantly moral. In structure the novels are carefully and tightly worked out, as if in advance; "the tone of the new writing is decorous, subdued, in the best of taste, and every sentence is clear in itself."

THE NEW FICTION can be recognized in the bookstores without reading a page of the text. Almost always it consists of thin books about the size of printed plays and hardly thicker than volumes of poetry. Fat novels are either naturalistic or else they are historical romances.

On the back of the dust wrapper there is a posed cabinet-size photograph of the author, who usually wears an intent and otherworldly look around the eyes. Beneath the photograph—if it doesn't fill the page, like the famous picture of Truman Capote brooding on a couch—there are critical comments, often calling attention to the depth or inwardness of the novel, its graceful irony, its meanings "on different levels," and its effective use of symbols. Naturalistic novels wear a different type of dressing gown. They give the blurb writer so much to talk about that there is room for only a small photograph, and the advance critical comments are supposed to be written by booksellers on order blanks.

Opening the book to the front matter, we usually find an epigraph or inscription. If it consists of a quotation from Rimbaud or Dante (in French or Italian), or from a seventeenth-century English author, or if there are several quotations, including one from T. S. Eliot, and another from a Greek or Roman classic, preferably Longinus *On the Sublime,* then we can be certain that the book is new-fictional and can go on to examine the text. Let us see what remarks are suggested by its various features, including time, setting, point of view, characters, themes, structure, and style.

The *time* of the new fiction is vaguely the present, or rather it is a recent but undated yesterday. Not much time elapses from beginning to end of the action; it may be a few days or weeks, perhaps a summer (*Wait, Son, October Is Near*), at most an academic year of two semesters. Sometimes the foreground of the novel is confined to a single day, but in that case it is rounded out with memories, so that we learn to know the principal character from birth.

The *setting* is seldom one of the centers where policy decisions are made; it is never Capitol Hill or the Pentagon or the boardroom of any corporation or political London or Paris or Army headquarters in the field. These are backgrounds for novels with public or social subjects. Preferring to deal with private lives, the new fiction is likely to have a remote and peripheral scene, for example—as I think of some recent novels—a lonely ranch in Colorado, a village in East Texas, a small town in Georgia, various plantation houses in Louisiana and Mississippi (all rotting into the dank loam), a country house in Maine, a "happy rural seat" in Ontario that haunts a house in Cleveland (don't ask how), an abandoned summer hotel, two beach resorts full of homosexuals, several freshwater colleges, a private asylum, the international colony in Rome, the still more international colony in Tangier, and a caravan crossing the Sahara under the sheltering sky. There is always an excuse for assembling the characters in one of these out-of-the-way places. Sometimes it is merely the accidents of travel; more often it is a house party, a vacation, a deathbed, a wedding (dozens of weddings), a family reunion—at any rate the device permits the novelist to present his story without any of the frayed edges that are so irritating when we encounter them in life.

The *point of view* from which the story will be told is chosen with extreme care so as to give an effect of depth and immediacy. The author with X-ray eyes who could look at a scene and know what everybody was thinking—but without penetrating deeply into anyone's mind—has practically vanished from American fiction. With him has vanished the museum-guide type of author who kept judging his characters and explaining them to the reader. The new author hides his personality in the background, like a dramatist. He tries to submerge himself in one or more of the characters and he tells the story as the character sees, hears, and feels it.

This concern with point of view is not exclusively a mark of the new fiction, since it extends to almost all our postwar writing. The "new" novelists, however, have devices and refinements of their own. One device is to describe a series of events through the eyes of a first character, then of a second, then of a third, then back to the first again, and so to the end of the novel (which might be *The Disguises of Love,* by Robie Macauley). Each character offers a different picture of the situation, and the author makes no explanatory comments, thus leaving the reader with a much-desired effect of irony or ambiguity, or plain confusion. Another device is for the novelist to pretend that he is a very young or stupid person who watches the behavior of grown-ups with an innocent eye. Very often the young person is a pre-adolescent girl vaguely resembling Henry James's Maisie; there are heroines of about her age in *The Member of the Wedding,* by Carson McCullers, *The Mountain Lion,* by Jean Stafford, and *The Strange Children,* by Caroline Gordon. Again the central intelligence may be a boy, also pre-adolescent, as in Truman Capote's *Other Voices, Other Rooms* and Peter Taylor's *A Woman of Means.* The hero of *Wait, Son, October is Near,* by John Bell Clayton, is a bright ten-year-old. In *The Caged Birds,* by Leroy Leatherman, an adult drama is rather dimly registered on the rather dim consciousness of a little boy of eight. All these books, except the last, are effectively written, and two or three of them are distinguished, but there are others in the same genre that give the effect of a country-club masquerade where busty debutantes and hairy-legged attorneys come dressed as babies.

The *characters* in the new fiction are distinguished by their lack of a functional relationship with American life. They don't sow or reap, build, mine, process, promote or sell, repair, heal, plead, administer, or legislate. In a still broader sense they don't join or belong. One widely observed feature of present-day America is that the lives of most individuals are defined by their relations with an interlocking series of institutions—for example, government bureaus, churches, schools and universities, the armed services, labor unions, chambers of commerce, farm bureaus, veterans' organizations, and, for most of us, that center of our daily activities, the office. But characters in the new fiction are exceptional persons who keep away from offices—at least for the duration of the novel—and are generally as unattached as Daniel Boone.

It is true that some of them are teachers, but they don't engage in faculty politics and seldom enter a classroom. Some are housewives who never cook or clean, and some are businessmen who have retired or are on vacation or play subordinate roles as fathers of the heroes and heroines. The characters likely to be treated at length are students of both sexes, young artists and writers, gentlemen on their travels, divorced or widowed mothers, gay boys, neurotic bitches, virtuous grandfathers, old women on their deathbeds, and preternaturally wise little girls. As compared with the population at large, the characters include an abnormally large number of persons living on inherited incomes. They also include more than the average proportion of very old people and children, with a smaller proportion of men and women in the active or money-earning ages. The women, down to the age of six, are more forceful or malignant and less inhibited than the men, most of whom are victims rather than heroes or villains. Some of the men are likely to be symbolic figures—for example, a scientist as prototype of evil, a doctor or a priest to represent spiritual wisdom, and a reformer as an object of scorn.

Instead of political or social subjects the new fiction has *themes* that are taken from individual lives. The distinction becomes clear if you ask one of the authors what is the subject of his next book.

"It's hard to say," he will answer; then, after a pause, he will add brightly, "I guess it's just about people." On reading the manuscript you will find that it is about people in some private crisis or dilemma that serves as the novelist's theme and his excuse for presenting a picture of human destinies.

So far the themes considered suitable for the new fiction have proved to be limited in number, and many of them keep reappearing in one book after another. One of the most popular is the initiation of a pre-adolescent girl or boy into the knowledge of sex or evil (as in *The Mountain Lion* and *Other Voices, Other Rooms*). Another is the mad infatuation of a middle-aged man or woman with a predatory younger person (as in *The Disguises of Love*, and in *The Roman Spring of Mrs. Stone*, by Tennessee Williams). Still another is the heroine's flight from reality, involving her surrender to drugs, nymphomania, or catatonic dementia (as in Paul Bowles' *The Sheltering Sky*). Some of the novels deal with the interplay between a religiously inspired character and a group of unbelievers; some show the hero or heroine struggling toward and finally reaching maturity; others, by contradiction, exalt the innocent world of childhood and depict grown persons as dangerous hypocrites. Later I shall have more to say about the novels—there are scores of them circulating in manuscript—that describe the ruin of a sensitive and truly artistic young man by his possessive mother.

The new fiction seldom deals with the familiar American theme of social mobility. In the old fiction one expected the hero (or the heroine, if she was the central character) to rise in the world like Silas Lapham and Sister Carrie and Susan Lenox. Sometimes he surprised us by falling, like Sister Carrie's lover and Dr. Richard Diver of *Tender Is The Night,* but in any case there was a vertical movement through different layers of society. In the new fiction there is little movement of the sort. Both the hero and the heroine can be expected to stay in the same position, socially speaking, though sometimes one of them suffers a moral decline. If the other characters include a man making his fortune, he is likely to be presented as a disagreeable person. Often the novelist seems to be making a plea for social stability and inherited position.

That is not the only social or political idea implied by the new fiction. Another idea suggested in many novels, including some but not all of those with a Southern background, is the foolishness of racial prejudice. Still another is the weakness and cowardice of liberals, and a fourth, expressed in terms of character, is the selfishness of reformers. Very old men and women are often depicted admiringly, as if to demonstrate that the past, with its widely accepted values and simple code of conduct, is better than the present. It remains true, however, that most of the ideas to be deduced from the new fiction are moral rather than social or political. Usually they can be translated into statements of a highly generalized type: for example, "Evil is in the human heart," "We must have compassion," "Let us be content with our lot," "Ripeness is all," "Little children, love one another!" or simply, "Mother was to blame."

The *structure* of the novels is usually balanced, efficient, economical, and tightly joined. A reader is left with the impression —which may be false in some cases—that the author has made a complete plan for the novel before setting to work on the first chapter. That is a comparatively safe method of writing novels and it has been followed by many distinguished authors. There are others, perhaps including more of the great, who have started with characters involved in a situation and have allowed them to work out their own destinies. "I write the first sentence," said Laurence Sterne, "and trust in God for the next." Dickens and most of the famous Victorians began publishing their novels by installments before they were finished and before the novelists knew how the stories would end. Jean Giraudoux said that he liked to go to the country with a ream of paper and an empty mind; when he came back to Paris his novel would be ready for publication.

There are all sorts of middle courses for novelists, but I am trying to suggest the two extremes. The second, that of Sterne and Giraudoux, implies a great deal of self-confidence, or trust in God. Even when followed by men of talent it is likely to produce formless, wasteful, inconsistent books, but the stories will flow like rivers or music and the characters may be a continual surprise to the author as well as the reader. The other method, that of the new fictionists, involves so much planning and preparation that the characters are no longer free to develop as in life. At best the stories will have an architectural form; their music is frozen and has ceased to flow; their economic structure is balanced in repose.

As for the *style* of the new fiction, there seems to be an im-

pression that it is precious and hard to understand. The impression
is justified in the case of a very few authors. Frederick Buechner,
for example, likes to use glittering phrases that seem to have been
picked from a jeweler's tray with a pair of tweezers. William
Goyen (*The House of Breath*) writes as if from a twilight region
where extreme sensitivity is on the point of being transformed
into simple hallucination. Neither of them is typical of the "new"
novelists. The typical style is simple and correct; often it is the
sort of language that one of the characters, chosen as observer,
would use in his daily life. The storytelling character is seldom or
never a foul-mouthed person, and it is safe to assume that any
novel peppered with obscenities belongs to the old-fictional or
naturalistic school. The tone of the new writing is decorous, subdued, in the best of taste, and every sentence is clear in itself.
The difficulty for the reader lies in recognizing the symbols and
what the author intends by them, or—in view of the author's
aloof and ironic attitude—in finding the meaning of the story as a
whole.

"Before I could hope to write
about anything else"

JAMES BALDWIN

Much of the social controversy of our day centers on the
role of the Negro in American society. The peculiar difficulties
that this situation poses for the serious Negro novelist are
outlined by James Baldwin in his *Notes of a Native Son* (1955).
From the social point of view, the Negro can only look with
approval upon the betterment of his position in society; as a
writer, however, the Negro must not look forward to a better
day, but back at his past, his relationship to Western culture
and society. Yet his social situation serves as a barrier to his

From James Baldwin, *Notes of a Native Son* (Boston: Beacon Press, 1955),
pp. 5–9.

examination of his own experience. The Negro writer must
struggle through this barrier before he can produce
distinguished work.

O NE OF THE DIFFICULTIES about being a Negro writer
(and this is not special pleading, since I don't mean to suggest
that he has it worse than anybody else) is that the Negro problem is written about so widely. The bookshelves groan under the
weight of information, and everyone therefore considers himself
informed. And this information, furthermore, operates usually
(generally, popularly) to reinforce traditional attitudes. Of traditional attitudes there are only two—For or Against—and I, personally, find it difficult to say which attitude has caused me the
most pain. I am speaking as a writer; from a social point of view
I am perfectly aware that the change from ill-will to good-will,
however motivated, however imperfect, however expressed, is
better than no change at all.

But it is part of the business of the writer—as I see it—to examine attitudes, to go beneath the surface, to tap the source. From
this point of view the Negro problem is nearly inaccessible. It is
not only written about so widely; it is written about so badly.
It is quite possible to say that the price a Negro pays for becoming
articulate is to find himself, at length, with nothing to be articulate
about. ("You taught me language," says Caliban to Prospero, "and
my profit on't is I know how to curse.") Consider: the tremendous
social activity that this problem generates imposes on whites and
Negroes alike the necessity of looking forward, of working to
bring about a better day. This is fine, it keeps the waters troubled;
it is all, indeed, that has made possible the Negro's progress.
Nevertheless, social affairs are not generally speaking the writer's
prime concern, whether they ought to be or not; it is absolutely
necessary that he establish between himself and these affairs a distance which will allow, at least, for clarity, so that before he can
look forward in any meaningful sense, he must first be allowed
to take a long look back. In the context of the Negro problem
neither whites nor blacks, for excellent reasons of their own, have
the faintest desire to look back; but I think that the past is all
that makes the present coherent, and further, that the past will

remain horrible for exactly as long as we refuse to assess it honestly.

I know, in any case, that the most crucial time in my own development came when I was forced to recognize that I was a kind of bastard of the West; when I followed the line of my past I did not find myself in Europe but in Africa. And this meant that in some subtle way, in a really profound way, I brought to Shakespeare, Bach, Rembrandt, to the stones of Paris, to the Cathedral of Chartres, and to the Empire State Building, a special attitude. These were not really my creations, they did not contain my history; I might search in them in vain forever for any reflection of myself. I was an interloper; this was not my heritage. At the same time I had no other heritage which I could possibly hope to use—I had certainly been unfitted for the jungle or the tribe. I would have to appropriate these white centuries, I would have to make them mine—I would have to accept my special attitude, my special place in this scheme—otherwise I would have no place in *any* scheme. What was the most difficult was the fact that I was forced to admit something I had always hidden from myself, which the American Negro has had to hide from himself as the price of his public progress; that I hated and feared white people. This did not mean that I loved black people; on the contrary, I despised them, possibly because they failed to produce Rembrandt. In effect, I hated and feared the world. And this meant, not only that I thus gave the world an altogether murderous power over me, but also that in such a self-destroying limbo I could never hope to write.

One writes out of one thing only—one's own experience. Everything depends on how relentlessly one forces from this experience the last drop, sweet or bitter, it can possibly give. This is the only real concern of the artist, to recreate out of the disorder of life that order which is art. The difficulty then, for me, of being a Negro writer was the fact that I was, in effect, prohibited from examining my own experience too closely by the tremendous demands and the very real dangers of my social situation.

I don't think the dilemma outlined above is uncommon. I do think, since writers work in the disastrously explicit medium of language, that it goes a little way towards explaining why, out of the enormous resources of Negro speech and life, and despite the example of Negro music, prose written by Negroes has been generally speaking so pallid and so harsh. I have not written about being a Negro at such length because I expect that to be my only subject, but only because it was the gate I had to unlock before I could hope to write about anything else. I don't think that the Negro problem in America can be even discussed coherently without bearing in mind its context; its context being the history, traditions, customs, the moral assumptions and preoccupations of the country; in short, the general social fabric. Appearances to the contrary, no one in America escapes its effects and everyone in America bears some responsibility for it. I believe this the more firmly because it is the overwhelming tendency to speak of this problem as though it were a thing apart. But in the work of Faulkner, in the general attitude and certain specific passages in Robert Penn Warren, and, most significantly, in the advent of Ralph Ellison, one sees the beginnings—at least—of a more genuinely penetrating search. Mr. Ellison, by the way, is the first Negro novelist I have ever read to utilize in language, and brilliantly, some of the ambiguity and irony of Negro life.

About my interests: I don't know if I have any, unless the morbid desire to own a sixteen-millimeter camera and make experimental movies can be so classified. Otherwise, I love to eat and drink—it's my melancholy conviction that I've scarcely ever had enough to eat (this is because it's *impossible* to eat enough if you're worried about the next meal)—and I love to argue with people who do not disagree with me too profoundly, and I love to laugh. I do *not* like bohemia, or bohemians, I do not like people whose principal aim is pleasure, and I do not like people who are *earnest* about anything. I don't like people who like me because I'm a Negro; neither do I like people who find in the same accident grounds for contempt. I love America more than any other country in the world, and, exactly for this reason, I insist on the right to criticize her perpetually. I think all theories are suspect, that the finest principles may have to be modified, or may even be pulverized by the demands of life, and that one must find, therefore, one's own moral center and move through the world hoping that this center will guide one aright. I consider that I have many responsibilities, but none greater than this: to last, as Hemingway says, and get my work done.

I want to be an honest man and a good writer.

"*Revolt so absolute that its elders cannot even recognize it*"

KENNETH REXROTH

While numerous journalists and critics called the 1950's the Age of Conformity in American writing, there burst onto the scene a school of authorship that denied most of the accepted literary values of the day. Centered about San Francisco, the Beat Generation dramatically proclaimed its absolute disaffiliation from American society, its rejection of "the official highbrow culture." While it is still too early to predict what the future of Beat literature may be, a novelist such as Jack Kerouac has undoubtedly added a new and quite different note to the contemporary American novel. In the passage that follows, the poet and critic Kenneth Rexroth, who though older than most of the Beat writers found strong affinities with them, discusses the Beat Generation's place in our literature and society.

LITERATURE GENERALLY, but literary criticism in particular, has always been an area in which social forces assume symbolic guise, and work out—or at least exemplify—conflicts taking place in the contemporary, or rather, usually the just-past wider arena of society. Recognition of this does not imply the acceptance of any general theory of social or economic determinism. It is a simple, empirical fact. Because of the pervasiveness of consent in American society generally, that democratic leveling up or down so often bewailed since de Tocqueville, American literature, especially literary criticism, has usually been

From Kenneth Rexroth, "Disengagement: the Art of the Beat Generation," in *The Beat Generation and the Angry Young Men*, ed. Gene Feldman and Max Gartenberg (New York: Citadel Press, 1958), pp. 323–324, 330–331, 337–338. Reprinted by permission of the author.

ruled by a "line." The fact that it was spontaneously evolved and enforced only by widespread consent has never detracted from its rigor—but rather the opposite. It is only human to kick against the prodding of an Erich Auerbach or an Andrey Zhdanov. An invisible, all-enveloping compulsion is not likely to be recognized, let alone protested against.

After World War I there was an official line for general consumption: "Back to Normalcy." Day by day in every way, we are getting better and better. This produced a literature which tirelessly pointed out that there was nothing whatsoever normal about us. The measure of decay in thirty years is the degree of acceptance of the official myth today—from the most obscure hack on a provincial newspaper to the loftiest metaphysicians of the literary quarterlies. The line goes: "The generation of experimentation and revolt is over." This is an etherealized corollary of the general line: "The bull market will never end."

I do not wish to argue about the bull market, but in the arts nothing could be less true. The youngest generation is in a state of revolt so absolute that its elders cannot even recognize it. The disaffiliation, alienation, and rejection of the young has, as far as their elders are concerned, moved out of the visible spectrum altogether. Critically invisible, modern revolt, like X-rays and radioactivity, is perceived only by its effects at more materialistic social levels, where it is called delinquency.

"Disaffiliation," by the way, is the term used by the critic and poet, Lawrence Lipton, who has written several articles on this subject, the first of which, in the *Nation*, quoted as epigraph, "We disaffiliate . . ."—John L. Lewis.

Like the pillars of Hercules, like two ruined Titans guarding the entrance to one of Dante's circles, stand two great dead juvenile delinquents—the heroes of the post-war generation: the great saxophonist, Charlie Parker, and Dylan Thomas. If the word deliberate means anything, both of them certainly deliberately destroyed themselves.

. . . . .

The ready market for prose fiction—there is almost no market at all for modern painting, and very much less for poetry—has had a decisive influence on its development. Sidemen with Kenton or Herman may make a good if somewhat hectic living, but any novelist who can write home to mother, or even spell his own name, has a chance to become another Brubeck. The deliberately and painfully intellectual fiction which appears in the literary quarterlies is a by-product of certain classrooms. The only significant fiction in America is popular fiction. Nobody realizes this better than the French. To them our late-born imitators of Henry James and E. M. Forster are just *chiens qui fument,* and arithmetical horses and bicycling seals. And there is no more perishable commodity than the middle-brow novel. No one today reads Ethel L. Voynich or Joseph Hergesheimer, just as no one in the future will read the writers' workshop pupils and teachers who fill the literary quarterlies. Very few people, except themselves, read them now.

On the other hand, the connection between the genuine, highbrow writer and the genuinely popular is very close. Hemingway had hardly started to write before his style had been reduced to a formula in *Black Mask,* the first hard-boiled detective magazine. In no time at all he had produced two first-class popular writers, Raymond Chandler and Dashiell Hammett. Van Vechten, their middle-brow contemporary, is forgotten. It is from Chandler and Hammett and Hemingway that the best modern fiction derives; although most of it comes out in hard covers, it is always thought of as written for a typical pocketbook audience. Once it gets into pocketbooks it is sometimes difficult to draw the line between it and its most ephemeral imitators. Even the most *précieux* French critics, a few years ago, considered Horace McCoy America's greatest contemporary novelist. There is not only something to be said for their point of view; the only thing to be said against it is that they don't read English.

Much of the best popular fiction deals with the world of the utterly disaffiliated. Burlesque and carnival people, hipsters, handicappers and hop heads, wanted men on the lam, an expendable squad of soldiers being expended, anyone who by definition is divorced from society and cannot afford to believe even an iota of the social lie—these are the favorite characters of modern post-war fiction, from Norman Mailer to the latest ephemerid called *Caught,* or *Hung Up,* or *The Needle,* its bright cover winking invitingly in the drugstore. The first, and still the greatest, novelist of total disengagement is not a young man at all, but an elderly former I.W.W. of German ancestry, B. Traven, the author of *The Death Ship* and *The Treasure of Sierra Madre.*

It is impossible for an artist to remain true to himself as a man, let alone an artist, and work within the context of this society. Contemporary mimics of Jane Austen or Anthony Trollope are not only beneath contempt. They are literally unreadable. It is impossible to keep your eyes focused on the page. Writers as far apart as J. F. Powers and Nelson Algren agree in one thing— their diagnosis of an absolute corruption.

. . . . .

There is no question but that the San Francisco renaissance is radically different from what is going on elsewhere. There are hand presses, poetry readings, young writers elsewhere—but nowhere else is there a whole younger generation culture pattern characterized by total rejection of the official high-brow culture —where critics like John Crowe Ransom or Lionel Trilling, magazines like the *Kenyon, Hudson* and *Partisan* reviews, are looked on as "The Enemy"—the other side of the barricades.

There is only one trouble about the renaissance in San Francisco. It is too far away from the literary market place. That, of course, is the reason why the Bohemian remnant, the avant garde have migrated here. It is possible to hear the story about what so-and-so said to someone else at a cocktail party twenty years ago just one too many times. You grab a plane or get on your thumb and hitchhike to the other side of the continent for good and all. Each generation, the great Latin poets came from farther and farther from Rome. Eventually, they ceased to even go there except to see the sights.

Distance from New York City does, however, make it harder to get things, if not published, at least nationally circulated. I recently formed a collection for one of the foundations of avant garde poetry printed in San Francisco. There were a great many items. The poetry was all at least readable, and the hand printing and binding were in most cases very fine indeed. None of these books were available in bookstores elsewhere in the country, and only a few of them had been reviewed in newspapers or magazines with national circulation.

Anyway, as an old war horse of the revolution of the word, things have never looked better from where I sit. The avant garde has not only not ceased to exist. It's jumping all over the place. Something's happening, man.

The disengagement of the creator, who, as creator, is necessarily judge, is one thing, but the utter nihilism of the emptied-out hipster is another. What is going to come of an attitude like this? It is impossible to go on indefinitely saying: "I am proud to be a delinquent," without destroying all civilized values. Between such persons no true enduring interpersonal relationships can be built, and, of course, nothing resembling a true "culture"—an at-homeness of men with each other, their work, their loves, their environment. The end result must be the desperation of ship-wreck—the despair, the orgies, ultimately the cannibalism of a lost lifeboat. I believe that most of an entire generation will go to ruin—the ruin of Céline, Artaud, Rimbaud, voluntarily, even enthusiastically. What will happen afterwards I don't know, but for the next ten years or so we are going to have to cope with the youth we, my generation, put through the atom smasher. Social disengagement, artistic integrity, voluntary poverty—these are powerful virtues and may pull them through, but they are not the virtues we tried to inculcate—rather they are the exact opposite.

"The spirit of men who are after strange gods"

WRIGHT MORRIS

The true American novelist must live in the present, and that present he discovers within his imagination, declares the novelist Wright Morris. Life—experience—is not real enough; the nature of man requires its transformation into art. For the American novelist "the true territory ahead is what he must imagine for himself." His freedom to search out strange gods is essential: "the spirit of the place, this American place, as it is revealed in Thoreau, Whitman, Melville, and Twain, is the spirit of men who are after strange gods."

From *The Territory Ahead*, pp. 228–231. © 1957, 1958 by Wright Morris, © The Macmillan Company, 1957. Reprinted by permission of Harcourt, Brace and Company, Inc.

Life, raw life, the kind we lead every day, whether it leads us into the past or the future, has the curious property of not seeming real *enough*. We have a need, however illusive, for a life that is more real than life. It lies in the imagination. Fiction would seem to be the way it is processed into reality. If this were not so we should have little excuse for art. Life, raw life, would be more than satisfactory in itself. But it seems to be the nature of man to transform—himself, if possible, and then the world around him—and the technique of this transformation is what we call art. When man fails to transform, he loses consciousness, he stops living.

Like Walt Whitman, we were there, we saw, and we suffered, but *where* we were, *what* we saw, and *how* we suffered are a mystery to us until the imagination has given them form. And yet imagination, both talent and imagination are of little value without conception. They are merely the tools, and it is conception that puts them to use. In the novel it is conceptual power, not style or sensibility, that indicates genius, since only conception responds to the organic pressures of life. The conceptual act is the most organic act of man. It is this that unites him with the processes of nature, with the nature of life. If man is nature self-conscious, as we have reason to believe, art is his expanding consciousness, and the creative act, in the deepest sense, is his expanding universe.

The essential ingredient in any artist—essential to what is conceptual in his talent—is his freedom to describe what he sees, and what he feels: his freedom to realize, like Cézanne, his sensations. Essential to him is his freedom to be after strange gods. It is by their strangeness that he will know them, since he conjured them up. They are, by definition, the gods that beckon him into the territory ahead. The spirit of the place, this American place, as it is revealed in Thoreau, Whitman, Melville, and Twain, is the spirit of men who are after strange gods.

To be after them is the artist's calling: to find and serve them is his proper function. His individual talent, if he has one, will displace an old god with a new one—but the new one will bear an astonishing resemblance to the one it displaced. Tradition, insofar as it is living, lives on in him, and he is powerless to thwart it; but what is dead in tradition, the heavy hand of it, he destroys. In this act of destruction he achieves his freedom as an artist, and what is vital in his art is the tradition that he sustains.

The man who lives in the present—in his own present—lives to that extent in both the past and the future: the man who seeks to live elsewhere, both as an artist and as a man, has deceived himself. This is an old deception. It is one of the crowded provinces of art.

As Lawrence reminds us:

. . . there is another kind of poetry; the poetry of that which is at hand: the immediate present. In the immediate present there is no perfection, no consummation, nothing finished. The strands are all flying, quivering, intermingling into the web, the waters shaking the moon.

The artist might well ask how, in such a spinning world as ours, he is to know that he stands in the *present*. There are no pat answers, but there are clues. Since he must live and have his being in a world of clichés, he will know this new world by their absence. He will know it by the fact that he has not been there before. The true territory ahead is what he must imagine for himself. He will recognize it by its strangeness, the lonely pilgrimage through which he attained it, and through the window of his fiction he will breathe the air of his brave new world. Strange, indeed, will be the gods found to inhabit it.

VII

Novels and Novelists

JAMES FENIMORE COOPER

"A kind of guardian spirit of the wilderness"

MARIUS BEWLEY

Fenimore Cooper (1789–1851) is the first American novelist
for whom considerable claims are still made today. His most
successful creation was the Leatherstocking series of five novels
whose hero, Natty Bumppo, symbolizes a kind of innocence
and integrity peculiarly American. Marius Bewley discusses the
symbolic meaning of Cooper's hero.

Probably no other novel in the language has first presented its principal character to us in so heroic a way. It is remarkable that Leatherstocking manages to sustain the implications
of this introduction, which would be impossible were he to be
considered a naturalistic character in Mr. Grossman's* sense.
. . . Cooper gives him to us almost as a natural evocation of
the land itself—a kind of guardian spirit of the wilderness and
the prairies who stands directly across the path of the spoilers. The
Bush family regards the figure with supernatural awe, and to the
reader, for whom the figure as its stands magnified in fiery light
remains unidentified until the end of the chapter—to the reader
also it is not a *human* form. The unusual power of the passage
flows, as nearly always with Cooper, from a perfect sense of tim-
ing, and from a remarkable plastic vision that enables him to
group details into palpable and contrasting masses. The Bush

From Marius Bewley, *The Eccentric Design* (New York: Columbia University Press, 1959), pp. 110–112. Reprinted by permission of Columbia University Press.

* [James Grossman, *James Fenimore Cooper* (New York: William Sloane
Associates, 1949).]

family, themselves a remarkable achievement in the creation of character, are the perfect spectators for this vision of Natty Bumppo. Their brooding heaviness, their sinister quality, the torpid but sure movement of their imaginations under powerful stimulus, provide exactly the right preparation for Cooper's baroque description of the colossal fiery figure in the sky. For several pages Cooper leads us towards the vision with the slow-moving wagon train, the teams growing tired as daylight fades, the prairie grass longer and more matted. The reader himself begins to participate in that general fatigue which will permit the vision to react on him with maximum effect. This is not simply a dramatic entrance made by the chief character. Cooper never allows Natty to lose entirely that aura of almost supernatural power that he acquires here.

With the exception of *The Pioneers* all the Leatherstocking tales are stories of flight and pursuit; yet the chase, as it occurs in the individual novels, is merely a matter of plot mechanics. But on the other hand, the flight of Natty Bumppo before the wood-choppers as they move steadily into the West, clearing the forest before them, is a flight charged with deeper significance, and despite the futility of paraphrase here, I wish to consider a little more fully what this flight means when we consider it as a symbol. Perhaps one of the characters in *The Prairie* gives as adequate a description of Natty's meaning as anyone is ever likely to:

The man I speak of was of great simplicity of mind, but of sterling worth. Unlike most of those who live a border life, he united the better instead of the worse qualities of the two people. He was a man endowed with the choicest—and perhaps the rarest—gift of nature—that of distinguishing good from evil. His virtues were those of simplicity. In courage he was the equal of his red associates. In short, he was a noble shoot from the stock of human nature, which could never attain its proper elevation and importance, for no other reason than because it grew in the forest.

This ability to distinguish good from evil is the ultimate note of Natty Bumppo's character, and it provides the moral passion of his flight. This flight before the advance of American civilization is virtually a moral judgement on it. Cooper presents it most often in terms of Natty's hatred of the destructive waste and

selfishness of the settlements, and yet it is much more complex
than that. We have glanced briefly at Cooper's indignant social
criticisms of America in the Effingham novels; we have looked
more carefully at his astute political criticisms, and have considered his despair in the face of agrarian reforms that he thought
spelled the downfall of aristocratic thought and feeling in his
country. Certainly, the medium of Cooper's mind was subtle
enough to permit an attitude of great complexity to take shape.
In his political and agrarian novels he enlarged the scope of the
novel itself by introducing ideas in a functional and structural
way. These ideas became the very substance of the novels. Important as this was technically in the development of fictional
form, the novels remain very incomplete successes because Cooper's personal feelings and imagination never seem wholly involved. In the Leatherstocking tales the reverse is true. The ideas
are not present as such, although they may make their presence
felt indirectly. Instead, the imagination takes over. Natty Bumppo
is not a 'character' in the sense Mr. Grossman implies, but a symbol
thrown up from the depths of Cooper's own response to America,
a response that involved both love and revulsion. Natty's love for
the land of America is mystical in its proportions, and yet the
civilization she was producing seemed a violation of that land
itself. Natty's flight across the continent is an unconscious but
profoundly realized symbol of Cooper's own recoil. But whereas
in the Effingham novels we are mainly conscious of the hatred
Cooper felt for the national manners and ideas that he believed
had betrayed America's spiritual obligations and possibilities, in
the Leatherstocking tales we are aware of that tolerance and
charity that was, after all, the prime mover in his complicated
attitude.

In *The Prairie*, then, Cooper endows Natty Bumppo in his
symbolic role with heroic grandeur. In the opening chapter he
steps into our vision from a heaven on fire, and in his magnificent
death scene, which is the finest thing in the book, the old man
sits facing the setting sun with his old hunting dog dead at his
feet. It is not accidental that Cooper has managed to suggest that
Natty Bumppo steps back into the flaming heavens from which
he seemed to come. The scene has a largeness and simplicity that
carries the mind back to some remote heroic age, and it places a

seal of consecration on Cooper's response to American society and reality. And at the same time it carries intimations of impending tragedy that look forward to Gatsby's death some eighty years later in Scott Fitzgerald's novel.

"*A work of art?*"

MARK TWAIN

In "Fenimore Cooper's Literary Offenses," Mark Twain (1835– 1910) demolishes Cooper's claims to being an artist to his own complete satisfaction and the reader's delectation.

I MAY BE MISTAKEN, but it does seem to me that *Deerslayer* is not a work of art in any sense; it does seem to me that it is destitute of every detail that goes to the making of a work of art; in truth, it seems to me that *Deerslayer* is just simply a literary *delirium tremens*.

A work of art? It has no invention; it has no order, system, sequence, or result; it has no lifelikeness, no thrill, no stir, no seeming of reality; its characters are confusedly drawn, and by their acts and words they prove that they are not the sort of people the author claims that they are; its humor is pathetic; its pathos is funny; its conversations are—oh! indescribable; its love-scenes odious; its English a crime against the language.

Counting these out, what is left is Art. I think we must all admit that.

From Mark Twain, "Fenimore Cooper's Literary Offenses," *North American Review,* CLXI (July, 1895), 12. Reprinted in *The Shock of Recognition,* ed. Edmund Wilson (New York: Farrar, Straus & Cudahy, Inc., 1955), p. 594.

"You can see Fenimore. . . .
You see Natty Bumppo"

D. H. LAWRENCE

In 1922 *Studies in Classic American Literature,* a very
personal and challenging interpretation of several of our
great writers by D. H. Lawrence (1885–1930), appeared.
Many later critics have drawn on this work, sometimes
without acknowledgment. To Lawrence, Natty Bumppo
represents Cooper's wish-fulfilment as well as an aspect of
the American myth.

FENIMORE LYING IN his Louis Quatorze hôtel in Paris,
passionately musing about Natty Bumppo and the pathless forest,
and mixing his imagination with the Cupids and Butterflies on the
painted ceiling, while Mrs. Cooper was struggling with her latest
gown in the next room, and déjeuner was with the Countess at
eleven. . . .

Men live by lies.

In actuality, Fenimore loved the genteel continent of Europe,
and waited gasping for the newspapers to praise his WORK.

In another actuality, he loved the tomahawking continent of
America, and imagined himself Natty Bumppo.

His actual desire was to be: *Monsieur Fenimore Cooper, le
grand écrivain américain.*

His innermost wish was to be: Natty Bumppo.

Now Natty and Fenimore arm-in-arm are an odd couple.

You can see Fenimore: blue coat, silver buttons, silver-and-
diamond buckle shoes, ruffles.

You see Natty Bumppo: a grizzled, uncouth old renegade, with gaps in his old teeth and a drop on the end of his nose.

But Natty was Fenimore's great Wish: his wish-fulfilment.

"It was a matter of course," says Mrs. Cooper, "that he should dwell on the better traits of the picture rather than on the coarser and more revolting, though more common points. Like West, he could see Apollo in the young Mohawk."

The coarser and more revolting, though more common points.

You see now why he depended so absolutely on MY WIFE. She had to look things in the face for him. The coarser and more revolting, and certainly more common points, she had to see.

He himself did so love seeing pretty-pretty, with the thrill of a red scalp now and then.

Fenimore, in his imagination, wanted to be Natty Bumppo, who, I am sure, belched after he had eaten his dinner. At the same time Mr. Cooper was nothing if not a gentleman. So he decided to stay in France and have it all his own way.

In France, Natty would not belch after eating, and Chingachgook could be all the Apollo he liked.

As if ever any Indian was like Apollo. The Indians, with their curious female quality, their archaic figures, with high shoulders and deep, archaic waists, like a sort of woman! And their natural devilishness, their natural insidiousness.

But men see what they want to see: especially if they look from a long distance, across the ocean, for example.

Yet the Leatherstocking books are lovely. Lovely half-lies.

They form a sort of American Odyssey, with Natty Bumppo for Odysseus.

Only, in the original Odyssey, there is plenty of devil, Circes and swine and all. And Ithacus is devil enough to outwit the devils. But Natty is a saint with a gun, and the Indians are gentlemen through and through, though they may take an occasional scalp.

There are five Leatherstocking novels: a *decrescendo* of reality, and a crescendo of beauty.

1. *Pioneers:* A raw frontier-village on Lake Champlain, at the end of the eighteenth century. Must be a picture of Cooper's home, as he knew it when a boy. A very lovely book. Natty Bumppo an old man, an old hunter half civilized.

2. *The Last of The Mohicans:* A historical fight between the British and the French, with Indians on both sides, at a Fort by Lake Champlain. Romantic flight of the British general's two daughters, conducted by the scout, Natty, who is in the prime of life; romantic death of the last of the Delawares.

3. *The Prairie:* A wagon of some huge, sinister Kentuckians trekking west into the unbroken prairie. Prairie Indians, and Natty, an old, old man; he dies seated on a chair on the Rocky Mountains, looking east.

4. *The Pathfinder:* The Great Lakes. Natty, a man of about thirty-five, makes an abortive proposal to a bouncing damsel, daughter of the Sergeant at the Fort.

5. *Deerslayer:* Natty and Hurry Harry, both quite young, are hunting in the virgin wild. They meet two white women. Lake Champlain again.

These are the five Leatherstocking books: Natty Bumppo being Leatherstocking, Pathfinder, Deerslayer, according to his ages.

Now let me put aside my impatience at the unreality of this vision, and accept it as a wish-fulfilment vision, a kind of yearning myth. Because it seems to me that the things in Cooper that make one so savage, when one compares them with actuality, are perhaps, when one considers them as presentations of a deep subjective desire, real in their way, and almost prophetic.

The passionate love for America, for the soil of America, for example. As I say, it is perhaps easier to love America passionately, when you look at it through the wrong end of the telescope, across all the Atlantic water, as Cooper did so often, than when you are right there. When you are actually *in* America, America hurts, because it has a powerful disintegrative influence upon the white psyche. It is full of grinning, unappeased aboriginal demons, too, ghosts, and it persecutes the white men like some Eumenides, until the white men give up their absolute whiteness. America is tense with latent violence and resistance. The very common-sense of white Americans has a tinge of helplessness in it, and deep fear of what might be if they were not common-sensical.

Yet one day the demons of America must be placated, the ghosts must be appeased, the Spirit of Place atoned for. Then the true passionate love for American Soil will appear. As yet, there is too much menace in the landscape.

But probably, one day America will be as beautiful in actuality as it is in Cooper. Not yet, however. When the factories have fallen down again.

And again, this perpetual blood-brother theme of the Leather-stocking novels, Natty and Chingachgook, the Great Serpent. At present it is a sheer myth. The Red Man and the White Man are not blood-brothers: even when they are most friendly. When they are most friendly, it is as a rule the one betraying his race-spirit to the other. In the white man—rather highbrow—who "loves" the Indian, one feels the white man betraying his own race. There is something unproud, underhand in it. Renegade. The same with the Americanised Indian who believes absolutely in the white mode. It is a betrayal. Renegade again.

In the actual flesh, it seems to me the white man and the red man cause a feeling of oppression, the one to the other, no matter what the good will. The red life flows in a different direction from the white life. You can't make two streams that flow in opposite directions meet and mingle soothingly.

Certainly, if Cooper had had to spend his whole life in the backwoods, side by side with a Noble Red Brother, he would have screamed with the oppression of suffocation. He had to have Mrs. Cooper, a straight strong pillar of society, to hang on to. And he had to have the culture of France to turn back to, or he would just have been stifled. The Noble Red Brother would have smothered him and driven him mad.

So that the Natty and Chingachgook myth must remain a myth. It is a wish-fulfilment, an evasion of actuality. As we have said before, the folds of the Great Serpent would have been heavy, very heavy, too heavy, on any white man. Unless the white man were a true renegade, hating himself and his own race spirit, as sometimes happens.

NATHANIEL HAWTHORNE

"But, one idle and rainy day"

Nathaniel Hawthorne (1804–1864) is most famous for his
novel *The Scarlet Letter* (1850), generally considered one of
the masterpieces of the nineteenth century. In a letter to a
friend Hawthorne described the effect his reading of the
conclusion of his new novel the night before had had on his
wife Sophia. "It broke her heart, and sent her to bed with a
grievous headache, which I look upon as a triumphant success.
. . . To tell you the truth it is . . . positively a hell-fired story,
into which I found it almost impossible to throw any cheering
light." When Hawthorne reluctantly gave the manuscript to
his publisher James T. Fields, he knew what he was giving
was "either very good or very bad—I don't know which." In
his long introductory essay to the novel Hawthorne describes
his life when he was surveyor at the Salem Custom House and
tells how the idea of the book came to him.

BUT THE SENTIMENT has likewise its moral quality. The
figure of that first ancestor, invested by family tradition with a
dim and dusky grandeur, was present to my boyish imagination,
as far back as I can remember. It still haunts me, and induces a
sort of home-feeling with the past, which I scarcely claim in reference to the present phase of the town. I seem to have a stronger
claim to a residence here on account of this grave, bearded, sable-
cloaked and steeple-crowned progenitor—who came so early, with

From Nathaniel Hawthorne, "The Custom House: Introductory," in *The
Scarlet Letter* in *The Collected Works* (Boston, 1880), pp. 8–10, 28–29,
32–33, 34–37.

his Bible and his sword, and trode the unworn street with such a
stately port, and made so large a figure, as a man of war and
peace—a stronger claim than for myself, whose name is seldom
heard and my face hardly known. He was a soldier, legislator,
judge; he was a ruler in the Church; he had all the Puritanic
traits, both good and evil. He was likewise a bitter prosecutor;
as witness the Quakers, who have remembered him in their his-
tories, and relate an incident of his hard severity toward a woman
of their sect, which will last longer, it is to be feared, than any
record of his better deeds, although these were many. His son,
too, inherited the persecuting spirit, and made himself so conspicuous in the martyrdom of the witches, that their blood may
fairly be said to have left a stain upon him. So deep a stain, indeed, that his old dry bones, in the Charter street burial-ground,
must still retain it, if they have not crumbled utterly to dust! I
know not whether these ancestors of mine bethought themselves
to repent, and ask pardon of heaven for their cruelties; or whether
they are now groaning under the heavy consequences of them
in another state of being. At all events, I, the present writer, as
their representative, hereby take shame upon myself, for their
sakes, and pray that any curse incurred by them—as I have heard,
and as the dreary and unprosperous condition of the race, for
many a long year back, would argue to exist—may be now and
henceforth removed.

Doubtless, however, either of these stern and black-browed
Puritans would have thought it quite a sufficient retribution for
his sins, that, after so long a lapse of years, the old trunk of the
family tree, with so much venerable moss upon it, should have
borne, as its topmost bough, an idler like myself. No aim, that
I have ever cherished, would they recognize as laudable; no success of mine—if my life, beyond its domestic scope, had ever been
brightened by success—would they deem otherwise than worth-
less, if not positively disgraceful. "What is he?" murmurs one gray
shadow of my forefathers to the other. "A writer of story-books!
What kind of a business in life—what mode of glorifying God, or
being serviceable to mankind in his day and generation—may that
be? Why, the degenerate fellow might as well have been a
fiddler!" Such are the compliments bandied between my great-
grandsires and myself, across the gulf of time! And yet, let them

scorn me as they will, strong traits of their nature have inter-
twined themselves with mine.

. . . . .

Literature, its exertions and objects, were now of little moment
in my regard. I cared not, at this period, for books; they were
apart from me. Nature—except it were human nature—the nature
that is developed in earth and sky, was, in one sense, hidden from
me; and all the imaginative delight, wherewith it had been
spiritualized, passed away out of my mind. A gift, a faculty, if
it had not departed, was suspended and inanimate with me. There
would have been something sad, unutterably dreary, in all this,
had I not been conscious that it lay at my own option to recall
whatever was valuable in the past. It might be true, indeed, that
this was a life which could not, with impunity, be lived too long;
else, it might make me permanently other than I had been, without transforming me into any shape which it would be worth my
while to take. But I never considered it as other than a transitory
life. There was always a prophetic instinct, a low whisper in my
ear, that, within no long period, and whenever a new change of
custom should be essential to my good, a change would come.

. . . . .

But, one idle and rainy day, it was my fortune to make a discovery of some little interest. Poking and burrowing into the
heaped-up rubbish in the corner; unfolding one and another document, and reading the names of vessels that had long ago foun-
dered at sea or rotted at the wharves, and those of merchants,
never heard of now on 'Change, nor very readily decipherable on
their mossy tombstones; glancing at such matters with the sad-
dened, weary, half reluctant interest which we bestow on the
corpse of dead activity, and exerting my fancy, sluggish with
little use, to raise up from these dry bones an image of the old
town's brighter aspect, when India was a new region and only
Salem knew the way thither, I chanced to lay my hand on a small
package, carefully done up in a piece of ancient yellow parchment. This envelope had the air of an official record of some
period long past, when clerks engrossed their stiff and formal
chirography on more substantial materials than at present. There
was something about it that quickened an instinctive curiosity,
and made me undo the faded red tape, that tied up the package,

with the sense that a treasure would here be brought to light. Unbending the rigid folds of the parchment cover, I found it to be a commission, under the hand and seal of Governor Shirley, in favor of one Jonathan Pue, as Surveyor of his Majesty's Customs for the port of Salem, in the Province of Massachusetts Bay. I remembered to have read (probably in Felt's Annals) a notice of the decease of Mr. Surveyor Pue, about fourscore years ago; and likewise, in a newspaper of recent times, an account of the digging up of his remains in the little grave-yard of St. Peter's Church, during the renewal of that edifice. Nothing, if I rightly call to mind, was left of my respected predecessor, save an imperfect skeleton, and some fragments of apparel, and a wig of majestic frizzle; which, unlike the head that it once adorned, was in very satisfactory preservation. But, on examining the papers which the parchment commission served to envelop, I found more traces of Mr. Pue's mental part, and the internal operations of his head, than the frizzled wig had contained of the venerable skull itself.

. . . . .

But the object that most drew my attention, in the mysterious package, was a certain affair of fine red cloth, much worn and faded. There were traces about it of gold embroidery, which, however, was greatly frayed and defaced; so that none, or very little, of the glitter was left. It had been wrought, as was easy to perceive, with wonderful skill of needlework; and the stitch (as I am assured by ladies conversant with such mysteries) gives evidence of a now forgotten art, not to be recovered even by the process of picking out the threads. This rag of scarlet cloth—for time, and wear, and a sacrilegious moth, had reduced it to little other than a rag—on careful examination, assumed the shape of a letter. It was the capital letter A. By an accurate measurement, each limb proved to be precisely three inches and a quarter in length. It had been intended, there could be no doubt, as an ornamental article of dress; but how it was to be worn, or what rank, honor, and dignity, in by-past times, were signified by it, was a riddle which (so evanescent are the fashions of the world in these particulars) I saw little hope of solving. And yet it strangely interested me. My eyes fastened themselves upon the old scarlet letter, and would not be turned aside. Certainly, there was some deep meaning in it, most worthy of interpretation, and which, as it were, streamed forth from the mystic symbol, subtly communicating itself to my sensibilities, but evading the analysis of my mind.

While thus perplexed—and cogitating, among other hypotheses, whether the letter might not have been one of those decorations which the white man used to contrive, in order to take the eyes of Indians—I happened to place it on my breast. It seemed to me —the reader may smile, but must not doubt my word—it seemed to me, then, that I experienced a sensation not altogether physical, yet almost so, as of burning heat; and as if the letter were not of red cloth, but red-hot iron. I shuddered, and involuntarily let it fall upon the floor.

In the absorbing contemplation of the scarlet letter, I had hitherto neglected to examine a small roll of dingy paper, around which it had been twisted. This I now opened, and had the satisfaction to find, recorded by the old Surveyor's pen, a reasonably complete explanation of the whole affair. There were several foolscap sheets, containing many particulars respecting the life and conversation of one Hester Prynne, who appeared to have been rather a noteworthy personage in the view of our ancestors. She had flourished during the period between the early days of Massachusetts and the close of the seventeenth century. Aged persons, alive in the time of Mr. Surveyor Pue, and from whose oral testimony he had made up his narrative, remembered her, in their youth, as a very old, but not decrepit woman, of a stately and solemn aspect. It had been her habit, from an almost immemorial date, to go about the country as a kind of voluntary nurse, and doing whatever miscellaneous good she might; taking upon herself, likewise, to give advice in all matters, especially those of the heart; by which means, as a person of such propensities inevitably must, she gained from many people the reverence due to an angel, but I should imagine, was looked upon by others as an intruder and a nuisance. Prying further into the manuscript, I found the record of other doings and sufferings of this singular woman, for most of which the reader is referred to the story entitled *The Scarlet Letter;* and it should be borne carefully in mind that the main facts of that story are authorized and authenticated by the document of Mr. Surveyor Pue. The original papers, together with the scarlet letter itself—a most curious relic—are still in my possession, and shall be freely exhibited to whomsoever, induced by the great interest of the narrative, may desire a sight of them. I must not be understood as affirming that, in the dressing up of the tale, and imagining the motives and modes of passion that influenced the characters who figure in it, I have invariably confined myself within the limits of the old Surveyor's half a dozen sheets of foolscap. On the contrary, I have allowed myself, as to such points, nearly or altogether as much license as if the facts had been entirely of my own invention. What I contend for is the authenticity of the outline.

"Out of the very heart of New England"

HENRY JAMES

In perhaps the first full-length critical study of an American writer, Henry James (1843–1916) writes both affectionately and perceptively on Hawthorne. James has just described Hawthorne's modesty about the success of *The Scarlet Letter* (he thought the introductory chapter we have just cited from probably accounted for its "vogue"). After mentioning the historical significance of the novel's success, James goes on to consider the book as the culmination of a long Puritan tradition, as "the vessel that gathered up the last of the precious drops."

IN FACT, THE PUBLICATION of *The Scarlet Letter* was in the United States a literary event of the first importance. The book was the finest piece of imaginative writing yet put forth in

From Henry James, *Hawthorne* (New York, 1880), pp. 108–110. Reprinted in *The Shock of Recognition,* ed. Edmund Wilson (Farrar, Straus & Cudahy, Inc., 1955), pp. 511–513.

the country. There was a consciousness of this in the welcome that was given it—a satisfaction in the idea of America having produced a novel that belonged to literature, and to the forefront of it. Something might at last be sent to Europe as exquisite in quality as anything that had been received, and the best of it was that the thing was absolutely American; it belonged to the soil, to the air; it came out of the very heart of New England.

It is beautiful, admirable, extraordinary; it has in the highest degree that merit which I have spoken of as the mark of Hawthorne's best things—an indefinable purity and lightness of conception, a quality which in a work of art affects one in the same way as the absence of grossness does in a human being. His fancy, as I just now said, had evidently brooded over the subject for a long time; the situation to be represented had disclosed itself to him in all its phases. When I say in all its phases, the sentence demands modification; for it is to be remembered that if Hawthorne laid his hand upon the well-worn theme, upon the familiar combination of the wife, the lover, and the husband, it was, after all but to one period of the history of these three persons that he attached himself. The situation is the situation after the woman's fault has been committed, and the current of expiation and repentance has set in. In spite of the relation between Hester Prynne and Arthur Dimmesdale, no story of love was surely ever less of a "love-story." To Hawthorne's imagination the fact that these two persons had loved each other too well was of an interest comparatively vulgar; what appealed to him was the idea of their moral situation in the long years that were to follow. The story, indeed, is in a secondary degree that of Hester Prynne; she becomes, really, after the first scene, an accessory figure; it is not upon her the dénoûement depends. It is upon her guilty lover that the author projects most frequently the cold, thin rays of his fitfully-moving lantern, which makes here and there a luminous circle, on the edge of which hovers the livid and sinister figure of the injured and retributive husband. The story goes on, for the most part, between the lover and the husband—the tormented young Puritan minister, who carries the secret of his own lapse from pastoral purity locked up beneath an exterior that commends itself to the reverence of his flock, while he sees the softer partner of his guilt standing in the full

glare of exposure and humbling herself to the misery of atone-
ment—between this more wretched and pitiable culprit, to whom
dishonor would come as a comfort and the pillory as a relief, and
the older, keener, wiser man, who, to obtain satisfaction for the
wrong he has suffered, devises the infernally ingenious plan of con-
joining himself with his wronger, living with him, living upon him;
and while he pretends to minister to his hidden ailment and to
sympathize with his pain, revels in his unsuspected knowledge of
these things, and stimulates them by malignant arts. The attitude
of Roger Chillingworth, and the means he takes to compensate
himself—these are the highly original elements in the situation
that Hawthorne so ingeniously treats. None of his works are so
impregnated with that after-sense of the old Puritan consciousness of life to which allusion has so often been made. If, as M.
Montégut says, the qualities of his ancestors *filtered* down through
generations into his composition, *The Scarlet Letter* was, as it
were, the vessel that gathered up the last of the precious drops.
And I say this not because the story happens to be of so-called
historical cast, to be told of the early days of Massachusetts, and
of people in steeple-crowned hats and sad-colored garments. The
historical coloring is rather weak than otherwise; there is little
elaboration of detail, of the modern realism of research; and the
author has made no great point of causing his figures to speak
the English of their period. Nevertheless, the book is full of the
moral presence of the race that invented Hester's penance—
diluted and complicated with other things, but still perfectly
recognizable. Puritanism, in a word, is there, not only objectively,
as Hawthorne tried to place it there, but subjectively as well.
Not, I mean, in his judgment of his characters in any harshness
of prejudice, or in the obtrusion of a moral lesson; but in the
very quality of his own vision, in the tone of the picture, in a certain coldness and exclusiveness of treatment.

"*That blue-eyed darling Nathaniel knew disagreeable things in his inner soul*"

D. H. LAWRENCE

The idea of romance again. D. H. Lawrence sees *The Scarlet Letter* as an example of the split in the American psyche: the surface decorum masks a diabolic content. Hester Prynne is a hunter who brings down her bird of prey, Arthur Dimmesdale. It is interesting to speculate on what Hawthorne would have made of Lawrence's comment. Perhaps he would have been shocked and horrified. But perhaps not.

NATHANIEL HAWTHORNE writes romance.

And what's romance? Usually, a nice little tale, where you have everything As You Like It, where rain never wets your jacket and gnats never bite your nose and it's always daisy-time. *As You Like It* and *Forest Lovers*, etc. *Morte D'Arthur.*

Hawthorne obviously isn't this kind of romanticist: though nobody has muddy boots in *The Scarlet Letter*, either.

But there is more to it. *The Scarlet Letter* isn't a pleasant, pretty romance. It is a sort of parable, an earthly story with a hellish meaning.

All the time there is this split in the American art and art-consciousness. On the top it is as nice as pie, goody-goody and lovey-dovey. Like Hawthorne being such a blue-eyed darling, in life, and Longfellow and the rest such sucking doves. Hawthorne's

From D. H. Lawrence, *Studies in Classic American Literature*, pp. 121–122, 138–141. Copyright 1923 by Thomas Seltzer, Inc., 1951 by Frieda Lawrence. Reprinted by permission of The Viking Press, Inc. Reprinted in *The Shock of Recognition* ed. Edmund Wilson (New York: Farrar, Straus & Cudahy, Inc., 1955), pp. 984, 995–997.

wife said she "never saw him in time," which doesn't mean she
saw him too late. But always in the "frail effulgence of eternity."

Serpents they were. Look at the inner meaning of their art and
see what demons they were.

You *must* look through the surface of American art, and see
the inner diabolism of the symbolic meaning. Otherwise it is all
mere childishness.

That blue-eyed darling Nathaniel knew disagreeable things in
his inner soul. He was careful to send them out in disguise.

. . . . .

Hester Prynne was a devil. Even when she was so meekly going round as a sick-nurse. Poor Hester. Part of her wanted to be
saved from her own devilishness. And another part wanted to
go on and on in devilishness, for revenge. Revenge! REVENGE!
It is this that fills the unconscious spirit of woman to-day. Revenge against man, and against the spirit of man, which has betrayed her into unbelief. Even when she is most sweet and a salvationist, she is her most devilish, is woman. She gives her man
the sugar-plum of her own submissive sweetness. And when he's
taken this sugar-plum in his mouth, a scorpion comes out of it.
After he's taken this Eve to his bosom, oh, so loving, she destroys
him inch by inch. Woman and her revenge! She will have it, and go
on having it, for decades and decades, unless she's stopped. And
to stop her you've got to believe in yourself and your gods, your
own Holy Ghost, Sir Man; and then you've got to fight her, and
never give in. She's a devil. But in the long run she is conquerable.
And just a tiny bit of her wants to be conquered. You've got to
fight three-quarters of her, in absolute hell, to get at the final
quarter of her that wants a release, at last, from the hell of her
own revenge. But it's a long last. And not yet.

"She had in her nature a rich, voluptuous, oriental characteristic
—a taste for the gorgeously beautiful." This is Hester. This is
American. But she repressed her nature in the above direction.
She would not even allow herself the luxury of labouring at fine,
delicate stitching. Only she dressed her little sin-child Pearl
vividly, and the scarlet letter was gorgeously embroidered. Her
Hecate and Astarte insignia.

"A voluptuous, oriental characteristic——" That lies waiting in
American women. It is probable that the Mormons are the forerunners of the coming real America. It is probable that men will

have more than one wife, in the coming America. That you will have again a half-oriental womanhood, and a polygamy.

The grey nurse, Hester. The Hecate, the hell-cat. The slowly-evolving voluptuous female of the new era, with a whole new submissiveness to the dark, phallic principle.

But it takes time. Generation after generation of nurses and political women and salvationists. And in the end, the dark erection of the images of sex worship once more, and the newly submissive women. That kind of depth. Deep women in that respect. When we have at last broken this insanity of mental-spiritual consciousness. And the women *choose* to experience again the great submission.

"The poor, whom she sought out to be the objects of her bounty, often reviled the hand that was stretched to succour them."

Naturally. The poor hate a salvationist. They smell the devil underneath.

"She was patient—a martyr indeed—but she forbore to pray for her enemies, lest, in spite of her forgiving aspirations, the words of the blessing should stubbornly twist themselves into a curse."

So much honesty, at least. No wonder the old witch-lady Mistress Hibbins claimed her for another witch.

"She grew to have a dread of children; for they had imbibed from their parents a vague idea of something horrible in this dreary woman gliding silently through the town, with never any companion but only one child."

"A vague idea!" Can't you see her "gliding silently"? It's not a question of a vague idea imbibed, but a definite feeling directly received.

"But sometimes, once in many days, or perchance in many months, she felt an eye—a human eye—upon the ignominious brand, that seemed to give a momentary relief, as if half her agony were shared. The next instant, back it all rushed again, with a still deeper throb of pain; for in that brief interval she had sinned again. Had Hester sinned alone?"

Of course not. As for sinning again, she would go on all her life silently, changelessly "sinning." She never repented. Not she. Why should she? She had brought down Arthur Dimmesdale, that too-too snow-white bird, and that was her life-work.

HERMAN MELVILLE

"He can neither believe, nor be comfortable in his unbelief"

NATHANIEL HAWTHORNE

Rather late in Hawthorne's life, Herman Melville (1819–1891) became an admirer and friend. He met Hawthorne in 1850 shortly after his review of Hawthorne's *Mosses from an Old Manse,* thus beginning a friendship which Mark Van Doren calls "one of the major events in literary history." Melville found in Hawthorne a "great power of blackness," a result of his "calvinistic sense of Innate Depravity and Original Sin"; Hawthorne found in Melville "a very high and noble nature . . . better worth immortality than most of us." This selection, from Hawthorne's journal for 1856, commemorates a meeting in Southport, England, when Hawthorne was consul at Liverpool and Melville had just come abroad.

M ELVILLE HAS NOT BEEN WELL of late; he has been affected with neuralgic complaints in his head and his limbs, and no doubt has suffered from too constant literary occupation, pursued without much success latterly; and his writings, for a long while past, have indicated a morbid state of mind. So he left his place at Pittsfield, and has established his wife and family, I believe, with his father-in-law in Boston, and is thus far on his way to Constantinople. I do not wonder that he found it necessary to take an airing through the world, after so many years of toilsome pen-labor following after so wild and adventurous a youth as his was. I invited him to come and stay with us at Southport

From *The Heart of Hawthorne's Journals,* ed. Newton Arvin (Boston: Little, Brown & Company, 1929), pp. 230–231.

as long as he might remain in this vicinity; and, accordingly, he did come, on the next day, taking with him, by way of luggage, the least little bit of a bundle, which, he told me, contained a nightshirt and a toothbrush. He is a person of very gentlemanly instincts in every respect, save that he is a little heterodox in the matter of clean linen.

He stayed with us from Tuesday till Thursday; and, on the intervening day, we took a pretty long walk together, and sat down in a hollow among the sandhills (sheltering ourselves from the high, cool wind) and smoked a cigar. Melville, as he always does, began to reason of Providence and futurity, and of everything that lies beyond human ken, and informed me that he had 'pretty much made up his mind to be annihilated'; but still he does not seem to rest in that anticipation, and, I think, will never rest until he gets hold of a definite belief. It is strange how he persists—and has persisted ever since I knew him, and probably long before—in wandering to and fro over these deserts, as dismal and monotonous as the sandhills amid which we were sitting. He can neither believe, nor be comfortable in his unbelief; and he is too honest and courageous not to try to do one or the other. If he were a religious man, he would be one of the most truly religious and reverential; he has a very high and noble nature and is better worth immortality than most of us.

"I have written a wicked book, and feel spotless as the lamb"

HERMAN MELVILLE

The disappearance of Hawthorne's letter to Melville in which he "allegorized" *Moby Dick* is one of our great literary losses. The best we can do is to give Melville's reply, full of his

Herman Melville, letter to Nathaniel Hawthorne, November, 1851, in Eleanor Metcalf Melville, *Herman Melville—Cycle and Epicycle* (Cambridge, Mass.: Harvard University Press, 1953), pp. 128–130.

exuberant gratitude for a fellow soul capable of understanding
him and his masterpiece.

Dear Hawthorne,—People think that if a man has
undergone any hardship, he should have a reward; but for my
part, if I have done the hardest possible day's work, and then
come to sit down in a corner and eat my supper comfortably—
why, then I don't think I deserve any reward for my hard day's
work—for am I not now at peace? Is not my supper good? My
peace and my supper are my reward, my dear Hawthorne. So
your joy-giving and exultation-breeding letter is not my reward
for my ditcher's work with that book, but is the good goddess's
bonus over and above what was stipulated for—for not one man
in five cycles, who is wise, will expect appreciative recognition
from his fellows, or any one of them. Appreciation! Recognition!
Is love appreciated? Why, ever since Adam, who has got to
the meaning of this great allegory—the world? Then we pygmies
must be content to have our paper allegories but ill comprehended.
I say your appreciation is my glorious gratuity. In my proud,
humble way,—a shepherd-king,—I was lord of a little vale in the
solitary Crimea; but you have now given me the crown of India.
But on trying it on my head, I found it fell down on my ears,
notwithstanding their asinine length—for it's only such ears that
sustain such crowns.

Your letter was handed me last night on the road going to Mr.
Morewoods's, and I read it there. Had I been at home, I would
have sat down at once and answered it. In me divine magnanimi-
ties are spontaneous and instantaneous—catch them while you
can. The world goes round, and the other side comes up. So now
I can't write what I felt. But I felt pantheistic then—your heart
beat in my ribs and mine in yours, and both in God's. A sense of
unspeakable security is in me this moment, on account of your
having understood the book. I have written a wicked book, and
feel spotless as the lamb. Ineffable socialities are in me. I would
sit down and dine with you and all the gods in old Rome's
Pantheon. It is a strange feeling—no hopefulness is in it, no
despair. Content—that is it; and irresponsibility; but without
licentious inclination. I speak now of my profoundest sense of being, not of an incidental feeling.

Whence come you, Hawthorne? By what right do you drink from my flagon of life? And when I put it to my lips—lo, they are yours and not mine. I feel that the Godhead is broken up like the bread at the Supper, and that we are the pieces. Hence this infinite fraternity of feeling. Now, sympathizing with the paper, my angel turns over another page. You did not care a penny for the book. But, now and then as you read, you understood the pervading thought that impelled the book—and that you praised. Was it not so? You were archangel enough to despise the imperfect body, and embrace the soul. Once you hugged the ugly Socrates because you saw the flame in the mouth, and heard the rushing of the demon,—the familiar,—and recognized the sound; for you have heard it in your own solitudes.

My dear Hawthorne, the atmospheric skepticisms steal into me now, and make me doubtful of my sanity in writing you thus. But, believe me, I am not mad, most noble Festus! But truth is ever incoherent, and when the big hearts strike together, the concussion is a little stunning. Farewell. Don't write a word about the book. That would be robbing me of my miserly delight. I am heartily sorry I ever wrote anything about you—it was paltry. Lord, when shall we be done growing? As long as we have anything more to do, we have done nothing. So now, let us add Moby Dick to our blessing, and step from that. Leviathan is not the biggest fish;—I have heard of Krakens.

This is a long letter, but you are not at all bound to answer it. Possibly, if you do answer it, and direct it to Herman Melville, you will missend it—for the very fingers that now guide this pen are not precisely the same that just took it up and put it on this paper. Lord, when shall we be done changing? Ah! It's a long stage, and no inn in sight, and night coming, and the body cold. But with you for a passenger, I am content and can be happy. I shall leave the world, I feel, with more satisfaction for having come to know you. Knowing you persuades me more than the Bible of our immortality.

What a pity, that, for your plain, bluff letter, you should get such gibberish! Mention me to Mrs. Hawthorne and to the children, and so, good-by to you, with my blessing. Herman.

P.S. I can't stop yet. If the world was entirely made up of Magians, I'll tell you what I should do. I should have a paper-mill established at one end of the house, and so have an endless

riband of foolscap rolling in upon my desk; and upon that endless
riband I should write a thousand—a million—billion thoughts, all
under the form of a letter to you. The divine magnet is on you,
and my magnet responds. Which is the biggest? A foolish question—they are *One*.

P.P.S. Don't think that by writing me a letter, you shall always
be bored with an immediate reply to it—and so keep both of us
delving over a writing-desk eternally. No such thing! I sh'n't always answer your letters, and you may do just as you please.

"A new work by Herman Melville"

GEORGE RIPLEY

Today there are few critics that would not rate *Moby Dick*
(1851) the high mark of American imaginative writing in the
nineteenth century, but it was not until the 1920's that
Melville's greatness began to be widely recognized.
Nevertheless, this early review shows that at least a few others
besides Hawthorne realized that *Moby Dick* was an
extraordinary work at the time it appeared. George Ripley
(1802–1880) notes in his review Melville's encyclopedic
range, his skill at characterization, his humor, and his epic
power.

A NEW WORK BY Herman Melville, entitled *Moby Dick;
or, The Whale*, has just been issued by Harper and Brothers,
which, in point of richness and variety of incident, originality of
conception, and splendor of description, surpasses any of the
former productions of this highly successful author. *Moby Dick*
is the name of an old White Whale; half fish and half devil; the
terror of the Nantucket cruisers; the scourge of distant oceans;
leading an invulnerable, charmed life; the subject of many grim

[George Ripley] "Literary Notices," *Harper's Magazine*, IV (December,
1851), 137.

and ghostly traditions. This huge sea monster has a conflict with
one Captain Ahab; the veteran Nantucket salt comes off second
best; not only loses a leg in the affray, but receives a twist in the
brain; becomes the victim of a deep, cunning monomania; believes
himself predestined to take a bloody revenge on his fearful
enemy; pursues him with fierce demoniac energy of purpose; and
at last perishes in the dreadful fight, just as he deems that he has
reached the goal of his frantic passion. On this slight framework,
the author has constructed a romance, a tragedy, and a natural
history, not without numerous gratuitous suggestions on psychology, ethics, and theology. Beneath the whole story, the subtle,
imaginative reader may perhaps find a pregnant allegory, intended to illustrate the mystery of human life. Certain it is that
the rapid, pointed hints which are often thrown out, with the
keenness and velocity of a harpoon, penetrate deep into the heart
of things, showing that the genius of the author for moral analysis
is scarcely surpassed by his wizard power of description.

In the course of the narrative the habits of the whale are fully
and ably described. Frequent graphic and instructive sketches of
the fishery, of sea-life in a whaling vessel, and of the manners
and customs of strange nations are interspersed with excellent
artistic effect among the thrilling scenes of the story. The various
processes of procuring oil are explained with the minute, pains-
taking fidelity of a statistical record, contrasting strangely with
the weird, phantom-like character of the plot, and of some of
the leading personages, who present a no less unearthly appearance than the witches in Macbeth. These sudden and decided
transitions form a striking feature of the volume. Difficult of
management, in the highest degree, they are wrought with con-
summate skill. To a less gifted author, they would inevitably have
proved fatal. He has not only deftly avoided their dangers, but
made them an element of great power. They constantly pique the
attention of the reader, keeping curiosity alive, and presenting
the combined charm of surprise and alternation.

The introductory chapters of the volume, containing sketches
of life in the great marts of Whalingdom, New Bedford and Nantucket, are pervaded with a fine vein of comic humor, and reveal
a succession of portraitures, in which the lineaments of nature shine
forth, through a good deal of perverse, intentional exaggeration.
To many readers, these will prove the most interesting portions of

the work. Nothing can be better than the description of the owners of the vessel, Captain Peleg and Captain Bildad, whose acquaintance we make before the commencement of the voyage. The character of Captain Ahab also opens upon us with wonderful power. He exercises a wild, bewildering fascination by his dark and mysterious nature, which is not at all diminished when we obtain a clearer insight into his strange history. Indeed, all the members of the ship's company, the three mates, Starbuck, Stubbs, and Flash, the wild, savage Gayheader, the case-hardened old blacksmith, to say nothing of the pearl of a New Zealand harpooner, the bosom friend of the narrator—all stand before us in the strongest individual relief, presenting a unique picture gallery, which every artist must despair of rivaling.

The plot becomes more intense and tragic, as it approaches toward the denouement. The malicious old Moby Dick, after long cruisings in pursuit of him, is at length discovered. He comes up to the battle, like an army with banners. He seems inspired with the same fierce, inveterate cunning with which Captain Ahab has followed the traces of his mortal foe. The fight is described in letters of blood. It is easy to foresee which will be the victor in such a contest. We need not say that the ill-omened ship is broken in fragments by the wrath of the weltering fiend. Captain Ahab becomes the prey of his intended victim. The crew perish. One alone escapes to tell the tale. Moby Dick disappears unscathed, and for aught we know, is the same "delicate monster," whose power in destroying another ship is just announced from Panama.

"The alternative of Narcissus"

RICHARD CHASE

In his revaluation of the tradition of the American novel, Richard Chase shows that typically the American novelist deals in extremes, that he has "a certain intrepid and penetrating

From Richard Chase, *The American Novel and Its Tradition*, pp. 105–113. Copyright 1955 by the American Jewish Committee, copyright © 1957 by Richard Chase. Reprinted by permission of Doubleday & Company, Inc.

dialectic of action and meaning, a radical skepticism about ultimate questions." Melville's *Moby Dick* is the case *par excellence* for Chase's theory of the American novel. Beside *King Lear, The Divine Comedy,* or *The Iliad,* Melville's great book seems profound but narrow; the issues are simplified though "the states of mind and feeling they generate" are not. But Chase finds *Moby Dick* "at once the most startling and the most characteristic product of the American imagination."

IF WE THINK of the dramatic action involving Ahab and the pursuit of the whale, isolating this in our minds from the almost encyclopedic context in which it occurs, we are conscious of a meaning, even of a didactic purpose. Just what the meaning is has been the subject of much speculation. Undoubtedly the first step towards understanding *Moby-Dick* is to observe what is really very obvious: it is a book about the alienation from life that results from an excessive or neurotic self-dependence. Melville has conceived of his moral fable in a way which makes *Moby-Dick* distinctly a book of its time and place and allies it intimately with the work of other American writers. As Newton Arvin demonstrates, there is some reason to think of Ahab as guilty of *hybris,* in the Greek sense, or of excessive pride, in the Christian sense; but there is more reason to think of him as guilty of or victimized by a distorted "self-reliance." An alternative to Ahab's suicidal course is proposed by the author. But since Mr. Arvin explains this in a way which seems generally to confirm the view of the American imagination as we are attempting to understand it in the present book, let us listen to him. Mr. Arvin begins by saying that "the alternative to Ahab's egotism" is not the Greek "ideal of 'nothing too much'" nor the Christian ideal of "a broken and contrite heart." Rather, he says,

On one level it is an intuition that carries us beyond morality, in the usual sense, into the realm of cosmic piety; on the usual ethical level, however, it is a strong intuition of human solidarity as a priceless good. Behind Melville's expression of this, one is conscious of the gravity and the tenderness of religious feeling, if not of religious belief; it came to him in part from the Christian tradition in which he had been nurtured. The form it took in him, however, is no longer specifically Christian; as with Hawthorne and Whitman, it was the natural recoil of a sensitive imagination, enriched by the humanities of romantic idealism, against the ruinous individualism of the age. It is Melville's version of Hawthorne's "magnetic chain of humanity," of Whitman's "manly attachment": so far, it is an essentially humanistic and secular principle.

The only caveat that needs to be added to these words is that the "intuition of human solidarity as a priceless good" is stronger in Melville and Whitman than in Hawthorne and that for all of them "human solidarity" means not a settled social order but a more or less unstable idyllic relationship, a personal and ideal sharing of the human fate among people temporarily brought together by chance or by a common purpose. The intuition of solidarity tends to come to American writers only when the solidarity is precarious and doomed by the passing of time or by the mere anarchic instinct of the individual. And so the American novel is full of idealized momentary associations—Natty Bumppo and his companions, Hawthorne's Blithedalers, Ishmael, Queequeg and the crew of the Pequod, Huck Finn and Nigger Jim on their raft, or—that classic example of the instability and mixed motives that characterize united action among Americans— the Bundren family in Faulkner's *As I Lay Dying*. Even such relatively stable social orders as that of the Bostonians described in James's *The Europeans* or that of the New Yorkers in Edith Wharton's *Age of Innocence* have to regroup themselves and suffer a good deal of agony in order to put up a united front against the foreigner who, in each novel, threatens invasion.

But to take up Mr. Arvin's argument again, one notes, in carrying it a step further, that the moral action of *Moby-Dick* is not strictly tragic or Christian. It is an action conceived as taking place in a universe of extreme contradictions. There is death and there is life. Death—spiritual, emotional, physical—is the price of self-reliance when it is pushed to the point of solipsism, where the world has no existence apart from the all-sufficient self. Life is to be clung to, if only precariously and for the moment, by natural piety and the ability to share with others the common vicissitudes of the human situation. These are the clear alternatives.

What must be remembered is that this is a melodramatic view of things. Strictly speaking, both Greek and Christian tragedy offer an ideal of catharsis or redemption—forms of harmonious life that come about *through* death. It is this life through death that Ishmael seems to have been given in the Epilogue, when he alone is saved by the coffin-life-buoy. But is this really a catharsis, a redemption, a rebirth? The momentary sense of harmony and joy is all too easily dispelled by the chilly gloom, the final despair, of the last words. "On the second day, a sail drew near, nearer, and picked me up at last. It was the devious-cruising Rachel, that in her retracing search after her missing children, only found another orphan."

For Melville there is little promise of renewal and reward after suffering. There is no transcendent ground where the painful contradictions of the human dilemma are reconciled. There is no life *through* death. There is only life *and* death, and for any individual a momentary choice between them. What moves Melville most powerfully is the horror that is the violent result of making the wrong choice. He is moved too by the comic aspect of the spectacle, the absurdity of such a creature as man, endowed with desires and an imagination so various, complex, and procreative yet so much the prisoner of the cruel contradictions with which, in his very being, he is inexorably involved. Finally, he is moved by the blissful, idyllic, erotic attachment to life and to one's ideal comrades, which is the only promise of happiness.

Solipsism, hypnotic self-regard, imprisonment within the self —these themes have absorbed American novelists. The Concord transcendentalism, of which Melville was very much aware and whose sensibility he in many ways shared, was a philosophy—or rather an ethical poetry—of the self. The idea of the image reflected in the mirror or in the water appeals as strongly to Melville as to Hawthorne, and like Hawthorne he uses this literary convention to point up the dangers of an exaggerated self-regard, rather than, as Whitman and Emerson loved to do, to suggest the vital possibilities of the self. At the very beginning of *Moby-Dick* we are shown "crowds of water-gazers" who are "posted like silent sentinels" around the shores of Manhattan and are "fixed in ocean reveries." And then, says Melville, amplifying his effect with his usual semi-humorous parody of learning, there is the still deeper "meaning of that story of Narcissus, who because he could not grasp the tormenting, mild image he saw in the fountain, plunged into it and was drowned. But that same image, we ourselves see in all rivers and oceans. It is the image of the ungraspable phantom of life; and this is the key to it all."

This last statement is tantalizing and although it sounds a little offhand, like a too facile way to end a paragraph, it also sounds and *is* important. For the book is to offer the alternative of Narcissus. One may, like Ahab, look into the water, or into the profound and ultimately unknowable abyss of nature, and see only one's own image or an ungraspable phantom, a white whale which is only a projection of self. Or, like Ishmael or Starbuck, one may see one's own image but in a context of life and reality which is *not* one's self. To be Ahab is to be unable to resist the hypnotic attraction of the self with its impulse to envelop and control the universe. To be Ishmael is to be able at the last minute to resist the plunge from the masthead into the sea one has with rapt fascination been gazing at, to assert at the critical moment the difference between the self and the not-self. To be Starbuck is to understand what the white whale might mean to a man like Ahab but to insist "with the stubbornness of life" that the whale is merely "a dumb brute" to seek vengeance on which is "blasphemous" and "madness."

Chapter 99, "The Doubloon," tells us much about the meaning of *Moby-Dick*. The doubloon is a gold coin Ahab has nailed to the main mast. It is to be won by whoever first sees the white whale. Ishmael describes the coin in detail (if indeed Ishmael can be called the narrator at this point; he is always ostensibly the narrator but in much of the latter part of the novel he is not *felt* as such). The coin is from Ecuador. "So this bright coin came from a country planted in the middle of the world, and beneath the great equator, and named after it; and it had been cast midway up the Andes, in the unwaning climate that knows no autumn." In the ambiguous symbolism of the coin, involving three mountains crowned respectively with a flame, a tower, and a crowing cock, we see "the keystone sun entering the equinoctial point at Libra" (the Scales). Without worrying over the rather labored symbolism, we note that for author-Ishmael the coin represents the equator, the dividing line in the dualistic world. From the point of view of the equator, there are in human destiny two grand alternatives: the self-absorption which leads to isolation, madness, and suicide, or the imperfect but more or less objective perceptions of the world which allow one to cling to life. All this is shown in the procession of the main figures of the drama as each in turn meditates momentarily on the coin.

Ahab soliloquizes thus:

the firm tower, that is Ahab; the volcano, that is Ahab; the courageous, the undaunted, and victorious fowl, that, too, is Ahab; all are Ahab; and this round gold is but the image of the rounder globe, which, like a magician's glass, to each and every man in turn but mirrors back his own mysterious self.

The others respond to the symbolism of the coin in their different ways, but each is free of Ahab's imprisonment. Starbuck sees the symbolism of the ordinary pious Christian life. Stubb is reminded of his *carpe diem* philosophy, his jolly acceptance of life and death. Flask, even less imaginative, sees simply a gold coin that, as he pauses to calculate, would buy nine hundred and sixty cigars. The Manxman, a primitive soothsayer, sees merely a vague doom. Fedallah, the Parsee harpooner Ahab has smuggled aboard, sees the fire worshipped in his religion. Pip, rather reminiscent of King Lear's fool, expresses with a theological despair, one may think, the impossibility of seeing anything, the impossibility of knowledge. To him it is not only Ahab who is imprisoned within the self; it is in the nature of man to seek but not to find, to look but not to see. Thus he mutters: "I look, you look, he looks; we look, ye look, they look." Little Pip is Melville's Christian caveat. As we are told in "The Castaway" (Chapter 93), Pip "saw God's foot upon the treadle of the loom, and spoke it; and therefore his shipmates called him mad. So man's insanity is heaven's sense. . . ." Heaven's sense may be glimpsed by visionaries, Melville concedes, but it cannot be brought to bear on such actions as are reported in *Moby-Dick*.

As a symbol the whale is endlessly suggestive of meanings. It is as significant and manifold as Nature herself, and, of course, that is the point. Like nature the whale is paradoxically benign and malevolent, nourishing and destructive. It is massive, brutal, monolithic, but at the same time protean, erotically beautiful, infinitely variable. It appears to be unpredictable and mindless; yet it is controlled by certain laws. The chapter on "The Whiteness of the Whale" is a *tour de force* of learning and ingenuity such as Melville liked to get off. It remains, however, rather inert, and like some of the excessively extended chapters on cetology,

or the interpolated story of the Town-Ho, it forces us to step outside the action of the book in order to take in a sort of sideshow
at a moment when we are all for getting on with the main event.
Still the idea of the whale's whiteness is indispensable. Whiteness
is the paradoxical color, the color that involves all the contradictions Melville attributes to nature. It signifies death and corruption as readily as virginal purity, innocence, and youth. It has
the advantage of being, from one point of view, the color that
contains all colors, whereas from another point of view, it suggests
a *tabula rasa* which may be imaginatively endowed with significance according to the desire or obsession of him who beholds it.
It also readily suggests the sense of the uncanny or the preter-
natural out of which mythic and religious ideas are formed.

As Melville writes:

> Is it that by its indefiniteness it shadows forth the heartless voids and
> immensities of the universe, and thus stabs us from behind with the
> thought of annihilation, when beholding the white depths of the milky
> way? Or is it, that as in essence whiteness is not so much a color as the
> visible absence of color, and at the same time the concrete of all colors;
> is it for these reasons that there is such a dumb blankness, full of mean-
> ing, in a wide landscape of snows—a colorless, all-color of atheism from
> which we shrink?

These rhetorical questions help us to understand what Melville
has in mind. Yet the most memorable passages about the whiteness of the whale are in other chapters where Melville the unsur-
passable poet lays aside the rather awkward philosophizings that
encumber portions of his book. The essential voice of Melville
is to be heard in the half humorous, subtly erotic lyric tone
which is peculiar to *Moby-Dick:*

> A gentle joyousness—a mighty mildness of repose in swiftness, in-
> vested the gliding whale. Not the white bull Jupiter swimming away
> with ravished Europa clinging to his graceful horns; his lovely, leering
> eyes sideways intent upon the maid; with smooth bewitching fleetness,
> rippling straight for the nuptial bower in Crete; not Jove, not that great
> majesty Supreme! did surpass the glorified White Whale as he so
> divinely swam.

But we should not think Melville a very great poet if he had not
written passages like the following (from "The Funeral," Chapter
69):

The vast tackles have now done their duty. The peeled white body of the beheaded whale flashes like a marble sepulchre; though changed in hue, it has not perceptibly lost anything in bulk. It is still colossal. Slowly it floats more and more away, the water round it torn and splashed by the insatiate sharks, and the air above vexed with rapacious flights of screaming fowls, whose beaks are like so many insulting poniards in the whale. The vast white headless phantom floats further and further from the ship, and every rod that it so floats, what seem square roods of sharks and cubic roods of fowls, augment the murderous din. For hours and hours from the almost stationary ship that hideous sight is seen. Beneath the unclouded and mild azure sky, upon the fair face of the pleasant sea, wafted by the joyous breezes, that great mass of death floats on and on, till lost in infinite perspectives.

The point of these remarks on "the meaning of *Moby-Dick*" will have been missed unless it is seen that they attribute a less manifold meaning to the book than is sometimes attributed to it. The symbols are manifold and suggestive; the epic scope is opulent; the rhetoric is full and various; the incidental actions and metaphors are richly absorbing. The meaning is profound. But at the same time it is narrow. The issues, as opposed to the states of mind and feeling they generate, are all simplified; they are abstracted and compressed to a degree incompatible with the broader reach, the more comprehensive concreted significance of greater poems like *King Lear*, *The Divine Comedy*, or *The Iliad*. These poems bring to the given facts of human destiny a universal tragic conception of their meaning. Melville's mind, no less profound in its intuitive sense of life, is nevertheless comparatively narrow and abstract. In this as in its incomparable discoveries of language, its appropriation of new subject matters, and its opening out of new aesthetic experience, *Moby-Dick* is at once the most startling and the most characteristic product of the American imagination.

WILLIAM DEAN HOWELLS

"Mr. James is cosmopolitan and Mr. Howells is American"

THE SATURDAY REVIEW

Starting with a comparison between Henry James (1843–1916) and his friend William Dean Howells (1837–1920), somewhat to the advantage of the latter, the writer of this article (which originally appeared in the British periodical *The Saturday Review* and was reprinted in *The Critic* of New York) then chooses *The Rise of Silas Lapham* (1885) as showing Howells' "Americanness" at its most conspicuous. For in the novel Howells has portrayed a type ("There are thousands of Silas Laphams throughout the United States"). Bret Harte, George W. Cable, Mark Twain, Henry James—none of them gives us "the average American of to-day." Howells not only gives us real people, he gives us pleasant people, for he "thoroughly understands the Great American Joke." The reviewer, however, does not neglect form; he praises Howells' skill in construction, comparing him to "the masters of the Dutch school" in his infinite care for detail and his finished composition.

SAINTE-BEUVE WAS wont to be severe on those who are prone to repeat ready-made opinions got one one scarce knows how. Reviewers have as much of the parrot in them as have other people, perhaps, and they are as carelessly likely to echo an error —for even the critic is human and liable to err. We must needs bear this in mind when we see the frequent setting apart and together of the writings of Mr. W. D. Howells and of Mr. Henry

"The Rise of Silas Lapham," in *The Critic*, n. s., IV (November 7, 1885), 224–225.

James, as though they were essentially alike and closely related. Both of these accomplished authors are Americans; both have resided at or near the Hub of the Universe, and have breathed the air of culture which glistens with the gilt reflection of the dome of Boston Courthouse; both came before the British public at almost the same time, and were accepted as writers of remarkable gifts; and both, finally, write novels in accordance with the tenets of realistic art. But here, in the main, the resemblance ceases. Mr. James, the novelist, is a very different person from Mr. Howells, the novelist; and the novels of Mr. James are very different in matter and in manner from the novels of Mr. Howells. The most striking and radical difference between the two writers is that Mr. James is cosmopolitan and Mr. Howells is American. Mr. James might take for his motto that scrap from some forgotten Italian *opera-buffa* which, as M. Bourget has recently reminded us, was adopted by Stendhal, 'Vengo di cosmopoli.' Mr. Howells has been in Italy; but he felt no temptations to belong to other nations, and he remains an American. Mr. James is not a New-Yorker, though he was born in New York; nor a Bostonian, though he has lived in Boston; he is not even an American, and as certainly he is not an Englishman or a Frenchman. He is an observer of extraordinary keenness of insight into national characteristics; but American critics maintain that he understands the Englishman and the Frenchman quite as well as he understands the American. To say this is to say that Mr. James is a foreigner even in the land of his birth, and that his Americans, like his English and his French, clever as they are, brilliantly as they are painted, and sharply as they are drawn, are all of them seen from the outside only, and are never illumined by the penetrating inner light of national sympathy. Now Mr. Howells knows his America, and he feels it; he is in sympathy with it; he knows what it means; he enjoys it, and he loves it. Mr. Howells has travelled; he is not in the least provincial; he has dwelt in Italy and absorbed its beauty, and he has studied its literature with loving delight; but he remains an American to the backbone.

In none of Mr. Howells's books is his Americanness more conspicuous than in his latest, and perhaps this is one of the reasons why we are inclined to think that 'The Rise of Silas Lapham' is in many respects the best novel he has yet written. Of his earlier stories, 'The Undiscovered Country' has always been our favorite;

and it may be that there is nothing in 'The Rise of Silas Lapham' more skilful than the way in which Mr. Howells mingled the mysterious with the commonplace, the natural with the super-natural, without shock or jar or discordance. But, although Mr. Howells may not be any more adroit in his later story, he has had a finer subject—a subject more characteristically American, a subject far broader in its interest, and the result is a very re-markable story. 'The Rise of Silas Lapham' is a novel which no one can neglect who cares to understand American character. Any one who wishes to gain an insight into the conditions of life in America, and to peer into its social complexities, cannot do better than to give his days and nights to the study of Mr. Howells's stories in general and of 'The Rise of Silas Lapham' in particular. America, and the average American of to-day, are not to be found in the picturesque pages of Mr. Bret Harte or of Mr. George W. Cable, any more than they are to be sought in the 'Biglow Papers,' or in Mark Twain's joyful pages, or in the very clever tales of Mr. Henry James. They are here—in the pages of Mr. Howells— as they are to be found nowhere else, except in real life. Mr. Howells has seen and he has understood and he has recorded, and his record is true. Of the truth of the characters in 'The Rise of Silas Lapham' there can be no doubt in the mind of any one who knows the American people of to-day. Silas Lapham himself is a type. There are thousands of Silas Laphams throughout the United States. Mr. John T. Raymond, the comedian who acts Colonel Sellers with so comic a zest, has said that there is not a town in the United States in which he has played the part where some one has not represented himself as the original of the sanguine and chivalric speculator. And there is hardly a village in the United States—at least in that part of the United States which is peopled by the original New England stock—where Silas Lapham has not many originals. Strong, gentle, pushing, perti-nacious, bragging unconsciously, scrupulous with the scrupulous-ness of the New England conscience, provincial, limited in his ideas, and yet not hostile to the light in so far as he can perceive it, Silas Lapham is an American type which has never before been so boldly presented. As characteristically American, however, and as true to life, is the elder Corey, the man of family, of breed-ing, of culture, of inherited traditions; but where there are ten thousand Silas Laphams there are only a thousand, or perhaps a hundred, Coreys. The contrast between Lapham and Corey, between Mrs. Lapham and Mrs. Corey, between Lapham's daughters and the more remotely presented daughters of Mr. Corey, is admirable in its truth and in its humor. Indeed the humor of Mr. Howells's story is quite as remarkable as its truth. Mr. Howells himself thoroughly understands the Great American Joke. Many, if not most, of his characters have a leaven of comedy—and Mr. Howells's comedy is always delightful. Mr. Corey on one side, and Penelope Lapham on the other, are not only humorous in themselves, but they have a strong sense of humor—and that toleration of others which only a strong sense of humor can give. In 'A Modern Instance' many, too many, of the people presented to us were unpleasant persons, whose acquaintance in real life we should not desire to cultivate; but in 'The Rise of Silas Lapham' most of the people are as pleasant as may be, honest, kindly, good people, good-looking, and taking the world easily; and yet even under these circumstances the quenching, or overshadowing rather, of Penelope Lapham's humor when there comes to her the great joy, which is a great sorrow also, and which leaves her long in doubt and darkness, is resented by the reader almost as though there were a falling-off in the *vis comica* of the writer.

Another of the many differences which divide Mr. Howells from Mr. James is the disagreement in their views as to the construction of a story. Mr. James, it seems to us, has been too long and too much under the influence of the latter-day French novelists, and from them he has caught the contagion of Impressionism —if we may venture to use the term. By this we mean chiefly that he seems to think it sufficient to give an impression of life, however brief and fleeting; and also that he inclines to hold manner more important than matter, and to think that how a thing is told is of higher value than what the thing told is in itself. As in real life a story does not come to an end symmetrically, so in his tales Mr. James is willing to let the tags of his threads hang out of the pattern, dangling, while the pattern itself fades away indefinitely. Now Mr. Howells clings firmly to the good old doctrine that art is not raw nature, and that a work of literary art must have a beginning, a middle, and an end, as a work of pictorial art must have a corresponding composition. Mr. James, only too often, offers us a cross-section of life seen under a microscope. Mr. Howells always attempts a finished picture—in the manner of

the masters of the Dutch school, it is true, and with infinite care
in the proper portrayal of the infinitely little. But his picture,
however small its scale, is a work of art; it is not a photograph
or a microscopic mount. His composition—what the French playwrights would call his *charpente*—is as careful and as skillful as
though he were about to attempt a historic battle-piece of the
most heroic proportions. Mr. Howells plans his tiny little garden
with as much fore-thought and ingenuity as Walter Scott, for
example, laid out his large parks. The movement of one of his
novels may be languid or even sluggish, but it is unhesitating,
and direct, and resistless. To any one who has followed Mr.
Howells's literary career with attention, it is evident that he has
studied the art of the novelist with increasing attention and that
he has slowly taught himself the trade. He began with the sketches
of Italian life and character; then he returned to America, and
used the skill thus acquired on the more familiar American subjects. We see the result in the volume called 'Suburban Sketches,'
not yet, we think, reprinted in England. Then he ventured on
'Their Wedding Journey,' a sketch of travel, with only the very
slightest thread of a story. This was followed by 'A Chance Acquaintance,' in which the texture of the story was a little stronger,
although even here the scenery was quite as important as the
characters. And thus he has gone on slowly proving himself and
training his hand until he has at last attained the mastery of narrative which we see in 'The Rise of Silas Lapham.' In the first
chapter we are plunged at once *in medias res,* and we learn the
history of Silas Lapham, and we get an insight into his character,
and we glean hints as to the other members of his family, all by
the simple device, as ingenious and novel as it is simple, of giving
the reader an exact report of the conversation which took place
between Silas Lapham and the reporter who was sent to interview him for the series of interviews which was to be called 'The
Solid Men of Boston.' Not less skilful is the author's setting forth
of Lapham's final fall, with the intervals of doubt and hope and
fear, with the occasional moments when it again seemed possible
that financial ruin might be averted, and with the perfectly steady
movement towards the inevitable crash at last. The effect of
these apparent fluctuations on the family, on the wife and on the
two daughters who are the two heroines of the story, is wonder-

fully well told. Of these two daughters the elder, Penelope, is at once more lifelike and more interesting than the younger and more beautiful Irene, who is well conceived and well presented, and who, however, does not impress the reader as quite as near to the real flesh and blood of womanhood as her plainer sister. As to the story itself, we have left ourselves space to say nothing. It is a love story, of course, for Mr. Howells clings to the old formulas in more ways than one; but the love interest is altogether subsidiary to the development, or rather to the presentation, of the character of Silas Lapham. It is a love story with a happy ending; although the heroine is for a while tossed between the horns of a most delightful dilemma, as perplexing as it is novel.

"A vivifying faith Mr. Howells may distinctly be said to possess"

HENRY JAMES

The friendship between William Dean Howells and Henry James lasted all their lives. When this article was written, in 1886, James had gone to live in England, and henceforth the scene of most of his novels was to be European. Their conceptions of realism were to diverge more and more widely. In this appreciative comment on his friend, James reveals his sense of the inadequacy of Howells's realism when he says of it, "If American life is on the whole, as I make no doubt whatever, more innocent than that of any other country, nowhere is the fact more patent than in Mr. Howells's novels, which exhibit so constant a study of the actual and so small a perception of evil."

From Henry James, "William Dean Howells," *Harper's Weekly*, XXX (June 19, 1886), 394. Reprinted in *The Shock of Recognition*, ed. Edmund Wilson (Farrar, Straus & Cudahy, Inc., 1955), pp. 575–577.

It is a singular circumstance that to know what one wishes to do should be, in the field of art, a rare distinction; but it is incontestable that, as one looks about in our English and American fiction, one does not perceive any very striking examples of a vivifying faith. There is no discussion of the great question of how best to write, no exchange of ideas, no vivacity nor variety of experiment. A vivifying faith Mr. Howells may distinctly be said to possess, and he conceals it so little as to afford every facility to those people who are anxious to prove that it is the wrong one. He is animated by a love of the common, the immediate, the familiar and vulgar elements of life, and holds that in proportion as we move into the rare and strange we become vague and arbitrary; that truth of representation, in a word, can be achieved only so long as it is in our power to test and measure it. He thinks scarcely anything too paltry to be interesting, that the small and the vulgar have been terribly neglected, and would rather see an exact account of a sentiment or a character he stumbles against every day than a brilliant evocation of a passion or a type he has never seen and does not even particularly believe in. He adores the real, the natural, the colloquial, the moderate, the optimistic, the domestic, and the democratic; looking askance at exceptions and perversities and superiorities, at surprising and incongruous phenomena in general. One must have seen a great deal before one concludes; the world is very large, and life is a mixture of many things; she by no means eschews the strange, and often risks combinations and effects that make one rub one's eyes. Nevertheless, Mr. Howells' standpoint is an excellent one for seeing a large part of the truth, and even if it were less advantageous, there would be a great deal to admire in the firmness with which he has planted himself. He hates a "story," and (this private feat is not impossible) has probably made up his mind very definitely as to what the pestilent thing consists of. In this respect he is more logical than M. Émile Zola, who partakes of the same aversion, but has greater lapses as well as greater audacities. Mr. Howells hates an artificial fable and a *denouément* that is pressed into the service; he likes things to occur as they occur in life, where the manner of a great many of them is not to occur at all. He has observed that heroic emotion and brilliant opportunity are not particularly interwoven with our days, and indeed, in the way of omission, he *has* often practiced in his pages a very considerable boldness. It has not, however, made what we find there any less interesting and less human.

The picture of American life on Mr. Howells' canvas is not of a dazzling brightness, and many readers have probably wondered why it is that (among a sensitive people) he has so successfully escaped the imputation of a want of patriotism. The manners he describes—the desolation of the whole social prospect in *A Modern Instance* is perhaps the strongest expression of those influences —are eminently of a nature to discourage the intending visitor, and yet the westward pilgrim continues to arrive, in spite of the Bartley Hubbards and the Laphams, and the terrible practices at the country hotel in *Doctor Breen,* and at the Boston boarding-house in *A Woman's Reason.* This tolerance of depressing revelations is explained partly, no doubt, by the fact that Mr. Howells' truthfulness imposes itself—the representation is so vivid that the reader accepts it as he accepts, in his own affairs, the mystery of fate—and partly by a very different consideration, which is simply that if many of his characters are disagreeable, almost all of them are extraordinarily good, and with a goodness which is a ground for national complacency. If American life is on the whole, as I make no doubt whatever, more innocent than that of any other country, nowhere is the fact more patent than in Mr. Howells' novels, which exhibit so constant a study of the actual and so small a perception of evil. His women, in particular, are of the best—except, indeed, in the sense of being the best to live with. Purity of life, fineness of conscience, benevolence of motive, decency of speech, good nature, kindness, charity, tolerance (though, indeed, there is little but each other's manners for the people to tolerate), govern all the scene; the only immoralities are aberrations of thought, like that of Silas Lapham, or excesses of beer, like that of Bartley Hubbard. In the gallery of Mr. Howells' portraits there are none more living than the admirable, humorous images of those two ineffectual sinners. Lapham, in particular, is magnificent, understood down to the ground, inside and out—a creation which does Mr. Howells the highest honor. I do not say that the figure of his wife is as good as his own, only because I wish to say that it is as good as that of the minister's wife in the history of *Lemuel Barker,* which is unfolding itself from month to month at the moment I write. These two ladies are exhaustive renderings of the type of virtue that worries. But everything in Silas Lapham is superior—nothing more so than the whole picture of casual female youth and contemporaneous "engaging" one's self, in the daughters of the proprietor of the mineral paint.

"He was the dean of the national letters"

H. L. MENCKEN

This half-mocking tribute by the champion of a new kind of realism to the dean of the older kind expresses relief at the close of an era but a real sense of loss as well. Few literary men since William D. Howells have been able to play such a distinguished public role and at the same time preserve their artistic integrity.

THE DEATH OF William Dean Howells in 1920 brought to an end a decorous and orderly era in American letters, and issued in a sort of anarchy. One may best describe the change, perhaps, by throwing it into dramatic form. Suppose Joseph Conrad and Anatole France were still alive and on their way to the United States on a lecture tour, or to study Prohibition or sex hygiene, or to pay their respects to Henry Ford. Suppose they were to arrive in New York at 2 p.m. today. Who would go down the bay on a revenue-cutter to meet them—that is, who in addition to the newspaper reporters and baggage-searchers—who to represent American Literature? I can't think of a single fit candidate. So long as Howells kept to his legs he was chosen almost

Reprinted from H. L. Mencken, "Want Ad," in *Prejudices: Fifth Series*, by permission of Alfred A. Knopf, Inc. Copyright 1926 by Alfred A. Knopf, Inc. Reprinted in *The Shock of Recognition*, ed. Edmund Wilson (New York: Farrar, Straus & Cudahy, Inc., 1955), pp. 1238–1241.

automatically for all such jobs, for he was the dean of the national letters, and acknowledged to be such by everyone. Moreover, he had experience at the work and a natural gift for it. He looked well in funeral garments. He had a noble and ancient head. He made a neat and caressing speech. He understood etiquette. And before he came to his growth, stretching back into the past, there was a long line precisely like him—Mark Twain, General Lew Wallace, James Russell Lowell, Edmund Clarence Stedman, Richard Watson Gilder, Bryant, Emerson, Irving, Cooper, and so on back to the dark abysm of time.

Such men performed a useful and highly onerous function. They represented letters in all public and official ways. When there was a grand celebration at one of the older universities they were present in their robes, freely visible to the lowliest sophomore. When there was a great banquet, they sat between generals in the Army and members of the firm of J. P. Morgan & Company. When there was a solemn petition or protest to sign— against fiat money, the massacres in Armenia, municipal corruption, or the lack of international copyright—they signed in fine round hands, not for themselves alone, but for the whole fraternity of American literati. Most important of all, when a literary whale from foreign parts was sighted off Fire Island, they jumped into their frock coats, clapped on their plug-hats, and made the damp, windy trip through the Narrows on the revenue-cutter, to give the visitor welcome in the name of the eminent living and the illustrious dead. It was by such men that Dickens was greeted, and Thackeray, and Herbert Spencer, and Max O'Rell, and Blasco Ibáñez, and Matthew Arnold, and James M. Barrie, and Kipling, and (until they found his bootleg wife under his bed) Maxim Gorky. I name names at random. No worthy visitor was overlooked. Always there was the stately committee on the revenue-cutter, always there was the series of polite speeches, and always there was the general feeling that the right thing had been done in the right way—that American literature had been represented in a tasteful and resounding manner.

Who is to represent it today? I search the country without finding a single suitable candidate, to say nothing of a whole posse. Turn, for example, to the mystic nobles of the American Academy of Arts and Letters. I pick out five at random: William C. Brownell, Augustus Thomas, Hamlin Garland, Owen Wister, and Henry van Dyke. What is wrong with them? The plain but dreadful fact that no literary foreigner has even heard of them —that their appearance on the deck of his incoming barge would puzzle and alarm him, and probably cause him to call for the police. These men do not lack the homely virtues. They spell correctly, write neatly, and print nothing that is not constructive. In the five of them there is not enough sin to raise a congressman's temperature one-hundredth of a degree. But they are completely devoid of what is absolutely essential to the official life: they have, so to speak, no stage presence. There is nothing rotund and gaudy about them. No public and unanimous reverence bathes them. What they write or say never causes any talk. To be welcomed by them, jointly or severally, would appear to Thomas Hardy or Gabriel D'Annunzio as equal to being welcomed by representatives of the St. Joe, Mo., Rotary Club. Nor do I find any better stock among their heirs and apprentices in the National Institute. Put Henry Sydnor Harrison, say, against Howells: it is a wart succeeding Ossa. Match Clayton Hamilton with Edmund Clarence Stedman: Broadway against Wall Street. Shove Robert W. Chambers or Herman Hagedorn into the coat of Lowell: he would rattle in one of its pockets.

Worse, there are no better candidates outside the academic cloister. I daresay that most literate foreigners, asked to name the principal American novelist in practice today, would nominate Theodore Dreiser. He would get probably 75 per cent of the votes, with the rest scattered among Upton Sinclair, Sinclair Lewis, Cabell, Hergesheimer, and Sherwood Anderson. But try to imagine any of these gentlemen togged out in a long-tailed coat, shivering on the deck of a revenue-cutter while Gerhart Hauptmann got a grip on himself aboard the *Majestic!* Try to imagine Cabell presiding at a banquet to Knut Hamsun, with Dr. A. Lawrence Lowell to one side of him and Otto Kahn to the other! Try to picture Sinclair handing James Joyce a wreath to put upon the grave of James Whitcomb Riley! The vision, indeed, is more dismal than ludicrous. Howells, the last of his lordly line, is missed tremendously; there is something grievously lacking in the official hospitality of the country. The lack showed itself the instant he was called away. A few weeks later Columbia University gave a soirée in honor of the centenary of Lowell. The president of Columbia, Dr. Nicholas Murray Butler, is a realist. Moreover, he is a member of the American Academy himself, elected as a wet to succeed Edgar Allan Poe. He was thus privy to the deficiencies of his colleagues. To conceal the flabbiness of the evening he shoved them into back seats—and invited John D. Rockefeller, Jr., Tex Rickard, General Pershing, and the board of governors of the New York Stock Exchange to the platform!

I believe that, of living masters of letters, H. G. Wells was the first to feel the new chill. When he last visited the republic he was made welcome by a committee of ship-news reporters. It was as if one of the justices of the King's Bench, landing in America, had been received by a committee of police-court lawyers from Gary, Ind. Later on American literature bestirred itself and gave Wells a banquet in New York. I was present at this feast, and a singular one it was. Not a single author read in Iowa or taught at Harvard was present. The principal literatus at the board was the late Frank A. Munsey, author of *Derringforth* and *The Boy Broker*, and the principal address was made by Max Eastman, formerly editor of the *Masses!* . . .

I come to a constructive suggestion. Let the literati of America meet in their respective places of social relaxation, each gang determining the credentials of its own members, and elect delegates to a national convention. Then let the national convention, by open ballot, choose ten spokesmen and ten alternates to represent the national letters on all formal occasions—not only when an eminent foreigner is to be made welcome, but also when Columbia University holds memorial services, when a President is inaugurated, when Harvard meets Yale, when monuments are unveiled —in brief, at all times of solemn public ceremonial. Let these representatives practice deportment and elocution. Let them employ good tailors and trustworthy bootleggers. I have, alas, no candidates for the committee. As I have said, there is a dreadful dearth of them. Does Dr. Frank Crane wear whiskers? If so, I nominate him.

HENRY JAMES

"The passion of it, the continual passion of it in this man who, fools said, didn't 'feel'"

EZRA POUND

In 1918 Ezra Pound, as foreign editor of the *Little Review*, instituted the first symposium (many were to follow) on Henry James, contributing himself the essay from which we quote. Pound enjoyed nothing more than a good literary battle, and probably did more to get a hearing for new writers, including Joyce, Eliot, and Wyndham Lewis, than anybody else. But he also changed the literary landscape of the past. This essay shows the kind of importance Pound felt James to have, an importance more and more critics have come to agree on since Pound published his essay.

NO MAN who has not lived on both sides of the Atlantic can well appraise Henry James; his death marks the end of a period. *The Times* says: 'The Americans will understand his changing his nationality,' or something of that sort. The 'Americans' will understand nothing whatsoever about it. They have understood nothing about it. They do not even know what they lost. They have not stopped for eight minutes to consider the

From Ezra Pound, "Henry James," in *Literary Essays of Ezra Pound*, ed. T. S. Eliot, pp. 295–296, 297–298. All rights reserved. Reprinted by permission of New Directions. This essay originally appeared in the *Little Review*, V (August, 1918), 6–9.

meaning of his last public act. After a year of ceaseless labour, of letter writing, of argument, of striving in every way to bring in America on the side of civilization, he died of apoplexy. On the side of civilization—civilization [1] against barbarism, civilization, not Utopia, not a country or countries where the right always prevails in six weeks! After a lifetime spent in trying to make two continents understand each other, in trying, and only his thoughtful readers can have any conception of how he had tried, to make three nations intelligible one to another. I am tired of hearing pettiness talked about Henry James's style. The subject has been discussed enough in all conscience, along with the minor James. Yet I have heard no word of the major James, of the hater of tyranny; book after early book against oppression, against all the sordid petty personal crushing oppression, the domination of modern life; not worked out in the diagrams of Greek tragedy, not labelled 'epos' or 'Aeschylus.' The outbursts in *The Tragic Muse,* the whole of *The Turn of the Screw,* human liberty, personal liberty, the rights of the individual against all sorts of intangible bondage! [2] The passion of it, the continual passion of it in this man who, fools said, didn't 'feel.' I have never yet found a man of emotion against whom idiots didn't raise this cry.

And the great labour, this labour of translation, of making America intelligible, of making it possible for individuals to meet across national borders. I think half the American idiom is recorded in Henry James' writing, and whole decades of American life that otherwise would have been utterly lost, wasted, rotting in the unhermetic jars of bad writing, of inaccurate writing. No

---

[1] 1929. I should probably be incapable of writing this paragraph now. But that is how things looked in 1918 and I see no reason to pretend that I saw them otherwise. I still believe that a Hohenzollern victory would have meant an intolerable post-war world. I think I write this without animus, and that I am quite aware of the German component indispensable to a complete civilization.

[2] This holds, despite anything that may be said of his fuss about social order, social tone. I naturally do not drag in political connotations, from which H.J. was, we believe, wholly exempt. What he fights is 'influence,' the impinging of family pressure, the impinging of one personality on another; all of them in highest degree damn'd, loathsome and detestable. Respect for the peripheries of the individual may be, however, a discovery of our generation; I doubt it, but it seems to have been at low ebb in some districts (not rural) for some time.

English reader will ever know how good are his New York and his New England; no one who does not see his grandmother's friends in the pages of the American books. The whole great assaying and weighing, the research for the significance of nationality, French, English, American.

. . . . .

I am not here to write a full volume of detailed criticism, but two things I do claim which I have not seen in reviewers' essays. First, that there was emotional greatness in Henry James' hatred of tyranny; secondly, that there was titanic volume, weight, in the masses he sets in opposition within his work. He uses forces no whit less specifically powerful than the proverbial 'doom of the house'—Destiny, *Deus ex machina,*—of great traditional art. His art was great art as opposed to over-elaborate or over-refined art by virtue of the major conflicts which he portrays. In his books he showed race against race, immutable; the essential Americanness, or Englishness or Frenchness—in *The American,* the difference between one nation and another; not flag-waving and treaties, not the machinery of government, but 'why' there is always misunderstanding, why men of different race are not the same.

We have ceased to believe that we conquer anything by having Alexander the Great make a gigantic 'joy-ride' through India. We know that conquests are made in the laboratory, that Curie with his minute fragments of things seen clearly in test tubes, in curious apparatus, makes conquests. So, too, in these novels, the essential qualities which make up the national qualities, are found and set working, the fundamental oppositions made clear. This is no contemptible labour. No other writer had so assayed three great nations or even thought of attempting it.

"He had a mind so fine that no idea could violate it"

T. S. ELIOT

In the same number of the *Little Review* (1918) that Pound wrote for, T. S. Eliot was a contributor. His emphasis is somewhat different from Pound's. What Eliot admires is a particular quality of James's intelligence: his ability to apply his analytic acuteness to "a situation, a relation, an atmosphere" and to make everything else—character, plot, general ideas— contributory but subordinate. The penetration we are accustomed to from Mr. Eliot is here, but there is also a sprightliness sometimes missing from his later criticism.

HE WAS A CRITIC who preyed not upon ideas, but upon living beings. It is criticism which is in a very high sense creative. The characters, the best of them, are each a distinct success of creation: Daisy Miller's small brother is one of these. Done in a clean, flat drawing, each is extracted out of a reality of its own, substantial enough; everything given is true for that individual; but what is given is chosen with great art for its place in a general scheme. The general scheme is not one character, nor a group of characters in a plot or merely in a crowd. The focus is a situation, a relation, an atmosphere, to which the characters pay tribute, but being allowed to give only what the writer wants. The real hero, in any of James's stories, is a social entity of which men and women are constituents. It is, in *The Europeans,* that particular conjunction of people at the Wentworth house, a situation in which several memorable scenes are merely timeless parts,

From T. S. Eliot, "Henry James," *Little Review,* V (August, 1918), 45–47. Reprinted in *The Shock of Recognition,* ed. Edmund Wilson (New York: Farrar, Straus & Cudahy, Inc., 1955), 856–858.

only occurring necessarily in succession. In this aspect, you can say that James is dramatic; as what Pinero and Mr. Jones used to do for a large public, James does for the intelligent. It is in the chemistry of these subtle substances, these curious precipitates and explosive gases which are suddenly formed by the contact of mind with mind, that James is unequaled. Compared with James's, other novelists' characters seem to be only accidentally in the same book. Naturally, there is something terrible, as disconcerting as a quicksand, in this discovery, though it only becomes absolutely dominant in such stories as *The Turn of the Screw*. It is partly foretold in Hawthorne, but James carried it much farther. And it makes the reader, as well as the personae, uneasily the victim of a merciless clairvoyance.

James's critical genius comes out most tellingly in his mastery over, his baffling escape from, Ideas; a mastery and an escape which are perhaps the last test of a superior intelligence. He had a mind so fine that no idea could violate it. Englishmen, with their uncritical admiration (in the present age) for France, like to refer to France as the Home of Ideas; a phrase which, if we could twist it into truth, or at least a compliment, ought to mean that in France ideas are very severely looked after; not allowed to stray, but preserved for the inspection of civic pride in a Jardin des Plantes, and frugally dispatched on occasions of public necessity. England, on the other hand, if it is not the Home of Ideas, has at least become infested with them in about the space of time within which Australia has been overrun by rabbits. In England ideas run wild and pasture on the emotions; instead of thinking with our feelings (a very different thing) we corrupt our feelings with ideas; we produce the political, the emotional idea, evading sensation and thought. George Meredith (the disciple of Carlyle) was fertile in ideas; his epigrams are a facile substitute for observation and inference. Mr. Chesterton's brain swarms with ideas; I see no evidence that it thinks. James in his novels is like the best French critics in maintaining a point of view, a viewpoint untouched by the parasite idea. He is the most intelligent man of his generation.

The fact of being everywhere a foreigner was probably an assistance to his native wit. Since Byron and Landor, no Englishman appears to have profited much from living abroad. We have had Birmingham seen from Chelsea, but not Chelsea seen (really *seen*) from Baden or Rome. There are advantages, indeed, in coming from a large flat country which no one wants to visit: advantages which both Turgenev and James enjoyed. These advantages have not won them recognition. Europeans have preferred to take their notion of the Russian from Dostoevski and their notion of the American from, let us say, Frank Norris if not O. Henry. Thus, they fail to note that there are many kinds of *their* fellow-countrymen, and that most of these kinds, similarly to the kinds of their fellow-countrymen, are stupid; likewise with Americans. Americans also have encouraged this fiction of a general type, a formula or idea, usually the predaceous square-jawed or thin-lipped. They like to be told that they are a race of commercial buccaneers. It gives them something easily escaped from, moreover, when they wish to reject America. Thus the novels of Frank Norris have succeeded in both countries; though it is curious that the most valuable part of *The Pit* is its satire (quite unconscious, I believe; Norris was simply representing faithfully the life he knew) of Chicago society after business hours. All this show of commercialism which Americans like to present to the foreign eye James quietly waves aside; and in pouncing upon his fellow-countryman after the stock exchange has closed, in tracking down his vices and absurdities across the Atlantic, and exposing them in their highest flights of dignity or culture, James may be guilty of what will seem to most Americans scandalously improper behavior. It is too much to expect them to be grateful. And the British public, had it been more aware, would hardly have been more comfortable confronted with a smile which was so far from breaking into the British laugh. Henry James's death, if it had been more taken note of, should have given considerable relief "on both sides of the Atlantic," and cemented the Anglo-American Entente.

"He is the culmination of the Superficial type"

H. G. WELLS

H. G. Wells (1866–1946) probably met Henry James in 1898, when Wells was thirty-two and James was fifty-five. Their association was a curious one, and though there is little doubt of its original warmth and sincerity, from the beginning their opposed attitudes toward life and art held the seeds of their famous later disagreement. In 1914 James wrote an article for *The Times Literary Supplement* called "The Younger Generation" in which he took the measure of his rising juniors and in which he saw Wells and Arnold Bennett as writers who "squeeze out to the utmost the plump and more or less juicy orange of a particular acquainted state and let this affirmation of energy, however directed or undirected, constitute for them the 'treatment' of the theme." Wells had been working on *Boon*, a book in which the imaginary George Boon gives his frank opinions of the literary world, for more than a decade. But it was only after reading James's article that Wells added his notorious chapter of parody and criticism of James. Wells's attitude is by no means dead even today.

"BUT JAMES has never discovered that a novel isn't a picture. . . . That life isn't a studio. . . .

"He wants a novel to be simply and completely *done*. He wants it to have a unity, he demands homogeneity. . . . Why *should* a book have that? For a picture it's reasonable, because you have

From H. G. Wells, "Of Art, of Literature, of Mr. Henry James," in *Boon* (London, 1915), pp. 101–105. Copyright 1915 by T. Fisher. Reprinted by permission of Paul Reynolds & Son, 599 Fifth Avenue, New York 17, New York. Reprinted in *Henry James and H. G. Wells*, ed. Leon Edel and Gordon N. Ray (Urbana, Ill.: University of Illinois Press, 1958), pp. 244–247.

to see it all at once. But there's no need to see a book all at once. It's like wanting to have a whole county done in one style and period of architecture. It's like insisting that a walking tour must stick to one valley. . . .

"But James *begins* by taking it for granted that a novel is a work of art that must be judged by its oneness. Judged first by its oneness. Some one gave him that idea in the beginning of things and he has never found it out. He doesn't find things out. He doesn't even seem to want to find things out. You can see that in him; he is eager to accept things—elaborately. You can see from his books that he accepts etiquettes, precedences, associations, claims. That is his peculiarity. He accepts very readily and then—elaborates. He has, I am convinced, one of the strongest, most abundant minds alive in the whole world, and he has the smallest penetration. Indeed, he has no penetration. He is the culmination of the Superficial type. Or else he would have gone into philosophy and been greater even than his wonderful brother. . . . But here he is, spinning about, like the most tremendous of water-boatmen—you know those insects?—kept up by surface tension. As if, when once he pierced the surface, he would drown. It's incredible. A water-boatman as big as an elephant. I was reading him only yesterday—'The Golden Bowl'; it's dazzling how never for a moment does he go through."

"Recently he's been explaining himself," said Dodd.

"His 'Notes on Novelists.' It's one sustained demand for the picture effect. Which is the denial of the sweet complexity of life, of the pointing this way and that, of the spider on the throne. Philosophy aims at a unity and never gets there. . . . That true unity which we all suspect, and which no one attains, if it is to be got at all it is to be got by penetrating, penetrating down and through. The picture, on the other hand, is forced to a unity because it can see only one aspect at a time. I am doubtful even about that. Think of Hogarth or Carpaccio. But if the novel is to follow life it must be various and discursive. Life is diversity and entertainment, not completeness and satisfaction. All actions are half-hearted, shot delightfully with wandering thoughts—about something else. All true stories are a felt of irrelevances. But James sets out to make his novels with the presupposition that they can be made continuously relevant. And perceiving the discordant things, he tries to get rid of them. He sets himself to pick the straws out of the hair of Life before he paints her. But without the straws she is no longer the mad woman we love. He talks of 'selection,' and of making all of a novel definitely *about* a theme. He objects to a 'saturation' that isn't oriented. And he objects, if you go into it, for no clear reason at all. Following up his conception of selection, see what in his own practice he omits. In practice James's selection becomes just omission and nothing more. He omits everything that demands digressive treatment or collateral statement. For example, he omits opinions. In all his novels you will find no people with defined political opinions, no people with religious opinions, none with clear partisanships or with lusts or whims, none definitely up to any specific impersonal thing. There are no poor people dominated by the imperatives of Saturday night and Monday morning, no dreaming types—and don't we all more or less live dreaming? And none are ever decently forgetful. All that much of humanity he clears out before he begins his story. It's like cleaning rabbits for the table."

"An absorbing figure, an immortal symbol"

VAN WYCK BROOKS

Henry James's long self-imposed exile from America has been variously evaluated. To some of his contemporaries it seemed a kind of treachery, whereas to more recent critics it has seemed a peculiar and necessary advantage for his kind of art. To Van Wyck Brooks in 1925 James seemed to have lost a great deal both as man and artist by uprooting himself. The following passage eloquently recreates the nostalgia for home Brooks imagined James to have felt.

From Van Wyck Brooks, *The Pilgrimage of Henry James* (New York: E. P. Dutton & Co., Inc., 1925), p. 169. Reprinted by permission of the publisher.

A$_N$ ABSORBING FIGURE, an immortal symbol. For is he not the embodiment, complete and unparalleled, of that deep, that impossible yearning of which Hawthorne somewhere speaks—the yearning of the American in the Old World, "of the blood within his veins, for that from which it has been estranged, the half-fanciful regret that he should ever have been separated from these woods, these fields, these natural features of scenery, to which his nature was moulded, from the men who are still so like himself, from these habits of life and thought (though he may not have known them for two centuries) he still perceives to have remained in some mysterious way latent in the depths of his character, and soon to be reassumed, not as a foreigner would do it, but like habits native to him, and only suspended for a season"?

"Can it be true that he is the novelist of haters?"

SHERWOOD ANDERSON

Sherwood Anderson (1876–1941) is about as different a writer from Henry James as H. G. Wells is. But Anderson's admiration for Van Wyck Brooks led him to try James out. Is his comment a penetrating truth or a misunderstanding?

Y$_{OU}$ HAVE A KIND of power over my mind, Van Wyck, of making me think of what you are thinking, and so I got James on my mind after you got to work at him. You may be interested

Sherwood Anderson, letter to Van Wyck Brooks (Reno, before July 30, 1923) in *Letters of Sherwood Anderson*, ed. Howard Mumford Jones and Walter B. Rideout (Boston: Little, Brown & Company, 1953), pp. 102–103. Copyright 1953 by Eleanor Anderson. Reprinted by permission of Little, Brown & Company.

to know my reactions to some solid weeks of James reading—the feeling of him as a man who never found anyone to love—who did not dare love. I really can't care much for any character after he gets through with it; he, in short, takes my love from me too.

I've a fancy—can it be true that he is the novelist of the haters? O[h], the thing infinitely refined and carried far into the field of intellectuality, as skillful haters find out how to do.

It is, you see, but a notion, but I thought it might interest you. . . .

"Fashion took him abroad—
fashion made it natural for
him to go—but it was not
fashion that led him to stay"

WRIGHT MORRIS

Sometimes the conflict between attitudes toward art and experience takes the form we have seen in the difference between Henry James and H. G. Wells; the latter wanted to use art to change the world whereas the former accepted the world and used art as a way of perceiving and evaluating experience. Unlike Thoreau, Whitman, Melville, Mark Twain—men who sought escape from civilization in their various ways—James plunged into "the wilderness of culture." Wright Morris in his recent survey (1958) of American literature sees James as a bridge between the past and the present, and as deeply and truly American. The problem of James's exile is not *his* problem, it is ours.

From *The Territory Ahead*, pp. 97–99. © 1957, 1958 by Wright Morris. Reprinted by permission of Harcourt, Brace and Company, Inc.

THE CENTRAL DEFECT in the mind and art of James is a defect of riches—he is simply too much for us. In James, and in James alone, the prevailing tendency of Thoreau's countrymen did not prevail. He did not take to the woods, to the open road, to his idyllic childhood, or to the high seas. He went east and not west. He took to the wilderness of culture, instead. The young and talented aesthete, who at twenty-two reviewed and dispensed with Whitman's barbaric yawp, had a lot to learn about both the old world and the new. He was buoyant on the high and rolling seas of the fashionable cliché. Fashion took him abroad—fashion made it natural for him to go—but it was not fashion that led him to stay. He was the first, of course, to both sense and define his predicament. With his customary insistence on the nuance, since that alone would give him the correct shade of meaning, he coined a word to describe his situation.

The word "*dis*patriot" carries the same charge, and much the same meaning, as the word "disinterested." It was *dis*interest that encouraged real interest. It was *dis*patriation that encouraged patriation. Expatriate he became when sentiment and passion led him to throw in *his* lot with England—his America, that is—when he felt she was threatened with barbarism. It is likely that his sensitivity to the charge that he had left America led him to coin certain remarks to the contrary—but the place to look for his dispatriation is not in his rejoinders, but in his works. There it is clear that his exile was less a problem for him than it is for us. The question of his exile, if it still exists, is rooted in the need some Americans feel to rid themselves of a problem they do not like, a problem too deep and too thorny to be ignored or absorbed.

James is the archetype of this problem, brought up from our own depths to goad and haunt us, a now-immortal reminder of our fear and distrust of real intelligence. In leaving the country he almost spared us the trouble of *exiling* him. But he was intelligent; even more, he was a writer and craftsman of genius, incurably engaged in the art and practice of prophecy. So he came back—never truly having been away. The only writer who had not taken to the woods, he alone confronted the new culture of cities. He confronted and described the new *business* culture, with its downtown men and its uptown women, its out-of-town children, and its mindless cultural problems. The busy, the tipsy, and Daniel Webster still ruled—but there were changes. What were they? Were they for the better, or the worse?

Of Lady Barberina he wrote:

> It was not in the least of American barbarism that she was afraid. Her dread was all of American civilization.

This will stand as one indictment he never departed from. It was not our barbarism, but our civilization that gave him dread.

"His great theme became that of deprivation—deprivation of life"

MARIUS BEWLEY

In his discussion of what "life" means in Henry James's work, Marius Bewley carries further the analysis that we have already found central in the criticism of James's art. For the American writer, Mr. Bewley says, the first question was to decide what life was not. Isabel Archer, the heroine of *Portrait of a Lady* (1881), is typically Jamesian in finding like the hero of *The Ambassadors* later, that the fuller life "is a matter of refining her consciousness by an ordeal of fire." Because of their Puritan background, James's Americans can never simply enjoy life; to be worth his attention they must discover life by looking for it in themselves, to paraphrase Mr. Bewley. James's greatness lies in his knowledge of the "terrible loss" that being American "foredoomed them to suffer."

J AMES IS THE FIRST great American novelist to have been consciously and explicitly concerned with 'life' in the way that

From Marius Bewley, *The Eccentric Design* (New York: Columbia University Press, 1959), pp. 238–240. Reprinted by permission of Columbia University Press.

D. H. Lawrence, for example, was concerned with it. But to say this is to point, paradoxically, to the impassable abyss that separates them. We are not so much faced with a radical difference between two sensibilities (though there is certainly that) as with a radical difference between two traditions. Lawrence 'treated' life; it was for him the native, natural subject matter, the raw material that was simply there. But in the abstract, intellectualizing, democratic, American tradition, filled with disembodied ideas and aspirations, and empty of the concrete, man-soiled evidences of a living humanity, the first problem was to say what life was. In such a tradition, it is hardly remarkable that the artist, like the theologian proving God's existence, arrived at his positive concept by saying what life was not. James's art is deeply concerned with life, but, confronted with such a problem, 'life' in his fictions often ends up with a negative look. Among the major characters in his work, where is there one to whom we can point as having realized 'life' in larger terms than those supplied by a more deeply sensitized consciousness of the possibilities and values of an experience from which he is usually excluded? Strether, who may be taken as James's ultimate portrayal of the American who has discovered life in Europe, discovers it only to make sure that he keeps nothing for himself. His discovery enables him only to renounce more largely, and on the level of practical living I do not see how his final plight is much better than Bernard Longmore's. James's finest female character (apart from little Maisie), Isabel Archer, relates to Strether in these respects. The fuller life she finds in Europe is a matter of refining her consciousness by an ordeal of fire. If, in the end, she registers more finely, she is left with nothing to register but a life of wretchedness and emotional frustration. The best that James's Americans can do for themselves is to look for a moment at the young artist and his sweetheart in the French inn yard, and deeply recognize that life lies *there*. It is the moment in the rose garden recollected through a life of democratic abstraction and Puritan deprivation.

But this must not be construed as criticism of James. It is only a recognition of the character of his particular problem. I do not like critics who attack James for having 'failed' to treat life, for being sensuously thin, or for not dealing, in more blatant terms, with sexual love. These are the people who mistake the smell of the manured field for the harvested crop. James's fictions are the record of men and women, bleakly deprived through their Puritan, democratic, and American traditions of much that constitutes life for the European artist, searching for means to satisfy their spiritual and emotional needs without sacrificing the good that they already possess, and which Europe cannot provide. It is a search for life, but it is a search in which, by the nature of the case, most are bound to fail. It was only a single couple, after all, that Hawthorne permitted to glimpse the Great Carbuncle, although many began the search. And even for that couple, the vision of the mystic jewel forced them to recognize that the reality they sought was in their own hearts. Europe is a symbol that acts in James's fictions rather like Hawthorne's Great Carbuncle. It shows everybody up for what they really are. In the end, those characters discover life who look for it in themselves, and in this sense Strether and Isabel find it. But this leaves us with a version of 'life' in James that will be almost as unsatisfactory to most people as Hawthorne's 'inner sphere of reality.'

This is not James's fault. Life does not exist in a vacuum. It may be 'the force that through the green fuse drives the flower,' but there has to be a pre-existent pattern of petals for it to actualize, and through which its radiance can glow greenly as the animating impulse sustained through a protracted creative moment. Such conventions as the American tradition could claim tended towards abstraction and speculativeness. Their direction was democratic and levelling, or puritan and repressive. The life of the senses contributed almost nothing. Love between the sexes is handled with a good deal of embarrassment in such a tradition, and the great loves in American literature are between Ishmael and Queequeg, Natty and Chingachgook, Huck and Jim, even perhaps Gatsby and Nick Carraway. For the artist intent on 'treating life,' as James was, the American scene yielded few places for its cultivation. When the American artist dealt with it successfully, it was in the primitive wilderness, on a raft in the middle of the Mississippi, or on a whaling boat in the Pacific, and it is difficult to imagine James at home in any of these places.

James had to find a theme which would make life accessible to 'treatment' in the American world that was inevitably his subject, and with the impoverished materials at hand his great theme became that of deprivation—deprivation of life. And in James the theme *is* a great one because he knew what life was, and what his characters were being deprived of. He not only measured exactly their terrible loss, he understood as well the conditions that foredoomed them to suffer—those native conditions through which James's deprived Americans relate to Hawthorne's excluded ones. But James is far greater than Hawthorne because he possessed a positive knowledge of, and a feeling for, life that eluded the older novelist, and that feeling and knowledge is implicit in what he writes.

MARK TWAIN

"Clemens was sole, incomparable, the Lincoln of our literature"

WILLIAM DEAN HOWELLS

The affection of William Dean Howells for Mark Twain
(Samuel Langhorne Clemens, 1835–1910) comes through with
an intensity and eloquence seldom surpassed in his voluminous
writings. Equally the friend of Clemens and Henry James,
Howells showed a catholicity of taste which does much to
explain his special position in the literary world of his time.

Out of a nature rich and fertile beyond any I have
known, the material given him by the Mystery that makes a man
and then leaves him to make himself over, he wrought a character of high nobility upon a foundation of clear and solid truth.
At the last day he will not have to confess anything, for all his life
was the free knowledge of anyone who would ask him of it. The
Searcher of hearts will not bring him to shame at that day, for
he did not try to hide any of the things for which he was often
so bitterly sorry. He knew where the Responsibility lay, and he
took a man's share of it bravely; but not the less fearlessly he left
the rest of the answer to the God who had imagined men.

It is in vain that I try to give a notion of the intensity with
which he pierced to the heart of life, and the breadth of vision
with which he compassed the whole world, and tried for the
reason of things, and then left trying. We had other meetings,
insignificantly sad and brief; but the last time I saw him alive

From William Dean Howells, *My Mark Twain* (New York: Harper &
Brothers, 1910). Reprinted in *The Shock of Recognition*, ed. Edmund Wilson
(New York: Farrar, Straus & Cudahy, Inc., 1955), pp. 740–741.

was made memorable to me by the kind, clear judicial sense with which he explained and justified the labor unions as the sole present help of the weak against the strong.

Next I saw him dead, lying in his coffin amid those flowers with which we garland our despair in that pitiless hour. After the voice of his old friend Twichell had been lifted in the prayer which it wailed through in broken-hearted supplication, I looked a moment at the face I knew so well; and it was patient with the patience I had so often seen in it: something of puzzle, a great silent dignity, an assent to what must be from the depths of a nature whose tragical seriousness broke in the laughter which the unwise took for the whole of him. Emerson, Longfellow, Lowell, Holmes—I knew them all and all the rest of our sages, poets, seers, critics, humorists; they were like one another and like other literary men; but Clemens was sole, incomparable, the Lincoln of our literature.

"Mark got to that once— when he wrote Huck Finn"

SHERWOOD ANDERSON

Writing to Van Wyck Brooks, Sherwood Anderson suggests an interpretation of Mark Twain that is later developed in Brooks's book on Twain. As we can see, Anderson felt a real kinship for his famous predecessor. For Anderson, the *real* Mark Twain was the man who heard "the whispering of the gods."

A s far as Twain is concerned, we have to remember the influences about him. Remember how he came into literature—the

Sherwood Anderson, letter to Van Wyck Brooks (Chicago, early April, 1918) in *Letters of Sherwood Anderson,* ed. Howard Mumford Jones and Walter B. Rideout (Boston: Little, Brown & Company, 1953), pp. 32–33.

crude buffoon of the early days in the mining camps, the terrible cheap and second-rate humor of much of *Innocents Abroad*. It seems to me that when he began he addressed an audience that gets a big laugh out of the braying of a jackass, and without a doubt Mark often brayed at them. He knew that later. There was tenderness and subtlety in Mark when he grew older.

You get the picture of him, Brooks—the river man who could write going East and getting in with that New England crowd, the fellows from barren hills and barren towns. The best he got out of the bunch was Howells, and Howells did Twain no good.

There's another point, Brooks. I can't help wishing Twain hadn't married such a good woman. There was such a universal inclination to tame the man—to save his soul, as it were. Left alone, I fancy Mark might have been willing to throw his soul overboard and then—ye gods, what a fellow he might have been, what poetry might have come from him. . . .

Well now you see I'm coming around. The cultural fellows got hold of Mark. They couldn't hold him. He was too big and too strong. He brushed their hands aside.

But their words got into his mind. In the effort to get out beyond that he became a pessimist.

Now, Brooks, you know a man cannot be a pessimist who lives near a brook or a cornfield. When the brook chatters or at night when the moon comes up and the wind plays in the corn, a man hears the whispering of the gods.

Mark got to that once—when he wrote Huck Finn. He forgot Howells and the good wife and everyone. Again he was the half savage, tender, god-worshiping, believing boy. He had proud conscious innocence.

I believe he wrote that book in a little hut on a hill on his farm. It poured out of him. I fancy that at night he came down from his hill stepping like a king—a splendid playboy, playing with rivers and men, ending on the Mississippi, on the broad river that is the great artery flowing out of the heart of the land.

"He had reached, in short, the heaven of literature and found it empty"

VAN WYCK BROOKS

The shock of contact between East and West sometimes produced startling results in literary matters. In his *The Ordeal of Mark Twain*, Van Wyck Brooks argues that Howells, far from being a help to his friend, actually contributed to Mark Twain's destruction as an artist. Perhaps it is the sort of thing represented here that Henry James had in mind when he said of his Lady Barberina, "It was not in the least of American barbarism that she was afraid. Her dread was all of American civilization."

PLAINLY IT WAS very little encouragement that Mark Twain's natural genius received from these relentless critics to whom he stood in such subjection, to whom he offered such devotion; for Mr. Howells, too, if we are to accept Mr. Paine's record, seconded him as often as not in these innocuous, infantile ventures, abetting him in the production of "blindfold novelettes" and plays of an abysmal foolishness. As for Mark Twain's unique masterpiece, "Huckleberry Finn," "I like it only tolerably well, as far as I have got," he writes, "and may possibly pigeonhole or burn the MS. when it is done": to which Mr. Paine adds: "It did not fascinate him as did the story of the wandering prince. He persevered only as the story moved him. . . . Apparently, he had not yet acquired confidence or pride enough in poor Huck to exhibit him, even to friends." And quite naturally! His artistic self-respect had been so little developed, had been, in fact, so baffled and abashed by all this mauling and fumbling that he could take no pride in a book which was, precisely, the mirror of the unregenerate past he was doing his best to live down.

Behold Mrs. Clemens, then, in the rôle of critic and censor. A memorandum Mark Twain made at the time when he and she were going over the proofs of "Following the Equator" shows us how she conceived of her task. It is in the form of a dialogue between them:

Page 1,020, 9th line from the top. I think some other word would be better than "stench." You have used that pretty often.

But can't I get it in *any*where? You've knocked it out every time. Out it goes again. And yet "stench" is a noble, good word.

Page 1,038. I hate to have your father pictured as lashing a slave boy.

It's out, and my father is whitewashed.

Page 1,050, 2nd line from the bottom. Change "breech-clout." It's a word that you love and I abominate. I would take that and "offal" out of the language.

You are steadily weakening the English tongue, Livy.

We can see from this that to Mrs. Clemens virility was just as offensive as profanity, that she had no sense of the difference between virility and profanity and vulgarity, that she had, in short, no positive taste, no independence of judgment at all. We can see also that she had no artistic ideal for her husband, that she regarded his natural liking for bold and masculine language, which was one of the outward signs of his latent greatness, merely as a literary equivalent of bad manners, as something that endangered their common prestige in the eyes of conventional public opinion. She condemned his writings, says Mr. Paine, specifically, "for the offense they might give in one way or another"; and that her sole object, however unconscious, in doing this was to further him, not as an artist but as a popular success, and especially as a candidate for gentility, is proved by the fact that she made him, as we observe in the incident of his father and the slave boy, whitewash not only himself but his family history also. And in all this Mr. Howells seconded her. "It skirts a certain kind of fun which you can't afford to indulge in," he reminds our shorn Samson in one of his letters; and again, "I'd have that swearing

out in an instant," the "swearing" in this case being what he himself admits is "so exactly the thing Huck would say"—namely,
"they comb me all to hell." As for Mark Twain himself, he took
it as meekly as a lamb. Mr. Paine tells of a certain story he had
written that was disrespectful to the Archbishop of Canterbury.
Forbidden to print it, he had "laboriously translated it into German, with some idea of publishing it surreptitiously; but his conscience had been too much for him. He had confessed, and even
the German version had been suppressed." And how does he
accept Mr. Howell's injunction about the "swearing" in "Huckleberry Finn"? "Mrs. Clemens received the mail this morning," he
writes, "and the next minute she lit into the study with danger in
her eye and this demand on her tongue, 'Where is the profanity
Mr. Howells speaks of?' Then I had to miserably confess that I
had left it out when reading the MS. to her. Nothing but almost
inspired lying got me out of this scrape with my scalp. Does your
wife give you rats, like that, when you go a little one-sided?"

They are very humiliating, these glimpses of great American
writers behind the scenes, given "rats" by their wives whenever
they stray for an instant from the straight and narrow path that
leads to success. "Once," writes Mr. Paine, "when Sarah Orne
Jewett was with the party—in Rome—he remarked that if the
old masters had labeled their fruit one wouldn't be so likely to
mistake pears for turnips. 'Youth,' said Mrs. Clemens, gravely, 'if
you do not care for these masterpieces yourself, you might at
least consider the feelings of others'; and Miss Jewett, regarding
him severely, added, in her quaint Yankee fashion: 'Now you've
been spoke to!'" Very humiliating, very ignominious, I say, are
these tableaux of "the Lincoln of our literature" in the posture of
an ignorant little boy browbeaten by the dry sisters of Culture-
Philistia. Very humiliating, and also very tragic!

Mark Twain had come East with the only conscious ambition
that Western life had bred in him, the ambition to succeed in a
practical sense, to win wealth and fame. But the poet in him was
still astir, still seeking, seeking, seeking for corroboration, for the
frank hand and the gallant word that might set it free. We know
this from the dim hope of liberation he had associated with the
idea of marriage, and we can guess that his eager desire to meet
"men of superior intellect and character" was more than half a

desire to find some one who could give him that grand conception of the literary life which he had never been able to formulate, some one who could show him how to meet life in the proud, free way of the artist, how to unify himself and focus his powers. Well, he had met the best, the greatest, he had met the man whom the Brahmins themselves had crowned as their successor, he had met Mr. Howells. And in this man of marvelous talent, this darling of all the gods and all the graces, he had encountered once more the eternal, universal, instinctive American subservience to what Mr. Santayana calls "the genteel tradition." He had reached, in short, the heaven of literature and found it empty, and there was nothing beyond for the poet in him to seek.

"The influence of Mark Twain has encouraged discipline and craftsmanship"

HENRY NASH SMITH

With Mark Twain we see another aspect of the problem of Europe for Americans, opposed but complementary to that of Henry James. In the first part of this selection from Henry Nash Smith, we have an acute analysis of Twain's social attitudes and of the meaning of "innocent" as it is used in Twain's *Innocents Abroad* (1869). For Twain the past in Europe represents all that is socially backward and repressive—"monarchy, poverty, illiteracy, dirt, and perhaps most of all, the Church, which stands as the embodiment of all these aspects of the historic past." In the second part Mr. Smith, using *Huckleberry Finn,* points to the

From Henry Nash Smith, "Origins of a Native American Tradition," in *The American Writer and the European Tradition,* ed. Margaret Denny and William H. Gilman (Minneapolis: University of Minnesota Press, 1950), pp. 70–71, 75–77. Copyright 1950 by the University of Minnesota.

inadequacies of the Western literary tradition but concludes
with a demonstration of the importance that book has had
in our literary development.

Iₙ READING Mark Twain's early books we discover at
once that if the westerner turned away from Europe, he frequently
felt the impulse to look over his shoulder. He understood perfectly
that Europe had a monopoly of traditional culture, and that he was
undertaking an audacious experiment when he proposed to get
along without the aid of tradition. The repudiation of Europe is
a different thing from indifference to it.

The most obvious, perhaps the inevitable, attitude which a westerner would take up when he confronted the momentous phenomenon of the Old World was that of an ignoramus, a barbarian—
or, as Mark Twain himself accurately puts it, an innocent. But
these are ambiguous terms. Barbarism implies ignorance and crudity and lack of ethical discipline. Yet it also has its positive aspect: the barbarian can conceive of himself according to the time-
honored conception of the Noble Savage, the man who lacks the
vices as well as the virtues of civilization, and who has an innate
integrity based upon communion with nature. From the earliest
discovery of America, a long succession of writers both in Europe
and later in this country had conceived the Americans in general
after this fashion; and with the increasing social maturity of the
Eastern Seaboard of the United States, the attributes of the Noble
Savage had been ascribed to westerners. Mark Twain alludes to
this set of attitudes when he classes himself as an innocent.

The critique of Europe (or, if you like, of the exaggerated ven-
eration for Europe which Mark Twain detected in his fellow countrymen) that is set forth in *Innocents Abroad* is not merely negative, not merely a destructive burlesque. It is built upon an
affirmation. The Americans, including the author's imaginative projection of himself, stand for purity, for naiveté, for progress and
democracy and the future. The Europe against which they array
themselves is not merely acres of Rubenses, but the past in general:
monarchy, poverty, illiteracy, dirt, and perhaps most of all, the
Church, which stands as the embodiment of all these aspects of
the historic past. In other words, Mark Twain's social judgments
tend again and again toward the general position of eighteenth-

century radicalism. Minnie Brashear has demonstrated that these ideas were current in the Missouri of Mark Twain's youth, where they had been conveyed through the instrumentality of Tom Paine's works. Church and throne—these are the twin evils that the unsophisticated westerner can see at the root of everything that disgusts him in Europe. His emphasis is political. His awareness of social wrongs is so vivid that the problem of whether the art of the Old World may actually embody a value inaccessible to him becomes irrelevant. Mark Twain was willing to forgive Louis XIV for his tyranny when he saw the gardens of Versailles, but this was a passing mood and he returned more often to indignation like that he felt in Rome when he contrasted the gorgeous marble of St. Peter's with the wretchedness of the common people who filled the slums of the city.

. . . . .

But there was a price to be paid for the freedom and freshness American writers could attain when they cut themselves loose from literary tradition. For one thing, backwoods humor was of little help in solving the architectural problems of the novel. It provided an abundance of characters and incident, a prose of rich texture, a literary strategy with fertile possibilities of variation, but it developed no tradition of major form. *Huckleberry Finn* is a series of anecdotes rather than an organized work of art. The voyage down the river gives it narrative shape of a sort, but the theme of Jim's escape to freedom up the Ohio does not harmonize with the steady southward sweep of the current of the Mississippi and is eventually abandoned. The moral crisis in which Huck decides to help Jim escape even though this means defying all the mores of his society, with its climax in his superb exclamation, "All right, then, I'll go to hell!" is grievously undercut by Mark Twain's subsequent revelation that Jim had already been freed in Miss Watson's will. The effort to supply a plot by introducing the complications surrounding Peter Wilks' will is a feeble borrowing from the melodramatic stage. And the long extravaganza at the end, when we are invited to enjoy a hundred pages of Tom Sawyer's rigmarole of rescuing Jim, is a source of discomfort to every reader.

As these final chapters suggest, moreover, the western tradition had not developed canons of taste to replace the ones it had abandoned. Mark Twain is an unreliable writer. He seems unable to distinguish between his best pages and his worst. Long after he wrote *Huckleberry Finn* he was capable of building two novelettes around the theme of Siamese twins. Even in his greatest book he can lose himself in a parody of Hamlet's soliloquy and can ask us to believe that the campmeeting crowd is taken in by the King's tale of being a pirate from the Indian Ocean. It is equally important to realize that the western tradition was intellectually naive. It could not deal with ideas in any profound or creative fashion. The abstract conceptions that Mark Twain had derived from the Enlightenment had become thin and shopworn indeed by the end of the nineteenth century. The philosophy of determinism, for example, which he elaborated with so much effort and viewed with so much awe, is a restatement of ideas that were commonplaces to thinkers like Helvetius and are simple-minded even in the eighteenth-century versions which were Mark Twain's ultimate sources.

And yet American literature of the twentieth century owes a substantial debt to the author of *Huckleberry Finn.* Writers as different from one another as Sherwood Anderson and Ernest Hemingway have acknowledged the influence of this book on their prose, and in addition one has to take into account the development of the humorous mode by writers like E. B. White, James Thurber, S. J. Perelman, and A. J. Liebling. These evidences demonstrate an important continuity in literary technique and attitude. Where the followers of Whitman have too often moved toward the loose oratory of Thomas Wolfe or Carl Sandburg, the influence of Mark Twain has encouraged discipline and craftsmanship. Paradoxically enough, the rank rabble party of Jacksonism turns out to have set in motion an austere cult of style that has given to American literature an esthetic tradition as pure and rigorous as that of the Symbolists themselves.

"*A hymn to an older America forever gone*"

LIONEL TRILLING

After the Civil War, a change came over American life that was remarked on by many of our leading intellectual and literary figures with regret. They spoke of "some simplicity, some innocence, some peace" that was gone forever. The new attitude toward money introduced a way of life that most of our greater artists instinctively despised. *Huckleberry Finn* is, among other things, a commemoration of the departed time when the Mississippi River was not primarily a highway of commerce but a place of "sunlight, space, uncrowded time, stillness, and danger." Lionel Trilling explores the form and style of *Huckleberry Finn* and defines the classic style that Mark Twain achieved.

W E ARE NOT LIKELY to miss in *Huckleberry Finn* the subtle, implicit moral meaning of the great river. But we are likely to understand these moral implications as having to do only with personal and individual conduct. And since the sum of individual pettiness is on the whole pretty constant, we are likely to think of the book as applicable to mankind in general and at all times and in all places, and we praise it by calling it "universal." And so it is; but like many books to which that large adjective applies, it is also local and particular. It has a particular moral reference to the United States in the period after the Civil War. It was then when, in Mr. Eliot's phrase, the river was for-

From Lionel Trilling's Introduction to *The Adventures of Huckleberry Finn*, Rinehart Editions. Copyright 1948 by Lionel Trilling. Reprinted by permission of the publishers, Holt, Rinehart and Winston, Inc. Reprinted in Lionel Trilling, *The Liberal Imagination* (New York: The Viking Press, Inc., 1950), pp. 113–117.

gotten, and precisely by the "dwellers in cities," by the "worshippers of the machine."

The Civil War and the development of the railroads ended the great days when the river was the central artery of the nation. No contrast could be more moving than that between the hot, turbulent energy of the river life of the first part of *Life on the Mississippi* and the melancholy reminiscence of the second part. And the war that brought the end of the rich Mississippi days also marked a change in the quality of life in America which, to many men, consisted of a deterioration of American moral values. It is of course a human habit to look back on the past and to find it a better and more innocent time than the present. Yet in this instance there seems to be an objective basis for the judgment. We cannot disregard the testimony of men so diverse as Henry Adams, Walt Whitman, William Dean Howells, and Mark Twain himself, to mention but a few of the many who were in agreement on this point. All spoke of something that had gone out of American life after the war, some simplicity, some innocence, some peace. None of them was under any illusion about the amount of ordinary human wickedness that existed in the old days, and Mark Twain certainly was not. The difference was in the public attitude, in the things that were now accepted and made respectable in the national ideal. It was, they all felt, connected with new emotions about money. As Mark Twain said, where formerly "the people had desired money," now they "fall down and worship it." The new gospel was, "Get money. Get it quickly. Get it in abundance. Get it in prodigious abundance. Get it dishonestly if you can, honestly if you must." [1]

With the end of the Civil War capitalism had established itself. The relaxing influence of the frontier was coming to an end. Americans increasingly became "dwellers in cities" and "worshippers of the machine." Mark Twain himself became a notable part of this new dispensation. No one worshiped the machine more than he did, or thought he did—he ruined himself by his devotion to the Paige typesetting machine, by which he hoped to make a fortune even greater than he had made by his writing, and he sang the praises of the machine age in *A Connecticut Yankee in King Arthur's Court*. He associated intimately with the dominant figures of American business enterprise. Yet at the same

---

[1] *Mark Twain in Eruption,* edited by Bernard De Voto, p. 77.

time he hated the new way of life and kept bitter memoranda of his scorn, commenting on the low morality or the bad taste of the men who were shaping the ideal and directing the destiny of the nation.

Mark Twain said of *Tom Sawyer* that it "is simply a hymn, put into prose form to give it a worldly air." He might have said the same, and with even more reason, of *Huckleberry Finn*, which is a hymn to an older America forever gone, an America which had its great national faults, which was full of violence and even of cruelty, but which still maintained its sense of reality, for it was not yet enthralled by money, the father of ultimate illusion and lies. Against the money-god stands the river-god, whose comments are silent—sunlight, space, uncrowded time, stillness, and danger. It was quickly forgotten once its practical usefulness had passed, but, as Mr. Eliot's poem says, 'The river is within us. . . .'

In form and style *Huckleberry Finn* is an almost perfect work. Only one mistake has ever been charged against it, that it concludes with Tom Sawyer's elaborate, too elaborate, game of Jim's escape. Certainly this episode is too long—in the original draft it was much longer—and certainly it is a falling off, as almost anything would have to be, from the incidents of the river. Yet it has a certain formal aptness—like, say, that of the Turkish initiation which brings Molière's *Le Bourgeois Gentilhomme* to its close. It is a rather mechanical development of an idea, and yet some device is needed to permit Huck to return to his anonymity, to give up the role of hero, to fall into the background which he prefers, for he is modest in all things and could not well endure the attention and glamour which attend a hero at a book's end. For this purpose nothing could serve better than the mind of Tom Sawyer with its literary furnishings, its conscious romantic desire for experience and the hero's part, and its ingenious schematization of life to achieve that aim.

The form of the book is based on the simplest of all novel-forms, the so-called picaresque novel, or novel of the road, which strings its incidents on the line of the hero's travels. But, as Pascal says, "rivers are roads that move," and the movement of the road in its own mysterious life transmutes the primitive simplicity of the form: the road itself is the greatest character in this novel of the road, and the hero's departures from the river and his returns to it compose a subtle and significant pattern. The linear simplicity of the picaresque novel is further modified by the story's having a clear dramatic organization: it has a beginning, a middle, and an end, and a mounting suspense of interest.

As for the style of the book, it is not less than definitive in American literature. The prose of *Huckleberry Finn* established for written prose the virtues of American colloquial speech. This has nothing to do with pronunciation or grammar. It has something to do with ease and freedom in the use of language. Most of all it has to do with the structure of the sentence, which is simple, direct, and fluent, maintaining the rhythm of the word-groups of speech and the intonations of the speaking voice.

In the matter of language, American literature had a special problem. The young nation was inclined to think that the mark of the truly literary product was a grandiosity and elegance not to be found in the common speech. It therefore encouraged a greater breach between its vernacular and its literary language than, say, English literature of the same period ever allowed. This accounts for the hollow ring one now and then hears even in the work of our best writers in the first half of the last century. English writers of equal stature would never have made the lapses into rhetorical excess that are common in Cooper and Poe and that are to be found even in Melville and Hawthorne.

Yet at the same time that the language of ambitious literature was high and thus always in danger of falseness, the American reader was keenly interested in the actualities of daily speech. No literature, indeed, was ever so taken up with matters of speech as ours was. "Dialect," which attracted even our serious writers, was the accepted common ground of our popular humorous writing. Nothing in social life seemed so remarkable as the different forms which speech could take—the brogue of the immigrant Irish or the mispronunciation of the German, the "affectation" of the English, the reputed precision of the Bostonian, the legendary twang of the Yankee farmer, and the drawl of the Pike County man. Mark Twain, of course, was in the tradition of humor that exploited this interest, and no one could play with it nearly so well. Although today the carefully spelled-out dialects of nineteenth-century American humor are likely to seem dull enough, the subtle variations of speech in *Huckleberry Finn,* of which Mark Twain was justly proud, are still part of the liveliness and flavor of the book.

Out of his knowledge of the actual speech of America Mark Twain forged a classic prose. The adjective may seem a strange one, yet it is apt. Forget the misspellings and the faults of grammar, and the prose will be seen to move with the greatest simplicity, directness, lucidity, and grace. These qualities are by no means accidental. Mark Twain, who read widely, was passionately interested in the problems of style; the mark of the strictest literary sensibility is everywhere to be found in the prose of *Huckleberry Finn*.

It is this prose that Ernest Hemingway had chiefly in mind when he said that "all modern American literature comes from one book by Mark Twain called *Huckleberry Finn*." Hemingway's own prose stems from it directly and consciously; so does the prose of the two modern writers who most influenced Hemingway's early style, Gertrude Stein and Sherwood Anderson (although neither of them could maintain the robust purity of their model); so, too, does the best of William Faulkner's prose, which, like Mark Twain's own, reinforces the colloquial tradition with the literary tradition. Indeed, it may be said that almost every contemporary American writer who deals conscientiously with the problems and possibility of prose must feel, directly or indirectly, the influence of Mark Twain. He is the master of the style that escapes the fixity of the printed page, that sounds in our ears with the immediacy of the heard voice, the very voice of unpretentious truth.

STEPHEN CRANE

"The new man as a typical young American"

H. G. WELLS

Stephen Crane (1871–1900) is famous as the man who wrote a great war novel before he had ever seen a battlefield. In his work, American literary realism changed from something warm and common into a starker, more unsparing view of man in a hostile, pitiless universe. *The Red Badge of Courage* (1894), Crane's second novel, found a first reception in England that was considerably more perceptive and favorable than in his own country. What struck H. G. Wells was that the young American novelist had done something new: he had applied "to the literary work the conception and theories of the cosmopolitan studio with a quite American directness and vigor." In its uncompromising realism the book was a symbol of the American novelist's new literary independence.

H IS SUCCESS in England began with the *Red Badge of Courage*, which did, indeed, more completely than any other book has done for many years, take the reading public by storm. Its freshness of method, its vigor of imagination, its force of color and its essential freedom from many traditions that dominate this side of the Atlantic, came—in spite of the previous shock of Mr. Kipling—with a positive effect of impact. It was a new thing, in a new school. When one looked for sources, one thought at once of Tolstoy; but, though it was clear that Tolstoy had exerted a powerful influence upon the conception, if not the actual writ-

From H. G. Wells, "Stephen Crane from an English Standpoint," *North American Review*, CLXXI (August, 1900), 234.

273

ing, of the book, there still remained something entirely original and novel. To a certain extent, of course, that was the new man as an individual; but, to at least an equal extent, it was the new man as a typical young American, free at last, as no generation of Americans have been free before, of any regard for English criticism, comment, or tradition, and applying to literary work the conception and theories of the cosmopolitan studio with a quite American directness and vigor. For the great influence of the studio on Crane cannot be ignored; in the persistent selection of the essential elements of an impression, in the ruthless exclusion of mere information, in the direct vigor with which the selected points are made, there is Whistler even more than there is Tolstoy in the *Red Badge of Courage*.

" 'Good Lord, what's the matter with me?' "

JOSEPH CONRAD

Joseph Conrad (1857–1924) felt an immediate kinship with the young writer of *The Red Badge of Courage*. Both were fascinated by the psychological crisis confronting an individual (often a young man in Conrad's tales too) in a group of men when moral and physical danger suddenly forces him to come to terms with himself—to prove his loyalty and endurance and courage. In Crane's Young Soldier Conrad saw "the symbol of all untried men," and in the book a virile and gentle sympathy expressed in a style unmarred by "a single declamatory sentiment."

Joseph Conrad, "His War Book—A Preface to Stephen Crane's *The Red Badge of Courage*," in *Last Essays* (London: J. M. Dent & Sons Ltd. and New York: Doubleday, Doran & Company, Inc., 1926). Reprinted by permission of J. M. Dent & Sons Ltd.

O NE OF THE MOST enduring memories of my literary life is the sensation produced by the appearance in 1895 of Crane's "Red Badge of Courage" in a small volume belonging to Mr. Heinemann's Pioneer Series of Modern Fiction—very modern fiction of that time, and upon the whole not devoid of merit. I have an idea the series was meant to give us shocks, and as far as my recollection goes there were, to use a term made familiar to all by another war, no "duds" in that small and lively bombardment. But Crane's work detonated on the mild din of that attack on our literary sensibilities with the impact and force of a twelve-inch shell charged with a very high explosive. Unexpected it fell amongst us; and its fall was followed by a great outcry.

Not of consternation, however. The energy of that projectile hurt nothing and no one (such was its good fortune), and delighted a good many. It delighted soldiers, men of letters, men in the street; it was welcomed by all lovers of personal expression as a genuine revelation, satisfying the curiosity of a world in which war and love have been subjects of song and story ever since the beginning of articulate speech.

Here we had an artist, a man not of experience but a man inspired, a seer with a gift for rendering the significant on the surface of things and with an incomparable insight into primitive emotions, who, in order to give us the image of war, had looked profoundly into his own breast. We welcomed him. As if the whole vocabulary of praise had been blown up sky-high by this missile from across the Atlantic, a rain of words descended on our heads, words well or ill chosen, chunks of pedantic praise and warm appreciation, clever words, and words of real understanding, platitudes, and felicities of criticism, but all as sincere in their response as the striking piece of work which set so many critical pens scurrying over the paper.

One of the most interesting, if not the most valuable, of printed criticisms was perhaps that of Mr. George Wyndham, soldier, man of the world, and in a sense a man of letters. He went into the whole question of war literature, at any rate during the nineteenth century, evoking comparisons with the *Memoires* of General Marbot and the famous *Diary of a Cavalry Officer* as records of a personal experience. He rendered justice to the interest of what soldiers themselves could tell us, but confessed that to gratify the curiosity of the potential combatant who lurks in most men as to the picturesque aspects and emotional reactions of a battle we must go to the artist with his Heaven-given faculty of words at the service of his divination as to what the truth of things is and must be. He comes to the conclusion that:

"Mr. Crane has contrived a masterpiece."

"Contrived"—that word of disparaging sound is the last word I would have used in connection with any piece of work by Stephen Crane, who in his art (as indeed in his private life) was the least "contriving" of men. But as to "masterpiece," there is no doubt that "The Red Badge of Courage" is that, if only because of the marvellous accord [*sic*] of the vivid impressionistic description of action on that woodland battlefield, and the imaged style of the analysis of the emotions in the inward moral struggle going on in the breast of one individual—the Young Soldier of the book, the protagonist of the monodrama presented to us in an effortless succession of graphic and coloured phrases.

Stephen Crane places his Young Soldier in an untried regiment. And this is well contrived—if any contrivance there be in a spontaneous piece of work which seems to spurt and flow like a tapped stream from the depths of the writer's being. In order that the revelation should be complete, the Young Soldier has to be deprived of the moral support which he would have found in a tried body of men matured in achievement to the consciousness of its worth. His regiment had been tried by nothing but days of waiting for the order to move; so many days that it and the Youth within it have come to think of themselves as merely "a part of a vast blue demonstration." The army had been lying camped near a river, idle and fretting, till the moment when Stephen Crane lays hold of it at dawn with masterly simplicity: "The cold passed reluctantly from the earth. . . ." These are the first words of the war book which was to give him his crumb of fame.

The whole of that opening paragraph is wonderful in the homely dignity of the indicated lines of the landscape, and the shivering awakening of the army at the break of the day before the battle. In the next, with a most effective change to racy colloquialism of narrative, the action which motivates, sustains and feeds the inner drama forming the subject of the book, begins with the Tall Soldier going down to the river to wash his shirt. He returns waving his garment above his head. He had heard at fifth-hand from somebody that the army is going to move tomorrow. The only immediate effect of this piece of news is that a Negro teamster, who had been dancing a jig on a wooden box in a ring of laughing soldiers, finds himself suddenly deserted. He sits down mournfully. For the rest, the Tall Soldier's excitement is met by blank disbelief, profane grumbling, an invincible incredulity. But the regiment is somehow sobered. One feels it, though no symptoms can be noticed. It does not know what a battle is, neither does the Young Soldier. He retires from the babbling throng into what seems a rather comfortable dugout and lies down with his hands over his eyes to think. Thus the drama begins.

He perceives suddenly that he had looked upon wars as historical phenomenons of the past. He had never believed in war in his own country. It had been a sort of play affair. He had been drilled, inspected, marched for months, till he has despaired "of ever seeing a Greek-like struggle. Such were no more. Men were better or more timid. Secular and religious education had effaced the throat-grappling instinct, or else firm finance held in check the passions."

Very modern this touch. We can remember thoughts like these round about the year 1914. That Young Soldier is representative of mankind in more ways than one, and first of all in his ignorance. His regiment had listened to the tales of veterans, "tales of gray bewhiskered hordes chewing tobacco with unspeakable valour and sweeping along like the Huns." Still, he cannot put his faith in veterans' tales. Recruits were their prey. They talked of blood, fire, and sudden death, but much of it might have been lies. They were in no wise to be trusted. And the question arises before him whether he will or will not "run from a battle"? He does not know. He cannot know. A little panic fear enters his mind. He jumps up and asks himself aloud, "Good Lord, what's the matter with me?" This is the first time his words are quoted, on this day before the battle. He dreads not danger, but fear itself. He stands before the unknown. He would like to prove to himself by some reasoning process that he will not "run from the battle." And in his unblooded regiment he can find no help. He is alone with the problem of courage.

In this he stands for the symbol of all untried men.

Some critics have estimated him a morbid case. I cannot agree to that. The abnormal cases are of the extremes; of those who crumple up at the first sight of danger, and of those of whom their fellows say "He doesn't know what fear is." Neither will I forget the rare favourites of the gods whose fiery spirit is only soothed by the fury and clamour of a battle. Of such was General Picton of Peninsular fame. But the lot of the mass of mankind is to know fear, the decent fear of disgrace. Of such is the Young Soldier of "The Red Badge of Courage." He only seems exceptional because he has got inside of him Stephen Crane's imagination, and is presented to us with the insight and the power of expression of an artist whom a just and severe critic, on a review of all his work, has called the foremost impressionist of his time; as Sterne was the greatest impressionist, but in a different way, of his age.

This is a generalized, fundamental judgment. More superficially both Zola's "La Débâcle" and Tolstoi's "War and Peace" were mentioned by critics in connection with Crane's war book. But Zola's main concern was with the downfall of the imperial regime he fancied he was portraying; and in Tolstoi's book the subtle presentation of Rostov's squadron under fire for the first time is a mere episode lost in a mass of other matter, like a handful of pebbles in a heap of sand. I could not see the relevancy. Crane was concerned with elemental truth only; and in any case I think that as an artist he is non-comparable. He dealt with what is enduring, and was the most detached of men.

That is why his book is short. Not quite two hundred pages. Gems are small. This monodrama, which happy inspiration or unerring instinct has led him to put before us in narrative form, is contained between the opening words I have already quoted and a phrase on page 194 of the English edition, which runs: "He had been to touch the great death, and found that, after all, it was but the great death. He was a man."

On these words the action ends. We are only given one glimpse of the victorious army at dusk, under the falling rain, "a procession of weary soldiers became a bedraggled train, despondent and muttering, marching with churning effort in a trough of liquid brown mud under a low wretched sky . . . ," while the last ray of the sun falls on the river through a break in the leaden clouds.

This war book, so virile and so full of gentle sympathy, in which not a single declamatory sentiment defaces the genuine verbal felicity, welding analysis and description in a continuous fascination of individual style, had been hailed by the critics as the herald of a brilliant career. Crane himself very seldom alluded to it, and always with a wistful smile. Perhaps he was conscious that, like the mortally wounded Tall Soldier of his book, who, snatching at the air, staggers out into a field to meet his appointed death on the first day of battle—while the terrified Youth and the kind Tattered Soldier stand by silent, watching with awe "these ceremonies at the place of meeting"—it was his fate, too, to fall early in the fray.

THEODORE DREISER

"His talent is essentially feminine, as Conrad's is masculine"

H. L. MENCKEN

H. L. Mencken (1880–1956), like Ezra Pound later, enjoyed
socking the "booboisie." And also like Pound, he was a doughty
champion of genius unjustly neglected. He did more than
anyone else to win recognition for Theodore Dreiser (1871–
1945), though he pulled no punches in criticizing what he
regarded as Dreiser's limitations. Mencken's admiration for
Dreiser's "gigantic steadfastness" under abuse and pressure to
change, and his scorn for the "infantile smugness and
hopefulness" of "the normal American novel" are equally
evident in his essay on Dreiser. In spite of Dreiser's lack of
self-conscious artistry, almost because of the lack, Mencken is
sure the artistic instinct is authentic. Dreiser "gets his effects,
one might say, not by designing them, but by living them."

OUT OF THE DESERT of American fictioneering, so populous and yet so dreary, Dreiser stands up—a phenomenon un-
escapably visible, but disconcertingly hard to explain. What forces
combined to produce him in the first place, and how has he managed to hold out so long against the prevailing blasts—of dis-
heartening misunderstanding and misrepresentation, of Puritan
suspicion and opposition, of artistic isolation, of commercial seduction? There is something downright heroic in the way the

Reprinted from "Theodore Dreiser," as found in *A Book of Prefaces* by
H. L. Mencken, pp. 67–70, 93–96. Reprinted by permission of Alfred A. Knopf,
Inc. Copyright 1917 by Alfred A. Knopf, Inc.

man has held his narrow and perilous ground, disdaining all compromise, unmoved by the cheap success that lies so inviting around the corner. He has faced, in his day, almost every form of attack that a serious artist can conceivably encounter, and yet all of them together have scarcely budged him an inch. He still plods along in the laborious, cheerless way he first marked out for himself; he is quite as undaunted by baited praise as by bludgeoning, malignant abuse; his later novels are, if anything, more unyieldingly dreiserian than his earliest. As one who has long sought to entice him in this direction or that, fatuously presuming to instruct him in what would improve him and profit him, I may well bear a reluctant and resigned sort of testimony to his gigantic steadfastness. It is almost as if any change in his manner, any concession to what is usual and esteemed, any amelioration of his blind, relentless exercises of *force majeure*, were a physical impossibility. One feels him at last to be authentically no more than a helpless instrument (or victim) of that inchoate flow of forces which he himself is so fond of depicting as at once the answer to the riddle of life, and a riddle ten times more vexing and accursed.

. . . . .

All the latter-day American novelists of consideration are vastly more facile than Dreiser in their philosophy, as they are in their style. In the fact, perhaps, lies the measure of their difference. What they lack, great and small, is the gesture of pity, the note of awe, the profound sense of wonder—in a phrase, that "soberness of mind" which William Lyon Phelps sees as the hallmark of Conrad and Hardy, and which even the most stupid cannot escape in Dreiser. The normal American novel, even in its most serious forms, takes colour from the national cocksureness and superficiality. It runs monotonously to ready explanations, a somewhat infantile smugness and hopefulness, a habit of reducing the unknowable to terms of the not worth knowing. What it cannot explain away with ready formulae, as in the later Winston Churchill, it snickers over as scarcely worth explaining at all, as in the later Howells. Such a brave and tragic book as "Ethan Frome" is so rare as to be almost singular, even with Mrs. Wharton. There is, I daresay, not much market for that sort of thing. In the arts, as in the concerns of everyday, the American seeks escape from the insoluble by pretending that it is solved. A comfortable phrase is what he craves beyond all things—and comfortable phrases are surely not to be sought in Dreiser's stock. . . .

. . . . .

The truth about Dreiser is that he is still in the transition stage between Christian Endeavour and civilization, between Warsaw, Indiana and the Socratic grove, between being a good American and being a free man, and so he sometimes vacillates perilously between a moral sentimentalism and a somewhat extravagant revolt. "The 'Genius,'" on the one hand, is almost a tract for rectitude, a Warning to the Young; its motto might be *Scheut die Dirnen!* And on the other hand, it is full of a laborious truculence that can only be explained by imagining the author as heroically determined to prove that he is a plain-spoken fellow and his own man, let the chips fall where they may. So, in spots, in "The Financier" and "The Titan," both of them far better books. There is an almost moral frenzy to expose and riddle what passes for morality among the stupid. The isolation of irony is never reached; the man is still evangelical; his ideas are still novelties to him; he is as solemnly absurd in some of his floutings of the Code Américain as he is in his respect for Bouguereau, or in his flirtings with the New Thought, or in his naïve belief in the importance of novel-writing. Somewhere or other I have called all this the Greenwich Village complex. It is not genuine artists, serving beauty reverently and proudly, who herd in those cockroached cellars and bawl for art; it is a mob of half-educated yokels and cockneys to whom the very idea of art is still novel, and intoxicating—and more than a little bawdy.

Not that Dreiser actually belongs to this ragamuffin company. Far from it, indeed. There is in him, hidden deep-down, a great instinctive artist, and hence the makings of an aristocrat. In his muddled way, held back by the manacles of his race and time, and his steps made uncertain by a guiding theory which too often eludes his own comprehension, he yet manages to produce works of art of unquestionable beauty and authority, and to interpret life in a manner that is poignant and illuminating. There is vastly more intuition in him than intellectualism; his talent is essentially feminine, as Conrad's is masculine; his ideas always seem to be deduced from his feelings. The view of life that got into "Sister Carrie," his first book, was not the product of a conscious thinking out of Carrie's problems. It simply got itself there by the force of the artistic passion behind it; its coherent statement had to wait for other and more reflective days. The thing began as a vision, not as a syllogism. Here the name of Franz Schubert inevitably comes up. Schubert was an ignoramus, even in music; he knew less about polyphony, which is the mother of harmony, which is the mother of music, than the average conservatory professor. But nevertheless he had such a vast instinctive sensitiveness to musical values, such a profound and accurate feeling for beauty in tone, that he not only arrived at the truth in tonal relations, but even went beyond what, in his day, was known to be the truth, and so led an advance. Likewise, Giorgione da Castelfranco and Masaccio come to mind: painters of the first rank, but untutored, unsophisticated, uncouth. Dreiser, within his limits, belongs to this cabot-shod company of the elect. One thinks of Conrad, not as artist first, but as savant. There is something of the icy aloofness of the laboratory in him, even when the images he conjures up pulsate with the very glow of life. He is almost as self-conscious as the Beethoven of the last quartets. In Dreiser the thing is more intimate, more disorderly, more a matter of pure feeling. He gets his effects, one might almost say, not by designing them, but by living them.

"'Dat's very good of yer ter say, Missus Rettle'"

ROBERT BENCHLEY

If Dreiser's work is in some ways the most impressive example of American naturalism, it also offers the broadest target for parody. This piece by Robert Benchley (1889–1945) epitomizes "in action" the objections to naturalism better than most formal critics could do.

SUGGESTIONS AS TO HOW THEODORE DREISER MIGHT WRITE
HIS NEXT HUMAN DOCUMENT AND SAVE FIVE YEARS' WORK

Chapter I

Up East Division Street, on a hot day in late July, walked two
men, one five feet four, the other, the taller of the two, five feet
six, the first being two inches shorter than his more elongated
companion, and consequently giving the appearance to passers-by
on East Division Street, or, whenever the two reached a cross
street, to the passers-by on the cross street, of being at least a
good two inches shorter than the taller of the little group.

Walking up East Division Street they came, in two or three
minutes, to Division Street proper, which runs at right angles and
a little to the left of East Division Street, but not so much to the
left as Marcellus Street, or Ransome Street, for that matter. As
the two continued strolling, in that fashion in which two men
of their respective heights are likely to stroll, they came in succession to—

(Note to printer: *Attached find copy of Thurston's Street Guide.
Print names of every street listed therein, beginning with East
Division and up to, and including, Dawson.*)

Chapter II

That these two men, presented in the last chapter, would
eventually stop walking up Division Street and enter a house of
some sort or description, might well be anticipated by the reader,
and, in fact, such was the case.

It was, indeed, the house of the shorter of the two, of the one
whom we have seen in the last chapter to have been five feet
four, if, indeed, he was. It was a typical dwelling, or home, of
a man of the middle class in a medium-sized city such as the one
in which these men found themselves living.

(Note To Printer: *Attached find insurance inventory of house-
hold-effects and architect's specifications. Reproduce in toto.*)

Chapter III

Reaching the living room described above, Tom Rettle, for
such was the name of the shorter of the two—the one to whom
the house, or home, or dwelling, belonged—was greeted by his
wife, Anna, a buxom woman of perhaps thirty-four or thirty-five,
certainly not *more* than thirty-five, if one were to judge by her

fresh, wholesome color and the sparkle of her brownish-gray eyes, or even by her well-rounded form, her—

(*Print attached passport description of Anna Rettle.*)

"Well, hello, Anna," said Tom, pleasantly, for Tom Rettle was, as a matter of fact, a very pleasant man unless he were angered, and his blue eyes smiled in a highly agreeable manner.

"Well, hello, Tom," replied Anna, for it was indeed Anna who spoke, in a soft, well-modulated voice, too, giving the impression of being an extremely agreeable sort of a woman.

"Anna, I want you to meet a very good friend of mine, Arthur Berolston, a very good friend of mine," said Tom, politely, looking, at the same time, at both Anna and Berolston.

"I'm very happy to meet Mr. Berolston," added Anna, genially, although one could see that in her heart she wished that Tom would bring a little different type of friend home, a thing she had often spoken to him about when they were alone, as they often were.

"Dat's very good of yer ter say, Missus Rettle," replied Berolston, in modern slang, which made him sound even more uncouth than he looked, which was uncouth enough. "For de love o' Mike!"

At this indication of a rough bringing-up on the part of her husband's acquaintance, Anna Rettle winced slightly but showed no other sign of her emotions. Tom was such a kind-hearted fellow! So good! So kind-hearted! Tom was.

"What is there for supper tonight, Anna?" asked Tom, when the wincing had died down. "You know how well I like cole slaw, and have always liked it."

"I certainly do know your fondness for cole slaw, Tom," replied his wife, but with a note of regret in her voice, for she was thinking that she had no cole slaw for supper on the particular night of which we are speaking. "But you will remember that we had cole slaw last night with the cold tongue, and night before last with the baked beans and—"

(*Run attached "Fifteen Midsummer Menus for Cole Slaw Lovers."*)

Chapter IV

Prepared as Tom was not to have cole slaw for supper, he could not hide his disappointment. Anna had been a good wife to him.

But somehow tonight, when he had brought Arthur Berolston

home to supper, his disappointment was particularly keen, for he and Arthur had been discussing cole slaw all the way up East Division Street, across Division Street and through to the southwest corner of Dawson and Margate, where Tom lived, and each had said how much he liked it.

Should he strike Anna for failing him at this juncture? He, Tom Rettle, strike his wife, Anna Rettle? And, even if he should decide to strike her, *where* should he direct the blow? Tom's mind was confused with all these questions.

(*Reprint the above paragraph twenty-five times.*)

Chapters V–LXXXII Inclusive

To Printer: *With the above copy you will find a briefcase containing newspaper clippings giving the complete testimony of Anna Rettle, Thomas Rettle and Arthur Berolston in the case of "Anna Rettle vs. Thomas Rettle," tried in the Criminal Court of Testiman County, September 2–28, 1925. There is also transcript of the testimony of three neighbors of the Rettles' (Herman Nordquist, Ethel Nordquist and Junior Nordquist), and of Officer Louis M. Hertzog of the Fifth Precinct. Reprint all these and, at the bottom of the last page, put "THE END."*

"Dreiser and James: With that juxtaposition we are immediately at the dark and bloody crossroads where literature and politics meet"

LIONEL TRILLING

The action and reaction of literature and politics on each other has been a special interest of Lionel Trilling. His book of essays *The Liberal Imagination* (1950) explored this subject in terms both of general ideas and of individual writers. He suggests

that the whole idea of "reality" in American liberal criticism
has been oriented toward "the awkwardness, the chaos, the
heaviness" typical of Dreiser's work, and that "the electric
qualities of mind" characteristic of Henry James have been a
source of anxious suspicion. Mr. Trilling's insistence that
Dreiser's style is no mere unruly irrelevance in estimating
Dreiser's final importance is an example of a basic principle no
good critic can afford to forget.

THIS BELIEF in the incompatibility of mind and reality
is exemplified by the doctrinaire indulgence which liberal intellectuals have always displayed toward Theodore Dreiser, an indulgence which becomes the worthier of remark when it is contrasted with the liberal severity toward Henry James. Dreiser and
James: with that juxtaposition we are immediately at the dark
and bloody crossroads where literature and politics meet. One
does not go there gladly, but nowadays it is not exactly a matter
of free choice whether one does or does not go. As for the particular juxtaposition itself, it is inevitable and it has at the present
moment far more significance than the juxtaposition which once
used to be made between James and Whitman. It is not hard to
contrive factitious oppositions between James and Whitman, but the
real difference between them is the difference between the moral
mind, with its awareness of tragedy, irony, and multitudinous distinctions, and the transcendental mind, with its passionate sense
of the oneness of multiplicity. James and Whitman are unlike not
in quality but in kind, and in their very opposition they serve
to complement each other. But the difference between James and
Dreiser is not of kind, for both men addressed themselves to virtually the same social and moral fact. The difference here is one
of quality, and perhaps nothing is more typical of American
liberalism than the way it has responded to the respective qualities of the two men.

Few critics, I suppose, no matter what their political disposition, have ever been wholly blind to James's great gifts, or even
to the grandiose moral intention of these gifts. And few critics

have ever been wholly blind to Dreiser's great faults. But by liberal critics James is traditionally put to the ultimate question: of
what use, of what actual political use, are his gifts and their intention? Granted that James was devoted to an extraordinary
moral perceptiveness, granted too that moral perceptiveness has
something to do with politics and the social life, of what possible
practical value in our world of impending disaster can James's
work be? And James's style, his characters, his subjects, and even
his own social origin and the manner of his personal life are ad-
duced to show that his work cannot endure the question. To James
no quarter is given by American criticism in its political and liberal aspect. But in the same degree that liberal criticism is moved
by political considerations to treat James with severity, it treats
Dreiser with the most sympathetic indulgence. Dreiser's literary
faults, it gives us to understand, are essentially social and political
virtues. It was Parrington who established the formula for the
liberal criticism of Dreiser by calling him a "peasant": when
Dreiser thinks stupidly, it is because he has the slow stubbornness of a peasant; when he writes badly, it is because he is impatient of the sterile literary gentility of the bourgeoisie. It is as
if wit, and flexibility of mind, and perception, and knowledge
were to be equated with aristocracy and political reaction, while
dullness and stupidity must naturally suggest a virtuous democracy, as in the old plays.

The liberal judgment of Dreiser and James goes back of politics,
goes back to the cultural assumptions that make politics. We are
still haunted by a kind of political fear of the intellect which
Tocqueville observed in us more than a century ago. American
intellectuals, when they are being consciously American or political, are remarkably quick to suggest that an art which is marked
by perception and knowledge, although all very well in its way,
can never get us through gross dangers and difficulties. And their
misgivings become the more intense when intellect works in art
as it ideally should, when its processes are vivacious and interesting and brilliant. It is then that we like to confront it with the
gross dangers and difficulties and to challenge it to save us at
once from disaster. When intellect in art is awkward or dull we
do not put it to the test of ultimate or immediate practicality.
No liberal critic asks the question of Dreiser whether *his* moral

preoccupations are going to be useful in confronting the disasters that threaten us. And it is a judgment on the proper nature of mind, rather than any actual political meaning that might be drawn from the works of the two men, which accounts for the unequal justice they have received from the progressive critics. If it could be conclusively demonstrated—by, say, documents in James's handwriting—that James explicitly intended his books to be understood as pleas for co-operatives, labor unions, better housing, and more equitable taxation, the American critic in his liberal and progressive character would still be worried by James because his work shows so many of the electric qualities of mind. And if something like the opposite were proved of Dreiser, it would be brushed aside—as his doctrinaire anti-Semitism has in fact been brushed aside—because his books have the awkward-ness, the chaos, the heaviness which we associate with "reality." In the American metaphysic, reality is always material reality, hard, resistant, unformed, impenetrable, and unpleasant. And that mind is alone felt to be trustworthy which most resembles this reality by most nearly reproducing the sensations it affords.

In *The Rise of American Civilization,* Professor Beard uses a significant phrase when, in the course of an ironic account of James's career, he implies that we have the clue to the irrelevance of that career when we know that James was "a whole generation removed from the odors of the shop." Of a piece with this, and in itself even more significant, is the comment which Granville Hicks makes in *The Great Tradition* when he deals with James's stories about artists and remarks that such artists as James por-trays, so concerned for their art and their integrity in art, do not really exist: "After all, who has ever known such artists? Where are the Hugh Verekers, the Mark Ambients, the Neil Paradays, the Overts, Limberts, Dencombes, Delavoys?" This question, as Mr. Hicks admits, had occurred to James himself, but what an-swer had James given to it? "If the life about us for the last thirty years refused warrant for these examples," he said in the preface to volume XII of the New York Edition, "then so much the worse for that life. . . . There are decencies that in the name of the general self-respect we must take for granted, there's a rudi-mentary intellectual honor to which we must, in the interest of civilization, at least pretend." And to this Mr. Hicks, shocked beyond argument, makes this reply, which would be astonishing had we not heard it before: "But this is the purest romanticism, this writing about what ought to be rather than what is!"

The "odors of the shop" are real, and to those who breathe them they guarantee a sense of vitality from which James is debarred. The idea of intellectual honor is not real, and to that chimera James was devoted. He betrayed the reality of what is in the interests of what ought to be. Dare we trust him? The question, we remember, is asked by men who themselves have elaborate transactions with what ought to be. Professor Beard spoke in the name of a growing, developing, and improving America. Mr. Hicks, when he wrote *The Great Tradition*, was in general sympathy with a nominally radical movement. But James's own transaction with what ought to be is suspect because it is carried on through what I have called the electrical qualities of mind, through a complex and rapid imagination and with a kind of authoritative immediacy. Mr. Hicks knows that Dreiser is "clumsy" and "stupid" and "bewildered" and "crude in his statement of materialistic monism"; he knows that Dreiser in his personal life —which is in point because James's personal life is always supposed to be so much in point—was not quite emancipated from "his boyhood longing for crass material success," showing "again and again a desire for the ostentatious luxury of the successful business man." But Dreiser is to be accepted and forgiven because his faults are the sad, lovable, honorable faults of reality itself, or of America itself—huge, inchoate, struggling toward expression, caught between the dream of raw power and the dream of morality.

"The liability in what Santayana called the genteel tradition was due to its being the product of mind apart from experience. Dreiser gave us the stuff of our common experience, not as it was hoped to be by any idealizing theorist, but as it actually was in its crudity." The author of this statement certainly cannot be accused of any lack of feeling for mind as Henry James represents it; nor can Mr. Matthiessen be thought of as a follower of Parrington—indeed, in the preface to *American Renaissance* he has framed one of the sharpest and most cogent criticisms of Parrington's method. Yet Mr. Matthiessen, writing in the *New York Times Book Review* about Dreiser's posthumous novel, *The Bulwark*, accepts the liberal cliché which opposes crude experience to mind and establishes Dreiser's value by implying that the mind which Dreiser's crude experience is presumed to confront and refute is the mind of gentility.

This implied amalgamation of mind with gentility is the rationale of the long indulgence of Dreiser, which is extended even to the style of his prose. Everyone is aware that Dreiser's prose style is full of roughness and ungainliness, and the critics who admire Dreiser tell us it does not matter. Of course it does not matter. No reader with a right sense of style would suppose that it does matter, and he might even find it a virtue. But it has been taken for granted that the ungainliness of Dreiser's style is the only possible objection to be made to it, and that whoever finds in it any fault at all wants a prettified genteel style (and is objecting to the ungainliness of reality itself). For instance, Edwin Berry Burgum, in a leaflet on Dreiser put out by the Book Find Club, tells us that Dreiser was one of those who used—or, as Mr. Burgum says, utilized— "the diction of the Middle West, pretty much as it was spoken, rich in colloquialism and frank in the simplicity and directness of the pioneer tradition," and that this diction took the place of "the literary English, formal and bookish, of New England provincialism that was closer to the aristocratic spirit of the mother country than to the tang of everyday life in the new West." This is mere fantasy. Hawthorne, Thoreau, and Emerson were for the most part remarkably colloquial—they wrote, that is, much as they spoke; their prose was specifically American in quality, and, except for occasional lapses, quite direct and simple. It is Dreiser who lacks the sense of colloquial diction—that of the Middle West or any other. If we are to talk of bookishness, it is Dreiser who is bookish; he is precisely literary in the bad sense; he is full of flowers of rhetoric and shines with paste gems; at hundreds of points his diction is not only genteel but fancy. It is he who speaks of "a scene more distingué than this," or of a woman "artistic in form and feature," or of a man who, although "strong, reserved, aggressive, with an air of wealth and experience, was *soi-disant* and not particularly eager to stay at home." Colloquialism held no real charm for him and his natural tendency is always toward the "fine":

. . . Moralists come and go; religionists fulminate and declare the pronouncements of God as to this; but Aphrodite still reigns. Embowered in the festal depths of the spring, set above her altars of porphyry, chalcedony, ivory and gold, see her smile the smile that is at once the texture and essence of delight, the glory and despair of the world! Dream on, oh Buddha, asleep on your lotus leaf, of an undisturbed Nirvana! Sweat, oh Jesus, your last agonizing drops over an unregenerate world! In the forests of Pan still ring the cries of the worshippers of Aphrodite! From her altars the incense of adoration ever rises! And see, the new red grapes dripping where votive hands new-press them!

Charles Jackson, the novelist, telling us in the same leaflet that Dreiser's style does not matter, remarks on how much still comes to us when we have lost by translation the stylistic brilliance of Thomas Mann or the Russians or Balzac. He is in part right. And he is right too when he says that a certain kind of conscious, supervised artistry is not appropriate to the novel of large dimensions. Yet the fact is that the great novelists have usually written very good prose, and what comes through even a bad translation is exactly the power of mind that made the well-hung sentence of the original text. In literature style is so little the mere clothing of thought—need it be insisted on at this late date?— that we may say that from the earth of the novelist's prose spring his characters, his ideas, and even his story itself.[1]

To the extent that Dreiser's style is defensible, his thought is also defensible. That is, when he thinks like a novelist, he is worth

[1] The latest defense of Dreiser's style, that in the chapter on Dreiser in the *Literary History of the United States,* is worth noting: "Forgetful of the integrity and power of Dreiser's whole work, many critics have been distracted into a condemnation of his style. He was, like Twain and Whitman, an organic artist; he wrote what he knew—what he was. His many colloquialisms were part of the coinage of his time, and his sentimental and romantic passages were written in the language of the educational system and the popular literature of his formative years. In his style, as in his material, he was a child of his time, of his class. Self-educated, a type or model of the artist of plebeian origin in America, his language, like his subject matter, is not marked by internal inconsistencies." No doubt Dreiser was an organic artist in the sense that he wrote what he knew and what he was, but so, I suppose, is every artist; the question for criticism comes down to *what* he knew and *what* he was. That he was a child of his time and class is also true, but this can be said of everyone without exception; the question for criticism is how he transcended the imposed limitations of his time and class. As for the defense made on the ground of his particular class, it can only be said that liberal thought has come to a strange pass when it assumes that a plebeian origin is accountable for a writer's faults through all his intellectual life.

following—when by means of his rough and ungainly but no doubt cumulatively effective style he creates rough, ungainly, but effective characters and events. But when he thinks like, as we say, a philosopher, he is likely to be not only foolish but vulgar. He thinks as the modern crowd thinks when it decided to think: religion and morality are nonsense, "religionists" and moralists are fakes, tradition is a fraud, what is man but matter and impulses, mysterious "chemisms," what value has life anyway? "What, cooking, eating, coition, job holding, growing, aging, losing, winning, in so changeful and passing a scene as this, important? Bunk! It is some form of titillating illusion with about as much import to the superior forces that bring it all about as the functions and gyrations of a fly. No more. And maybe less." Thus Dreiser at sixty. And yet there is for him always the vulgarly saving suspicion that maybe, when all is said and done, there is Something Behind It All. It is much to the point of his intellectual vulgarity that Dreiser's anti-Semitism was not merely a social prejudice but an idea, a way of dealing with difficulties.

No one, I suppose, has ever represented Dreiser as a masterly intellect. It is even commonplace to say that his ideas are inconsistent or inadequate. But once that admission has been made, his ideas are hustled out of sight while his "reality" and great brooding pity are spoken of. (His pity is to be questioned: pity is to be judged by kind, not amount, and Dreiser's pity—*Jennie Gerhardt* provides the only exception—is either destructive of its object or it is self-pity.) Why has no liberal critic ever brought Dreiser's ideas to the bar of political practicality, asking what use is to be made of Dreiser's dim, awkward speculation, of his self-justification, of his lust for "beauty" and "sex" and "living" and "life itself," and of the showy nihilism which always seems to him so grand a gesture in the direction of profundity? We live, understandably enough, with the sense of urgency; our clock, like Baudelaire's, has had the hands removed and bears the legend, "It is later than you think." But with us it is always a little too late for mind, yet never too late for honest stupidity; always a little too late for understanding, never too late for righteous, bewildered wrath; always too late for thought, never too late for naïve moralizing. We seem to like to condemn our finest but not our worst qualities by pitting them against the exigency of time.

"Dreiser had to be a pioneer"

JAMES T. FARRELL

This elegiac piece, written by James T. Farrell, a friend and follower of Theodore Dreiser, on the occasion of the latter's death, gives us a good idea of what it was about Dreiser that so impressed his admirers. His desire to learn from experience, to forge his own way as an artist, to feel himself into the heart of things, to tell the truth as he saw it—these things won over many people superior in knowledge of culture to him.

AND THEODORE DREISER was a boy, son of a pious and frustrated immigrant from Germany. He was shy, awkward, callow, moody, dreaming, brooding, eager. He wanted to live: he wanted to grow: he wanted to learn. He looked at everything. He was always looking. In his major writing, we can notice that he writes from the standpoint of a spectator. He became a spectator early in life. In the fields and small towns of Indiana, in the ugly, semi-primitive, violently alive streets of Chicago, this boy looked, looked and dreamed. He felt a need to grow; to learn; to be somebody; to rise in the world; to make a name for himself. He was a sensitive child of this period. But above all else, he wanted to understand. He learned, and it will still take time before many really come to know how much he learned. But he learned from life. In "Jennie Gerhardt," there is a passing little comment which is a clue to Dreiser and to his times. Jennie gets a job as a maid in a rich household. And her author tells us that as a maid in this house, she learned, she learned much: and she gained a theory of existence. This suggests Dreiser. When looking

From "Dreiser: In Memoriam," in *Literature and Morality* by James T. Farrell. Reprinted by permission of the publisher, The Vanguard Press. Copyright 1947 by James T. Farrell. This essay also appeared in *The Saturday Review of Literature*, 29 (January 12, 1946), 17, 27–28.

at factories, he learned; when he worked as an order boy in a wholesale hardware concern, he learned; when he drove a laundry wagon, he learned. When he watched his family, he learned. When he overheard neighbors quarreling in the flat above that of the Dreisers in Chicago, he learned. The boy, Theodore, learned from everything, and out of his learning, he sought a theory of existence. Later, he was to speak again and again of the mystery, the wonder, the terror, the beauty of life. His endless ponderings —these were part of his lifelong quest—were for a theory of existence. He sought it in life, life that was new, dynamic, growing, terrible, fascinating.

What literary and cultivated tradition was there for Dreiser to have taken and used in describing this world with its gigantic changes, its fresh cultural lift, its dramatic struggles? Where in the culture of the past could he have found more adequate tools than he did find? What could he have done that he did not do in order to have forged a better style with which to give shape and depth of meaning to this raw world?

Dreiser did learn—from Balzac, from Spencer. He tried, tried seriously, to assimilate the best ideas of his time. But as for the cultivated traditions of Europe, the cultivation of New England, the culture of Victorian England—how could it have given enough to such a boy, to such a youth when face to face with this American world? Dreiser had to be a pioneer. He had to plough his own way. He had to educate himself. He had to learn from life. Much that has been described as the weakness of Dreiser—that was in reality his strength. Dreiser's task was to describe the changing face of America. He was more than adequate to his task.

And in being adequate to his task, Theodore Dreiser became the great novelist of the period of capitalist growth and expansion, the period of urbanization in American life. In his youth, the city was the most powerful of all social magnets. It attracted youth, eager youth, ambitious boys and beautiful girls. It attracted swarms from all of Europe. Some rose in the city to great success. Many, thousands and thousands, were crushed, destroyed. And in the city the sound of the hammer was never still. Everywhere something was happening. And all this Dreiser saw, saw and remembered. And he told us about this with depths of compassion, with depths of feeling for the condition of man, and also, with wonder, with love of beauty, with anger at the sight of squalor, and above all else with objectivity.

His great books are not only works which convey to us an awesome depth of feeling for the condition of man. Also, they try to tell the truth. Filled with pity and compassion for men and women, for boys and girls involved in a tragic web of life, they are also pitiless in their delineation of the way circumstances drive man, the way impulses in man's organism, and tendencies in society, are more powerful than the will of man. And to give added humanness to such pictures, he also recounts with sad eyes, with a sorrowing pen, the terrible meaning of the biological tragedy of mankind.

SINCLAIR LEWIS

"In being grasped with such cruel fresh firmness as Mr. Lewis's the whole nation may be felt to squirm"

FRANCIS HACKETT

It is interesting to compare later opinion of an author or work that has become famous with contemporary reviews. Mr. Hackett's review of *Main Street* (1920), allowing for changes in the American scene which Sinclair Lewis's (1885–1951) work may have helped to bring about, still seems an accurate account of Lewis's merits and demerits at the time he wrote this novel.

CAN YOU IMAGINE Henry James deposited for five or six years in McHenry, Illinois, or Sun Prairie, Wisconsin, or Eldora, Iowa? Or can you imagine George Meredith coming to anchor in any of these hard-shelled villages? Or, for that matter, Joseph Conrad? A Kalmuk village might easily engage Conrad, or a London village hold Henry James, but there is something about the American town of small size that says no to the idea of these artists. The small American town, that is to say, presents a fictional problem all its own, and one can only imagine Henry James pathetically groping for the handle as one imbecilly gropes for a strange door-handle in the dark.

The immense interest of *Main Street* is not simply that Mr. Sinclair Lewis has written his best novel, but that his best novel should cope with this flatness and hardness and thinness which is

F[rancis] H[ackett], "God's Country," *The New Republic*, 25 (December 1, 1920), 20–21.

the small, new American prairie town. He calls it Gopher Prairie, Minnesota, and because it is Minnesota the facts group around Swedes rather than Germans, around the Cities rather than St. Louis or Chicago. But his village is not a special village. It is, as he himself says, a representative specimen, standing for something to be found anywhere and everywhere in the length and breadth of the Middle West. It is, so to say, the heart of American Philistia, the perfect nodulation of the plutocratic middle class. It has its college graduates, its clergymen, its Reds, its Whites, its Single Taxers, its Protective Tariff disciples, its smart set, (who has not heard of the Four Hundred of Chillecothe, Illinois?), its club-women, its bankers and bakers and butchers and undertakers, its doctors and lawyers and odd-job men and dead-beats and Joans of Arc. But the collection, the agglomeration, of all these is, necessarily, a specimen of pluto-democratic American society, earmarked by the Saturday Evening Post. Man, of course, does not live by Fords alone. Even among the dreariest of American institutions and under their heavy multiplicity and monotony there does sprout an occasional surprising difference. That Mr. Lewis shows. But his Gopher Prairie stands out precisely because it is like all the other Gopher Prairies. And in being grasped with such cruel fresh firmness as Mr. Lewis's the whole nation may be felt to squirm.

The method is H. G. Wells's. To Gopher Prairie—the one that is part of the author's own being, the one he grew up with and the one to which he has brought his biting observation—Mr. Lewis has applied not merely the imagination of the artist, but the ravenous curiosity of the political animal. And to that ravenous curiosity, like his master Wells, Mr. Lewis has sacrificed much of the mood of art. To put in evidence his full theory of this nation of villagers Mr. Lewis has been ready all through his book to represent his men and women as actually saying those things about themselves and their socio-political situation which, per-haps, they ought to say, but don't. He has, indeed, a briskness and naturalness of discourse which almost induces one to believe that Gopher Prairie can be articulate. But the articulateness is Mr. Lewis's. He has a stinging perceptiveness of practically every-thing that pertains to the jays and super-jays of this United States. He knows the Busy Booster. He knows the "gentleman hen" who loves art. He knows the hearty people whose sympathies are warm, but stationary. He knows the self-effacing couple who are worth several millions and who take themselves and their Gopher atmosphere to Pasadena—the last way-station en route to those new, decorous, expensive, cemeteries which cater only to hearse-automobiles. Mr. Lewis possesses the 'orrible details about the town's bad boy, the town's diabolic gossip, the wife of repressed sex instinct who is like the moist plant that envelops flies. He understands and exposes the ghastly boredom diffused by the Baptists, the Congregationalists, the Methodists and all the other gentry who have a vested interest in the conformity of nonconformity and the dissidence of dissent. Mr. Lewis pinions these professional Christians. He also pinions the cut-up, the bright reforming librarian, the person who does a stunt at the party, the person who makes the "servant problem" and later discovers it. But while he is much too mobile to accept the matter as settled, when he exposes boredom or triteness or inflexibility, he does— like H. G. Wells, or, to be fair all round, Wells does, like Sinclair Lewis—push the classificatory tendency so far that the whole fascinating circumstance of personality is subordinated.

It is subordinated even in Will Kennicott, the doctor, and Carol Kennicott, the doctor's wife. At times Will Kennicott is very real —sound, generous, reliable, wholesome, facetious, executive, crude and the rest. He does all the things that ought to make him real. He amputates in a farm-house at night, Carol giving the ether. He goes hunting, in all the sports-goods that are needed to bring about the death of two or three rabbits. He talks about cars and other tangible objects in a bright stream of slang that shines like the coffee-urn in an American restaurant—and pours forth the same staleness. Mr. Lewis apprehends every necessary convincing detail. And yet, captious though it may sound, this rich chunkiness of detail does not establish the insideness of Kennicott, or give us that entente with him which is the triumph of imagination. Toward the end, when Kennicott comes to see his wife in Washington and dimly perceives that there is in the world such a thing as another personality, we have a glimpse of his being. But this is a small macaroon to satisfy the reader's long hunger.

The woman of the story (for this is The Story of Carol Kennicott) is placed more gently and tenderly, but not in any degree more securely. She is a super-jay who reacts against Gopher Prairie as a person coming in out of the fresh air reacts against stale travelers in a day-coach. This Mr. Lewis depicts admirably. But her repeated efforts to maintain a full personality against the tribal fear of personality Mr. Lewis fails to encircle because he gives these efforts a sort of sociological twist. Her stabs at the new library, the new theatre, a friendship with the pale-gray lawyer, or the Greek-faced tailor's assistant, her attempts to take an interest in Kennicott's work—these could not be more vivid, but they would gain depth of intelligibility if Mr. Lewis himself had more interest in the specific "otherness" of this undeveloped, striving person.

The same exterior vision is seen in the get-it-over-the-footlights emphasis on the stage Swedes who come in and out. And even the conscientious imagism of the nature-descriptions is not the same as feeling.

But *Main Street* is pioneer work. Some formulae it does help to perpetuate. Some garishness and crudity it does unpleasantly employ in its anxiety to be effective and pat. But while the novelistic hen does not necessarily lay better if surrounded by strong artificial light, the light in *Main Street* is on the whole natural, honest and oh so amazingly illuminating. No one who reads *Main Street* can remain a stranger to Gopher Prairie. There are things about Swedes and the Kennicotts that perhaps Sinclair Lewis is not interested in knowing or cannot ever know. He, like the rest of his country, is touched with utilitarianism, wants his analysis to answer "do" rather than "be." But even if he pelts himself at taste and hits it too hard occasionally, his novel is immeasurably better, better-experienced and seasoned and lived and thought and felt, than most of the American novels. Out of his "land of dairy herds and exquisite lakes, of new automobiles and tar-paper shanties and silos like red towers, of clumsy speech and a hope that is boundless," he has created a reality. And while he is much too tender to it, in the end, he has given American herd-life something of which it had seemed scarcely capable—a literary domicile.

"*The folksiest and most comradely of American novelists*"

ALFRED KAZIN

From a wider perspective than Mr. Hackett's in his review of *Main Street*, Alfred Kazin surveys Sinclair Lewis's career and remarks the irony of the iconoclast who became the delight of the very people he had set out to satirize. But Mr. Kazin sees terror in Lewis too, "the terror immanent in the commonplace" when a Babbitt ventures outside the conventions. Lewis's mimetic gift came to seem a limitation, and his books "not so much revelations of life as brilliant equivalents of it." Yet he sounded the authentic note of American shyness, yearning, and loneliness as well as catching the vulgarity of an era.

For there is a certain irony in Lewis's career that is now impossible to miss, and one that illuminates it as a whole. Here was the bright modern satirist who wrote each of his early books as an assault on American smugness, provincialism, ignorance, and bigotry; and ended up by finding himself not an enemy, not a danger, but the folksiest and most comradely of American novelists. Here was the young rebel who had begun *Main Street* as his spiritual autobiography, who even wrote dashingly in his foreword that it preached "alien" doctrine and painted that whole world of endless Main Streets where "dullness is made God"— and found that people merely chortled with delight over how well he had hit off the village butcher, the somnolent afternoons on Main Street, the hysterical Sunday-night suppers, and the genteel moneylender's wife, with her "bleached cheeks, bleached hair, bleached voice, and a bleached manner." Here was the crusading satirist who spared none of the hypocrisies by which Babbitt and his group lived, least of all their big and little cruelties, and gave Babbitt back to his people as a friendly, browbeaten, noisy good fellow. Here was the indignant critic of commercialism in science who portrayed the tragedy of Max Gottlieb in *Arrowsmith* and the struggles of Martin Arrowsmith against those who threatened his disinterested worship of truth, yet succeeded even more significantly in making out of Arrowsmith a gangling romantic American hero. Here was the topical novelist, with his genius for public opinion, who tried to describe the nightmare coming of Fascism to America in *It Can't Happen Here,* but really described his own American optimism in the affectionate portrait of Doremus Jessup, that good American small-town liberal.

In the first flush of his triumph in the twenties, when Lewis did seem to be the bad boy breaking out of school, the iconoclast who was Mencken's companion in breaking all the traditional American commandments, it was easy enough to enjoy his satiric bitterness and regard him as a purely irreverent figure. But today, when his characters have entered so completely into the national life and his iconoclasm has become so tedious and safe, it is impossible to look back at Lewis himself without seeing how much native fellowship he brought into the novel and how deeply he has always depended on the common life he satirized. The caricature will always be there, and the ugly terror that Babbitt felt when he tried to break away for a moment from the conventional life of his society. There is indeed more significant terror of a kind in Lewis's novels than in a writer like Faulkner or the hard-boiled novelists, for it is the terror immanent in the commonplace, the terror that arises out of the repressions, the meanness, the hard jokes of the world Lewis had soaked into his pores. But in a larger sense his whole significance as a writer rests on just his absorption of all those commonplaces, for Lewis has seemed not merely to live on the surface of public reality, but for it. It was this that so many critics have felt when they have accused him of living intellectually from hand to mouth, and what T. K. Whipple meant when he so cleverly compared Lewis to a Red Indian stalking the country of his enemies. For Lewis has always led so mimetic an existence that his works have even come to seem an uncanny reproduction of surface reality. Not so much revelations of life as brilliant equivalents of it, his books have really given back to Americans a perfect symbolic myth, the central image of what they have believed themselves to be; and it is this which has always been the source of his raucous charm and his boisterous good-fellowship with the very people and ideas he has caricatured.

For what is it about Lewis that strikes one today but how deeply he has always enjoyed people in America? What is it but the proud gusto and pleasure behind his caricatures that have always made them so funny—and so comfortable? Only a novelist fundamentally uncritical of American life could have brought so much zest to its mechanics; only a novelist anxious not to surmount the visible scene, but to give it back brilliantly, could have presented so vivid an image of what Americans are or believe themselves to be. It was the satire that always gave Lewis's books their design, but the life that streamed out of them impressed people most by giving them a final *happy* recognition. Lewis caught the vulgarity and the perpetual salesmanship, and caught it as effortlessly as he caught the sights and sounds, the exact sound of a Ford car being cranked on a summer morning in Zenith in 1922, the exact resemblance of Chum Frinkley to Eddie Guest and of Sharon Falconer to Aimée Semple McPherson. But he caught also, as almost no one did before him, the boyish helplessness of a Babbitt, the stammering romance of a Martin Arrowsmith on his first day at the McGurk Institute, the loneliness of a great Sam Dodsworth before all those Europeans in Paris. Even his novel on Fascism reminded Americans that when an exiled American Hitler like Buzz Windrip goes to Paris, he yearns only for Lucky Strikes and the smoking-car jokes of his pals. Even his assault on small-town ignorance and bigotry in *Main Street* suggested that if Carol Kennicott was heroically unhappy on Main Street, she was just a little silly with her passion for uplift.

ERNEST HEMINGWAY

"He is not a propagandist even for humanity"

A revolutionist in style, Ernest Hemingway has had a more
powerful effect on other writers than any other American
novelist since the first World War. Edmund Wilson's review
(the *Dial* for October, 1924) of Hemingway's *In Our Time*
(1924) immediately registered the original quality of this
new work, and as Hemingway's letter shows, he was properly
pleased.

M R. HEMINGWAY'S POEMS are not particularly impor-
tant, but his prose is of the first distinction. He must be counted
as the only American writer but one—Mr. Sherwood Anderson
—who has felt the genius of Gertrude Stein's *Three Lives* and has
evidently been influenced by it. Indeed, Miss Stein, Mr. Anderson
and Mr. Hemingway may now be said to form a school by themselves. The characteristic of this school is a naïveté of language,
often passing into the colloquialism of the character dealt with,
which serves actually to convey profound emotions and complex
states of mind. It is a distinctively American development in prose
—as opposed to more or less successful American achievements
in the traditional style of English prose—which has artistically
justified itself at its best as a limpid shaft into deep waters.

Not, however, that Mr. Hemingway is imitative. On the con-

From Edmund Wilson, "Emergence of Ernest Hemingway," in *The Shores
of Light: A Literary Chronicle of the Twenties and Thirties* (New York:
Farrar, Straus and Young, Inc., 1952), pp. 119–124. Reprinted by permission
of the author.

trary, he is rather strikingly original, and in the dry compressed little vignettes of *In Our Time*, has almost invented a form of his own:

> They shot the six cabinet ministers at half-past six in the morning against the wall of a hospital. There were pools of water in the courtyard. There were dead leaves on the paving of the courtyard. It rained hard. All the shutters of the hospital were nailed shut. One of the ministers was sick with typhoid. Two soldiers carried him downstairs and out into the rain. They tried to hold him up against the wall but he sat down in a puddle of water. The other five stood very quietly against the wall. Finally the officer told the soldiers it was no good trying to make him stand up. When they fired the first volley he was sitting down in the water with his head on his knees.

Mr. Hemingway is remarkably successful in suggesting moral values by a series of simple statements of this sort. His more important book is called *In Our Time*, and, behind its cool objective manner, it constitutes a harrowing record of the barbarities of the period in which we live: you have not only political executions, but hangings of criminals, bull-fights, assassinations by the police and the cruelties and horrors of the war. Mr. Hemingway is unperturbed as he tells us about these things: he is not a propagandist even for humanity. His bull-fight sketches have the dry sharpness and elegance of the bull-fight lithographs of Goya. And, like Goya, he is concerned first of all with making a fine picture. Too proud an artist to simplify in the interests of conventional pretenses, he is showing you what life is like. And I am inclined to think that his little book has more artistic dignity than anything else about the period of the war that has as yet been written by an American.

Not perhaps the most vivid book, but the soundest. Mr. Hemingway, who can make you feel the poignancy of the Italian soldier deciding in his death agony that he will "make a separate peace," has no anti-militarist parti pris which will lead him to suppress from his record the exhilaration of the men who had "jammed an absolutely perfect barricade across the bridge" and who were "frightfully put out when we heard the flank had gone, and we had to fall back." It is only in the paleness, the thinness of some of his effects that Mr. Hemingway sometimes fails. I am thinking especially of the story called *Up in Michigan*, which should have been a masterpiece, but has the curious defect of dealing with rude and primitive people yet leaving them rather shadowy.

In Our Time has a pretty and very amusing cover designed from scrambled newspaper clippings. The only objection I have to its appearance is that the titles are printed throughout without capitals—thus: "in our time by ernest hemingway—paris." This device, which had a certain effectiveness when the modernists used it first to call attention to the newness of what they were offering, is now becoming a bore. The American advertisers have taken it over as one of their stock tricks. And it is so unsightly in itself that one does not like to see it become—as in the case of Mr. Hemingway's book and Mr. Hueffer's *trans-atlantic review*— a kind of badge for all that is freshest and most interesting in contemporary writing.   October, 1924

In connection with this review, Hemingway wrote me the following letter:

> 113 Rue Notre Dame des Champs
> Paris VII
> October 18, 1924

Dear Wilson:

Thank you so much for writing the review in the October *Dial*. I liked it very much. You are very right about the lack of capital letters—which seemed very silly and affected to me—but Bird had put them in and as he was printing the *In Our Time* himself and that was all the fun he was getting out of it I thought he could go ahead and be a damn fool in his own way if it pleased him. So long as he did not fool with the text.

I'm awfully glad you liked it.

How are you anyway? and did you ever get Chaplin for your ballet?

We have lived very quietly, working hard, except for a trip to Spain, Pamplona, where we had a fine time and I learned a lot about bull fighting, the inside the ring scene. We had a lot of minor adventures.

I've worked like hell most of the time and think the stuff gets better. Finished the book of 14 stories with a chapter on *In Our Time* between each story—that is the way they were meant to go—to give the picture of the whole between examining it in detail. Like looking with your eyes at something, say a passing coast line, and then looking at it with 15X binoculars. Or rather, maybe, looking at it and then going in and living in it—and then coming out and looking at it again.

I sent the book to Don Stewart at the Yale Club about three weeks ago. When he was here he offered to try and sell it for me. I think you would like it, it has a pretty good unity. In some of the stories since the *In Our Time* I've gotten across both the people and the scene. It makes you feel good when you can do it. It feels now as though I had gotten on top of it.

Will you get over here this winter do you think? We will probably be in Paris all winter. Not enough money to get out. The baby is very well and husky. Hadley is working on the piano.

She sends her best regards to you and Mrs. Wilson.

Hope everything is going well with you and that you have a good winter. I would like to hear from you and I did appreciate the review. It was cool and clear minded and decent and impersonal and sympathetic. Christ how I hate this terrible personal stuff. Do you remember my writing from Toronto wanting some reviews and publicity? and then got some and it turned me sick.

I think there's nothing more discouraging than unintelligent appreciation. Not really discouraging; but just driving something back inside of you. Some bright guy said *In Our Time* was a series of thumbnail sketches showing a great deal of talent but obviously under the influence of Ring Lardner. Yeah! That kind of stuff is fine. It doesn't bother. But these wordy, sentimental bastards. You are the only man writing criticism who or whom I can read when the book being criticized is one I've read or know something about. I can read almost anybody when they write on things I don't know about. Intelligence is so damn rare and the people who have it often have such a bad time with it that they get bitter or propagandistic and then it's not much use.

With best wishes to you and to your wife.

Very sincerely,

ERNEST HEMINGWAY

Is this *What Price Glory?* really a good play. I don't mean a good *play*—it sounds fine over here.

"Hemingway has always shown the integrity which only the true masters of a style or subject can claim"

MORTON DAUWEN ZABEL

The careers and reputations of American writers seem peculiarly liable to severe ups and downs. After Hemingway wrote *Across the River and into the Trees* (1950) he seemed to have reached an impasse, but with *The Old Man and the Sea* (1952) he reasserted his powers. Now he is riding high again. Morton Dauwen Zabel indicates how autobiographical all Hemingway's writing has been and yet how severe his self-criticism has also been. "Hemingway has been from the beginning his own first, last, and consistent critic."

WHEN HEMINGWAY PUBLISHED *Across the River and into the Trees* he gave his strongest followers reason to believe that his resources had been depleted. This was not a new experience for them, but it had never been quite so emphatic. The novel gave every possible sign of marking an impasse not only in his subject matter and moral assumptions but in its style and method. The book was, as we now know, written at a point of crisis in his life. He found himself seriously, perhaps fatally, ill. The tale was apparently conceived as a personal valedictory, an act of conscious stock-taking and intimate moral self-projection. And as so often in books of such motivation—*Pierre, The Sacred Fount, The "Genius," L'Immoraliste, The Arrow of Gold,* to some extent in a

From Morton Dauwen Zabel, *Craft and Character in Modern Fiction*, pp. 323–326. Copyright © 1957 by Morton Dauwen Zabel. Reprinted by permission of The Viking Press, Inc.

finer novel than any of these, *Tender Is The Night*—it showed, but in an extreme degree, the liability of that order of inspiration. The writer's persona proved almost abjectly inadequate to the use exacted of it; the personal usurped the functions of the intimate; imaginative projection yielded to defensive apology. The result was a failure not only of imagination but of language, of insight and expression as much as of drama, with results not only embarrassing but fundamentally disastrous in fiction or any other kind of writing: the book gave away its secret and so offended the first law of its art. *Across the River* has already been treated to some misspent ingenuity of analysis and symbolic interpretation by unflinching admirers of its author. This has possibly yielded some interesting psychological evidence; on the score of its critical or aesthetic relevance it has amounted to little but a documentation of the obvious. For let us make no mistake about it. It was a bad book, an almost desperately miscalculated performance; it had the effect of certifying the latent weaknesses in Hemingway's equipment; and to rate it as anything else is to do his finer powers a disservice.

Those powers, which for thirty years have been among the major assets and one of the surest reasons for pride in the American creative achievement, reappear in strength in *The Old Man and the Sea*. The tale is so admirably written, so beautifully conceived and stated, so firmly controlled and so accurately condensed to its essence, that it invites rating as one of the finest things Hemingway has ever done. Perhaps it should be said at the outset that this may not be the case. It does not show the strongest implicitness of conception and feeling he has been capable of in the past, in "Big Two-Hearted River," or "The Killers," or "The Undefeated," or "Fathers and Sons." It does not show the specific dramatic force of "Francis Macomber" or "Fifty Grand," or the intensity of tragic pathos of "An Alpine Idyll," "A Canary for One," "Cat in the Rain," and "Hills Like White Elephants." Its emblematic theme of heroism and endurance in old age recalls the similar themes of "The Undefeated" and "Old Man at the Bridge" without quite achieving the emotional reality of the first or the steel-cut precision, so perfectly laconic yet so bitterly and classically accurate, of the second. And of course it deliberately avoids the fuller dramatic and psychological body of the longer novels. Hemingway has always shown the integrity which only the true masters of a style or a subject can claim: he has from the first supplied his own standard of value, and it asserts itself as urgently in relation to his best work as to his weakest. The *Old Man* recapitulates his powers as unmistakably as *Across the River* summed up his failings, and both of them do so by measures he himself has supplied. Just as there has been something remorseless about the lengths to which he has indulged his shortcomings, so there is something ruthless about the test to which he can rise when he recovers his strength and about the way he in turn imposes that test on his readers.

Another matter in which he has always kept company with the masters of his art is the combination in his work of an intense personal necessity for expression and self-realization and of the objective intelligence, severe and unsparing, by which his art judges and controls that intimate personal need. Everything he has written—including this story—has issued from his own personality, ordeal, conflict, self-doubt and self-concern. His themes, all the way from the stories of boyhood in Michigan and soldiering in war, to the tales of France, Africa, Spain, and Cuba, suggest their autobiographical origins. He is always himself present in his lines, whether they describe action or dream, objective events and characters or the moral commentary drawn from these. (*In Our Time*, with its alternation of anecdote and personal asides or epiphanic comments, gave a perfect and permanent definition of the elements at work in his mind and imagination, and its method has been projected for better or worse into everything he has written since.)

But against this insistent personal claim in his work there has always operated the critical force of his style and symbolic insights—the severe language, the spare accuracy of statement, the lean form, the precision in allegoric suggestion, the austere authority of his imagery and symbols. The intimate personality that speaks in his pages has never spared itself the checks and severity of this implicit discipline. The moment the personality indulges itself extravagantly, defensively, apologetically, or histrionically, it is made to feel the lash of the critical whip in his words, images, and rhythms. The overwrought reveries in "The Snows of Kilimanjaro," the self-justifying diatribes in *Death in the Afternoon* or

To Have and Have Not, the excesses of melodrama in *For Whom the Bell Tolls,* never escape the reproof of that latent honesty, even when the surface appearances of those books give every sign that it has been violated. Hemingway has been from the beginning his own first, last, and consistent critic. His essential art and drama derive from a persistent critical instinct in his style and method. It has made possible the authority of his genius, given him his originality and success, provided the surest standard by which to judge his lapses, made a continuous moral drama of his career in art, and made of himself a classic example of the aesthetic conscience in his age and generation.

His own moral drama has given him the subject of *The Old Man and the Sea.* Its story of the old Cuban fisherman Santiago, famous for his skill and cunning, now deserted by his sacred luck, abandoned by everything but his hope and courage, desperate to catch the fish that still eludes him after eighty-four days of failure, successful at last in catching a fabulous giant marlin only to have it attacked by sharks and reduced to a skeleton, returning finally to port with his mutilated trophy, defeated in everything but faith and his determination to try once more, and blessed in nothing but his knowledge that life is tragic and survival alone a reason for gratitude—this is obviously susceptible to a large amount of personal interpretation. The degree to which it overtly invites such a reading may keep it from achieving the purer integrity of "The Undefeated" and "Old Man at the Bridge," but its superb sincerity of language and moral dignity removes it by miles from the messy apologetic and crude rancors of *Across The River.* As by a kind of systolic rhythm, the moral force of Hemingway's art has reasserted itself. Once more he has recovered the essential powers that have enabled him to mark a stage in the maturity of American writing and to declare his authority in the literature of his time. The authority has redefined itself; it returns unmistakably; but what makes it a particular lesson for his fellow-artists is the struggle that has gone into its making, the self-respect that has survived its abuses, and the hard tenacity by which it has endured.

"*All modern American literature comes from one book by Mark Twain called* Huckleberry Finn"

ERNEST HEMINGWAY

Ernest Hemingway's little lecture on American writers, though mannered and evasive, is undeniably interesting because it is so personal and succinct. It provides another testament to the difficulty of being a serious creative writer in America and reveals as no one else could the ambiguous feelings Hemingway has about his own country. Notice that *both* Henry James and Mark Twain are on his select list (only three) of "good writers."

W₁ HAVE BOOKS," he said. "I cannot buy new books now but we can always talk. Ideas and conversation are very interesting. We discuss all things. Everything. We have a very interesting mental life. Formerly, with the shamba, we had the *Querschnitt.* That gave you a feeling of belonging, of being made a part of, to a very brilliant group of people. The people one would see if one saw whom one wished to see. You know all of those people? You must know them."

"Some of them," I said. "Some in Paris. Some in Berlin."

I did not wish to destroy anything this man had, and so I did not go into those brilliant people in detail.

"They're marvellous," I said, lying.

"I envy you to know them," he said. "And tell me, who is the greatest writer in America?"

"My husband," said my wife.

Reprinted with the permission of Charles Scribner's Sons from *Green Hills of Africa* by Ernest Hemingway, pp. 18–25. Copyright 1935, Charles Scribner's Sons.

"No. I do not mean for you to speak from family pride. I mean who really? Certainly not Upton Sinclair. Certainly not Sinclair Lewis. Who is your Thomas Mann? Who is your Valery?"

"We do not have great writers," I said. "Something happens to our good writers at a certain age. I can explain but it is quite long and may bore you."

"Please explain," he said. "This is what I enjoy. This is the best part of life. The life of the mind. This is not killing kudu."

"You haven't heard it yet," I said.

"Ah, but I can see it coming. You must take more beer to loosen your tongue."

"It's loose," I told him. "It's always too bloody loose. But *you* don't drink anything."

"No, I never drink. It is not good for the mind. It is unnecessary. But tell me. Please tell me."

"Well," I said, "we have had, in America, skillful writers. Poe is a skillful writer. It is skillful, marvellously constructed, and it is dead. We have had writers of rhetoric who had the good fortune to find a little, in a chronicle of another man and from voyaging, of how things, actual things, can be, whales for instance, and this knowledge is wrapped in the rhetoric like plums in a pudding. Occasionally it is there, alone, unwrapped in pudding, and it is good. This is Melville. But the people who praise it, praise it for the rhetoric which is not important. They put a mystery in which is not there."

"Yes," he said. "I see. But it is the mind working, its ability to work, which makes the rhetoric. Rhetoric is the blue sparks from the dynamo."

"Sometimes. And sometimes it is only blue sparks and what is the dynamo driving?"

"So. Go on."

"I've forgotten."

"No. Go on. Do not pretend to be stupid."

"Did you ever get up before daylight—"

"Every morning," he said. "Go on."

"All right. There were others who wrote like exiled English colonials from an England of which they were never a part to a newer England that they were making. Very good men with the small, dried, and excellent wisdom of Unitarians; men of letters; Quakers with a sense of humor."

"Who were these?"

"Emerson, Hawthorne, Whittier, and Company. All our early classics who did not know that a new classic does not bear any resemblance to the classics that have preceded it. It can steal from anything that it is better than, anything that is not a classic, all classics do that. Some writers are only born to help another writer to write one sentence. But it cannot derive from or resemble a previous classic. Also all these men were gentlemen, or wished to be. They were all very respectable. They did not use the words that people always have used in speech, the words that survive in language. Nor would you gather that they had bodies. They had minds, yes. Nice, dry, clean minds. This is all very dull, I would not state it except that you ask for it."

"Go on."

"There is one at that time that is supposed to be really good, Thoreau. I cannot tell you about it because I have not yet been able to read it. But that means nothing because I cannot read other naturalists unless they are being extremely accurate and not literary. Naturalists should all work alone and some one else should correlate their findings for them. Writers should work alone. They should see each other only after their work is done, and not too often then. Otherwise they become like writers in New York. All angleworms in a bottle, trying to derive knowledge and nourishment from their own contact and from the bottle. Sometimes the bottle is shaped art, sometimes economics, sometimes economic-religion. But once they are in the bottle they stay there. They are lonesome outside of the bottle. They do not want to be lonesome. They are afraid to be alone in their beliefs and no woman would love any of them enough so that they could kill their lonesomeness in that woman, or pool it with hers, or make something with her that makes the rest unimportant."

"But what about Thoreau?"

"You'll have to read him. Maybe I'll be able to later. I can do nearly everything later."

"Better have some more beer, Papa."

"All right."

"What about the good writers?"

"The good writers are Henry James, Stephen Crane, and Mark Twain. That's not the order they're good in. There is no order for good writers."

"Mark Twain is a humorist. The others I do not know."

"All modern American literature comes from one book by Mark Twain called *Huckleberry Finn*. If you read it you must stop where the Nigger Jim is stolen from the boys. That is the real end. The rest is just cheating. But it's the best book we've had. All American writing comes from that. There was nothing before. There has been nothing as good since."

"What about the others?"

"Crane wrote two fine stories. *The Open Boat* and *The Blue Hotel*. The last one is the best."

"And what happened to him?"

"He died. That's simple. He was dying from the start."

"But the other two?"

"They both lived to be old men but they did not get any wiser as they got older. I don't know what they really wanted. You see we make our writers into something very strange."

"I do not understand."

"We destroy them in many ways. First, economically. They make money. It is only by hazard that a writer makes money although good books always make money eventually. Then our writers when they have made some money increase their standard of living and they are caught. They have to write to keep up their establishments, their wives, and so on, and they write slop. It is slop not on purpose but because it is hurried. Because they write when there is nothing to say or no water in the well. Because they are ambitious. Then, once they have betrayed themselves, they justify it and you get more slop. Or else they read the critics. If they believe the critics when they say they are great then they must believe them when they say they are rotten and they lose confidence. At present we have two good writers who cannot write because they have lost confidence through reading critics. If they wrote, sometimes it would be good and sometimes not so good and sometimes it would be quite bad, but the good would get out. But they have read the critics and they must write masterpieces. The masterpieces the critics said they wrote. They weren't masterpieces, of course. They were just quite good books. So now they cannot write at all. The critics have made them impotent."

"Who are these writers?"

"Their names would mean nothing to you and by now they

may have written, become frightened, and be impotent again."

"But what is it that happens to American writers? Be definite."

"I was not here in the old days so I cannot tell you about them, but now there are various things. At a certain age the men writers change into Old Mother Hubbard. The women writers become Joan of Arc without the fighting. They become leaders. It doesn't matter who they lead. If they do not have followers they invent them. It is useless for those selected as followers to protest. They are accused of disloyalty. Oh, hell. There are too many things happen to them. That is one thing. The others try to save their souls with what they write. That is an easy way out. Others are ruined by the first money, the first praise, the first attack, the first time they find they cannot write, or the first time they cannot do anything else, or else they get frightened and join organizations that do their thinking for them. Or they do not know what they want. Henry James wanted to make money. He never did, of course."

"And you?"

"I am interested in other things. I have a good life but I must write because if I do not write a certain amount I do not enjoy the rest of my life."

"And what do you want?"

"To write as well as I can and learn as I go along. At the same time I have my life which I enjoy and which is a damned good life."

F. SCOTT FITZGERALD

"An heroic personification of the American romantic hero"

MARIUS BEWLEY

With *The Great Gatsby* (1925) F. Scott Fitzgerald (1896–1940) "arrived" as an artist. Analyzing the hero of the novel, Marius Bewley finds him "a 'mythic' character" who "wears [the word 'gorgeous'] with an archetypal American elegance." This mythic quality means Gatsby has a kind of "impersonal significance" which we must understand if we are to take in his full dimensions. One characteristic of mythic heroes is that "there is no distinction between their public and their private lives." Consequently Gatsby's personal concerns, his love affair with Daisy, are not what hold our interest; what grips our imagination is "his compelling desire to realize all the possibilities of existence."

THE GREAT GATSBY is an exploration of the American dream as it exists in a corrupt period, and it is an attempt to determine that concealed boundary that divides the reality from the illusions. The illusions seem more real than the reality itself. Embodied in the subordinate characters in the novel, they threaten to invade the whole of the picture. On the other hand, the reality is embodied in Gatsby; and as opposed to the hard, tangible illusions, the reality is a thing of the spirit, a promise rather than the possession of a vision, a faith in the half-glimpsed, but hardly

From Marius Bewley, *The Eccentric Design* (New York: Columbia University Press, 1959), pp. 270–272, 273–274, 276–278, 287. Reprinted by permission of Columbia University Press.

understood, possibilities of life. In Gatsby's America, the reality
is undefined to itself. It is inarticulate and frustrated. Nick Carraway, Gatsby's friend and Fitzgerald's narrator, says of Gatsby:

> Through all he said, even through his appalling sentimentality, I was
> reminded of something—an elusive rhythm, a fragment of lost words,
> that I had heard somewhere a long time ago. For a moment a phrase
> tried to take shape in my mouth and my lips parted like a dumb man's
> as though there was more struggling upon them than a wisp of startled
> air. But they made no sound, and what I had almost remembered was
> incommunicado forever.

This is not pretentious phrase-making performing a vague gesture towards some artificial significance. It is both an evocative
and an exact description of that unholy cruel paradox by which
the conditions of American history have condemned the grandeur
of the aspiration and vision to expend itself in a waste of shame
and silence. But the reality is not entirely lost. It ends by redeeming the human spirit, even though it live in a wilderness of illusions, from the cheapness and vulgarity that encompass it. In
this novel, the illusions are known and condemned at last simply
by the rank complacency with which they are content to be themselves. On the other hand, the reality is in the energy of the
spirit's resistance, which may not recognize itself as resistance at
all, but which can neither stoop to the illusions nor abide with
them when they are at last recognized. Perhaps it is really nothing
more than ultimate immunity from the final contamination, but
it encompasses the difference between life and death. Gatsby never
succeeds in seeing through the sham of his world or his ac-
quaintances very clearly. It is of the essence of his romantic
American vision that it should lack the seasoned powers of discrimination. But it invests those illusions with its own faith, and
thus it discovers its projected goodness in the frauds of its crippled
world. *The Great Gatsby* becomes the acting out of the tragedy
of the American vision. It is a vision totally untouched by the
scales of values that order life in a society governed by traditional manners; and Fitzgerald knows that although it would be
easy to condemn and 'place' the illusions by invoking these outside values, to do so would be to kill the reality that lies beyond
them, but which can sometimes only be reached through them.

For example, Fitzgerald perfectly understood the inadequacy of Gatsby's romantic view of wealth. But that is not the point. He presents it in Gatsby as a romantic baptism of desire for a reality that stubbornly remains out of his sight. It is as if a savage islander, suddenly touched with Grace, transcended in his prayers and aspirations the grotesque little fetish in which he imagined he discovered the object of his longing. The scene in which Gatsby shows his stacks of beautiful imported shirts to Daisy and Nick has been mentioned as a failure of Gatsby's, and so of Fitzgerald's, critical control of values. Actually, the shirts are sacramentals, and it is clear that Gatsby shows them, neither in vanity nor in pride, but with a reverential humility in the presence of some inner vision he cannot consciously grasp, but toward which he desperately struggles in the only way he knows.

In an essay called 'Myths for Materialists' Mr. Jacques Barzun once wrote that figures, whether of fact or fiction, in so far as they express destinies, aspirations, attitudes typical of man or particular groups, are invested with a mythical character. In this sense Gatsby is a 'mythic' character, and no other word will define him. Not only is he an embodiment (as Fitzgerald makes clear at the outset) of that conflict between illusion and reality at the heart of American life; he is an heroic personification of the American romantic hero, the true heir of the American dream. 'There was something gorgeous about him,' Nick Carraway says, and although 'gorgeous' was a favourite word with the 'twenties, Gatsby wears it with an archetypal American elegance.

. . . . .

Gatsby, for all his shimmer of representative surfaces, is never allowed to become soiled by the touch of realism. In creating him, Fitzgerald observed as high a decorum of character as a Renaissance playwright: for although Gatsby's parents were shiftless and unsuccessful farm people, Gatsby really 'sprang from his Platonic conception of himself. He was a son of God—a phrase which, if it means anything, means just that—and he must be about His Father's business, the service of a vast, vulgar, meretricious beauty'.

Fitzgerald created Gatsby with a sense of his own election; but the beauty it was in his nature to serve had already been betrayed by history. Even in the midst of the blighted earthly paradise of West Egg, Long Island, Gatsby bore about him the marks of his birth. He is a kind of exiled Duke in disguise. We know him by his bearing, the decorous pattern of his speech. Even his dress invariably touches the imagination: 'Gatsby in a white flannel suit, silver shirt, and gold coloured tie. . . .' There is something dogmatically Olympic about the combination. After Gatsby's death when his pathetic old father journeys east for the funeral, one feels that he is only the kindly shepherd who once found a baby on the cold hillside.

But so far I have been talking in general terms. This beautiful control of conventions can be studied more closely in the description of Gatsby's party at which (if we except that distant glimpse of him at the end of Chapter I, of which I shall speak later) we encounter him for the first time. We are told later that Gatsby was gifted with a 'hint of the unreality of reality, a promise that the rock of the world was founded securely on a fairy's wing.' Fitzgerald does not actually let us meet Gatsby face to face until he has concretely created this fantastic world of Gatsby's vision, for it is the element in which we must meet Gatsby if we are to understand his impersonal significance:

There was music from my neighbour's house through the summer nights. In his blue gardens men and girls came and went like moths among the whisperings and the champagne and the stars. At high tide in the afternoon I watched his guests diving from the tower of his raft, or taking the sun on the hot sand of his beach while his two motor-boats slit the waters of the Sound, drawing aquaplanes over cataracts of foam. On week-ends his Rolls-Royce became an omnibus, bearing parties to and from the city between nine in the morning and long past midnight, while his station wagon scampered like a brisk yellow bug to meet all trains. And on Mondays eight servants, including an extra gardener, toiled all day with mops and scrubbing-brushes and hammers and garden-shears, repairing the ravages of the night before.

The nostalgic poetic quality, which tends to leave one longing for sterner stuff, is, in fact, deceptive. It is Gatsby's ordeal that he must separate the foul dust that floated in the wake of his dreams from the reality of the dream itself: that he must find some vantage point from which he can bring the responsibilities and the possibilities of life into a single focus. But the 'ineffable gaudiness' of the world to which Gatsby is committed is a fatal deterrent. Even within the compass of this paragraph we see how the focus has become blurred: how the possibilities of life are conceived of in material terms. But in that heroic list of the vaster luxury items—motor-boats, aquaplanes, private beaches, Rolls-Royces, diving towers—Gatsby's vision maintains its gigantic unreal stature. It imposes a rhythm on his guests which they accept in terms of their own tawdry illusions, having no conception of the compulsion that drives him to offer them the hospitality of his fabulous wealth. They come for their week-ends as George Dane in Henry James's *The Great Good Place* went into his dream retreat. But the result is not the same: 'on Mondays eight servants, including an extra gardener, toiled all day with mops and scrubbing-brushes and hammers and garden-shears, repairing the ravages of the night before'. That is the most important sentence in the paragraph, and despite the fairy-story overtone, it possesses an ironic nuance that rises towards the tragic. And how fine that touch of the extra gardener is—as if Gatsby's guests had made a breach in nature. It completely qualifies the over-fragility of the moths and champagne and blue gardens in the opening sentences.

. . . . .

'Mythic' characters are impersonal. There is no distinction between their public and their private lives. Because they share their meaning with everyone, they have no secrets and no hidden corners into which they can retire for a moment, unobserved. An intimacy so universal stands revealed in a ritual pattern for the inspection and instruction of the race. The 'mythic' character can never withdraw from that air which is his existence—that is to say, from that area of consciousness (and hence of publicity) which every individual shares with the members, both living and dead, of his group or race. Gatsby is a 'mythic' character in this sense—he has no private life, no meaning or significance that depends on the fulfilment of his merely private destiny, his happiness as an individual in a society of individuals. In a transcendent sense he touches our imaginations, but in this smaller sense— which is the world of the realistic novel—he even fails to arouse our curiosity. At this level, his love affair with Daisy is too easily 'placed', a tawdry epic 'crush' of no depth or interest in itself. But Gatsby not only remains undiminished by what is essentially the meanness of the affair: his stature grows, as we watch, to the proportions of a hero. We must inquire how Fitzgerald managed this extraordinary achievement.

Daisy Buchanan exists at two well-defined levels in the novel. She is what she is—but she exists at the level of Gatsby's vision of her. Even Fitzgerald's admirers regard Daisy as rather a good, if somewhat silly, little thing; but Fitzgerald knew that at its most depraved levels the American dream merges with the American debutante's dream—a thing of deathly hollowness. Fitzgerald faces up squarely to the problem of telling us what Daisy has to offer in a human relationship. At one of Gatsby's fabulous parties —the one to which Daisy brings her husband, Tom Buchanan— Gatsby points out to Daisy and Tom, among the celebrated guests, one particular couple:

> 'Perhaps you know that lady,' Gatsby indicated a gorgeous, scarcely human orchid of a woman who sat in state under a white-plum tree. Tom and Daisy stared, with that peculiarly unreal feeling that accompanies the recognition of a hitherto ghostly celebrity of the movies.
> 'She's lovely,' said Daisy.
> 'That man bending over her is her director.'

Superficially, the scene is highly civilized. One fancies one has seen it in Manet. But in the context we know that it has no reality whatever—the star and her director can get no nearer reality than by rehearsing a scene. Our attention is then taken up by other scenes at the party, but by suddenly returning to this couple after an interval of two pages to make his point, Fitzgerald achieves a curious impression of static or arrested action. We have the feeling that if we walked behind the white-plum tree we should only see the back of a canvas screen:

> Almost the last thing I remember was standing with Daisy and watching the moving-picture director and his Star. They were still under the white-plum tree and their faces were touching except for a pale, thin ray of moonlight between. It occurred to me that he had been very slowly bending toward her all evening to attain this proximity, and even while I watched I saw him stoop one ultimate degree and kiss at her cheek.
> 'I like her,' said Daisy, 'I think she's lovely.'
> But the rest offended her—and inarguably, because it wasn't a gesture but an emotion.

Daisy likes the moving-picture actress because she has no substance. She is a gesture that is committed to nothing more real than her own image on the silver screen. She has become a gesture divorced forever from the tiresomeness of human reality. In effect, this passage is Daisy's confession of faith. She virtually announces here what her criteria of human emotions and conduct are. Fitzgerald's illustration of the emptiness of Daisy's character —an emptiness that we see curdling into the viciousness of a monstrous moral indifference as the story unfolds—is drawn with a fineness and depth of critical understanding, and communicated with a force of imagery so rare in modern American writing, that it is almost astonishing that he is often credited with giving in to those very qualities which *The Great Gatsby* so effectively excoriates.

. . . . .

We recognized that the great achievement of this novel is that it manages, while poetically evoking a sense of the goodness of that early dream, to offer the most damaging criticism of it in American literature. The astonishing thing is that the criticism— if indictment wouldn't be the better word—manages to be part of the tribute. Gatsby, the 'mythic' embodiment of the American dream, is shown to us in all his immature romanticism. His insecure grasp of social and human values, his lack of critical intelligence and self-knowledge, his blindness to the pitfalls that surround him in American society, his compulsive optimism, are realized in the text with rare assurance and understanding. And yet the very grounding of these deficiencies is Gatsby's goodness and faith in life, his compelling desire to realize all the possibilities of existence, his belief that we can have an Earthly Paradise populated by Buchanans. A great part of Fitzgerald's achievement is that he suggests effectively that these terrifying deficiencies are not so much the private deficiencies of Gatsby, but are deficiencies inherent in contemporary manifestations of the American vision itself—a vision no doubt admirable, but stupidly defenceless before the equally American world of Tom and Daisy. Gatsby's deficiencies of intelligence and judgment bring him to his tragic death—a death that is spiritual as well as physical. But the more important question that faces us through our sense of the immediate tragedy is where they have brought America.

"*The first step that American fiction has taken since Henry James*"

T. S. ELIOT

The following letter from T. S. Eliot is the kind of thing writers dream about receiving. The dream of F. Scott Fitzgerald came true.

FROM T. S. ELIOT

Faber and Gwyer Ltd.

Publishers

24 Russell Square,
London, W. C. 1.
31st December, 1925

F. Scott Fitzgerald, Esqre.,
c/o Charles Scribners & Sons,
New York City.

Dear Mr. Scott Fitzgerald,

The Great Gatsby with your charming and overpowering inscription arrived the very morning that I was leaving in some haste for a sea voyage advised by my doctor. I therefore left it behind and only read it on my return a few days ago. I have, however, now read it three times. I am not in the least influenced by your remark about myself when I say that it has interested and excited me more than any new novel I have seen, either English or American, for a number of years.

When I have time I should like to write to you more fully and tell you exactly why it seems to me such a remarkable book. In fact it seems to me to be the first step that American fiction has taken since Henry James. . . .

T. S. Eliot, letter to Scott Fitzgerald in F. Scott Fitzgerald, *The Crack-Up*, ed. Edmund Wilson, p. 310. Copyright 1945 by New Directions. Reprinted by permission of New Directions.

By the way, if you ever have any short stories which you think would be suitable for the *Criterion* I wish you would let me see them.
With many thanks, I am,

Yours very truly,

T. S. ELIOT

P. S. By a coincidence Gilbert Seldes in his New York Chronicle in the *Criterion* for January 14th has chosen your book for particular mention.

"In the fragments of The Last Tycoon, *you can see the beginning of a real grand style"*

JOHN DOS PASSOS

Using the occasion of his anger at the notices of Scott Fitzgerald's death, John Dos Passos delivers some home truths about the literary situation in America. He shows how Fitzgerald was a victim of this situation, and how in the end he transcended his own failings.

THE NOTICES in the press referring to Scott Fitzgerald's untimely death produced in the reader the same strange feeling that you have when, after talking about some topic for an hour with a man, it suddenly comes over you that neither you nor he has understood a word of what the other was saying. The gentlemen who wrote these pieces obviously knew something about writing the English language, and it should follow that they knew

John Dos Passos, "A Note on Fitzgerald," in F. Scott Fitzgerald, *The Crack-Up*, ed. Edmund Wilson, pp. 338–343. Copyright 1945 by New Directions. Reprinted by permission of New Directions.

how to read it. But shouldn't the fact that they had set themselves up to make their livings as critics of the work of other men furnish some assurance that they recognized the existence of certain standards in the art of writing? If there are no permanent standards, there is no criticism possible.

It seems hardly necessary to point out that a well written book is a well written book whether it's written under Louis XIII or Joe Stalin or on the wall of a tomb of an Egyptian Pharaoh. It's the quality of detaching itself from its period while embodying its period that marks a piece of work as good. I would have no quarrel with any critic who examined Scott Fitzgerald's work and declared that in his opinion it did not detach itself from its period. My answer would be that my opinion was different. The strange thing about the articles that came out about Fitzgerald's death was that the writers seemed to feel that they didn't need to read his books; all they needed for a license to shovel them into the ashcan was to label them as having been written in such and such a period now past. This leads us to the inescapable conclusion that these gentlemen had no other standards than the styles of window-dressing on Fifth Avenue. It means that when they wrote about literature all they were thinking of was the present rating of a book on the exchange, a matter which has almost nothing to do with its eventual value. For a man who is making his living as a critic to write about Scott Fitzgerald without mentioning *The Great Gatsby* just meant that he didn't know his business. To write about the life of a man as important to American letters as the author of *The Great Gatsby* in terms of last summer's styles in ladies' hats, showed an incomprehension of what it was all about, that, to anyone who cared for the art of writing, was absolutely appalling. Fortunately there was enough of his last novel already written to still these silly yappings. The celebrity was dead. The novelist remained.

It is tragic that Scott Fitzgerald did not live to finish *The Last Tycoon*. Even as it stands I have an idea that it will turn out to be one of those literary fragments that from time to time appear in the stream of a culture and profoundly influence the course of future events. His unique achievement, in these beginnings of a great novel, is that here for the first time he has managed to establish that unshakable moral attitude towards the world we live in and towards its temporary standards that is the basic essential of any powerful work of the imagination. A firmly anchored ethical standard is something that American writing has been struggling towards for half a century.

During most of our history our writers have been distracted by various forms of the double standard of morals. Most of our great writers of the early nineteenth century were caught on the tarbaby of the decency complex of the period, so much more painful in provincial America than on Queen Grundy's own isle. Since the successful revolt of the realists under Dreiser, the dilemma has been different, but just as acute. A young American proposing to write a book is faced by the world, the flesh and the devil on the one hand and on the other by the cramped schoolroom of the highbrows with its flyblown busts of the European great and its priggish sectarian attitudes. There's popular fiction and fortune's bright roulette wheel, and there are the erratic aspirations of the longhaired men and shorthaired women who, according to the folklore of the time, live on isms and Russian tea, and absinthe and small magazines of verse. Everybody who has put pen to paper during the last twenty years has been daily plagued by the difficulty of deciding whether he's to do "good" writing that will satisfy his conscience or "cheap" writing that will satisfy his pocketbook. Since the standards of value have never been strongly established, it's often been hard to tell which was which. As a result all but the most fervid disciples of the cloistered muse have tended to try to ride both horses at once, or at least alternately. That effort and the subsequent failure to make good either aim, has produced hideous paroxysms of moral and intellectual obfuscation. A great deal of Fitzgerald's own life was made a hell by this sort of schizophrenia, that ends in paralysis of the will and of all the functions of body and mind. No durable piece of work, either addressed to the pulps or to the ages, has ever been accomplished by a double-minded man. To attain the invention of any sound thing, no matter how trivial, demands the integrated effort of somebody's whole heart and whole intelligence. The agonized efforts of split personalities to assert themselves in writing has resulted, on the money side, in a limp pandering to every conceivable low popular taste and prejudice, and, on the angels' side, in a sterile connoisseur viewpoint that has made "good" writing, like vintage wines and old colonial chairs, a coefficient of the leisure of the literate rich.

One reason for the persistence of this strange dualism and the resulting inefficiency of the men and women who have tried to create literature in this country is that few of us have really faced the problem of who was going to read what we wrote. Most of us started out with a dim notion of a parliament of our peers and our betters through the ages that would eventually screen out the vital grain. To this the Marxists added the heady picture of the onmarching avenging armies of the proletariat who would read your books round their campfires. But as the years ground on both the aristocratic republic of letters of the eighteenth century and the dreams of a universal first of May have receded further and further from the realities we have had to live among. Only the simple requirements of the editors of mass circulation magazines with income based on advertising have remained fairly stable, as have the demands of the public brothels of Hollywood, where retired writers, after relieving their consciences by a few sanctimonious remarks expressing what is known in those haunts as "integrity," have earned huge incomes by setting their wits to work to play up to whatever tastes of the average man seemed easiest to cash in on at any given moment.

This state of things is based, not, as they try to make us believe, on the natural depravity of men with brains, but on the fact that for peace as well as for war industrial techniques have turned the old world upside down. Writers are up today against a new problem of illiteracy. Fifty years ago you either learned to read and write or you didn't learn. The constant reading of the bible in hundreds of thousands of humble families kept a basic floor of literacy under literature as a whole, and under the English language. The variety of styles of writing so admirably represented, the relative complexity of many of the ideas involved and the range of ethical levels to be found in that great compendium of ancient Hebrew culture demanded, in its reading and in its exposition to the children, a certain mental activity, and provided for the poorer classes the same sort of cultural groundwork that the study of Greek and Latin provided for the sons of the rich. A mind accustomed to the Old and New Testaments could easily admit Shakespeare and the entire range of Victorian writing: poetry, novels, historic and scientific essays, up to the saturation point of that particular intelligence. Today the English-speaking peoples have no such common basic classical education. The bottom level is the visual and aural culture of the movies, not a literary level at all. Above that appear all sorts of gradations of illiteracy, from those who, though they may have learned to read in school, are now barely able to spell out the captions in the pictures, to those who can take in, with the help of the photographs, a few simple sentences out of the daily tabloids, right through to the several millions of actively literate people who can read right through *The Saturday Evening Post* or *The Reader's Digest* and understand every word of it. This is the literal truth. Every statistical survey that has recently been made of literacy in this country has produced the most staggering results. We have to face the fact that the number of Americans capable of reading a page of anything not aimed at the mentality of a child of twelve is not only on the decrease but probably rapidly on the decrease. A confused intimation of this situation has, it seems to me, done a great deal to take the ground from under the feet of intelligent men who in the enthusiasm of youth decided to set themselves up to be writers. The old standards just don't ring true to the quicker minds of this unstable century. Literature, who for? they ask themselves. It is natural that they should turn to the easy demands of the popular market, and to that fame which if it is admittedly not deathless is at least ladled out publicly and with a trowel.

Scott Fitzgerald was one of the inventors of that kind of fame. As a man he was tragically destroyed by his own invention. As a writer his triumph was that he managed in *The Great Gatsby* and to a greater degree in *The Last Tycoon* to weld together again the two divergent halves, to fuse the conscientious worker that no creative man can ever really kill with the moneyed celebrity who aimed his stories at the twelve-year-olds. In *The Last Tycoon* he was even able to invest with some human dignity the pimp and pander aspects of Hollywood. There he was writing, not for highbrows or for lowbrows, but for whoever had enough elementary knowledge of the English language to read through a page of a novel.

Stahr, the prime mover of a Hollywood picture studio who is the central figure, is described with a combination of intimacy and detachment that constitutes a real advance over the treatment of such characters in all the stories that have followed Dreiser and Frank Norris. There is no trace of envy or adulation in the picture.

Fitzgerald writes about Stahr, not as a poor man writing about someone rich and powerful, nor as the impotent last upthrust of some established American stock sneering at a parvenu Jew; but coolly, as a man writing about an equal he knows and understands. Immediately a frame of reference is established that takes into the warm reasonable light of all-around comprehension the Hollywood magnate and the workers on the lot and the people in the dusty sunscorched bungalows of Los Angeles. In that frame of reference acts and gestures can be described on a broad and to a certain degree passionlessly impersonal terrain of common humanity.

This establishment of a frame of reference for common humanity has been the main achievement and the main utility of writing which in other times and places has come to be called great. It requires, as well as the necessary skill with the tools of the trade, secure standards of judgment that can only be called ethical. Hollywood, the subject of *The Last Tycoon*, is probably the most important and the most difficult subject for our time to deal with. Whether we like it or not it is in that great bargain sale of five and ten cent lusts and dreams that the new bottom level of our culture is being created. The fact that at the end of a life of brilliant worldly successes and crushing disasters Scott Fitzgerald was engaged so ably in a work of such importance proves him to have been the first-rate novelist his friends believed him to be. In *The Last Tycoon* he was managing to invent a set of people seen really in the round instead of lit by an envious spotlight from above or below. *The Great Gatsby* remains a perfect example of this sort of treatment at an earlier, more anecdotic, more bas relief stage, but in the fragments of *The Last Tycoon*, you can see the beginning of a real grand style. Even in their unfinished state these fragments, I believe, are of sufficient dimensions to raise the level of American fiction to follow in some such way as Marlowe's blank verse line raised the whole level of Elizabethan verse.

JOHN DOS PASSOS

"We begin to guess some stubborn sentimentalism"

EDMUND WILSON

This notice (April 17, 1929) of Edmund Wilson's was written before John Dos Passos had embarked on the trilogy called *U.S.A.* (1930–1936) for which he is remembered today, but some of the questions it raises are not obsolete.

Now, THE LIFE of middle-class America, even under capitalism and even in a city like New York, is not so unattractive as Dos Passos makes it—no human life under any conditions can ever have been so unattractive. Under however an unequal distribution of wealth, human beings are still capable of enjoyment, affection and enthusiasm—even of integrity and courage. Nor are these qualities and emotions entirely confined to class-conscious workers and their leaders. There are moments in reading a novel or seeing a play by Dos Passos when one finds oneself ready to rush to the defense of even the American bathroom, even the Ford car—which, after all, one begins to reflect, have perhaps done as much to rescue us from helplessness, ignorance and squalor as the prophets of revolution. We may begin to reflect upon the relation, in Dos Passos, of political opinions to artistic effects. Might it not, we ask ourselves, be possible—have we not, in fact, seen it occur—for a writer to hold Dos Passos's political opinions and yet not depict our middle-class republic as a place where no birds sing, no flowers bloom and where the very air is

From Edmund Wilson, "Dos Passos and the Social Revolution," in *The Shores of Light: A Literary Chronicle of the Twenties and Thirties* (New York: Farrar, Straus and Young, Inc., 1952), pp. 432–434. Reprinted by permission of the author.

almost unbreathable? For, in the novels and plays of Dos Passos, everybody loses out: if he is on the right side of the social question, he has to suffer, if he is not snuffed out; if he is on the oppressors' side, his pleasures are made repulsive. When a man as intelligent as Dos Passos—that is, a man a good deal more intelligent than, say, Michael Gold or Upton Sinclair, who hold similar political views—when so intelligent a man and so good an artist allows his bias so to falsify his picture of life that, in spite of all the accurate observation and all the imaginative insight, its values are partly those of melodrama—we begin to guess some stubborn sentimentalism at the bottom of the whole thing—some deeply buried streak of hysteria of which his misapplied resentments represent the aggressive side. And from the moment we suspect the processes by which he has arrived at his political ideas, the ideas themselves become suspect.

In the meantime, whatever diagnosis we may make of Dos Passos's infatuation with the social revolution, he remains one of the few first-rate figures among our writers of his generation, and the only one of these who has made a systematic effort to study all the aspects of America and to take account of all its elements, to compose them into a picture which makes some general sense. Most of the first-rate men of Dos Passos's age— Hemingway, Wilder, Fitzgerald—cultivate their own little corners and do not confront the situation as a whole. Only Dos Passos has tried to take hold of it. . . .

"Dos Passos has definitely
extended the art of narration"

DELMORE SCHWARTZ

In *U.S.A.* John Dos Passos's intention was to be nothing less than "the architect of history." Interspersing accounts of public persons and events with crisp narratives of the private lives of his invented characters, he achieved an effect of epic magnitude. In his article Delmore Schwartz praises Dos Passos's achievement but then turns to an examination of the inadequacies of the "truth" embodied in the novels. For one thing, he says, "The unity, the *felt* unity, is only the loose grab-bag of time and place, 1919 and the U.S.A." The absence of plot emphasizes the similarity to some of the best modern poetry ("The Waste Land," Pound's *Cantos*), but it is a sacrifice the novel cannot afford. Finally, Dos Passos's very skill in getting "under the skin of his characters" tends to drag down the level of sensibility of the book. "There is no imagination, and no Don Quixote" at the center.

I F WE THINK for a moment of the newspaper as a representation of American life, we get some idea of the basis of John Dos Passos' enormous novel. It is not merely that one of the devices of this novel is the "newsreel" and consists of an arrangement of quotations from newspapers of the past thirty years; nor that another device is the "camera eye," and still another consists of biographies of Americans who have for the most part been prominent in the newspaper. It is in its whole sense of American life and in its formal character—its omnibus, omnivorous span— that Dos Passos' novel seems to at least one reader to derive from the newspaper. The sense of the unknown lives behind the wedding announcements and the obituaries, the immense gap between private life and public events, and betweeen the private experience of the individual and the public experience represented in the newspaper as being constituted by accident, violence, scandal, the speeches of politicians, and the deliberations of Congress —all this would seem to have a good deal to do with determining Dos Passos' vision and his intention. There were concerts, club meetings, and lectures in St. Petersburg on the night in October, 1917, when the Russian Revolution occurred—it is such a curious mixture of the private worlds and the public world that seems to obsess Dos Passos.

Another and related way of characterizing his novels is through the names he has given them: *Three Soldiers,* a "picture" of the

From Delmore Schwartz, "John Dos Passos and the Whole Truth," *The Southern Review,* 4 (Autumn, 1938), 351–352, 353–355, 357–358, 359–361, 364–365. Reprinted by permission of the author.

World War (which, curiously enough, delighted Amy Lowell), *Manhattan Transfer*, a "picture" of New York City, *The 42nd Parallel*, and *1919*. And thus it is interesting to remark that the name of *U.S.A.* apparently was chosen for Dos Passos by the reviewer in *Time* who said, when a part of the book appeared as a separate novel, that "Alone among U. S. writers, John Dos Passos has taken as his subject the whole U.S.A. and attempted to organize its chaotic high-pressure life into an understandable artistic pattern." The source of the title suggests that Dos Passos' way of grasping experience has a good deal, although not everything, in common not only with the triumvirate of *Time, Life,* and *Fortune*, but also with the whole tendency to get documents, to record facts, and to swallow the whole rich chaos of modern life.

. . . . .

At the conclusion of the last book of *U.S.A.* and after having written some 1400 pages, Dos Passos wrote a brief chapter to head the whole book and called the chapter *U.S.A.*, and here defined his intention, at the conclusion of his efforts, when he would know it best.

The young man walks by himself through the crowd that thins into night streets. . . . eyes greedy for warm curves of faces. . . . mind a beehive of hopes . . . muscles ache for the knowledge of jobs. The young man walks by himself searching through the crowd with greedy eyes, greedy ears taut to hear, by himself, alone . . .

The young man walks by himself, fast but not fast enough, far but not far enough (faces slide out of sight, talk trails into tattered scraps, ...) he must catch the last subway, the streetcar, the bus, run up the gangplank of all the steamboats, register at all the hotels, work in the cities, answer the want-ads, live in all the boardinghouses. . . . one job is not enough, one life is not enough.

And the only link, we are told, between the young man walking alone and the life he wished to know so fully was in the speech of the people. U.S.A. meant and was many things—a part of a continent, a group of holding companies, the soldiers who died for the U.S.A., the letters on an address, a stack of newspapers on file—"but mostly U.S.A., is the speech of the people." And Dos Passos has told us this before, in the introduction written to *Three Soldiers*, in 1932, when that book was canonized by The Modern Library. Again what he says is worth quoting for its expression of the utter honesty and clarity of his intention.

You wake up one morning and find that what was to have been a *springboard into reality* [my italics] is a profession. Making a living by selling daydreams is all right, but few men feel it's much of a life for a man. . . . What I'm trying to get out is the difference in kind between the work of James Joyce, say, and that of any current dispenser of daydreams. . . . What do you write for, then? To convince people of something? That's preaching, and a part of the business of everyone who deals with words. . . . but outside of preaching I think there is such a thing as straight writing . . . . The mind of a generation is its speech. A writer makes aspects of that speech enduring . . . . makes of them forms to set the mind of tomorrow's generation. That's history. A writer who writes straight is the architect of history . . . . Those of us who have lived through [these times] have seen the years strip the bunting off the great illusions of our time. We must deal with the raw structure of history now, we must deal with it quick, before it stamps us out.

One may regret the slanging tone, as of Mr. Otis Ferguson (as if Dos Passos too were afraid that if he used abstract terms and an unconversational diction, he would be considered a sissy), and one may feel that an "architect of history" is rather a fancy claim, but one cannot deny that Dos Passos knows very well what he wants to do in his novels.

. . . . .

The major part of the novel, perhaps as much as 1200 pages, is, however, constituted by direct narratives of the lives of eleven leading characters and perhaps three times as many minor ones who are notable. In creating a mode in which to present the lives of these characters, Dos Passos has definitely extended the art of narration. It is difficult to describe what he has accomplished because it is so much a matter of the digestion of a great many details and the use of facts which rise from the historical sense— all caught into a smooth-running story which, taken in itself, cannot fail to hold the reader's attention. The narratives are always in the third person and yet have all the warm interior flow of a story presented through the medium of a stream-of-consciousness first-person. One remarkable achievement is the way in which the element of time is disposed. With no break or unevenness at all, the narrative passes quickly through several years of the character's life, presenting much that is essential briefly, and then contracts, without warning, without being noted, and focuses for several pages upon a single episode which is important. It is an ability which an apprentice writer can best appreciate and comes from the indispensable knowledge of how very much the writer can *omit*—Hemingway knows this very well also—and a knowledge of how each sentence can expand in the reader's mind to include a whole context of experience. Another feature to be noted is Dos Passos' immense command of details which seem to come from a thousand American places and to be invested with a kind of historical idiom at all times. There is, for example, the story of Eleanor Stoddard, which begins:

> When she was small she hated everything. She hated her father, a stout red haired man smelling of whiskers and stale pipe tobacco. He worked in an office in the stockyards . . . Nights she used to dream she lived alone with her mother in a big clean white house in Oak Park in winter when there was snow on the ground and she'd been setting a white linen table cloth with bright white silver . . . When she was sixteen in highschool she and a girl named Isabelle swore together that if a boy ever touched them they'd kill themselves . . . The only other person Eleanor liked was Miss Oliphant, her English teacher . . . It was Miss Oliphant who induced Eleanor to take courses at the Art Institute. She had reproductions on her walls of pictures by Rossetti and Burne-Jones . . . She made Eleanor feel that Art was something ivory white and very pure and noble and distant and sad . . . She was reading through the complete works of George Eliot.

The whiskers and stale pipe smoke, the white house and the snow, the pictures of Rossetti and Burne-Jones, and the novels of George Eliot (as understood by such a person)—with such qualitative details a whole type of girlhood is summoned up and placed in time. The utterance, as if from the movement of the character's mind, is completely convincing and is achieved by a discreet use of speech diction and speech rhythms and words of direct feeling. Dos Passos has had to work for a long time to attain to this kind of mastery. In his earlier novels, the description was always thick, heavy, isolated, and the use of dialects at times approximated a vaudeville show. But these faults have been pursued to the point where they are magnificent virtues.

. . . . .

Whatever else we may say of American life as represented in these narratives, there is one statement which we must make first: it is so, it is true; we have seen this with our own eyes and many of us have lived in this way. This is a true picture of the lives of many Americans, and anyone who doubts the fact can learn for himself very quickly how accurate Dos Passos is. But there is, on the other hand, a great deal more to be said about the truth which the novel as a form is capable of presenting.

To begin the attempt at a thorough judgment, the formal inadequacy of *U.S.A.*, taken as a whole, is the direct experience of every reader. There is no need to summon up abstract canons, nor to make that very interesting approach which can be summed up in the question: what would Henry James say? No reader can go from page one to page 1449 without feeling that the newsreels, camera eyes, and biographies, however good they may be in themselves, are interruptions which thwart his interest and break the novel into many isolated parts.* Even in the central narratives, where, as in the greatest pure prose (that of Stendhal and Tolstoy, where the word is transparent as glass), the reader passes without an awareness of style to the intense, ragged actuality presented, even here the novel falls into separate parts, even though there is an occasional interweaving of lives. The unity, the *felt* unity, is only the loose grab-bag of time and place, 1919 and the U.S.A. The binding together of lives (and thus of the reader's interest and gaze) into the progress of a plot—an element present even in a work of the scope of *War and Peace*— is wholly lacking. This heaping together of fragments of valuable perception is a characteristic of the best poetry of our time and the connection is interesting. *The Waste Land,* Pound's *Cantos, The Bridge,* and *The Orators* of Auden are all examples. And as there is a separation or gap between the sensibility of the camera eye and the narrative form in *U.S.A.*, so in the history of modern poetry we can remark the converse phenomenon, how, since Coleridge wrote marginal summaries of the narrative to "The Ancient Mariner," the capacity for a narrative framework has gradually disappeared from poetry of the first order: modern

---

* In his essay on Dos Passos, Malcolm Cowley insists that there is a sufficient connection between the narratives and the other forms. There is, for example, a biography of Wilson when the fictional persons are concerned with the aftermath of the World War, a biography of Rudolph Valentino when one of the characters is a movie star. The connection is thus general, tangential, and wholly external, and occurs to the reader only as a passing afterthought, if at all. This kind of connection can be compared with the *internal* unity of any biography or narrative in the book and then the difference between a unified whole and a loose collection will be clear in terms of the book itself.

poetic style can bear the utmost strain of sensibility, but it cannot tell a story. In the medium of poetry, however, a unity of tone and mood and theme can substitute, although imperfectly, for other kinds of unity. *U.S.A.* cannot be considered a poem, however, and even if it could, Dos Passos does not rise to the level of the poets in question. As a narrative, it becomes a suite of narratives in which panels without direct relation to the subject are inserted (one would suppose that Dos Passos in fact put the book together as a motion-picture director composes his film, by a procedure of cutting, arranging, and interposing parts). As a novel, it is not in any careful sense a novel, but rather an anthology of long stories and prose poems. And it is to be insisted that the unity and form in question are not the abstractions of the critic, but the generic traits of the actual experience of reading fiction.

．　．　．　．　．

What we want of literature is the truth, and the truth is the only intention of *U.S.A.* But, to repeat, the truth is not merely the way in which human beings behave and feel, nor is it wholly contained in their conscious experience. In Racine and in Henry James, to take extreme examples, many characters speak as no one has ever spoken, on land or sea. They speak so in order to contain many of the levels of truth present in any possible situation. The facts represented are always there, but a good many of them can never be consciously known by any actor involved up to his neck in the present moment, as the characters of *U.S.A.* usually are. Only through the focus of the imagination can the relevant facts be brought into the narrative. In Dos Passos, however, there is a beautiful imaginative sympathy which permits him to get under the skin of his characters, but there is no imagination, and no Don Quixote. Dos Passos testified to all this by his use of newsreels, just as he seeks the full sensibility in the impressions of the camera eye and the heroic character in the biographies; but in his central narratives the standpoint is always narrowed to what the character himself knows as the quality of his existence, life as it appears to him. And this leveling drags with it and tends to make rather crude and sometimes commonplace the sensibility shown in the other panels. If Dos Passos were not so wholly successful in grasping this level of experience, then, undoubtedly, he would be less aware of the need to jump back to the other levels of truth, and his novel would not break into four "eyes" of uncoördinated vision. Or to shift the metaphor, his novel attempts to achieve the whole truth by going rapidly in two opposite directions—the direction of the known experience of his characters, in all their blindness and limitation, and on the other hand, the direction of the transcendent knowledge of experience, the full truth about it. And thus the formal breakdown was scarcely avoidable.

JAMES T. FARRELL

" *He has a very serious view of the educational function of literature today*"

JOSEPH WARREN BEACH

U.S.A. was not the only famous trilogy of the 1930's. James T. Farrell's *Studs Lonigan* (*Young Lonigan*, 1932; *The Young Manhood of Studs Lonigan*, 1934; *Judgment Day*, 1935) was widely hailed and discussed as an important work of naturalism. As this selection shows, the naturalistic novelist by no means considers his function limited to the neutral representation of life. Though he may allow his themes to be implicit rather than explicit, his purpose (and Farrell seems typical in this) is broadly educational. At his most ambitious, the naturalist (like many non-naturalists) would like to help shape "the consciousness of an epoch." Mr. Beach's account of Farrell's aims and problems would apply to many novelists of the naturalistic school.

I DON'T KNOW whether Arnold would have judged that *Studs Lonigan* is done with high seriousness. We have to make our own judgment. It so happens that, in our day and in the United States, the most serious literary artists are much inclined to that tendency in literature which goes by the name of naturalism. Farrell is consciously of that school. And he is of that school partly, I suppose, because his personal need is to tell the unvar-

From Joseph Warren Beach, *American Fiction, 1920–1940* (New York: The Macmillan Company, 1941), pp. 280–283. Reprinted by permission of Russell & Russell, Inc., who have published a new edition (1960) of this book.

nished truth about the world from which he made his difficult escape. He had to get it out of his system. That is, psychologically considered, one of the chief functions of literary art. It is a therapeutic and health-giving function. It is one of man's chief instruments for getting the best of ugliness and evil. In *Studs Lonigan*, Farrell achieved his great triumph over hooliganism by thus objectifying it.

But this is not the whole story. Farrell considers that naturalism is the major trend of our literature today; he describes it, in his *Note on Literary Criticism*, as the school which "chooses understanding rather than myth, truth rather than comfort." And he regards it as more than the personal therapeutic referred to above. He has a very serious view of the educational function of literature today.

It makes the reader more intensely conscious of the problems of life, of the predicaments of people, the possibilities and the limitations of living, the diversities in human experience. It makes value judgments on conditions, actions, thoughts, situations, environments, hopes, despairs, ideals, dreams, fantasies. . . . It points [the readers'] emotions, their impulses, their wishes, and their thoughts toward or away from certain goals. It creates . . . the consciousness of an epoch, and is thus one of the instruments that work toward the molding and remolding of the human consciousness.

Thus it is clear that Farrell regards naturalistic fiction as properly more than a mere recording of truth. It is a criticism of life, making value judgments on actions and attitudes, setting ideal objectives for thought and feeling, and molding the spirit of men in more desirable patterns.

With such a humanistic program, and with his personal experience, he could not regard this thing which I have called hooliganism with anything but deadly seriousness. It was not possible to treat it in the romantic or sentimental vein, for that would falsify its essential nature. It was not possible with this theme to be entertaining in the ordinary story manner, or witty. The characters of this story were not conceived as people of fine feelings and noble aims at odds with a cruel and cynical world, triumphing over it in the end. They are rather people of the average neutral sort who take on the prevailing color of their environment, and who, being subjected to a social state of mind ugly and vile, are inevitably reduced themselves to the same uniform color of vileness and ugliness. Their instincts and intentions are normal enough, and with a different set of stimuli they might have developed into something fair and rich. But there is nothing in their environment to suggest ways of gratifying their instincts, or realizing their intentions, which might lead to fair and rich living.

The process of their degradation is a long and gradual one. It cannot be adequately presented in anything short of an extended narrative. In order to do justice to this process it was necessary for the author to set down scene after scene of talk and action gross, dreary, brutal, repelling, in an ascending scale of ugliness. The reader is caught in the pitiful web of this narrative; the people are so real and their plight so arresting that he cannot escape. He cries out over and over again at the cruelty of the thing; but he is held by its fatal fascination. When he is done, his first reaction is to repudiate it as one repudiates what is foul and wicked. But he cannot quite do that. It is too real, too serious, and too human. As time passes and he looks back on the thing from a certain distance, the ugliness gives place to a sense of pathos. His dominant feeling, so far as the characters are concerned, is that of pity. Poor bewildered humans who, by the circumstances of their lives, were condemned to live in hell! And so far as the literary work itself is concerned, he has the feeling of having looked upon some structure great and monumental in its proportions, something solidly based in earth and occupying space with an obstinate persistence like Dante's Hell or the Canterbury Tales or the novels of Zola.

There can be little doubt that Farrell's purpose was well served on the strictly esthetic side. On the moral side, and having in mind his own statement of the function of literature, there are two objections that might be raised. It is possible to hold that his record is more detailed and prolonged than is necessary to make his point. And as for "pointing emotions, etc., toward or away from certain goals," it might be urged that in this book he is too exclusively engaged in pointing away from undesirable goals, and does too little pointing toward desirable ones.

But I am not inclined to urge either of these objections. It is always questionable business trying to check the flow of imaginative creation. Too much is the fault of great artists. And while pointing toward ideal goals is certainly one of the noblest functions of literature, it cannot be required of everyone nor in every context. To require it of Farrell in *Studs Lonigan* might well mean the spoiling of something that is good in its own way in order to make it good in another.

THOMAS WOLFE

"No more sensuous novel has been written in the United States"

One of the most impressive entrances of modern American
literature was that of Thomas Wolfe (1901–1938). His *Look
Homeward, Angel* (1929) seemed to have all the virtues of
a richly talented youthfulness. John Chamberlain's review is a
typical example of the keen anticipation this first novel aroused.

Among young American writers who have made impressive débuts in recent years Thomas Wolfe is a distinct
anomaly: he has not a nostalgic temperament. *Look Homeward,
Angel* is not the book of a frayed spirit who is trying his level
best to escape through elegiac writing; it is a rich, positive
grappling with life, a remembrance of things past untinged by
the shadow of regret, of one who has found his youthful experiences full of savor. No more sensuous (not to be construed
as sensual) novel has been written in the United States. There
is an easy, unforced strength to it that should be the despair of
those beginners of the *New American Caravan* who have tossed
overboard one genteel tradition only to fall into another. Inas-
much as it is not a novelist's novel, there will be quite intelligent
devotees of fiction who will find its rough, fluid pattern too easy
for their tastes. The answer to them would be that it is unfair to
condemn a good chronicle novel simply because the chronicle,
through over-emphasis, is now falling out of fashion.

For a good chronicle novel is precisely what *Look Homeward,*

John Chamberlain, "Look Homeward, Angel," *The Bookman*, 70 (December, 1929), 449–450. Reprinted by permission of the author.

Angel is. The story is a familiar one: the life of a family set down as it progresses in time, with particular attention to one member who serves as a focal point. The Gants are middle-class people, living in a resort town in the southern mountains that is called Altamount [*sic*], but which is probably Asheville, N.C. Eugene Gant is born at the opening of the century, and his experiences have probably been matched by any number of our contemporaries. But Mr. Wolfe writes of Eugene's days with a difference. The sensitivity of the book is enormous, and it is not a sick sensitivity. There is either gusto or intensity to all of Eugene's activities; his fighting as a boy with the poor whites; his taste for foods; his mooning over the heroines of cheap American fiction (which recalls Joyce's Stephen Dedalus and his boyish maundering over Mercedes of the Dumas novel); and his relations with brothers and sisters, father and mother. His friendship with his elder brother Ben is particularly well set forth.

Mr. Wolfe's grasp of character is unhurried—a firm grasp in the old Thackeray sense. His people are "flat"; they are tagged by their idiosyncrasies of speech and action. They do not change greatly (old Gant always dissipates his energy, and Eliza, the mother, is a hoarder no matter what comes), but because they are the sort of people who are set in their ways (excepting Eugene) the imputation of flatness is no derogation. As for Mr. Wolfe's sheer dramatic power, we ask you to read the death of Ben and then compare it, as we did, with the death of Madame Bovary. Mr. Wolfe's scene is more intimate, it brings a sharper emotion of recognition to one who has been through such a ghastly ordeal. We do not say that it is greater artistically; we merely submit that it is substantially richer.

Look Homeward, Angel has its faults, but they are not those springing from a poverty of material. We might point out that a more logical effect would have been gained if Ben's adventure in the Greasy Spoon (which sets fineness against vulgarity in the manner of the Walpurgisnacht of *Ulysses*) had been left open somehow to the observation of Eugene, or if Gant's trip to California had been assimilated in some way to the narrative of Eugene's life. There are sentences that debouch here and there into meaningless rhetoric. But why seek flaws in the midst of abundance? Mr. Wolfe gives the impression of being inexhaustible, even though the book is largely autobiographical. His second novel will be his real test; for in it he will be forced to think more in terms of pattern and idea than he has in his first. But his observance is so inclusive, his antennae so sensitive to the world about him, that one can hardly regard *Look Homeward, Angel* as a flash in the pan.

"A sense, proud, lonely, exhilarating, of the immensity of the country"

JOHN PEALE BISHOP

John Peale Bishop, writing the year after Thomas Wolfe's death, found that Wolfe had caught the size and energy of America but that his work lacked "moral grandeur." As the economic depression of the 1930's grew worse, Wolfe could no longer "consent to the 'greatness of America' "; with "the loss of a controlling myth" he was unable to find a meaning in the sufferings of men.

THE TWO MOST CONSPICUOUS failures in American letters of recent years have been Thomas Wolfe and Hart Crane. What the one in his novels, the other in his poems, meant to write about was the greatness of America. As a theme, it was in the air when they began writing, and if they could have written of it, they should have done so. Both had gifts in abundance; both shared "the breath released" of a new world, a world of the machine whose accomplishments, great as they were, were as nothing to its promises of progress; both had access, almost at will, to that secret source of energy we call genius. America is great, in many ways; but the consciousness they had of a coun-

From "The Myth and Modern Literature," reprinted with the permission of Charles Scribner's Sons from *The Collected Essays of John Peale Bishop*, ed. Edmund Wilson, pp. 127–128. This essay originally appeared in *The Saturday Review of Literature*, July 22, 1939.

try which had spread across a continent in a grandeur of covetousness was scarcely a myth. The "greatness of America" was merely a particular phase of the myth of progress. To accept it was to limit moral criticism. To go contrary to it was something that Crane, once he had conceived *The Bridge,* was unwilling to do. And yet he found not much for his poem which was positive and concrete to celebrate. He had, I have been told by those who knew him, night after night crossed Brooklyn Bridge, prompted by impetuous needs, as personal as love and sleep, so that before he began to make of it a poem, it had become for him, not merely a complex of the engineer's skill, but a symbol of man's undaunted desire. But his faith was arbitrary and forced. He tried to believe in the greatness of America, and when, as a myth, it failed him, he attempted to make myths of his own. And that, I am inclined to think, is something no one man can do. Crane failed.

In working with the same myth, Thomas Wolfe did give, as no other American writer has done in prose, a sense, proud, lonely, exhilarating, of the immensity of the country. With his prodigious appetite for experience, Wolfe did record, so far as one not participating could, one after another, American scenes. His characters are huge, and they are American. But of moral grandeur there is none. Indeed, as the depression deepened, Wolfe grew more and more distressed. He could no longer consent to the "greatness of America"; for it was impossible any longer to hold to the myth of progress. Progress, of course, exists; and as long as science remains free, it can probably be counted on to continue. But progress as a be-all and end-all, progress as a word to give meaning to increasingly restless and more and more meaningless activities, that progress had suddenly stopped. And Wolfe was thrown back on man's capacity to endure suffering, both the suffering which he has brought on himself and the suffering with which others, willing or unwilling, have afflicted him. What else he could have done, had he lived longer, can only be conjectured. At present, it must be said that, for all his concern with myths, he did not and, working as he did, could not find a meaning for *Of Time and the River.*

"Thomas Wolfe has created for Eugene Gant a Shandean world"

C. HUGH HOLMAN

Looking back on *Look Homeward, Angel* from the perspective
of 1955, Hugh Holman sees an interesting comparison between
the world Wolfe has created and "the universe of Walter
Shandy and Uncle Toby" in Laurence Sterne's eighteenth
century masterpiece, *Tristram Shandy* (1760–1767).
Essentially "both books are family novels, peculiarly rich in
brilliantly realized, hyperbolically presented familial portraits."
And both authors "were oppressed with the tragic sense of
human insularity." Summing up, Mr. Holman finds that *Look
Homeward, Angel* "has much to offer us still."

FOR ALL ITS RHETORICAL exclamation about emotion,
Look Homeward, Angel is a book firmly fixed in a sharply realized
and realistically presented social environment. The book comes
to us almost entirely through Eugene Gant's perceptions, but what
he perceives is very often Altamont and Pulpit Hill (Asheville
and Chapel Hill, N.C.) and he perceives them with a wealth of
accurate detail. At this stage of his career, Thomas Wolfe had few
serious pronouncements to make about man as a social animal (in
his later career he was to attempt to make many), but he had a
realist's view of his world.

It is a view colored, too, by a broadly Agrarian attitude, however much he was contemptuous of the Agrarians as a group. His
picture of Altamont is a picture of a place mad with money and
size, of a people submerging everything of value in valueless

C. Hugh Holman, "The Loneliness at the Core," *The New Republic*, 133
(October 10, 1955), 16–17.

wealth. This view, the sword on which Eliza Gant is first hoist and then eviscerated, extends from the family to the life of the town and finally to the imagery of the whole book. As an example (and it is but one of hundreds), when he hears his idol-brother Ben talking sententious businessman nonsense, "Eugene writhed to hear this fierce condor prattle this stale hash of the canny millionaires, like any obedient parrot in a teller's cage."

Further, we perceive as a rediscovery that beneath the extravagant rhetoric, the badly and baldly rhythmic passages—the ones that eager young men reprint as bad free verse—there is a truly lyric quality in Wolfe's writing. With an abnormally keen memory for sensory perceptions, what Wolfe called his "more than ordinary . . . power to evoke and bring back the odors, sounds, colors, shapes, and feel of things with concrete vividness," he is able to bring to bear vicariously on our five senses the precise content of a given scene and to make it poignantly and palpably real.

And here he works, not as a rhetorician asking us to imagine an emotion, but as an imagist rubbing "the thing" against our exposed nerve ends and thereby calling forth the feeling. It is, perhaps, in this ability to use authentically "the thing" to evoke emotion that the finest aspect of Wolfe's very uneven talent appears.

A new look at *Look Homeward, Angel* shows us that it is a book, not only of Eugene's "buried life," but one about tragic loneliness. Few lonelier pictures exist than the ones here that show the insularity within which Eliza and W. O. Gant live. This W. O. Gant, a rich and hungry man in spirit, who was never called by his wife Eliza anything except "Mr. Gant," strove by rhetoric, invective, alcohol, and lust to make somehow an impress on the unresponsive world around him. He is the ultimate tragic center of a book which deals with spiritual isolation almost everywhere.

Certainly the book lacks formal novelistic structure. If its core, as I believe, is W. O. Gant, then it contains a wealth of unresolved irrelevancy. If its central pattern is somehow linked up with brother Ben, as Wolfe seems to feel that it is, then we must regretfully assert that Brother Ben is a failure, the only really dead person in a book noteworthy for the vitality of its characters.

Yet *Look Homeward, Angel* has a consistency and an integrity of its own. In a way different from those indicated above, it presents a world. And as we survey that world and its characteristics, it begins to appear very much like the universe of that surprisingly modern eighteenth century figure, Laurence Sterne; and the thought impresses itself upon us that Thomas Wolfe has created for Eugene Gant a Shandean world and that his book has something of the inspired illogic of the universe of Walter Shandy and Uncle Toby.

Both *Look Homeward, Angel* and *Tristram Shandy* defy formal analysis. Both are concerned with the education of the very young. Both see that education as essentially the product of the impact of the world outside upon the young mind. Both describe that education through memories in maturity. And both gain a certain quality of detachment through the comic or amused presentation of material, although Sterne's humor is better than Wolfe's and more pervasively a portion of his book.

Both Eugene and Tristram are the products of mismatched parents, both pairs of whom exist in their eternally separate worlds. Both heroes have older brothers who die; both are given to rhetorical excesses; both have a tendency toward unsatisfied concupiscence; and both embarrass us by "snickering," as Thackeray pointed out about Sterne. But these are superficial similarities; more real ones exist in method, language, and theme.

Look Homeward, Angel and *Tristram Shandy* are both ostensibly about their heroes, are records of these heroes' "life and opinions," yet neither Eugene nor Tristram is as real as other characters in their books. Uncle Toby, "My Father," and to a certain extent "My Mother" dominate *Tristram Shandy* and over-shadow its narrator-hero. W. O. Gant, Eliza Gant, and Helen Gant dominate *Look Homeward, Angel,* and beside them the viewpoint character, Eugene, pales into comparative unreality. Furthermore, both books are family novels, peculiarly rich in brilliantly realized, hyperbolically presented familial portraits.

Both Wolfe and Sterne were adept at the precise, fact-laden description in which the thing evokes the feeling. Both were given to the representation of emotional excess in terms of heightened sensibility. Sterne is famous for this characteristic; in Wolfe, one needs only to look at the Laura James sequence to see the "novel of sensibility" present with us again.

Both men were remarkably proficient at capturing the individual cadences of human speech and reproducing them with sharp accuracy, and both delighted in the rhetorically extravagant; so that their works present, not a unified style, but a medley of styles.

But most significantly of all, both Wolfe and Sterne were oppressed with the tragic sense of human insularity, with the ineffable loneliness at the core of all human life. Walter Shandy sought a word to communicate with wife and brother, and he sought in vain. His wife walked in inarticulate silence beside him. Eugene Gant was striving for "a stone, a leaf, an unfound door." W. O. Gant, with all his exuberance and overbrimming life, remained "Mr. Gant" to a wife who never understood "save in incommunicable gleams."

And the whole problem of life, loneliness, and memory with which in their different ways these two books are concerned is for both writers bound up in the mystery of time and memory. Uncle Toby and Tristram, as well as Sterne, brood amusingly and seriously about kinds of time. For Wolfe and his hero, Time is the great unanswerable mystery and villain of life.

The world of Eugene Gant is a Shandean world. And in that inconsistent, unbalanced, illogical, incongruous, incomplete, and lonely universe, the secret of *Look Homeward, Angel's* sprawling formlessness, its unevenness, and its passages of colossal failure and of splendid success exist.

Unless we demand that all novels be neat and concise, *Look Homeward, Angel* has much to offer us still: a clear, detailed picture of a town; two extravagantly drawn but very living people, Eliza and W. O. Gant; a comic sense that lends aesthetic distance; a poignantly lyrical expression of the physical world of youth; and a picture of the individual's incommunicable loneliness.

WILLIAM FAULKNER

"It is a nightmare world, wearing a mask of reality"

J. DONALD ADAMS

In the opinion of J. Donald Adams, book columnist for many years in *The New York Sunday Times* book review section, "Faulkner's work is fundamentally meaningless because there is no interaction in it between good and evil, to the end that the mystery of human life is absent from his writing." Mr. Adams wrote this piece several years before William Faulkner was awarded the Nobel Prize (1950).

HERE IS WILLIAM FAULKNER, potentially one of the ablest writers of his generation, hopelessly, as it seems to me, involved in his own technical virtuosity, and blocked by his pre-occupation with the pathological ills of mankind. No American writer's name has been more frequently coupled with that of Dostoevski, but Faulkner has never been able to balance the man-God against the man-beast as the Russian did. Dostoevski was as aware as Faulkner of the darkly evil in human life, but it did not engulf him as it has the strangely agonized romantic of Mississippi. Faulkner has written some of the most powerful scenes in American fiction, some of its most beautiful as well as some of its most tortured prose, but he has not been able to give meaning to his work. The world which he has created is as palpably unreal in its way as the world of Cabell. If one were to make a prolonged visit to a hospital for the insane, talking at length to its inmates, one would have as balanced a view of a

From J. Donald Adams, *The Shape of Books to Come*, pp. 91–92, 93, 95. Copyright 1944 by J. Donald Adams. Reprinted by permission of The Viking Press, Inc.

cross-section of humanity as one receives from the fiction of Faulkner.

In the entire range of his work—twelve novels and several volumes of short stories—there is not a single instance, so far as I can recall, of a normal and mature relationship between a man and a woman. Every such relationship remains of an infantile, depraved, or, at the best, an adolescent level. You may search his novels from end to end without finding a single family in which the relationships are not twisted either by perversion or insanity. The vital currents of life are stepped up in his pages to an unparalleled intensity, so that sexual intercourse is conducted always on the level either of rape or of nymphomania. It is a nightmare world, wearing a mask of reality. Is it any wonder, then, that in spite of quantities of solemn critical discussion and ecstatic praise, not one novel by Faulkner (generally accepted as one of the major American writers of his time) has been bought by as many as ten thousand persons, with the single exception of *Sanctuary*, a cheaply meretricious book, which he confessedly wrote as a shocker? There is nothing in *Sanctuary* to repay an intelligent reader, though there is plenty to titillate adolescent minds, whereas in Faulkner's other books there are pages of genuine power or beauty which are like the rational moments of a demented man. . . .

. . . . .

Now, there is no doubt that Faulkner has been painfully conscious of the decay of the old aristocratic Southern tradition in which he himself was nurtured, that he had observed with something like mingled fury and dismay the going to seed of some of the old families and the brutally forceful thrust for power of the formerly submerged poor whites; it is plain that he detests the Northern industrialism which shattered the pattern of life the old South had established. These reactions, so keenly felt by him, he has permitted to confuse and distort the social content of his novels, which I think has frequently been discussed with too great seriousness. Other factors contributed to the warping of Faulkner's mind: his experience of war for one, and whatever caused his bitterly malignant attitude toward women, expressed over and over again in his portraits of them, for another.

. . . . .

Faulkner's work is fundamentally meaningless because there is

no interaction in it between good and evil, to the end that the
mystery of human life is absent from his writing. One reads Faulkner as one watches, fascinated, while a cobra swallows a black
snake. Both exhibit the same intensity, and one is about as significant as the other.

"Inventiveness of the richest possible sort"

CONRAD AIKEN

This relatively early Faulkner appreciation (1939) by Conrad
Aiken displays an entirely different insight into Faulkner from
that of Mr. Adams. It is through his analysis of Faulkner's
form and style that Mr. Aiken arrives at his estimate of the high
significance of such novels as *The Sound and the Fury* (1929),
As I Lay Dying (1930), *Absalom, Absalom!* (1936), and *The
Wild Palms* (1939).

WHAT MR. FAULKNER IS AFTER, in a sense, is a *continuum.* He wants a medium without stops or pauses, a medium
which is always *of the moment,* and of which the passage from
moment to moment is as fluid and undetectable as in the life
itself which he is purporting to give. It is all inside and underneath, or as seen from within and below; the reader must therefore be steadily *drawn in;* he must be powerfully and unremit-
tingly hypnotized inward and downward to that image-stream;
and this suggests, perhaps, a reason not only for the length and
elaborateness of the sentence structure, but for the repetitiveness
as well. The repetitiveness, and the steady iterative emphasis—

Conrad Aiken, "William Faulkner: the Novel as Form," from *A Reviewer's
ABC,* pp. 203–207. Copyright © 1935, 1939, 1940, 1942, 1951, 1958 by Conrad Aiken. A Greenwich Edition, published by Meridian Books, Inc. This
article originally appeared in *The Atlantic,* 164 (November, 1939), 650–654.

like a kind of chanting or invocation—on certain relatively abstract words ("sonorous, latin, *vaguely* eloquent"), has the effect at last of producing, for Mr. Faulkner, a special language, a conglomerate of his own, which he uses with an astonishing virtuosity, and which, although in detailed analysis it may look shoddy, is actually for his purpose a life stream of almost miraculous adaptability. At the one extreme it is abstract, cerebral, time-and-space-obsessed, tortured and twisted, but nevertheless always with a living *pulse* in it; and at the other it can be as overwhelming in its simple vividness, its richness in the actual, as the flood scenes in *The Wild Palms*.

Obviously, such a style, especially when allied with such a method, and such a *concern* for method, must make difficulties for the reader; and it must be admitted that Mr. Faulkner does little or nothing as a rule to make his highly complex "situation" easily available or perceptible. The reader must simply make up his mind to go to work, and in a sense to cooperate; his reward being that there *is* a situation to be given shape, a meaning to be extracted, and that half the fun is precisely in watching the queer, difficult, and often so laborious, evolution of Mr. Faulkner's idea. And not so much idea, either, as form. For, like the great predecessor whom at least in this regard he so oddly resembles, Mr. Faulkner could say with Henry James that it is practically impossible to make any real distinction between theme and form. What immoderately delights him, alike in *Sanctuary, The Sound and the Fury, As I Lay Dying, Light in August, Pylon, Absalom, Absalom!* and now again in *The Wild Palms,* and what sets him above—shall we say it firmly—all his American contemporaries, is his continuous preoccupation with the novel *as form,* his passionate concern with it, and a degree of success with it which would clearly have commanded the interest and respect of Henry James himself. The novel as revelation, the novel as slice-of-life, the novel as mere story, do not interest him: these he would say, like James again, "are the circumstances of the interest," but not the interest itself. The interest itself will be the *use* to which these circumstances are put, the degree to which they can be organized.

From this point of view, he is not in the least to be considered as a mere "Southern" writer: the "Southernness" of his scenes and characters is of little concern to him, just as little as the question whether they are pleasant or unpleasant, true or untrue. Verisimilitude—or, at any rate, *degree* of verisimilitude—he will cheerfully abandon, where necessary, if the compensating advantages of plan or tone are a sufficient inducement. The famous scene in *Sanctuary* of Miss Reba and Uncle Bud, in which a "madam" and her cronies hold a wake for a dead gangster, while the small boy gets drunk, is quite false, taken out of its context; it is not endowed with the same *kind* of actuality which permeates the greater part of the book at all. Mr. Faulkner was cunning enough to see that a two-dimensional cartoon-like statement, at this juncture, would supply him with the effect of a chorus, and without in the least being perceived as a change in the temperature of truthfulness.

That particular kind of dilution, or adulteration, of verisimilitude, was both practiced and praised by James: as when he blandly admitted of *In the Cage* that his central character was "too ardent a focus of divination" to be quite credible. It was defensible simply because it made possible the coherence of the whole, and was itself absorbed back into the luminous texture. It was for him a device for organization, just as the careful cherishing of "viewpoint" was a device, whether simply or in counterpoint. Of Mr. Faulkner's devices, of this sort, aimed at the achievement of complex "form," the two most constant are the manipulation of viewpoint and the use of the flash-back, or sudden shift of time-scene, forward or backward.

In *Sanctuary,* where the alternation of viewpoint is a little lawless, the complexity is given, perhaps a shade disingenuously, by violent shifts in time; a deliberate disarrangement of an otherwise straightforward story. Technically, there is no doubt that the novel, despite its fame, rattles a little; and Mr. Faulkner himself takes pains to disclaim it. But, even done with the left hand, it betrays a genius for form, quite apart from its wonderful virtuosity in other respects. *Light in August,* published a year after *Sanctuary,* repeats the same technique, that of a dislocation of time, and more elaborately; the time-shifts alternate with shifts in the viewpoint; and if the book is a failure it is perhaps because Mr. Faulkner's tendency to what is almost a hypertrophy of form is not here, as well as in the other novels, matched with the characters and the theme. Neither the person nor the story of Joe Christmas is seen fiercely enough—by its creator—to carry off that immense machinery of narrative; it would have needed another Popeye, or another Jiggs and Shumann, another Temple Drake, and for once Mr. Faulkner's inexhaustible inventiveness seems to have been at fault. Consequently what we see is an extraordinary power for form functioning relatively *in vacuo,* and existing only to sustain itself.

In the best of the novels, however—and it is difficult to choose between *The Sound and the Fury* and *The Wild Palms,* with *Absalom, Absalom!* a very close third—this tendency to hypertrophy of form has been sufficiently curbed; and it is interesting, too, to notice that in all these three (and in that remarkable *tour de force, As I Lay Dying,* as well) while there is still a considerable reliance on time-shift, the effect of richness and complexity is chiefly obtained by a very skillful fugue-like alternation of viewpoint. Fugue-like in *The Wild Palms*—and fugue-like especially, of course, in *As I Lay Dying,* where the shift is kaleidoscopically rapid, and where, despite an astonishing violence to plausibility (in the reflections, and *language* of reflection, of the characters) an effect of the utmost reality and immediateness is nevertheless produced. Fugue-like, again, in *Absalom, Absalom!* where indeed one may say the form is really circular—there is no beginning and no ending, properly speaking, and therefore no *logical* point of entrance: we must just submit, and follow the circling of the author's interest, which turns a light inward towards the center, but every moment from a new angle, a new point of view. The story unfolds, therefore, now in one color of light, now in another, with references backward and forward: those that refer forward being necessarily, for the moment, blind. What is complete in Mr. Faulkner's pattern, *a priori,* must nevertheless remain *in*complete for us until the very last stone is in place; what is "real," therefore, at one stage of the unfolding, or from one point of view, turns out to be "unreal" from another; and we find that one among other things with which we are engaged is the fascinating sport of trying to separate truth from legend, watching the growth of legend from truth, and finally reaching the conclusion that the distinction is itself false.

Something of the same sort is true also of *The Sound and the Fury*—and this, with its massive four-part symphonic structure, is perhaps the most beautifully *wrought* of the whole series, and an indubitable masterpiece of what James loved to call the "fictive art." The joinery is flawless in its intricacy; it is a novelist's novel —a whole textbook on the craft of fiction in itself, comparable in its way to *What Maisie Knew* or *The Golden Bowl*.

But if it is important, for the moment, to emphasize Mr. Faulkner's genius for form, and his continued exploration of its possibilities, as against the usual concern with the violence and dreadfulness of his themes—though we might pause to remind carpers on this score of the fact that the best of Henry James is precisely that group of last novels which so completely concerned themselves with moral depravity—it is also well to keep in mind his genius for invention, whether of character or episode. The inventiveness is of the richest possible sort—a headlong and tumultuous abundance, an exuberant generosity and vitality, which makes most other contemporary fiction look very pale and chaste indeed. It is an unforgettable gallery of portraits, whether of character or caricature, and all of them endowed with a violent and immediate vitality.

He is at once [to quote once more from James] one of the most corrupt of writers and one of the most naif, the most mechanical and pedantic, and the fullest of *bonhomie* and natural impulse. He is one of the finest of artists and one of the coarsest. Viewed in one way, his novels are ponderous, shapeless, overloaded; his touch is graceless, violent, barbarous. Viewed in another, his tales have more color, more composition, more grasp of the reader's attention than any others. [His] style would demand a chapter apart. It is the least simple style, probably, that was ever written; it bristles, it cracks, it swells and swaggers; but it is a perfect expression of the man's genius. Like his genius, it contains a certain quantity of everything, from immaculate gold to flagrant dross. He was a very bad writer, and yet unquestionably he was a very great writer. We may say briefly, that in so far as his method was an instinct it was successful, and that in so far as it was a theory it was a failure. But both in instinct and in theory he had the aid of an immense force of conviction. His imagination warmed to its work so intensely that there was nothing his volition could not impose upon it. Hallucination settled upon him, and he believed anything that was necessary in the circumstances.

That passage, from Henry James's essay on Balzac, is almost word for word, with scarcely a reservation, applicable to Mr. Faulkner. All that is lacking is Balzac's greater *range* of understanding and tenderness, his greater freedom from special preoccupations. For this, one would hazard the guess that Mr. Faulkner has the gifts—and time is still before him.

"Within the traditional world there had been a notion of truth"

ROBERT PENN WARREN

In his Nobel Prize acceptance speech (1950) Faulkner affirmed his belief in man's capacity to survive "because he has a soul, a spirit capable of compassion and sacrifice and endurance." Robert Penn Warren emphasizes that "the constant ethical center of Faulkner's work is to be found in the glorification of human effort and human endurance, which are not confined to any one time." His essay (1946–1950) marks a change in emphasis in Faulkner criticism: the earlier criticism was predominantly concerned with Faulkner's picture of the decay of the Old South, with his hatred of "modernity," with his nightmare picture of sexual brutality and psychological abnormality; Mr. Warren explains Faulkner's concern with a timeless human truth. In Mr. Warren's opinion, "If respect for the human is the central fact of Faulkner's work, what makes that fact significant is that he realizes and dramatizes the difficulty of respecting the human."

I T IS SOMETIMES SAID that Faulkner's theme is the disintegration of the Southern traditional life. For instance, Malcolm Cowley, in his fine introduction to the *Portable Faulkner*, says that the violence of Faulkner's work is "an example of the Freudian method turned backward, being full of sexual nightmares that are in reality social symbols. It is somehow connected in the author's mind with what he regards as the rape and cor-

From Robert Penn Warren, "William Faulkner," in *Selected Essays*, pp. 65–68, 78–79. Copyright 1946, 1958 by Robert Penn Warren. Reprinted by permission of Random House, Inc.

ruption of the South." And Maxwell Geismar, whose lack of comprehension of Faulkner strikes me as monumental, interprets Faulkner's work as merely Southern apologetics, as "the extreme hallucinations" of a "cultural psychosis."

It is true that Faulkner deals almost exclusively with the Southern scene, it is true that the conflict between past and present is a constant concern for him, it is true that the Civil War is always behind his work as a kind of backdrop, and it is true, or at least I think it is true, that in Faulkner's work there is the implication that Northern arms were the cutting edge of modernism. But granting all this, I should put the emphasis not in terms of South and North, but in terms of issues common to our modern world.

The Faulkner legend is not merely a legend of the South but of a general plight and problem. The modern world is in moral confusion. It does suffer from a lack of discipline, of sanction, of community of values, of a sense of mission. We don't have to go to Faulkner to find that out—or to find that it is a world in which self-interest, workableness, success provide the standards of conduct. It was a Yankee who first referred to the bitch goddess Success. It is a world in which the individual has lost his relation to society, the world of the power state in which man is a cipher. It is a world in which man is the victim of abstraction and mechanism, or at least, at moments, feels himself to be. It can look back nostalgically upon various worlds of the past, Dante's world of the Catholic synthesis, Shakespeare's world of Renaissance energy, or the world of our grandfathers who lived before Shiloh and Gettysburg, and feel loss of traditional values and despair in its own aimlessness and fragmentation. Any of those older worlds, so it seems now, was a world in which, as one of Faulkner's characters puts it, men "had the gift of living once or dying once instead of being diffused and scattered creatures drawn blindly from a grab bag and assembled"—a world in which men were, "integer for integer," more simple and complete.

At this point we must pause to consider an objection. Someone will say, and quite properly, that there never was a golden age in which man was simple and complete. Let us grant that. But we must grant that even with that realistic reservation man's conception of his own role and position has changed from time to time. It is unhistorical to reduce history to some dead level, and the mere fact that man in the modern world is worried about his role and position is in itself significant.

Again, it may be objected, and quite properly, that any old order that had satisfied human needs would have survived; that it is sentimental to hold that an old order is killed from the outside by certain wicked people or forces. But when this objection is applied to Faulkner it is based on a misreading of his work. The old order, he clearly indicates, did *not* satisfy human needs, did *not* afford justice, and therefore was "accurst" and held the seeds of its own ruin. But the point is this: the old order, even with its bad conscience and confusion of mind, even as it failed to live up to its ideal, cherished the concept of justice. Even in terms of the curse, the old order as opposed to the new order (in so far as the new order is equated with Snopesism) allowed the traditional man to define himself as human by setting up codes, ideas of virtue, however mistaken; by affirming obligations, however arbitrary; by accepting the risks of humanity. But Snopesism has abolished the concept, the very possibility of entertaining the idea of virtue. It is not a question of one idea and interpretation. It is simply that no idea of virtue is conceivable in the world in which practical success is the criterion.

Within the traditional world there had been a notion of truth, even if man in the flow of things could not readily define or realize his truth. Take, for instance, a passage from "The Bear."

'All right,' he said. 'Listen,' and read again, but only one stanza this time and closed the book and laid it on the table. 'She cannot fade, though thou has not thy bliss,' McCaslin said: 'Forever wilt thou love, and she be fair.'

'He's talking about a girl,' he said

'He had to talk about something,' McCaslin said. Then he said, 'He was talking about truth. Truth is one. It doesn't change. It covers all things which touch the heart—honor and pride and pity and justice and courage and love. Do you see now?'

The important thing, then, is the presence of the concept of truth —that covers all things which touch the heart and defines the effort of man to rise above the mechanical process of life.

When it is said, as it is sometimes said, that Faulkner is "backward-looking," the answer lies, I think, in the notion expressed above. The "truth" is neither of the past nor of the future.

Or rather, it is of both. The constant ethical center of Faulkner's
work is to be found in the glorification of human effort and
human endurance, which are not confined to any one time. It is
true that Faulkner's work contains a savage attack on modernity,
but the values he admires *are* found in our time. The point is
that they are found most often in people who are outside the
stream of the dominant world, the "loud world," as it is called in
The Sound and the Fury. Faulkner's world is full of "good people"
—Byron Bunch, Lucas Beauchamp, Dilsey, Ike McCaslin, Uncle
Gavin, Benbow, the justice of peace in *The Hamlet*, Ratliff of the
same book, Hightower of *Light in August*—we could make an
impressive list, probably a longer list from Faulkner than from
any other modern writer. "There are good men everywhere, at
all times," Ike McCaslin says in "Delta Autumn."

It is not ultimately important whether the traditional order
(Southern or other) as depicted by Faulkner fits exactly the picture which critical historical method provides. Let it be granted
that Faulkner does simplify the matter. What remains important
is that his picture of the traditional order has a symbolic function
in contrast to the modern world which he gives us. It is a way
of embodying his values—his "truth."

. . . . .

That is the central fact in Faulkner's work, the recognition of
the common human bond, a profound respect for the human.
There are, in one way, no villains in his work, except those who
deny the human bond. Even some of the Snopes family are, after
all, human: the son of the barn-burner in the story "Barn-Burn-
ing," or Mink in *The Hamlet*. The point about the Gowries in
Intruder in the Dust is the same: the Gowries seem to be the
enemy, the pure villains, but in the end there is the pure grief
on old Stub's face, and he is human, after all.

If respect for the human is the central fact of Faulkner's work,
what makes that fact significant is that he realizes and dramatizes
the difficulty of respecting the human. Everything is against it,
the savage egotism, the blank appetite, stupidity and arrogance,
even virtues sometimes, the misreading of our history and tradition, our education, our twisted loyalties. That is the great drama,
however, the constant story. His hatred of "modernism"—and we
must quote the word to give it his special meaning—arises because
he sees it as the enemy of the human, as abstraction, as mecha-

nism, as irresponsible power, as the cipher on the ledger or the curve on a graph.

And the reference to modernism brings us back to the question of the past and the present. But what of the future? Does Faulkner come to a dead end, setting up traditional virtues against the blank present, and let the matter stand there? No, he does not. But he holds out no easy solutions for man's "struggle toward the stars in the stepping stones of his expiations." He does, however, give a sense of the future, though as a future of struggle in working out that truth referred to in "The Bear." We can remember that old Ike McCaslin, at the end of "Delta Autumn" gives General Compson's hunting horn to the mulatto girl who has been deserted by his young kinsman, saying, "We will have to wait." And *The Sound and the Fury,* which is Faulkner's *Waste Land,* ends with Easter and the promise of resurrection.

ROBERT PENN WARREN

"The problem lies precisely in his being so two-sidedly gifted"

ERIC BENTLEY

Beginning with the whole issue of naturalism in the modern
American novel, Eric Bentley finds "two false assumptions"
behind the complaints raised against the naturalistic novelists:
first, that morality can be conveyed only by elevated characters
and tone; second, that naturalism "implies amorality, not to
say prosaic dullness, excessive and mere factuality." In the best
of the naturalists, says Mr. Bentley, symbolism has become "a
'moral equivalent' of nobility," for "a naturalistic picture of
things *becomes* symbolic if it is well enough done." As for
Robert Penn Warren, although he fails sometimes through
not being naturalistic enough, "he is worth a dozen petty
perfectionists." His is "the type of romantic genius: robust,
fluent, versatile, at his worst clever and clumsy, at his best
brilliant and profound."

I<small>N A LECTURE</small> attacking modern novelists *en masse,* Professor Douglas Bush of Harvard not long ago * declared that

. . . the conflict within the individual, between his conscience and
his natural self, has been often replaced by a conflict between the individual and social forces. This may involve a struggle between good and
evil, but it is more likely to show a poor creature destroyed by the environment that created him. Moral responsibility is more or less shifted
from the individual to society.

* At the Conference on the Heritage of the English-speaking Peoples, at
Kenyon College, October, 1946.

From Eric Bentley, "The Meaning of Robert Penn Warren's Novels," *Kenyon Review,* X (Summer, 1948), 421–424. Reprinted by permission of the
author.

What is there here that Warren does not know? Yet Warren, I am told, was included in Mr. Bush's spoken indictment. (His name does not appear in the published version, though Faulkner's does.) Mr. Bush finds modern novels to be "clinical reports on the crude or vicious lives lived by crude or vicious people." He adds: "Indeed we may ask if, in their preoccupation with the sub-moral, they [the modern novelists] are not cutting the ground from under their own feet since the sub-moral level of experience cannot be the tragic level." He finds a formula for the modern novelist: "toughness plus sentimentality." And he expresses a strong preference for Shakespeare.

Well, Warren writes "tough" dialogue, and is capable of sentimentality. His five principal works to date—*Night Rider, At Heaven's Gate, The Ballad of Billie Potts, Proud Flesh,* and *All the King's Men*—are all murder stories in which neither the murderer nor the murdered are exactly—to use Mr. Bush's words—"noble characters, heroic examples." One might ask how an artist should be inspired by our sordid world—our century of the all too common man—to portray nobility and heroism. How should he avoid that abstraction from the actual situation which is fatal to literature? After all we have the "noble characters, heroic examples" of Socialist Realism to warn us. But if a man does not agree that work like Warren's is moral in its whole drift, questioning will not help.

Mr. Bush's account of modern fiction is virtually a rejection of the whole naturalistic tendency in modern literature. (I refer now, not to philosophical naturalism, but to the literary naturalism which we associate with Zola.) Two false assumptions, I believe, are involved. The first is that literature can be moral only through the agency of heroic characters, edifying surroundings, elevated tone, and the like. The second is that naturalism—the naturalistic method, not only of Zola and his disciples, but of most modern fiction—implies amorality, not to say prosaic dullness, excessive and mere factuality. It is true that something like the second assumption—without the pejorative implications— underlies Zola's theoretical writings. It does not, however, underlie his fiction or that of any modern novelist of rank. On the contrary, modern fiction, influenced as all of it is by naturalism, has found what Mr. Bush could, if he chose, regard as a "moral equivalent" of nobility, namely, a rich poetic symbolism. It is not

that James or Lawrence or Proust or Faulkner "combine" naturalism with symbolism. It is that a naturalistic picture of things
becomes symbolic if it is well enough done.

When Robert Penn Warren fails, as he sometimes does, it is
not because he is too naturalistic, but because he is not naturalistic
enough. His symbolism is too often something superimposed. The
vehicle which Warren devises to carry his meaning is not always
as "natural," as "real," as it should be. The worst thing you can
truthfully say about *All the King's Men* is that the almost Holly-
woodian thriller which is Warren's vehicle is all too easily separable from his theme. That of course is why the book could be a
best seller: the public read it *simply* as a thriller.

If the symbolist in Warren seems not to submerge himself in
the naturalist, the thinker in him seems not to submerge himself
in the artist. Trite as it is nowadays to stigmatize an author as a
dual personality, I cannot help pointing to a duality in Warren
that may well constitute his major problem: it is his combination
of critical and creative power. I am far from suggesting that the
critical and the creative are of their nature antithetic and I am
fully ready to grant that what makes Warren remarkable among
American writers is his double endowment. The problem lies
precisely in his being so two-sidedly gifted; he evidently finds
it endlessly difficult to combine his two sorts of awareness. There
is Warren the critic, the cosmopolitan, the scholar, the philosopher; and there is Warren the raconteur, the Kentuckian, the
humorist, the ballad maker. Sometimes the division becomes an
overt formal separation within a work—*The Ballad of Billie Potts*
is the obvious example. *Proud Flesh*, at its worst, wobbles awk-
wardly from one level to the other. *All the King's Men*, as I have
suggested, suffers a good deal from incomplete fusion of theme
and vehicle. The choice of such a Smart Alec as Jack Burden for
narrator may have unlocked Warren's marvelous store of humor,
but it sadly limited his chances of rendering (without reporting,
without too much explicit comment) his theme. And we cannot
forgive all the fancy writing, as some critics do, merely on the
grounds that the writer is supposed to be Burden and not Warren.
Burden was chosen and created by Warren. Critics who write the
exegesis of a great symbolic masterpiece in which every detail
is in place are writing of the book Warren *ought* to have written,
not of the one he wrote.

Warren is a faulty writer; but he is worth a dozen petty perfectionists. Though commonly associated with "formalists" and "classicists" in criticism, he is close to the type of romantic genius: robust, fluent, versatile, at his worst clever and clumsy, at his best brilliant and profound. On the other hand, he is remarkable for self-discipline. The pattern for the American novelist—Sinclair Lewis is the great example—is that he makes the bestseller list with a youthful *tour de force* and spends the rest of his life trying to live up to his reputation. Warren did not write a full-length book between 1929 and 1939. He did not meet with the blandishments of the publicity racket till 1946; too late, I trust, for him to suffer from it. He reminds us of the possibility of a better sort of "American" writing than, say, Howard Fast's, a better sort of "Southern" writing than, say, Margaret Mitchell's. At a time when Americanism in writing suggests the ugly cultural nationalism of Van Wyck Brooks and regionalism suggests the ugly cultural provinciality that allows Dante and Shakespeare to be replaced on college curricula by the poets of eastern South Dakota, it is very refreshing to find a good writer whom one may meaningfully call deeply American and genuinely regionalist. This means, paradoxically enough, that Warren is not *too* American and not *too* regionalist. He has room for the rest of the world, and I think the rest of the world will have room for him. For if you start somewhere you may end everywhere, but if you start nowhere that is also where you will end.

CODA

"I'm not trying to be rosy about things
like the atom bomb and war and
the failure of the Presbyterian Church.
Those things are awful"

WILLIAM STYRON

As a young writer confronted with the question of the
"morbidity and depression" of many writers today, William
Styron believes that "the terrific increase of the scientific
knowledge which has come to us about the human self"
accounts for more of the "new trend toward the introspective
in fiction" than the horrors of the public world. What should
the purpose of a young writer be? "The purpose of a young
writer is to write, and he shouldn't drink too much. He
shouldn't think that after he's written one book he's God
Almighty and air all his immature opinions in pompous
interviews."

INTERVIEWERS: But getting back to the original point—
in *Lie Down in Darkness* didn't your heroine commit suicide on
the day the atom bomb was dropped on Hiroshima? This seems
to us to be a little bit more than fortuitous symbolism, and perhaps to indicate a sense of that inescapable and overpowering
despair of our age which you just denied was our peculiar lot.

Excerpt of an interview with William Styron from *Writers at Work: "The
Paris Review" Interviews*, ed. Malcolm Cowley, pp. 281–282. Copyright ©
1958 by The Paris Review, Inc. Reprinted by permission of The Viking Press,
Inc.

STYRON: That was just gilding the lily. If I were writing the same thing now I'd leave that out and have her jump on the Fourth of July. Really, I'm not trying to be rosy about things like the atom bomb and war and the failure of the Presbyterian Church. Those things are awful. All I'm trying to say is that those things don't alter one bit a writer's fundamental problems, which are Love, Requited and Unrequited, Insult, et cetera.

INTERVIEWERS: Then you believe that young writers today have no cause to be morbid and depressing, which is a charge so often leveled at them by the critics?

STYRON: Certainly they do. They have a perfect right to be anything they honestly are, but I'd like to risk saying that a great deal of this morbidity and depression doesn't arise so much from political conditions, or the threat of war, or the atom bomb, as from the terrific increase of the scientific knowledge which has come to us about the human self—Freud, that is, abnormal psychology, and all the new psychiatric wisdom. My God, think of how morbid and depressing Dostoevski would have been if he could have gotten hold of some of the juicy work of Dr. Wilhelm Stekel, say *Sadism and Masochism*. What people like John Webster and, say, Hieronymus Bosch felt intuitively about some of the keen horrors which lurk in the human mind, we now have neatly catalogued and clinically described by Krafft-Ebing and the Menningers and Karen Horney, and they're available to any fifteen-year-old with a pass-card to the New York Public Library. I don't say that this new knowledge is *the* cause of the so-called morbidity and gloom, but I do think it has contributed to a new trend toward the introspective in fiction. And when you get an eminent journal like *Time* magazine complaining, as it often has, that to the young writers of today life seems short on rewards and that what they write is a product of their own neuroses, in its silly way the magazine is merely stating the status quo and obvious truth. The good writing of any age has always been the product of *someone's* neurosis, and we'd have a mighty dull literature if all the writers that came along were a bunch of happy chuckleheads.

INTERVIEWERS: To sort of round this out, we'd like to ask finally what might sound like a rather obvious question. That is, what should be the purpose of a young writer? Should he, for instance, be *engagé,* not concerned as much with the story aspects of the novel as with the problems of the contemporary world?

STYRON: It seems to me that only a great satirist can tackle the world problems and articulate them. Most writers write simply out of some strong interior need, and that I think is the answer. A great writer, writing out of this need, will give substance to and perhaps even explain all the problems of the world without even knowing it, until a scholar comes along a hundred years after he's dead and digs up some symbols. The purpose of a young writer is to write, and he shouldn't drink too much. He shouldn't think that after he's written one book he's God Almighty and air all his immature opinions in pompous interviews. Let's have another cognac and go up to Le Chapelain.

Bibliography

Bibliography

In addition to the books and essays from which selections have been chosen for this collection, none of which is listed below, there is a wealth of material on the American novel in both book and periodical form. Listed below are some additional book length studies. For periodical articles, the student is advised to consult Lewis Leary, comp., *Articles on American Literature, 1900–1950* (Durham, N.C.: Duke University Press, 1954). Three volumes of Jacob Blanck's projected *Bibliography of American Literature* (New Haven, Conn.: Yale University Press, 1955) have thus far appeared, of the projected six volume work. The most complete bibliography at present is Vol. III, compiled by Thomas H. Johnson, in Robert E. Spiller, *et al.*, *Literary History of the United States* (New York: The Macmillan Company, 1948), together with the *Bibliographical Supplement*, Richard M. Ludwig, ed. (New York: The Macmillan Company, 1959).

Aldridge, John W. *After the Lost Generation* (New York: McGraw-Hill Book Company, Inc., 1951).

Angoff, Allan (ed.). *American Writing Today: Its Independence and Vigor* (New York: New York University Press, 1957).

Beer, Thomas. *The Mauve Decade* (New York: Alfred A. Knopf, Inc., 1926).

Bewley, Marius. *The Complex Fate* (New York: Grove Press, 1954).

Blackmur, R. P. *The Expense of Greatness* (New York: Arrow Editions Co-operative Association, Inc., 1940).

Blankenship, Russell. *American Literature as an Expression of the National Mind* (New York: Henry Holt & Company, Inc., 1931).

Boynton, Percy H. *America in Contemporary Fiction* (Chicago: University of Chicago Press, 1940).

Bradbury, John M. *The Fugitives: A Critical Account* (Chapel Hill, N.C.: University of North Carolina Press, 1958).

Breit, Harvey. *The Writer Observed* (Cleveland: The World Publishing Company, 1956).

Brooks, Van Wyck. *The Confident Years, 1885–1915* (New York: E. P. Dutton & Co., Inc., 1952).

———. *Days of the Phoenix: The Nineteen-Twenties I Remember* (New York: E. P. Dutton & Co., Inc., 1957).

———. *The Flowering of New England, 1815–1865* (New York: E. P. Dutton & Co., Inc., 1936).

———. *New England: Indian Summer, 1865–1915* (New York: E. P. Dutton & Co., Inc., 1940).

———. *Opinions of Oliver Allston* (New York: E. P. Dutton & Co., Inc., 1941).

———. *The Times of Whitman and Melville* (New York: E. P. Dutton & Co., Inc., 1947).

———. *The World of Washington Irving* (New York: E. P. Dutton & Co., Inc., 1944).

Brownell, William Crary. *American Prose Masters* (New York: Charles Scribner's Sons, 1909).

Burgum, Edwin Berry. *The Novel and the World's Dilemma* (New York: Oxford University Press, 1947).

Cairns, William B. *A History of American Literature* (New York: Oxford University Press, 1930).

Calverton, V. F. *The Liberation of American Literature* (New York: Charles Scribner's Sons, 1932).

———. *The Newer Spirit: A Sociological Criticism of Literature* (New York: Boni & Liveright, 1925).

Campbell, Charles A., Jr. *The Great American Novel: A Study in Literary Nationalism, 1870–1900.* Unpublished doctoral dissertation, University of Minnesota, 1951. Microfilm reproduction, University Microfilms, Inc., Ann Arbor, Michigan.

Canby, Henry Seidel. *American Estimates* (New York: Harcourt, Brace & Company, Inc., 1929).

———. *Classic Americans* (New York: Harcourt, Brace & Company, Inc., 1931).

Cargill, Oscar. *Intellectual America: Ideas on the March* (New York: The Macmillan Company, 1941).

Carpenter, Frederic I. *American Literature and the Dream* (New York: Philosophical Library, Inc., 1955).

Clark, Harry Hayden (ed.). *Transitions in American Literary History* (Durham, N.C.: Duke University Press, 1953).

Commager, Henry Steele. *The American Mind* (New Haven, Conn.: Yale University Press, 1950).

Cowie, Alexander. *The Rise of the American Novel* (New York: American Book Company, 1948).

Cowley, Malcolm (ed.). *After the Genteel Tradition: American Writers Since 1910* (New York: W. W. Norton & Company, Inc., 1937).

Cunliffe, Marcus. *The Literature of the United States* (Baltimore: Penguin Books, Inc., 1954).

Curti, Merle E. *The Growth of American Thought* (New York: Harper & Brothers, 1943).

———. *The Roots of American Loyalty* (New York: Columbia University Press, 1946).

Duffey, Bernard. *The Chicago Renaissance in American Letters* (East Lansing: Michigan State University Press, 1954).

Erskine, John. *Leading American Novelists* (New York: Henry Holt & Company, Inc., 1910).

Farrell, James T. *The League of Frightened Philistines* (New York: Vanguard Press, Inc., 1945).

Fiedler, Leslie A. *Love and Death in the American Novel* (New York: Criterion Books, Inc., 1960).

Foerster, Norman. *Towards Standards* (New York: Farrar & Rinehart, Inc., 1930).

Frank, Waldo. *The Re-discovery of America* (Charles Scribner's Sons, 1929).

Frohock, W. M. *The Novel of Violence in America* (Dallas, Tex.: Southern Methodist University Press, 1957).

Gabriel, R. H. *The Course of American Democratic Thought* (New York: The Ronald Press Company, 1940).

Gardiner, Harold C. (ed.). *American Classics Reconsidered* (New York: Charles Scribner's Sons, 1958).

———. (ed.). *Fifty Years of the American Novel* (New York: Charles Scribner's Sons, 1952).

Geismar, Maxwell. *The Last of the Provincials* (Boston: Houghton Mifflin Company, 1947).

———. *Rebels and Ancestors, 1890–1915* (Boston: Houghton Mifflin Company, 1953).

———. *Writers in Crisis: the American Novel between Two Wars* (Boston: Houghton Mifflin Company, 1942).

Gelfant, Blanche Housman. *The American City Novel* (Norman, Okla.: University of Oklahoma Press, 1954).

Hart, James D. *Oxford Companion to American Literature* (New York: Oxford University Press, 1948).

Hartwick, Harry. *The Foreground of American Fiction* (New York: American Book Company, 1934).

Hatcher, Harlan H. *Creating the Modern American Novel* (New York: Farrar & Rinehart, Inc., 1935).

Hoffman, Frederick J. *The Modern Novel in America* (Chicago: Henry Regnery Co., 1951).

———. *The Twenties* (New York: The Viking Press, Inc., 1955).

Howard, Leon. *Literature and the American Tradition* (New York: Doubleday and Company, Inc., 1960).

Howells, William Dean. *Prefaces to Contemporaries, 1882–1920*. Introduction by George Arms, *et al.* (Gainesville, Fla.: Scholars' Facsimiles & Reprints, 1957).

Hubbell, Jay B. *The South in American Literature* (Durham, N.C.: Duke University Press, 1954).

Jones, Howard Mumford. *The Theory of American Literature* (Ithaca, N.Y.: Cornell University Press, 1948).

Knight, Grant C. *American Literature and Culture* (New York: Ray Long and Richard R. Smith, Inc., 1932).

———. *The Strenuous Age in American Literature, 1900–1910* (Chapel Hill, N.C.: University of North Carolina Press, 1954).

Kohn, Hans. *The Idea of Nationalism* (New York: The Macmillan Company, 1944).

Kunitz, S. J., and Howard Haycraft (eds.). *American Authors, 1600–1900* (New York: H. W. Wilson Company, 1942).

——— (eds.). *Twentieth Century Authors* (New York: H. W. Wilson Company, 1944).

Kunitz, S. J. (ed.). *Twentieth Century Authors: First Supplement* (New York: The H. W. Wilson Company, 1955).

Leavis, F. R. *The Great Tradition* (New York: George W. Stewart, Publisher, Inc., 1948).

Leisy, Ernest E. *The American Historical Novel* (Norman, Okla.: University of Oklahoma Press, 1950).

Levin, Harry. *The Power of Blackness* (New York: Alfred A. Knopf, Inc., 1958).

Lewis, R. W. B. *The American Adam* (Chicago: University of Chicago Press, 1955).

Lewisohn, Ludwig. *The Story of American Literature* (New York: Harper & Brothers, 1932).

Lynn, Kenneth. *The Dream of Success* (Boston: Little, Brown & Company, 1955).

Magny, Claude-Edmonde. *L'Age du roman americain* (Paris: Editions de Seuil, 1948).

Matthiessen, F. O. *American Renaissance* (New York: Oxford University Press, 1941).

Miller, Perry. *The Raven and the Whale* (New York: Harcourt, Brace & Company, Inc., 1956).

Millett, Fred B. *Contemporary American Authors: a Critical Survey and 219 Bio-Bibliographies* (New York: Harcourt, Brace & Company, Inc., 1940).

Muller, Herbert J. *Modern Fiction: A Study of Values* (New York: Funk and Wagnalls Company, 1937).

Mumford, Lewis. *The Brown Decades* (New York: Harcourt, Brace & Company, Inc., 1931).

————. *The Golden Day: A Study in American Experience and Culture* (New York: Boni and Liveright, 1926).

Munson, Gorham B. *Destinations* (New York: Sears Publishing Company, Inc., 1928).

O'Connor, William Van. *An Age of Criticism, 1900–1950* (Chicago: Henry Regnery Co., 1952).

———— (ed.). *Forms of Modern Fiction* (Minneapolis, Minn.: University of Minnesota Press, 1948).

Parrington, Vernon Louis. *Main Currents in American Thought* (3 vols.; New York: Harcourt, Brace & Company, Inc., 1927–1930).

Pattee, Fred L. *A History of American Literature Since 1870* (New York: Century Company, 1915).

————. *The American Literature, 1890–1930* (New York: D. Appleton-Century Company, Inc., 1930).

Prescott, Orville. *In My Opinion: an Inquiry into the Contemporary Novel* (Indianapolis: The Bobbs-Merrill Company, 1952).

Pritchard, John Paul. *Criticism in America* (Norman, Okla.: University of Oklahoma Press, 1956).

Quinn, Arthur Hobson, *et al. The Literature of the American People* (New York: Appleton-Century-Crofts, Inc., 1951).

Rahv, Philip (ed.). *Literature in America* (New York: Meridian Books, Inc., 1957).

Rideout, Walter B. *The Radical Novel in the United States, 1900–1954* (Cambridge, Mass.: Harvard University Press, 1957).

Rourke, Constance. *American Humor* (New York: Harcourt, Brace & Company, Inc., 1931).

Rubin, Louis D., Jr., and Robert D. Jacobs (eds.). *Southern Renascence: The Literature of the Modern South* (Baltimore, Md.: Johns Hopkins Press, 1953).

Shapiro, Charles (ed.). *Twelve Original Essays on Great American Novels* (Detroit, Mich.: Wayne State University Press, 1958).

Sherman, Stuart P. *Americans* (New York: Charles Scribner's Sons, 1922).

————. *The Main Stream* (New York: Charles Scribner's Sons, 1927).

Slochower, Harry. *No Voice Is Wholly Lost* (New York: Creative Age Press, Inc., 1945).

Smith, Bernard. *Forces in American Criticism* (New York: Harcourt, Brace & Company, Inc., 1939).

Smith, Henry Nash. *Virgin Land* (Cambridge, Mass.: Harvard University Press, 1950).

Snell, George D. *The Shapers of American Fiction, 1798–1947* (New York: E. P. Dutton & Co., Inc., 1947).

Spiller, Robert E. *The Cycle of American Literature* (New York: The Macmillan Company, 1955).

————, *et al.* (eds.). *Literary History of the United States* (3 vols.; New York: The Macmillan Company, 1948).

Stewart, Randall. *American Literature and Christian Doctrine* (Baton Rouge, La.: Louisiana State University Press, 1958).

Stovall, Floyd B. (ed.). *The Development of American Literary Criticism* (Chapel Hill, N.C.: University of North Carolina Press, 1955).

————. (ed.). *Eight American Authors: a Review of Research and Criticism* (New York: The Modern Language Association, 1956).

Taylor, Walter Fuller. *The Economic Novel in America* (Chapel Hill, N.C.: University of North Carolina Press, 1942).

————. *The Story of American Letters* (Chicago: Henry Regnery Co., 1956).

Trent, William P., *et al. Cambridge History of American Literature* (4 vols.; New York: The Macmillan Company, 1917–1921).

Van Doren, Carl. *The American Novel, 1789–1939* (rev. ed.; New York: The Macmillan Company, 1940).

Wagenknecht, Edward. *Cavalcade of the American Novel* (New York: Henry Holt & Company, Inc., 1952).

Walcutt, Charles C. *American Literary Naturalism: a Divided Stream* (Minneapolis, Minn.: University of Minnesota Press, 1956).

Wendell, Barrett. *A Literary History of America* (New York: Charles Scribner's Sons, 1900).

Williams, Stanley T. *The American Spirit in Letters* (New Haven, Conn.: Yale University Press, 1926).

Wilson, Edmund. *Classics and Commercials: A Literary Chronicle of the Forties* (New York: Farrar, Straus & Young, Inc., 1950).

Winters, Yvor. *Maule's Curse* (Norfolk, Conn.: New Directions, 1950).

Woodberry, George E. *American Literature* (New York: Charles Scribner's Sons, 1900).

Woodress, James (ed.). *Dissertations in American Literature, 1891–1955* (Durham, N.C.: Duke University Press, 1957).

INDIVIDUAL WRITERS

Only full length studies are listed, unless none is available. The student is cautioned that especially with the more recent novelists, much of the best material on their work is available in periodical form, or in some of the more general works cited above.

James Fenimore Cooper

Boynton, Henry W. *James Fenimore Cooper* (New York: D. Appleton-Century Company, Inc., 1931).

Grossman, James. *James Fenimore Cooper* (New York: William Sloane Associates, Inc., 1949).

Lounsbury, Thomas. *James Fenimore Cooper* (Boston: Houghton Mifflin Company, 1882).

Spiller, Robert E. *Fenimore Cooper: Critic of His Times* (New York: Minton, Balch & Company, 1931).

Waples, Dorothy. *The Whig Myth of Fenimore Cooper* (New Haven, Conn.: Yale University Press, 1938).

Nathaniel Hawthorne

Arvin, Newton. *Hawthorne* (Boston: Little, Brown & Company, 1929).

Fogle, Richard H. *Hawthorne's Fiction: the Light and the Dark* (Norman, Okla.: University of Oklahoma Press, 1952).

Hawthorne, Julian. *Nathaniel Hawthorne and His Wife* (Boston: James R. Osgood, 1885).

Stewart, Randall. *Nathaniel Hawthorne: A Biography* (New Haven, Conn.: Yale University Press, 1948).

Van Doren, Mark. *Nathaniel Hawthorne* (New York: William Sloane Associates, Inc., 1949).

Herman Melville

Arvin, Newton. *Herman Melville* (New York: William Sloane Associates, Inc., 1950).

Mumford, Lewis. *Herman Melville* (New York: Harcourt, Brace & Company, Inc., 1929).

Olson, Charles. *Call Me Ishmael* (New York: Reynal and Hitchcock, 1947).

Sedgwick, William Ellery. *Herman Melville: the Tragedy of Mind* (Cambridge, Mass.: Harvard University Press, 1944).

Weaver, Raymond. *Herman Melville: Mariner and Mystic* (New York: Doubleday, Doran & Company, Inc., 1921).

William Dean Howells

Cady, Edwin H. *The Realist at War* (Syracuse, N.Y.: Syracuse University Press, 1958).

Cady, Edwin H. *The Road to Realism* (Syracuse, N.Y.: Syracuse University Press, 1954).

Carter, Everett. *Howells and the Age of Realism* (Philadelphia: J. B. Lippincott Company, 1954).

Firkins, Oscar W. *William Dean Howells: A Study* (Cambridge, Mass.: Harvard University Press, 1924).

Howells, Mildred (ed.). *The Life and Letters of William Dean Howells* (New York: Doubleday, Doran & Company, Inc., 1928).

Henry James

Anderson, Quentin. *The American Henry James* (New Brunswick, N.J.: Rutgers University Press, 1957).

Beach, Joseph Warren. *The Method of Henry James* (New Haven, Conn.: Yale University Press, 1918).

Dupee, F. W. *Henry James* (New York: Doubleday & Company, Inc., 1951). A Doubleday Anchor Book.

———— (ed.). *The Quest of Henry James* (New York: Henry Holt & Company, Inc., 1947).

Edel, Leon. *Henry James, 1843–1870: The Untried Years* (Philadelphia: J. B. Lippincott Company, 1953).

Edgar, Pelham. *Henry James: Man and Author* (Boston: Houghton Mifflin Company, 1927).

Matthiessen, F. O. *Henry James: The Major Phase* (New York: Oxford University Press, 1944).

Mark Twain (Samuel L. Clemens)

Blair, Walter. *Mark Twain and Huck Finn* (Berkeley, Calif.: University of California Press, 1960).

DeVoto, Bernard. *Mark Twain's America* (Boston: Little, Brown & Company, 1932).

Ferguson, De Lancey. *Mark Twain: Man and Legend* (Indianapolis: The Bobbs-Merrill Company, Inc., 1943).

Long, E. Hudson. *The Mark Twain Handbook* (New York: Hendricks House, Inc., 1958).

Paine, Albert Bigelow. *Mark Twain, a Biography: The Personal and Literary Life of Samuel Langhorne Clemens* (New York: Harper & Brothers, 1912).

Wagenknecht, Edward. *Mark Twain: The Man and His Work* (New Haven, Conn.: Yale University Press, 1935).

Wecter, Dixon. *Sam Clemens of Hannibal* (Boston: Houghton Mifflin Company, 1952).

Stephen Crane

Beer, Thomas. *Stephen Crane* (New York: Alfred A. Knopf, Inc., 1923).

Berryman, John. *Stephen Crane* (New York: William Sloane Associates, Inc., 1950).

Linson, Corwin K. *My Stephen Crane,* ed. Edwin H. Cady (Syracuse, N.Y.: Syracuse University Press, 1958).

Theodore Dreiser

Elias, Robert. *Theodore Dreiser, Apostle of Nature* (New York: Alfred A. Knopf, Inc., 1949).

Kazin, Alfred, and Charles Shapiro (eds.). *The Stature of Theodore Dreiser* (Bloomington, Ind.: Indiana University Press, 1955).

Matthiessen, F. O. *Theodore Dreiser* (New York: William Sloane Associates, Inc., 1951).

Sinclair Lewis

Lewis, Grace Hegger. *With Love from Gracie: Sinclair Lewis, 1912–1925* (New York: Harcourt, Brace & Company, Inc., 1955).

Parrington, Vernon Lewis. *Sinclair Lewis: Our Own Diogenes* ("Chapbooks No. 5") (Seattle, Wash.: University of Washington Bookstore, 1927).

Sherman, Stuart P. *The Significance of Sinclair Lewis* (New York: Harcourt, Brace & Company, Inc., 1922).

Van Doren, Carl. *Sinclair Lewis: A Biographical Sketch* (Doubleday, Doran & Company, Inc., 1933).

Ernest Hemingway

Baker, Carlos. *Hemingway: The Writer as Artist* (Princeton, N.J.: Princeton University Press, 1952).

Fenton, Charles A. *The Apprenticeship of Ernest Hemingway: The Early Years* (New York: Farrar, Straus and Cudahy, Inc., 1954).

McCaffery, John K. (ed.). *Ernest Hemingway: the Man and His Work* (Cleveland: The World Publishing Company, 1950).

Young, Philip. *Ernest Hemingway* (New York: Rinehart & Company, Inc., 1953).

F. Scott Fitzgerald

Mizener, Arthur. *The Far Side of Paradise* (Boston: Houghton Mifflin Company, 1951).

Schulberg, Budd. *The Disenchanted* (New York: Random House, Inc., 1950), a novel.

John Dos Passos

There are no full-length books on Dos Passos. See Joseph Warren Beach, *American Fiction, 1920–1940* (New York: The Macmillan Company, 1941), and Alfred Kazin, *On Native Grounds* (New York: Reynal and Hitchcock, 1942).

James T. Farrell

There are no full-length books on Farrell. See Joseph Warren Beach, *American Fiction, 1920–1940* (New York: The Macmillan Company, 1941), and Blanche Housman Gelfant, *The American City Novel* (Norman, Okla.: University of Oklahoma Press, 1954).

Thomas Wolfe

Muller, Herbert J. *Thomas Wolfe* (Norfolk, Conn.: New Directions, 1947).

Nowell, Elizabeth. *Thomas Wolfe* (New York: Doubleday and Company, Inc., 1960).

Rubin, Louis D., Jr. *Thomas Wolfe, the Weather of His Youth* (Baton Rouge, La.: Louisiana State University Press, 1955).

Walser, Richard (ed.). *The Enigma of Thomas Wolfe* (Cambridge, Mass.: Harvard University Press, 1953).

Watkins, Floyd B. *Thomas Wolfe's Characters* (Norman, Okla.: University of Oklahoma Press, 1957).

William Faulkner

Hoffman, Frederick J., and Olga Vickery (eds.). *William Faulkner: Two Decades of Criticism* (East Lansing, Mich.: Michigan State College Press, 1954).

Howe, Irving. *William Faulkner: A Critical Study* (New York: Random House, Inc., 1952).

O'Connor, William Van. *The Tangled Fire of William Faulkner* (Minneapolis, Minn.: University of Minnesota Press, 1954).

Vickery, Olga. *Novels of William Faulkner* (Baton Rouge, La.: Louisiana State University Press, 1959).

Robert Penn Warren

There are no full-length books on Warren. See Members of the Department of English, Carnegie Institute of Technology: *"All the King's Men": A Symposium* (1957), and John M. Bradbury, *The Fugitives: A Critical Account* (Chapel Hill, N.C.: University of North Carolina Press, 1958).

Index

Page numbers in italics indicate sections devoted to a discussion of the author and his work.